Hiking
North Carolina

Hiking
North Carolina

by
Randy Johnson

FALCON™

Falcon Press® Publishing Co., Inc.
Helena, Montana

⩗FALCON GUIDE

Falcon Press is continually expanding its list of recreational guidebooks. All books include detailed descriptions, accurate maps, and all the information necessary for enjoyable trips. You can order extra copies of this book and get information and prices for other Falcon guidebooks by writing Falcon Press, P.O. Box 1718, Helena, MT 59624 or calling toll free 1-800-582-2665. Also, please ask for a free copy of our current catalog.

The author of this guidebook can be reached via e-mail at: ranjohns@aol.com

Printed in the United States of America.

All black-and-white photos by author unless noted otherwise.
Cover photo by Bill Lea.

Library of Congress Cataloging-in-Publication Data

Johnson, Randy 1951–
    Hiking North Carolina / by Randy Johnson.
        p.   cm.
    "A Falcon guide"—CIP t.p. verso.
    ISBN 1-56044-211-5 (pbk.)
    1. Hiking—North Carolina—Guidebooks. 2. North Carolina—
    Guidebooks. I. Title.
    GV199.42.N66J65 1996
    796.5'1'09756—dc20   96-1002
                                                          CIP

CAUTION

Outdoor recreation activities are by their very nature potentially hazardous. All participants in such activities must assume the responsibility for their own actions and safety. The information contained in this guidebook cannot replace sound judgment and good decision-making skills, which help reduce the risk exposure, nor does the scope of this book allow for disclosure of all the potential hazards and risks involved in such activities.

Learn as much as possible about the outdoor recreation activities you participate in, prepare for the unexpected, and be safe and cautious. The reward will be a safer and more enjoyable experience.

 Text pages printed on recycled paper.

To my Mother and Father.
My Dad —
for taking me to my first mountaintop.
My Mom —
for instilling an ability to appreciate it.

CONTENTS

CONTENTS

CONTENTS

CONTENTS

CONTENTS

CONTENTS

ACKNOWLEDGMENTS

Working with rangers, managers, volunteers, and aficionados of trails and parks is one of the wonderful things about writing a hiking guide. These people, especially parks employees, are dedicated, enthusiastic, and—in most cases—woefully underpaid. Nevertheless, they gladly send materials about their areas and answer all manner of questions. The best of these informants go beyond that. Some of the people I contacted dug into files; others created materials for me to use. They did this because they want hikers to appreciate the places to which they dedicate their energies. When you meet these people on the trail, take the time to thank them with your words and actions.

My involvement with North Carolina trails has been long and life-transforming. Many people influenced me. I've encountered people who inspired me to explore my own potential as I traveled spectacular trails, the backdrop for my life. I've hiked with them, crawled through the wilds with them, designed trails with them, spent hours dreaming with them. We worked together to protect and maintain the world we share.

I especially thank those in North Carolina who have walked my same path. First, thanks go to Hugh Morton, who saw in my endorsement of private-land trail fees a practical environmentalism that complements his own. I never could have created my own job and influenced Grandfather Mountain's backcountry hiking without his cooperation and encouragement. Nor could I have illustrated this book without his photos. After Hugh, I owe thanks to friends and coworkers at Grandfather: Harris Prevost, Winston Church, Tommy Huskins, and Catherine Morton. Trail aid and camaraderie came from Steve Miller (Grandfather's current trail manager), Ed Schultz, Kinney Baughman, Jim Morton, Scott Huffman, Jim Boone, and many others. Special thanks goes to those who labored long and hard with me on the Profile Trail, one of the accomplishments of which I am most proud.

I also thank the many volunteers at Grandfather Mountain, most of them dear friends: Steve Owen, Jeep Barrett, Robert Branch, Gerry McDade, and my brother Ken Johnson, without whose unpaid work I would not have been able to undertake the fee trail experiment. And I'm grateful for help from many others, among them dozens of Outward Bound crew members on countless rain and snow-splattered days.

My thanks range further. Ken Ketchie, editor and publisher of *The Mountain Times* in Boone, North Carolina, embraced my involvement in his award-winning newspaper from its third issue in 1978. I'm indebted to an array of outdoor professionals: William Bake, who defines the term "wilderness writer/ photographer"; Gary Everhardt, who guided the Blue Ridge Parkway around Grandfather Mountain and has been the consummate park professional. Parkway landscape architect Bob Hope also inspired me.

John Hendee, editor of the *International Journal of Wilderness*, and Joe Roggenbuck, professor of forestry at Virginia Polytechnic Institute, are wildlands scientists who have sparked my adulation and emulation. I remember fondly my Appalachian Mountain Club research days with Ed Spencer and Bob Proudman. May this book reflect the love we share for wild places.

As I prepared this book for press, some went beyond the call of duty. Lisa Davis's willingness to be extra helpful when no one else was in the Parkway office made it easier to bring the project to fruition. At Cape Hatteras National Seashore, Marcia Lyons and Chris Eckard were invaluable, as was Mary Jaeger-Gale at Chimney Rock Park. Holly Jenkins checked my Croatan copy with attention to minute detail and shared plans so hikers would find this book accurate long after publication. Thanks go to Judson Edeburn at Duke Forest and to Dave Cook at Eno River State Park, who was a giver of knowledge and a thorough reviewer. Michael Smith at Pilot Mountain State Park was similarly generous, as was Norris Baker of Hanging Rock State Park. Mike Simpson and Rick Bolin, both devoted urban trail enthusiasts, helped me cover trails at Greensboro's Lake Brandt.

I'm glad to have worked with Dwayne Stutzman of the North Carolina State Parks on diverse projects. I also enjoyed working with Bob Benner, the whitewater guidebook writer, on the Mountains To Sea Trail, and the time spent on Raleigh's greenway system with Victor Lebsock, Dick Bailey, and their pride in the trails. Judy Hunt of the Winston-Salem Parks and Recreation Department was instrumental to research on Salem Lake and Greenway; Laura Carathanasis at William B. Umstead State Park was a vital help.

From the USDA Forest Service, I received much. I have enjoyed a long trail association with Melinda McWilliams in Asheville. Darlene Huntsinger of the French Broad Ranger District deserves thanks for her quick response to my need for late-breaking information. Thanks, too, to Tanya E. Henderson of French Broad and Jose Zambrana, former superintendent of Uwharrie National Forest.

Lastly, I appreciate the folks at Falcon Press, especially Randall Green, for overlooking the problems of helping a full-time magazine editor publish his second Falcon guidebook. Thank you all for helping make this book, and my life in the outdoors, possible.

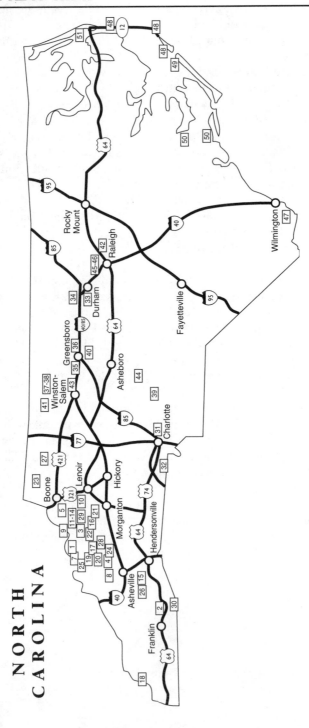

MAP LEGEND

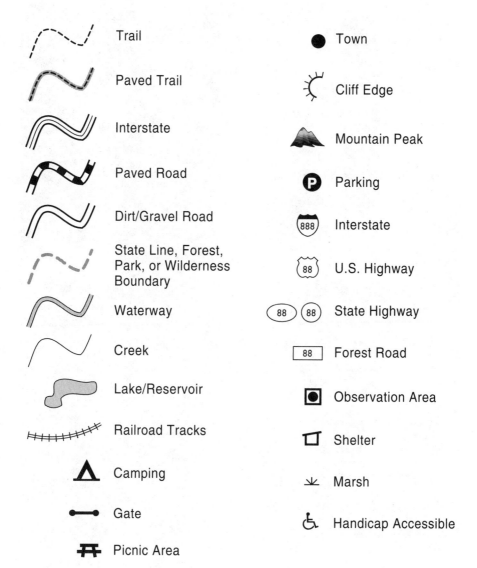

Trail

Paved Trail

Interstate

Paved Road

Dirt/Gravel Road

State Line, Forest, Park, or Wilderness Boundary

Waterway

Creek

Lake/Reservoir

Railroad Tracks

Camping

Gate

Picnic Area

Town

Cliff Edge

Mountain Peak

Parking

Interstate

U.S. Highway

State Highway

Forest Road

Observation Area

Shelter

Marsh

Handicap Accessible

Hickory Nut Falls in late fall, Forest Stroll Trail, Chimney Rock Park, North Carolina. *Photo by Emili Jurchynsky.*

INTRODUCTION

North Carolina forests rank among the nation's top ten in hiker days of trail activity. North Carolina's national parks, the Great Smokies and Blue Ridge Parkway (both partially in neighboring states), are among the most popular in the nation. But these are only part of North Carolina's natural appeal. Its long coastal arc of sand, called the Outer Banks, is as outstanding as any island chain in the continental United States. Add the distinctive appeal of the Piedmont, the foothills region in the middle of the state, and you realize that North Carolina spans a mountains-to-sea spectrum of scenic beauty.

The Regions

Like most southeastern states, North Carolina comprises three regions: the mountains, the Piedmont, and the coastal plain.

Its mountains are a massive, complex jumble of topography. The North Carolina/Tennessee border splits the Great Smoky Mountains, and parallel ridges spill in all directions from the nearly 7,000-foot ridge. South of the Smokies, smaller ranges cover hundreds of square miles. North of them, the Allegheny Front continues along the state's northern border; eastward, the Blue Ridge Mountains peel off as the front range of the Appalachians. In places such as Grandfather Mountain, this latter group towers nearly a vertical mile over the western Piedmont. North of Asheville a range called the

Rhododendron blooms on the Appalachian Trail over Jane Bald near Roan Mountain.

Black Mountains soars to the East's highest summits. On these and other lofty peaks, Canadian-zone forests alternate with crag-capped, alpine-like meadows. Much of this mountain land is federally owned.

The name Piedmont means "at the foot of the mountains." Appropriately, the North Carolina Piedmont runs from the foot of the Blue Ridge Mountains to the fall line, the dropoff where streams tumble to the coastal plain. Piedmont topography varies: rippling foothills on the west become noticeably flat on the east. A profusion of flowering shrubs and trees grows in this "flatland" forest. Trails cross undulating woods in the east and climb modest mountains. The tops of the Uwharrie Mountains, northeast of Charlotte, reach heights of just 1,000 feet. State parks in the Piedmont region preserve monadnocks, the isolated single summits such as Crowders Mountain (west of Charlotte) and Hanging Rock (north of Greensboro). And lakes here provide outstanding trail destinations.

The Coast region, or coastal plain, is indeed the flattest part of North Carolina. Its distinctively sandy soils run to the beaches and bays. In Croatan National Forest, the largest federal tract here, trails wander into cypress forests and onto saltwater marshes. Barrier islands may be the best part of far eastern North Carolina. From north to south, paths explore dunescapes and ponds, saltwater marshes and ancient maritime forests. Trails dot private lands all along the coast, in resorts or state and national wildlife preserves, as well as Cape Hatteras and Cape Lookout national seashores.

The Seasons

North Carolina's climatic contrasts create a range of options that is nothing short of wonderful. While summer hikers enjoy near-tropical temperatures on the coast and in the Piedmont, mountain goers find cool walks. In winter, it's possible to enjoy temperate outings at the beach while others on the same day make snowy winter hikes and cross-country ski in the mountains. The choice is yours. All you need is a refined idea of what conditions prevail in which region.

North Carolina's mountain climate is remarkably diverse due to the western part of the state's varying elevations. The southern mountains, from Asheville south of the Great Smoky Mountains to the state's southwestern tip, have a mild climate. Average summer days in the south will be around 80 degrees Fahrenheit. Summer temperatures (June through August) in southwestern mountain valleys can be hot: up to the low 90s. In the higher northern mountains, which include the Great Smokies and reach north to the Virginia border, normal summer days fall in the low to mid-70s; the hottest days will reach the mid-80s. Summer nights in the north dip to the mid-50s and mid-60s. On the highest peaks in both areas, summer days can be downright chilly. Misty conditions can drop temperatures to the 50s and 60s. The coolest summer nights can drop to the upper 40s at higher elevations. Part of the cool of North Carolina's loftiest peaks is due to the fact that they are home to a kind of temperate rain forest. You may encounter sunny periods there, but generally summer is a time for

Indian pipe, a sentinel of early summer in North Carolina's Canadian zone forests. *Photo by Hugh Morton.*

daily thunderstorms and, possibly, sustained periods of wet weather.

That changes in early fall. In September and October, days become drier, and temperatures cool on the highest peaks. The first light snow often dusts summits in October. Autumn color is best by October 10 in the northern mountains, and by October 25 in southwestern sites. Fall color lasts into early November in the lowest valleys, and often warm, summerlike spells delight November hikers. By late November and early December, the area sees its first significant snowfall.

The thumping heard during autumn in high elevation North Carolina forests is often the display of the ruffed grouse. *Photo by Hugh Morton.*

Hikers and skiers looking for snow should visit the mountains in January, February, and early March. Ample snowfalls often cover the trails, with temperatures dipping below 15 degrees Fahrenheit at night and staying below freezing during the day during surges of cold. Extremely high winds, arctic temperatures, and deep snow can make these mountains as challenging as those in New England. But the snow doesn't stay all winter. Coverage fluctuates with the weather; for a guide, turn to television's The

Weather Channel, which has been accurate in predicting and reporting the microclimatic weather here.

Spring may be the least appealing season in the mountains. Snow and rain are frequent, as is mud during March and April. When the area dries to warm, clear days, flowers bloom profusely—in early May in the south, by late May in the north. Budding trees don't reach the highest peaks until early June, and the spectacle of rhododendrons in bloom explodes across the highest elevations by the third weekend in the month.

In the Piedmont, summer (June through September) can be very hot and sticky, with daytime temperatures ranging from the mid-80s to low-90s. Thunderstorms are frequent, though not as prevalent as in the mountains. The northern Piedmont can be as much as five degrees cooler, and at times cloudier, than the southern Piedmont.

Fall (October through November) is wonderful in the midsection of the state. The summer heat is gone, though Indian summer days can still reach the 80s. Autumn color peaks by November 15, but colorful forests and invigorating weather can prevail into late November. Piedmont mountain parks, greenways, and lakeshore trails are best at this time of year.

Winter (December to March) often yields bright, dry, and crisp days. Rain falls here when the mountains receive snow. Very little snow falls on Piedmont trails; when it does, it's gone in a day or so.

Spring is another premier time to hike the Piedmont. It can be rainy, but flowers bloom here by mid-March. In April, the area's near-summer warmth produces explosive blossoms. May has more of the same, with summer-like temperatures arriving late in the month.

The coastal plain and the shore are a world apart. Summer at the coastal parks and Outer Banks trails is hot and sunny in spades. But like subtropical areas elsewhere, onshore breezes and thundershowers can make the trails (and camping) attractive for acclimatized hikers. Those who are least attracted to hot weather should consider the shoulder seasons of spring and fall. My favorite months at the beach are April, May, September, and October. From late-September to mid-November, the ocean is warm and lower humidity days (mid-70s to mid-80s) are perfect for walking. Spring is similar, except ocean water temperatures aren't inviting until late May.

On the coast, the north-to-south range in climate is as noticeable as it is in the mountains. Warmer, sunnier days occur earlier and stay later on the southeastern beaches, a fact reflected in the flora and fauna, which have much in common with areas much farther south.

BEING PREPARED

In North Carolina's varied climate and geography, there is no substitute for adequate planning. This section covers the most important elements involved in preparing for a safe, enjoyable outing; hikers should also check the information included in the overviews and details of each trail entry. The following are general tips and hiking advice—an orientation— to FalconGuides and this book.

Selecting a Trail

When you are deciding which one of the hikes from *Hiking North Carolina* to take, your first step is matching the trail with your level of ability. Hikes listed in this book are described as easy, moderate, or strenuous, with "moderately" and "extremely" added to these terms as modifiers. Generally, regardless of length, an easy trail has a graded or benched treadway, meaning that the tread has been excavated, like a mini road grade, to permit predictable footing. An easy hike is relatively level, meaning that its grade, or rate of rise, is gradual and consistent. A moderate trail involves a rougher, rockier treadway and fluctuations in the rate of rise, though the climb is usually gradual. Strenuous trails are steep overall or in places, require substantial exertion, and often have uneven footing or necessitate the use of ladders or climbing over rocks. When a trail is said to "slab around a peak," it means that it avoids a summit, generally keeping to a level grade at one elevation.

Add these basic terms to the descriptions in the trail entries. For instance, both the Chestnut Oak Nature Trail in Hanging Rock State Park (rated easy) and the Nuwati Trail on Grandfather Mountain (rated moderately easy are considered untaxing because of gradual grades. Nevertheless,

Vaseyi azalea blooms on the heights long after spring has come to the foothills.
Photo by Hugh Morton.

the text mentions that both trails have rocky footing, a fact that hikers will need to consider.

Trail entries often use the terms "loop" or "circuit" to describe a recommended hike. In general, a loop is a single trail that leaves a trailhead, splits at some point, then returns the hiker to the initial path and trailhead. A circuit is a hike that originates on one trail, but turns onto another trail to return to the same starting point. Either of these hikes resembles a circle of sorts.

Trail entries also specify various elevations at the trailhead and the highest or lowest point. Trailheads are generally a trail's low point, often where a trail reaches a road. The entry also specifies elevation gain and loss.

Mileages are given for most hikes, often with "about" appended to them. This is done where seemingly reliable data conflicts with other information, such as park brochures or official publications. All mileage information should be considered a best estimate. Certain kinds of terrain make it difficult to measure with certainty exactly how long a trail is. In addition, the varying levels of experience that hikers bring to the trails make mileage information less meaningful. Certainly, you don't want to set off on a 10-mile hike when a 2-mile hike is what you have in mind; nevertheless, trail descriptions and ratings are often more valuable than simple mileage figures.

To further inform your trail choices, we've included entries that suggest ways for inexperienced or less physically fit hikers to sample longer, more strenuous trails. Most entries, for instance, suggest places to turn around, or alternative routes that avoid the most difficult terrain. Still, a person in very poor condition could find an easy-rated trail to be a challenging hike, so the trail descriptions in this book are subjective. If you are considered overweight, do no regular exercise, or are unsure of foot, create your own hike rating system: expect an easy hike to feel moderately difficult, and a moderate hike to be strenuous. The nice thing is that, with consistent exercise, your rating system will change.

Don't Forget the Net

Perhaps, surprisingly, the nature-loving legion of hikers are the same educated group of people rushing to explore the global computer web called the Internet. If you're on-line, definitely check out the exploding trove of information about hiking to be found on the World Wide Web. The richness starts with homepages for individual national, state, and city parks where you'll find maps, directions, and even the latest campground rates.

But that's just the beginning. The Web even has homepages for mountain peaks! Many sites are linked to an amazing array of related resources such as hiking clubs and interest groups and commercial enterprises. You can even tap the NWS for weather forecasts. And on-line services such as America Online and CompuServe feature magazines and chatgroups of interest to hikers.

Turn to Appendix D for a listing of Internet sites of interest to NC hikers, including some hiking destinations that aren't covered in the text of this book.

What To Carry

The shortest, easiest nature trails in this book require that the hiker carry nothing other than a camera or binoculars. But hikers who venture more than 1 mile into fields or forests will want to carry a few basic essentials.

A small backpack or fanny pack can provide space for the essentials: a canteen of water, a snack or extra food, spare clothing and other protective items (sunscreen, insect repellent, sunglasses, a hat and raincoat), a small first-aid kit (bandages, antiseptic, extra-strength aspirin/acetaminophen, moleskin for blisters), this book, the recommended hiking maps, and any trail permits required by managing agencies. See Appendix B at the back of this book for an easy hiker's checklist to use before taking longer backpacking trips.

The ultimate item you'll want to carry isn't in your pack, but in your head: knowledge. The information contained here is timely and extensive, but no single trail guide can do it all. Prepare yourself by seeking out the variety of resources available to those who enjoy the outdoors, not the least of which are training courses in CPR and first aid. Read FalconGuides and other books on survival, route finding, mountaineering, backpacking, and many outdoor topics.

Clothes

Choose clothes that are comfortable and protective.

Any outdoor activity, regardless of the season, requires that you be able to exercise and remain comfortable. In summer, anywhere in the state, that often means wearing shorts and T-shirts. But climate and insects or poisonous plants can intervene. On the coast or in the Piedmont, you may find a hat, long-sleeved T-shirt, and long, loose pants necessary because of sun, bugs, or vegetation. A heavier version of the same outfit can be worn in the mountains' cooler conditions. And remember: a high-altitude sun can burn you as much or more than that at the beach.

When choosing clothing, the best policy is to be prepared for the worst weather the season and place can deliver. This means being flexible and dressing in layers. However lightly clothed you find yourself in summer, be prepared for rain and wind. The best choices are jackets made of new synthetic fabrics, which are waterproof and breathable. These are expensive but highly recommended for effectiveness and durability.

In spring, fall, and especially winter, waterproof outer garments are even more valuable. Whether you are reveling in cold salt spray or climbing into a Blue Ridge snowstorm, your outer layer of clothing, which can include shell jacket and pants, is your first line of defense. Under that, wear layers—how many varies by season. Synthetic fabrics, such as polypropylene, that are warm even when wet, are the best choices. Look for polypropylene T-shirts, long underwear, pants, and ubiquitous zip-up or pullover pile jackets, indispensable for cold weather.

Hiker climbs the ladders on MacRae Peak, Grandfather Mountain, North Carolina.

Major insulating garments are decidedly necessary in North Carolina's winter mountains. Your choice for thick insulation is, again, clothing made of synthetic fabric. Unlike down, synthetics won't lose their insulating value when wet. The serious winter backpacker would do well to carry both parkas and pants of such material.

Footwear

On easy trails, you'll need only a sturdy pair of walking or running shoes. But on moderate or more difficult hikes—or even easy hikes with rocky footing—you'll depend on hiking boots.

The newest generation of boots are light and relatively inexpensive compared with the heavy, costly leather boots associated with the 1970s backpacking boom. The new boots boast waterproof fabrics and various kinds of non-skid soles. They add comfort, safety, and enjoyment to any hike, and are a worthwhile purchase for even a casual hiker.

Serious hikers and backpackers would do well to consider that boots may not be the only kind of shoe you'll need on a hike. Specialty hikers, such as serious winter hikers, will need more than a three-season, lightweight boot. Those who walk North Carolina trails often will find that in many places paths cross streams without the aid of bridges. Rather than avoid these trails, consider carrying a pair of aqua shoes, which

Boone Bowl—a memorable winter vista up to Calloway Peak of Grandfather Mountain. Some say the high valley is a glacial cirque.

slip over bare feet, or sport sandals for wading. And, after a day on the trail, they make great in-camp wear.

Weather Dangers

Owning the proper clothing isn't enough. Be sure to use your high-tech garments before you become thoroughly wet or chilled.

Hypothermia results when lack of food and/or exposure to severe weather prevent the body from maintaining its core temperature. It can occur at any time of year, at temperatures well above freezing, with the dramatic cooling effects of wind and rain. To prevent it, stay dry and protected with the right clothing—especially a hat, since up to 70 percent of lost heat can emanate from your head. Don extra clothing when you stop for a rest, before you get chilled. Adequately fuel yourself with food and water; drink plenty of fluids (in winter, just breathing robs you of moisture) and nibble energy foods (such as trail mix, sandwiches, and hot soups). Set up camp earlier to accommodate an inexperienced or less physically fit member of your party. The best way to treat hypothermia is to stop it before it starts.

You may not be able to. Whatever you do, do not ignore the uncontrollable shivering and, later, slow and slurred speech, stumbling gait, clumsiness, and seeming disorientation of a hypothermic hiker. Take immediate

A snowfall begins highlighting trailside rhododendron in the Joyce Kilmer Slickrock Wilderness.

Snowy summits often linger while spring buds in North Carolina Mountain valleys. Don't underestimate High Country weather.

action to shelter and refuel anyone with these symptoms. If the victim is uncooperative, or unconscious, use a sleeping bag to sandwich the unclad hiker between two other similarly undressed helpers.

Frostbite is another danger. Frozen flesh that results from severe cold, its first sign is reddened skin. Next, the frozen site—often toes, fingers or portions of the face—will turn white or gray. The best prevention is to stay warm so your extremities receive the blood flow they need. If you can avoid it, do not venture into extreme conditions or exposed areas where wind-chill factors are below minus 20 degrees Fahrenheit. In severe conditions, hikers should monitor each others' faces and suggest shelter when the need arises. Do not rub frozen skin or slap frozen extremities together. When an area with severe frostbite begins to thaw, expect severe pain; use aspirin or acetaminophen on the way to medical assistance.

In summer, a hiker's major danger is **lightning,** especially on exposed mountaintops. Lightning is a complex combination of charges that bounce from cloud to ground and back. Suffice it to say take shelter before you have to decide which kind of lightning you're likely to be subject to. Other lightning safety tips include the following: move off ridgetops; seek shelter in a group of smaller trees rather than under one tall one; rest in a low, dry area (but not a gully or near a pond, where water can conduct the current); avoid overhangs or small caves where ground current might pass through you. In a lightning storm, it's best to sit in the open below surrounding high points and atop a rock that is detached and thus insulated from the ground. To further insulate yourself, crouch low or kneel on top of your pack or sleeping pad.

Heat stroke and heat exhaustion are summer equivalents of exposure to cold. North Carolina boasts more than its share of hot hikes, so carry and drink plenty of fluids if you're sweating heavily. Avoid hiking in the hottest part of the day; slip into one of the trailside pools so often mentioned in this book's hike descriptions. If you feel dizzy and drained, heat exhaustion may be the culprit. Relax, drink fluids, and let your body recover. Heat stroke is the more extreme condition: rather than being damp and drained, you'll be dry and feverish, dangerous signs that the body has given up its attempts to cool itself down by perspiring. If things get this bad, immediately cool the affected person with cold, wet compresses. Administer water. Hydration should resume.

Trailside Pests

Winter weather largely eradicates North Carolina's most bothersome bugs, reptiles, and plants. But spring, summer, and fall are different matters.

In mild and hot weather, **wasps, hornets, and bees** of various kinds are found across the state. Take every precaution to avoid contact with concentrations of bees. Be cautious when you see a large number of bees around fruit and flowers; be on the lookout for nests, both hanging from limbs and in hollow trees, logs, or on the ground. If you notice heightened activity and presence of bees, move away. And don't act like a flower. You can't avoid sweating, which attracts some bees, but don't entice them with perfume or scented body care products.

Most stings are minor and easily treated. Simply scrape an imbedded stinger out with a knife blade; another method, squeezing it out, releases more venom into your bloodstream. A paste made of water and unseasoned meat tenderizer that contains papain (a papaya enzyme) can neutralize bee venom. Baking soda paste does not. Some stings are not so simple. When a person is allergic to bee stings or stung enough times, the danger of anaphylactic shock and even death can be great. People die from bee stings each year in the United States. An over-the-counter antihistamine that contains diphenhidramine (such as Benadryl) can help control mild allergic reactions. Serious toxic reactions and anaphylactic shock can set in immediately or after some delay. If you know you are allergic to bee stings, always carry an epinephrine syringe bee sting kit—and be sure companions know where it is and how to use it.

Ticks are another source of potentially deadly bites. North Carolina's hot Piedmont and coastal forests are favorite habitats for ticks, especially late spring through summer. Hikers on the state's highest mountains are less likely to find ticks, especially where spruce and fir forests prevail. Lyme disease is one serious malady carried by ticks; Rocky Mountain spotted fever is another. North Carolina is infamous for the latter. Both diseases can take up to two weeks to gestate before symptoms develop. Among the signs are arthritis-like joint pain, high fever, and/or a circular rash.

The best defense against ticks is three-pronged. First, use a tick and insect repellent that contains N, N-diethyl-3-methylbenzamide, more widely known as DEET. Second, whether you use chemicals or not, wear long-sleeved shirts and long pants, and avoid walking through tall grass, brush, or dense woods. Third, frequently check yourself for ticks, especially at night and when you finish a hike. Focus on armpits, ears, scalp, groin, legs, and where clothes, such as socks, constrict the body. It takes a while for ticks to attach and transmit disease, so you have a good shot at preventing infection if you find ticks early.

If a tick becomes imbedded in your skin, use a bit of repellent, rubbing alcohol, or a hot, extinguished match to encourage it to back itself out. If you must use tweezers to remove it, grasp the head to avoid squeezing toxins into the wound. And don't hesitate to pull a little bit of your skin out with it so that mouth parts do not remain.

Flies can also be a problem in many areas of North Carolina. In spring (mid-April to mid-June), hikers on the state's highest peaks can be troubled by the same tiny black flies that pester North Country hikers in Minnesota and Maine. More often hikers here see common house flies and horse flies; the latter seem particularly vicious at the coast. The best defenses are to be sure to carry and use insect repellent, keep food and garbage covered or stored elsewhere when picnicking and camping, and cover your body. Consider wearing a repellent-coated cap.

Mosquitoes are prevalent in the state, especially on cool mountain evenings and on trails that pass coastal marshlands. In the latter locations, mosquitoes can be voracious. For most comfort, hike the buggiest locations, such as coastal marshes, in fall and winter; at other times, do not fail to carry and use repellent with DEET, because nothing else will do.

Insects find you, but North Carolina also has plant pests that you may step into. **Poison ivy, poison oak, and poison sumac** are all found here, though the highest peaks are free of these troublesome plants. All produce contact dermatitis—rash and watery blisters that appear from twelve to forty-eight hours after skin rubs against the plant resin. The outbreak usually runs its course in ten days, but isolated cases can be severe or cause allergic reactions. Learn to identify these plants (A tip to remember: "Leaves of three, let it be") and be wary of wading through brush in shorts.

If you realize you just touched one of these poisonous plants, remove and isolate contaminated clothing until it can be washed at home. Flush the affected skin with water but no soap; your skin's natural oils will temporarily protect you. Cover rash areas with calamine lotion. See a physician if face or genitals or more than 25 percent of your body is affected.

Snakes rank high on the list of hiker fears. Indeed, North Carolina's venomous vipers range from the timber rattler and copperhead (found across the state except for the highest peaks), to the cottonmouth moccasin, usually confined to the warmest, wettest coastal sites. Luckily, of the twenty thousand people a year who are bitten by poisonous snakes in the United States, only between six and fifteen die. The low death rate is due to several factors: snake venom is relatively slow acting; almost half of all snake bites do not include the injection of venom; and antivenin is widely available at hospitals.

The best bet is to be observant and be able to recognize poisonous snakes before they can bite. All of the above kinds of snakes are generally heftier than harmless snakes and have triangular or arrow-shaped heads and vertically slit pupils (versus tube-shaped heads and round pupils for nonpoisonous snakes). To avoid snakes, don't reach blindly behind logs and rocks, inspect wooded sites where you plan to sit, and watch where you step.

If bitten, be able to report what kind of snake attacked. Observe your wound: the bite of a pit viper includes two or more prominent fang marks, while a harmless snake bite usually leaves two rows of indentations and no big holes. If you can, use a commercial snake bite kit within three minutes of the bite. Immediately remove all watches and rings that may cause constriction from swelling, and do not make incisions with a knife or try to suck the venom out. Do not use tourniquets, cold water, or ice packs, since these heighten the possibility of gangrene. Instead, loosely splint and immobilize the affected limb, and with a pen, mark on the victim to record the time and spread of swelling. If you are within twenty minutes of the trailhead, carry the victim (or permit them to walk slowly, with frequent rests) to a vehicle for immediate transfer to a hospital. If hiking alone, walk as calmly as possible back to your car for help. Hikers who are far from a trailhead should send a companion for help and wait for emergency personnel to return with antivenin.

Most other animals in North Carolina are harmless for hikers. The exception is the rarely seen black bear. Most of the time, a backcountry glimpse of one of these reclusive mammals includes its rear end sprinting away. If you have a sudden encounter with a nearby bear, especially a mother with cubs, steadily and calmly back away. Leave the area. Do not run or climb a tree, since this may provoke a chase—and you cannot out-run a bear. Stand your ground in a charge: bears often bluff these.

The most problematic locations for bear encounters are in popular campsites, where marauding bears forage through garbage. There they can be aggressive, especially if you approach while they are enjoying food. Stay away. The best defense against such encounters with bears—and with skunks and other animals, even mice—is to keep your food away from camp. Safely hang bagged food by tossing a rope over a tree limb, tying on your food container, running the food up into midair away from the trunk, and tying the other end where you can reach it.

The other animal threat is a microscopic one. The ingestion of **waterborne pests** can cause a variety of backcountry infections. Perhaps the best known is *giardia lamblia*, but an *E. coli* infection can be deadly. Hikers have even contracted Type A hepatitis from drinking untreated water in the "wilderness." Giardia victims may not feel the effects for days or weeks, but you should see a physician if you develop foul-smelling gas, loss of appetite, bloating, stomach cramps, or nausea. Unfortunately, even pristine-looking streams may contain these and other disease-producing agents. All hikers should carry water from treated sources or include commercially bottled drinks among their trail beverages, or treat the water they use. Boiling water for at least 5 minutes (before adding food or flavoring) will kill the tiny cysts that cause giardia, so campers can often prepare hot foods with water from streams and springs. Boiling can cause drinking water to taste flat, though, so pour it back and forth between clean containers to restore its oxygen content or add flavorings. Better still, purchase a portable water purifier from an outdoor store or travel catalog. Do not disinfect water with Halazone, chlorine, or iodine.

LEAVE NO TRACE

Everyone's heard the dictum "Take only pictures, leave only footprints." Well, even footprints are a problem in many popular wilderness areas—causing soil compaction and erosion. Nevertheless, damage to the environment can be minimized.

The basic idea of leave-no-trace hiking and camping is to minimize your impact. That starts with staying on defined trails and restricting your outings to a small party of people. Intelligent strategies for protecting trails, such as not shortcutting switchbacks, also mean you won't brush directly through poison ivy or step on that snoozing copperhead. It's bad form to hike into the woods in a group of eight or more, because anyplace you choose to picnic or camp will be overwhelmed. Groups of four or six people are best, in part because they can more easily find campsites and deal with emergencies. And larger groups are noisier; most people prefer quiet or a natural noise level in the backcountry. However large your party, try to keep your noise level down, especially when camping in the vicinity of others. Noise travels in the damp after dark. There's no excuse for loud conversation or rowdy behavior after 9 p.m.

The other obvious no-no is littering, the number-one trail pollution problem. The dictum "Pack it in, pack it out" has become the basic credo of backcountry. Too many people lug food and drink into the woods in heavy containers, then leave the bottles and cans behind when they're empty. Pack properly, using lightweight plastic, and you won't be tempted to jettison the refuse. Also, bag refuse immediately to avoid attracting bugs and animals. And consider picking up litter left by others. It sets a good example.

Everyone generates waste in the woods, so proper disposal is another element of leaving no trace. At popular parks and trails, use the restrooms before hitting the trail. While hiking or camping, use proper methods of disposal to keep urine, feces, soap, and garbage out of water sources; these cause the increasing pollution of streams and springs. To make a "cat hole" for body waste, use a tiny trowel to remove a cap of sod (keep it intact) and dig a hole at least 6 inches deep in organic soil (damp but not wet), at least 200 feet from surface water, trails, campsites, or other places people congregate. This is your "toilet." Use natural toilet paper such as leaves, or pack out toilet paper in a plastic bag. After using your pit, mix soil into the waste to hasten decomposition, then cover with the sod cap. When urinating, avoid hitting plants and go into mineral soil or sand. Choose a sunny spot to hasten evaporation.

Camping impacts the environment in ways that hiking does not. Hikers who intend to camp should read up on clean camping: how to choose a campsite, the safety and environmental benefits of carrying a stove, and many other topics are addressed in several fine publications. A touchy topic for campers is how to keep your body and equipment clean without polluting streams and lakes. Some camping purists choose not to bathe in the backcountry; others wouldn't camp if they couldn't get clean. The best way to wash and not pollute nearby drinking water is to carry a large pot or bucket of water at least 200 feet from the water source. Lather minimally with biodegradable soap and rinse. Then disperse and dilute any suds on the ground with more water. To brush your teeth, go the same distance away and use the smallest amount of paste possible. Disperse it by spitting, and rinse away suds with water.

Huge stepping stones span the headwaters of the Watauga River on Grandfather Mountain's Profile Trail. *Photo by Hugh Morton.*

HIKING WITH KIDS

Hiking is a wonderful way to instill a love of the outdoors, an enjoyment of physical fitness and exercise, and less-tangible values of environmental and personal responsibility in young people.

You don't have to wait until a child is ten years old to take him or her out into the woods. Many of the easiest hikes in this book are great for kids. Trail descriptions highlight paths suitable for toddlers (on their first unaided woods walks), family hikes, beginner backpacking trips, and saunters with the elderly and physically challenged. Sample some of these, but don't expect to make the entire hike or reach that intended campsite. Be flexible with tiny hikers. Let them set the pace.

Many parents purchase sophisticated child-carrier packs that include a pouch for kid items. These increase your mobility, but remember to avoid tree limbs and other obstacles. Also, children often fall asleep in these packs, and few have a way to stabilize a sleeping hiker's head. Be prepared to use a scarf, pillow, or other items to cushion the napping kid. Work this out in advance of a longer hike.

Cool weather hiking with children poses more challenges. Since children in backpacks aren't active, it is easy for them to become cold, especially in winter. Don't overdo winter hikes and ski trips. Carry hot drinks or soup in a thermos; nothing is better if a child becomes cold. Be aware that just bundling a child in urban-style outerwear may not keep her or him warm. There is no substitute for effectively layered, high-quality clothing. Foam-lined, heavily insulated boots with polypropylene or wool socks and substantial mittens should also be basic requirements. Children who have a bad experience will not be enthusiastic about hiking in the future.

Focus on comfort and safety. Items such as sunscreen, hats, insect repellent, topical anesthetic for bug bites or sunburn, and others are the ingredients for a successful family hike.

BACKCOUNTRY ETIQUETTE

You can enhance your safety and limit human conflict in the backcountry, just as you can leave no trace of your passing. Backcountry conflict arises in many ways. Hikers have tempers, too: this topic has already been touched upon with the suggestion that campers keep noise to a minimum after 9 p.m. Serious campers cope with darkness by going to sleep; when nearby tenters build a giant bonfire and party until midnight, the result can be unpleasant.

You can avoid such conflicts by choosing your sites well. Know your preferences. Choose an isolated campsite if you are a wilderness purist; choose a car-accessible campground or other appropriate place if you're taking the neighborhood kids on their first camping trip. With a little forethought and consideration, you can minimize conflicts between users.

Trails have their own form of etiquette. Unless it's unsafe to do so, step aside when other hikers approach, even if you have the right of way. Be diplomatic at all times. If the chemistry in a given situation is wrong, be the first to back down and move on.

Criminal violence is rare on trails, but instances of robbery and rape seem to be increasing. For that reason, be friendly but reasonably wary. Do not hike alone; if you do, dress conservatively, don't flaunt expensive equipment or jewelry, and don't hesitate to say you're with a group of friends. Backcountry users have much in common, and the camaraderie of the woods can cause some people to treat everyone they meet as if they were old friends. But it is far better to keep an urban sense of security about you—which means not leaving your pack and other gear unattended, and not volunteering valuable information about yourself or your belongings.

And don't leave valuables in your vehicle. The number-one crime associated with hiking is the trailhead auto break-in. When your trek begins at an isolated trailhead, consider parking at a nearby business and arranging to be shuttled.

No matter what, let a responsible party know where you are and when you'll return. Religiously comply with hiker registration and user permit systems, which exist at many North Carolina parks and preserves. These function as a safety net and, where fees are collected, support the maintenance and management of the trails you've come to enjoy.

Enjoyment is what using trails is all about. There's the exercise, the good times you share with those who accompany you, and the scenic views, both vast and intimate. You'll savor the sound of wind as it rushes over a forest and be astounded by the way vegetation gives way to a dramatic vista. You will discover how sweat and hard work turn into rewards. It's no wonder that Henry David Thoreau and many soul-searchers have found that walking complements insight. Hiking has a way of leading your mind to new awareness as surely as it leads you to new settings. May you, and those you hike with, find both.

THE APPALACHIAN TRAIL

Each spring nearly fifteen hundred people hoist unbelievably heavy packs onto their backs and strain down a misty trail, intent on accomplishing the most difficult task of their lives: going the length of the Appalachian Mountains. The footpath links a tree-covered mountaintop in Georgia and a rock-capped summit in central Maine. The trail winds for 300 miles across western North Carolina, home to some of its highest elevations and most spectacular scenery. Nearly sixty years old, the Appalachian Trail (AT) was the first organized recreational avenue to wilderness. Today there are many long-distance trails, but none equal the AT.

When first proposed in 1921 by regional planner Benton MacKaye, the idea for a cross-Appalachian trail was labeled "an experiment in regional planning." Actually, it was a philosophical experiment, too, intended to dilute the hold that industrialism had on modern life. The AT would preserve the East's wilderness while offering the laboring masses an uplifting escape from the manufacturing economy. The idea caught on dramatically, since people recognized the unspoiled Appalachians—so different from other denuded and eroded lands—were at stake. And trail enthusiasts liked the idea of the path itself.

Creating the AT was a large task. Within two years of MacKaye's first article proposing the AT, the major trail organizations, including fledgling groups in the South, had endorsed the plan and built the first sections of the AT in New England. In 1925, a meeting held in Washington, D.C., formally created the Appalachian Trail Conference, Incorporated, forerunner of the organization that manages the path today. At these early starts, MacKaye's philosophical bent still shaped the trail's future; he announced at the conference that "the trailway should 'open up' a country as an escape from civilization....The path of the trailway should be as 'pathless' as possible."

In the late 1920s, that's exactly how the path was. The original route plan led from Cohutta Mountain, Georgia, across the Great Smoky Mountains, to Grandfather Mountain, North Carolina, through southwestern Virginia, across the Blue Ridge Mountains at what is now Shenandoah

National Park, and on to its terminus at Mount Washington, New Hampshire. With railroad imagery fostered by MacKaye, the trail's "main line" described above would link to various "branch lines." In the South, feeder trails were meant to reach Birmingham and Atlanta, funneling jaded urban workers into the refreshing green corridor of renewal. North Carolina's Mountains To Sea Trail and Bartram Trail are examples of branch lines.

In reality, the AT was built largely out of existing trails in the north, and through unexpected devotion from trail clubs and the Forest Service in the South. The Southern Appalachian section was finished quickly, surprising New Englanders who felt sure that their region's trail clubs would be the most active. The Southerners helped build other sections, too: the Potomac Appalachian Trail Club was instrumental in completing the trail through Maine to Mount Katahdin.

During AT construction, nearly 600 miles of road, including the Skyline Drive and Blue Ridge Parkway, were built. The building of those roads, opposed by many trail clubs, claimed dozens of miles of the AT's early route. Luckily, the Civilian Conservation Corps (CCC) was enlisted to revise the route; it built many of the three-sided lean-tos that line the trail. Nevertheless, Appalachian Trail Conference chairman Myron Avery called the scenic roads a "major catastrophe in Appalachian Trail history." Today, we nod at Avery's assertions. Although the Parkway boasts wonderful hiking opportunities, its leg-stretcher hikes do not a wilderness experience make.

The trail, in any form, became a symbol. Long before wilderness preservation was ever achieved in the East, diehard hikers followed ridgetops and linked remnants of a wild heritage as they built it. By 1937, the first version of the trail was complete. Thousands of minor catastrophes and positive changes have happened since then. The bad events range from hurricanes to commercial development of private land, all claiming portions of the trail. The good occurrences come, too, since at each time of loss, a new generation of trail enthusiasts has stepped in and carved a new path. The extension of the trail to Mount Katahdin, originally a branch site rather than a terminus, was one of thousands of changes that qualify the AT as a living thing. It was Myron Avery who said that the AT was the trail of which it could never be said, "It is finished—this is the end!"

The Appalachian Trail started as, and remains, an effort spearheaded by the public. But the Appalachian Trail Conference also enlisted the support and cooperation of the national parks, forests, state parks, and other agencies and individuals. Since 1938, when a minimum width was established for the trail corridor through federal land, the extent of cooperation between AT enthusiasts and the government has been astounding. In 1968, the AT became the first National Scenic Trail under the landmark National Trails System Act, which gave the Appalachian Trail Conference control. It also authorized that the 1,000 miles of trail in private hands be acquired, by eminent domain if necessary. But acquisition of land was slow. After pressure from the trail community, an Appalachian Trail bill passed Congress in the late 1970s; this has substantially speeded up land acquisition along the route. Today, almost all of the path is in public ownership.

The trail has elevated some isolated mountain burgs into backcountry boom towns. Hikers bring thousands of dollars into towns lacking mainstream tourist attractions. Hot Springs, North Carolina, is one place swelled by trail traffic. "The Appalachian Trail passes within 5 miles of 105 towns," says Brian King, Appalachian Trail Conference spokesman. "Many of those towns see the trail as their primary tourist attraction. Just the money spent on gas, food, and lodging is a significant transfer of wealth from urban areas to the Appalachians."

Maintenance of the path never wanes and is accomplished through the efforts of thirty-two organizations affiliated with the Appalachian Trail Conference. The Conference boasts 23,500 members, and affiliated clubs include another 70,000 trail enthusiasts. Many times each year, volunteers toil long hours in the task of maintaining their portions of the footpath and any of the 278 overnight shelters on the route. All told, about 5,300 volunteers work more than 145,000 hours each year on the path.

Because of such necessary efforts, the heart of the most populous part of the United States is today a forest trail. This premier hiking path is a world-class adventure covering about 2,143 miles. Only 150 to 200 people a year finish the complete hike over the loftiest mountains in eastern North America. Those who have accomplished the entire feat number fewer than 3,000. But about 4 million people take to part of the trail annually, enjoying a short stroll, a summit hike, a nearby point of interest, or a multinight backpacking trip. The Appalachian Trail in North Carolina is a wonderful string of day hikes.

The perils of the 2,143-mile trek might be unimaginable to sedentary Americans. If the sheer physical task weren't arduous enough, equipment and its failures pose other problems. If you've ever had a blister from new hiking boots, imagine having boot problems as you walk 10 or more miles daily. Even when a hiker's boots are comfortable, they wear out or fall apart on the trek, often at the least-opportune time. That kind of roulette plagues everything a hiker relies on, from a backpacking stove to a tent to a sleeping bag.

And the end-to-end AT hiker discovers that the human body is just another piece of equipment bound to fail. Most people find a three- or four-day backpacking trip ample undertaking; imagine walking for an entire summer. Your body really begins to lag at the daily chore of hoisting 40 pounds onto your back. Food can become an obsession after just three nights without a satisfying, multicourse repast. But that's the fun part; worse is yet to come. For some, the feet go first—blisters and other injuries plague these body parts that touch the trail. For others, the knees give in. A searing spike of pain with each step puts an end to many a hike. So can a sore back that just gets worse, or a bad cold that lingers long after your body's spare energy is gone. An end-to-end hike on the AT is a Herculean undertaking. And not everybody makes it. Not everybody is up to the simple mental and physical fatigue.

From the Boulevard Trail junction, this Appalachian Trail hiker only has another mile and a half to Charlie's Bunion—perhaps the scenic highpoint of the Smokies.

But that doesn't mean it's unrewarding. Within North Carolina alone, hikers pass through tree-covered, modest mountains that conjure the Appalachians of stereotype. And they see their share of poverty, what many hikers call the raw side of life in these stark, rugged hills. They also see some of the East's grandest, most spectacular views. And there is mud, cold summer rain, stinging spring snow, and just about everything else a mountain climate can deliver, including awesome solitude and pockets of virgin wilderness reminiscent of the forests Daniel Boone experienced.

More than a half-century after the trail was begun, the philosophical uplift that MacKaye hoped for has taken place. Our current outdoor lifestyle and environmental consciousness is traceable in part to the existence of the Appalachian Trail and the wildlands that enclose it. The path's enduring grandeur inspires generation after generation of hikers. Perhaps more than any other recreational facility in the world, the Appalachian Trail symbolizes the power of nature to work wonders in the hearts and minds of those who take the time to wander in the woods.

Hike 1 in this book explores the Southern Balds section of the AT in North Carolina. Appendix A, an annotated mileage log for the Appalachian Trail, lists several trail checkpoints and good day hikes. More information about the Appalachian Trail can be acquired from the Appalachian Trail Conference, see Appendix C, or from any of the trail guidebooks available in many libraries and outdoor shops.

1 APPALACHIAN TRAIL–SOUTHERN BALDS SECTION

Overview

Seen from the North Carolina section of the Appalachian Trail (AT), the Roan Mountain Highlands offer spectacular scenery and interesting natural history. Their meadow-covered mountaintops, called the Southern Balds, provide the most alpine-like scenery in the region.

Indian legends offer various explanations for the formation of the Southern Balds. One holds that the Catawba tribe challenged all tribes of earth to a great battle. The ensuing struggle denuded the summits, and where every Catawba brave fell, a blood-red rhododendron sprang up as a memorial. True or not, the late June bloom of rhododendrons across the Roan Mountain crest is one of the Southern Appalachians' premier natural events. Other theories about the Balds speculate that a major fire claimed the trees and made the soil unsuitable for immediate reforestation. The treeless landscape probably lasted because of extensive grazing by cattle from local farms.

In the mid-1980s, a conference weighed the future of the Balds. There "The alarms really went off," says Paul Bradley, a district ranger for the area that includes Hump, Yellow, and Roan Mountains, which are the summits crossed on this 13-mile section of the AT along the North Carolina/Tennessee border. "Scientists, Forest Service officials, and the public realized that

Rhododendron blooms on the Appalachian Trail near Roan Mountain.

if we didn't start doing something immediately we'd lose the Balds," he says. The statistics were ominous. Of 2,500 bald acres on and near the summits mentioned above, 1,641 acres had started growing in. The reforestation appeared to be a natural process; blackberry, hawthorn, and spruce were slowly taking over. Under the Forest Land Management Plan that coordinates Pisgah National Forest's multiple uses, the agency was directed to evaluate ways to keep the Balds. The program, now underway, includes methods such as mowing, controlled fires, and more. It could determine whether the scenic views on this section of the AT will remain for future generations.

The Southern Balds provide key habitat for more than thirty endangered and threatened plant species. These plants, among them Gray's lily, wretched sedge, and Roan Mountain bluets, constitute the greatest concentration of rare plants in the Southern Appalachians. The Forest Service plans to maintain 1,000 acres of the Balds and reclaim another 1,600 where trees, shrubs and briars are encroaching on this meadow plant community.

Revegetation of the balds may be accelerating because grazing slowed twenty years ago when the Forest Service acquired much of the land. At the time, grazing was considered incompatible with use of the Appalachian Trail. Now, ironically, grazing is at the top of the list of methods being used to keep the balds covered with grasses and sedges. On Roan Mountain, hikers now see goats grazing in summer. The animals are well suited to the heights, especially the Alpine and Angora breeds. Their droppings aren't as noticeable as cow waste, and their hooves do less damage to the fragile environment.

Balds near Engine Gap on Appalachian Trail.

General description: An inspiring hike on the Appalachian Trail (AT) over the mountaintop meadows called the Southern Balds. As a whole, this is a wonderful but strenuous backpacking trip. Hikers can also make day hikes to mountaintop views.

General location: Carvers Gap, near Boone.

Length: 13 miles total. Round-trip day hikes from Carvers Gap are as follows: 0.8 mile to Round Bald; 2.4 miles to Jane Bald; 4 miles to Grassy Ridge Bald. Round-trip hikes from Yellow Mountain Gap: 3 miles to views near Little Hump Mountain; 8 miles to Hump Mountain (10 miles from U.S. Highway 19-E).

Degree of difficulty: Moderately strenuous to nearby mountaintops; very strenuous for lengthy day hikes or a backpack of the entire ridgetop, especially north to south.

Maps: Appalachian Trail Conference AT map and guide; USGS Carvers Gap, Elk Park, and White Rocks Mountain quads.

Elevation gain and loss: 7,100 feet south to north.

Trailhead elevation: 5,512 feet at Carvers Gap; 2,880 feet at Elk Park.

High point: Just under 6,000 feet.

Water availability: A water fountain and restroom are located 1.8 miles from Carvers Gap at the Roan Mountain Gardens Forest Service station, open late spring through early fall. Nearby water sources are the community of Roan Mountain and Roan Mountain State Park, see Appendix C. Near the Elk Park trailhead, businesses can provide water. Water is also available at springs along the route.

For more information: Toecane Ranger District, Pisgah National Forest. Or contact Supervisor's Office, National Forests in North Carolina. See Appendix C.

Finding the trailheads: AT trailheads are 2.5 miles west of Elk Park and at Carvers Gap, a high crest in the Appalachians on the state line. Hikers who want to walk the entire ridge should begin at Carvers Gap.

From Boone, go though Linville and Newland (or Banner Elk) to reach US 19-E. Go west beyond the state line 0.9 mile to a small parking area on the left.

To reach the Carvers Gap trailhead, stay west on US 19-E, then turn left on Tennessee Highway 143 at the town of Roan Mountain. Carvers Gap is 14 miles from that junction. From Asheville and more southerly areas, take North Carolina Highway 261 from Bakersville about 14 miles to Carvers Gap. To reach Elk Park, cross into Tennessee and take TN 143 to US 19-E and take a right.

The Roaring Creek trailhead is on US 19-E. Between Elk Park and Newland, take US 19-E south toward Spruce Pine from the junction with North Carolina Highway 194. Go south past Minneapolis to a right on Roaring Creek Road at 8.6 miles. Keep right at all the forks to reach the trailhead below Yellow Mountain Gap, about 5 miles.

Parking overnight along US 19-E is not recommended, for your car's safety. Try to arrange for pickup and drop-off. Winter access to the

1 APPALACHIAN TRAIL—
SOUTHERN BALDS SECTION

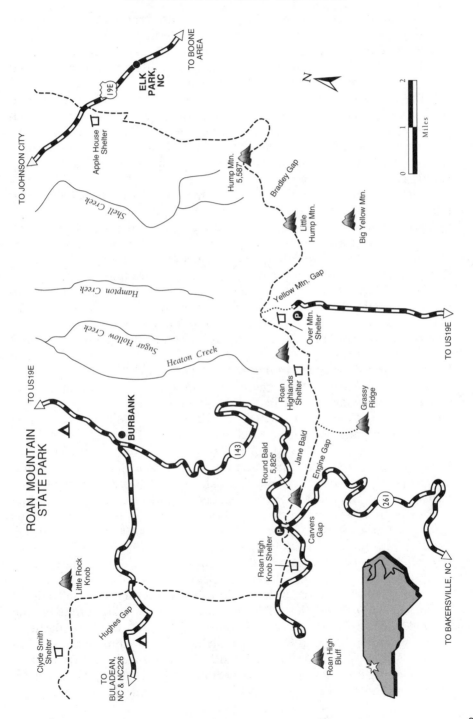

TO BOONE AREA

ELK PARK, NC

19E

Apple House Shelter

TO JOHNSON CITY

Shell Creek

Hump Mtn. 5,587'

Bradley Gap

Little Hump Mtn.

Big Yellow Mtn.

N

Miles

0 1 2

Hampton Creek

Sugar Hollow Creek

Heaton Creek

Yellow Mtn. Gap

Over Mtn. Shelter

P

TO US19E

Roan Highlands Shelter

Grassy Ridge

ROAN MOUNTAIN STATE PARK

TO US19E

BURBANK

143

Round Bald 5,826'

Jane Bald

Engine Gap

261

Little Rock Knob

Clyde Smith Shelter

Hughes Gap

TO BULADEAN, NC & NC226

Roan High Knob Shelter

P

Carvers Gap

Roan High Bluff

TO BAKERSVILLE, NC

27

trailheads can be complicated by deep snow; they are a low priority for plowing.

The hikes: The white-blazed **Appalachian Trail (AT)** traverses the entire ridge, sticking closely to the state line all the way. It winds farthest into North Carolina as it ascends the summit of Hump Mountain, then runs east before looping back toward the border. It ventures farthest into Tennessee as the trail descends to U.S. Highway 19-E.

The trail is well-marked, but the open terrain can provide substantial route-finding challenges in snow, fog, and rain. Use caution and take adequate maps. Expect unusual weather year-round. Though cool days are the norm in summer at these heights, high-altitude sun can be punishing, so take a hat and sunscreen. And remember that the Balds are brushy; woody plants can irritate bare legs.

Backpackers who intend to walk the trail end-to-end should hike from south to north, since the trail descends in that direction from Carvers Gap, at 5,512 feet, to Elk Park, at 2,880 feet. Though graded, the steep 5-mile climb from Elk Park to Hump Mountain rises 2,700 feet, more than the entire elevation gain going north from Carvers Gap to Elk Park. From either direction, hikers find campsites plentiful in the grassy gaps lining the trail.

From Carvers Gap, cross the stile at the fence line and ascend steps up the grassy bald mountain to the east. These wonderful log steps were placed by a crew from the Appalachian Mountain Club in the late 1970s. Views spread in all directions as the trail ascends Round Bald, a summit resembling the broad end of an egg. The 360-degree summit view, at 5,826 feet, is a steep but short 0.4 mile from Carvers Gap.

The trail descends then veers right on a nice route that gradually reaches Engine Gap at 0.8 mile. It then ascends a rock outcrop at 1 mile, and the summit of Jane Bald at about 1.2 miles, at 5,807 feet, both fine turnaround points for a shorter hike with fabulous views.

At 1.5 miles, the AT slides left. Straight ahead a side trail reaches Grassy Ridge, 6,000 feet, a bald summit, with spectacular views. Continuing left past the trail to Grassy Ridge Bald, the AT passes a spring on the right at about 1.7 miles. The trail reaches a spur of Grassy Ridge, then drops steeply left at 2 miles to Low Gap (5,000 feet) and Roan Highlands Shelter at 3 miles. A side trail south of the ridge leads 100 yards to a spring.

The trail climbs over Elk Hollow Ridge, then descends to Buckeye Gap at 4 miles. Hikers cross a nearly 5,000-foot summit with nice views at 4.5 miles. Bear right off the main ridge. At 4.7 miles, the trail drops into Yellow Mountain Gap (4,682 feet). The **Overmountain Victory Trail**, a National Historic Trail, crosses the AT here. This is the route of colonists who defeated British Colonel Patrick Ferguson's forces at the 1780 Battle of King's Mountain in South Carolina, a pivotal step in winning the Revolutionary War. To the right, the road-width colonial trace descends in about 0.7 mile to the Roaring Creek Road, North Carolina Highway 1132. A blue-blazed side trail leads right from the gap to a barn, the Overmountain

Shelter, where campers may sleep in the loft and cook downstairs. This is another good starting point for day hikes or an overnighter south to the Roan Highlands Shelter. Parking is about 0.7 mile south of the gap on Roaring Creek Road via a gated forest road or the OVT.

Leaving Yellow Mountain Gap, the trail ascends a steep meadow and gradually enters a woods road, bearing right. At a meadow with a fence on the left, about 5.7 miles, it turns and crosses a stile (the old road continues straight, eventually reaching Big Yellow Mountain, a Nature Conservancy Preserve). Follow the trail along the woods as it bears away from the trees into another meadow.

The trail reaches a small gap at 6 miles. Hikers can find water about 300 feet off the trail to the right. From the gap, the path ascends past a large rock outcrop. At 6.2 miles, it tops Little Hump Mountain (5,459 feet). Descending, at about 6.5 miles, it passes through a small gap between the two peaks of Little Hump. It climbs again to the second peak, then descends gradually into Bradley Gap (4,960 feet) at 7.1 miles. Trails to the left and right reach springs on the headwaters of Shell and Horse creeks, respectively.

Leaving Bradley Gap, the trail ascends the open summit ridge of Hump Mountain, an occasionally rocky, alpine-feeling, 1-mile hike to the peak (5,587 feet) at 8 miles. The views are all-encompassing and include Mount Mitchell, Roan Mountain, Grandfather Mountain, and Virginia's highest summits, Mount Rogers and Whitetop. Meadows sweep away, interspersed with crags. Returning to Yellow Mountain Gap from here is an 8-mile round-trip.

From Hump Mountain, the route to US 19-E has changed substantially in the last decade or so. The AT heads east from the summit on a new section of trail, actually an old vehicle route across the bald top, completed in the early 1980s. The trail turns left, enters the woods at 8.6 miles, then starts a graded descent back west (past a nice view of Elk Park at 8.9 miles). It slabs into the open meadows of Doll Flats, a good campsite, at just over 10 miles. From Doll Flats, the new trail leads northwest, down a narrow ridge, under a power line, then switchbacks into Wilder Mine Hollow at about 12 miles.

At 12.2 miles, hikers pass a spring on the right. The trail follows a road across a stream through the Wilder Mine area, where iron ore was mined in the late nineteenth and early twentieth centuries, and where rock was quarried in the 1950s. **CAUTION:** The mineshafts are dangerous; keep out! Continuing on the road, the trail crosses the stream to reach the Apple House Shelter on the left at 12.5 miles. Refurbished as a trail shelter in the mid-1980s, this old building once stored explosives for the mines. The shelter's name is appropriate given the plentiful apple orchards and cider stands in the Elk Park area.

Hikers will turn left from the road and pass an old railroad bridge support where the narrow-gauge Eastern Tennessee & Western North Carolina Railroad used to run between Johnson City, Tennessee, and Boone, North Carolina, from the late 1800s to its demise in a 1940s flood. The line carried ore from the Wilder Mine and another massive operation nearby at Cranberry, North Carolina. A trail bridge spans Buck Creek, the lowest stream along the trail, and an old driveway rises left to the edge of US 19-E at 13 miles.

A day hike or overnight backpacking trip from here to **Hump Mountain**, a 10-mile round-trip, would be rewarding but extremely strenuous.

2 BARTRAM TRAIL

Overview

The Bartram Trail was the dream of Walter G. McKelvey of Brevard, North Carolina, a retired landscape architect. McKelvey spent the early 1970s acquiring government approval and planning a route, but died just before the meeting he'd planned to charter the North Carolina Bartram Trail Society. Countless volunteers have contributed to his effort to build this trail honoring early botanist William Bartram, whom the Indians called "Puc Puggy," a Muskogean name meaning "the flower hunter."

Bartram was a Philadelphia-born naturalist and explorer whose trips expanded the world's awareness of Cherokee culture and the profuse flora and fauna of the Southern Appalachians. Sparked by his fascination with "primitive, unmodified nature," Bartram wandered southwestern North Carolina from 1773-1777 and published *The Travels of William Bartram* in 1791 (still in print and highly recommended). The book was immensely popular, especially in Europe, where it was praised by writers such as Carlyle and Coleridge.

Today, the yellow-blazed Bartram Trail has been largely completed. About 72 miles of the nearly 100-mile path are hikable. Seven sections of the Bartram Trail fall in North Carolina. The 11.5 miles of the trail from Wallace Branch to Wayah Bald, the trail's high point at 5,342 feet, were designated as a National Recreation Trail in 1985 and make a strenuous and spectacular backpacking trip. The Georgia section of the Bartram Trail is also an NRT (see *Hiking Georgia*, Falcon Press).

The section of trail described below is perhaps the Bartram Trail's best part.

General description: An outstanding ridge walk, perfect for backpacking or day hiking. The graded trail traverses a rarely visited ridge and spectacular summits.
General location: North of Highlands.
Length: 8.5 miles, with shorter out-and-back day hikes from either end.
Degree of difficulty: Moderate to moderately strenuous from Jones Gap; strenuous from Buckeye Creek.
Maps: USGS Scaly Mountain quad; the best map of the trail is a pamphlet published by the North Carolina Bartram Trail Society.
Elevation gain and loss: 2,600 feet for the entire section.

2 BARTRAM TRAIL

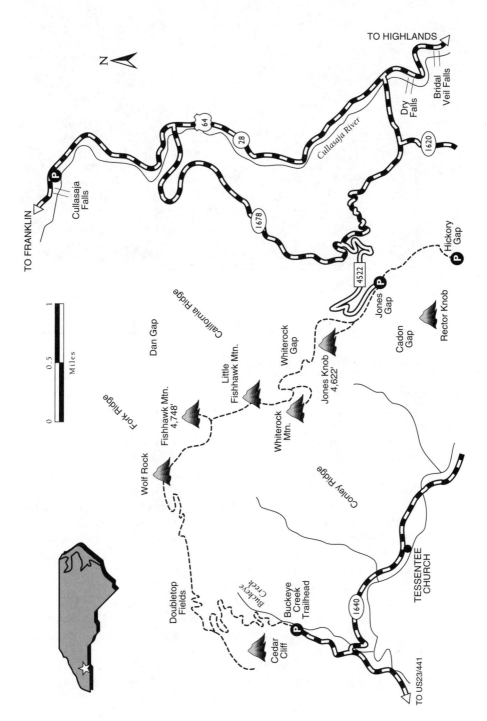

Lush ferns line the Bartram Trail near Cedar Cliff.

Trailhead elevation: 4,360 feet at Jones Gap; 2,400 feet at the Buckeye Creek trailhead.
High point: 4,620 feet at Little Fishhawk Mountain.
Low point: Buckeye Creek trailhead.
Water availability: Stephens Creek Spring, the only reliable water source, is just off the trail, 1.3 miles north from Jones Gap.
Best season: Year-round.
For more information: North Carolina Bartram Trail Society. Maps and a wealth of other materials about the national forest are available at the Highlands Ranger District Visitor Information Center, Main Street, Highlands, North Carolina. Open seven days per week during summer and fall, weekends before and after, and closed in winter. Or contact Highlands Ranger District, open weekdays year-round. See Appendix C.
Finding the trailheads: To reach the Jones Gap trailhead from Highlands, go west on U.S. Highway 64/North Carolina Highway 28 from downtown Highlands. At 4.7 miles, turn left on Turtle Pond Road. (From Franklin, at the U.S. Highways 64/441 junction, go south on US 64/NC 28 for 12.8 miles to Turtle Pond Rd.) After 1.1 miles, turn right onto a road marked SR 1678. At 1.4 miles, at the top of a hill, turn left on Forest Road 4522 (narrow but well-maintained) which reaches the trailhead in 2 miles. The trail leaves the parking area to the right.

To reach the Buckeye Creek trailhead from Dillard, Georgia, go a short distance north from Dillard on U.S. Highways 441/23. From where Georgia

Highway 246/North Carolina Highway 106 joins on the right, go 5.3 miles north and take a right on a road marked SR 1636. (This junction is 7 miles south of Franklin on US 441/23.) In 3.5 miles, turn left on SR 1640. In 0.3 mile, bear right immediately below and past a house. In another 0.2 mile, bear right at the entrance to Cedar Ridge Ranch and park at the beginning of an old logging road. Follow the road on foot to a gate and vertical Bartram Trail sign.

The hike: This hike combines easy access, masterful design, gradual grade, and backcountry character. Section 2 of the **Bartram Trail**, the route is a well-kept secret in the Highlands Ranger District of Nantahala National Forest. The trail was installed from scratch, so few people know about it; the area saw precious little visitation before, and is still rarely visited. So many other trails in the Highlands Ranger District are crowded, but hikers can enjoy relative solitude here. Another plus for the area: pristine scenery. With little evidence of logging, the forests on this hike are mature and inspiring. Combine that with spectacular views from rocky summits, and this becomes an unusually appealing destination. You'd want to hike here even if no trail existed.

From Jones Gap or Buckeye Creek, the trail makes a nice out-and-back day hike. The best hike for scenery and ease of walking involves going northwest from Jones Gap (4,360 feet); the greatest climb to the ridge occurs on the hike south from the Buckeye Creek trailhead (2,400 feet). Nevertheless, the climb from Buckeye Creek is graded and less frequented than

View from Whiterock Mountain on Bartram Trail.

the trail from Jones Gap, which spells solitude for the day hiker who wants a workout. The following hike description covers the route from Jones Gap.

From the trailhead, the path enters a wildlife plot, then the woods. A blue-blazed trail goes left; in 0.3 mile it reaches a western view from Jones Knob, 4,622 feet (a nice 0.8-mile round-trip day hike). Go right on the yellow-blazed Bartram Trail as it slabs east of Jones Knob through a fern-covered forest. As the trail descends north of the knob it passes through an impressive forest of rhododendron and along a moss-covered ledge. The trail crosses a small gap, slabs the west side of a small peak, and descends into Whiterock Gap. Just as it turns down, a view appears just beyond the trees on the left from a pristine exfoliated dome.

In Whiterock Gap, at 1.3 miles, is a campsite and an old sign directing you right to Stephens Creek Spring (about 800 feet off trail). The trail leaves the gap, slabbing gradually up the eastern side of Whiterock Mountain to a junction, at about 2 miles, with another blue-blazed side trail. This one leads to the summit of Whiterock Mountain (4,480 feet). In the 0.3-mile climb to the peak, the trail makes a neat passage between rocks and over domes to an expansive dome with an extended view north along the ridge. This is a great day hike, at about 4.6 miles round-trip. Use caution on the summit dome in wet weather.

The trail continues north on a sharp ridge through mature white oak forest to Little Fishhawk Mountain, at 3 miles. The trail dips off the summit, runs another sharp ridgeline, and bears left, skirting the cone of Fishhawk Mountain (4,748 feet), the highest summit on the entire ridge. Here a steep and primitive blue-blazed trail to the right ascends to the peak where a plaque commemorates Bartram's travels.

The main trail slabs past Fishhawk Mountain and descends the ridge west to a memorable view at Wolf Rock, at 3.9 miles. For the next 2 miles, the trail descends gradually to Double Top Fields, at 5.5 miles. Here is a surprise: a school bus sitting in the middle of the trail. The old, wheel-less Macon County bus obviously was the last vehicle to wander up here, who knows how, on a now overgrown road that descends north through an old apple orchard. It once became someone's house, too. The remains of an old deck lie on the side looking out over the orchard.

The trail descends through wildly wind-gnarled trees, switchbacks to a viewpoint on a crag, then exits through open forest on the gradual jog to the final gap on the ridge. The gap, just before Cedar Cliff, is high and breezy with a fine campsite (perfect for backpackers starting at the Buckeye Creek trailhead, 3 miles and 1,000 feet below).

The Bartram Trail continues through the gap from here, but ends in about 0.2 mile. The trail's sudden dwindling to trackless brush and bits of flagging tape will be a startling and enlightening experience for hikers who have never volunteered to build a trail. The treadway ends, then tiny bits of tape lead to a nice campsite. The trail will eventually descend to the valley.

Back at the gap, take a sharp left on a blue-blazed access trail and descend through a boulder strewn forest with plentiful ferns. The trail is gradual through mature forest, then switchbacks, passes through a massive wall of rhododendron, and joins an overgrown logging grade at about 7 miles. Soon, the old grade emerges into a recovering clearcut and a signed junction with a logging grade that goes left and right. Go right to descend.

The last 1.5 miles of this hike aren't pristine by any means. But the surrounding clearcut is buffered, and the grade is gradual. It can be hot on a summer day. Near the bottom, the logging grade enters the woods again and grass covers it. The path passes a gate and reaches the trailhead above audible Buckeye Creek at about 8.5 miles.

3 BEACON HEIGHTS

General description: A short leg-stretcher with spectacular views of Grandfather Mountain and its nearly vertical-mile drop to the Piedmont. By adding a stretch of the Mountains To Sea Trail, hikers can find solitude.
General location: Blue Ridge Parkway.
Length: 0.7 mile round-trip. Adding the Mountains To Sea Trail side trip creates a hike of about 1.1 miles.
Degree of difficulty: Easy.
Maps: USGS Grandfather quad. The Grandfather Mountain hiking map shows the trail and is available free at the Grandfather Mountain entrance, open daily year-round (see Hike 11). A strip map for finding the trailhead is available from Parkway headquarters.
Elevation gain and loss: 320 feet.
Trailhead elevation: 4,200 feet.
High point: 4,360 feet.
Water availability: No water is available on the trail, but the Grandfather Mountain entrance nearby has water year-round.
For more information: The Blue Ridge Parkway, Asheville, NC. Call for recorded information, weather road closures, mailing requests, etc. The trail is in the Parkway's Gillespie Gap District. See Appendix C.
Finding the trailhead: The trailhead is located at milepost 305 on the Blue Ridge Parkway, just south of the U.S. Highway 221 entrance to the Parkway, 2 miles east of Linville; 13.4 miles south of the U.S. Highway 321 access between Boone and Blowing Rock; and 12.3 miles north of the US 221 access north of Marion.

The hike: This is one of the Parkway's best leg-stretchers. The grades are gradual, the footing is never very difficult, and the views are outstanding. For these reasons it is also a popular hike, but by adding a short stretch of the Mountains To Sea Trail, hikers can outwit the crowds and picnic alone at scenic viewpoints. Signs at the bottom and top of the trail note that no camping or fires are permitted.

3 BEACON HEIGHTS AND MOUNTAINS TO THE SEA TRAILS

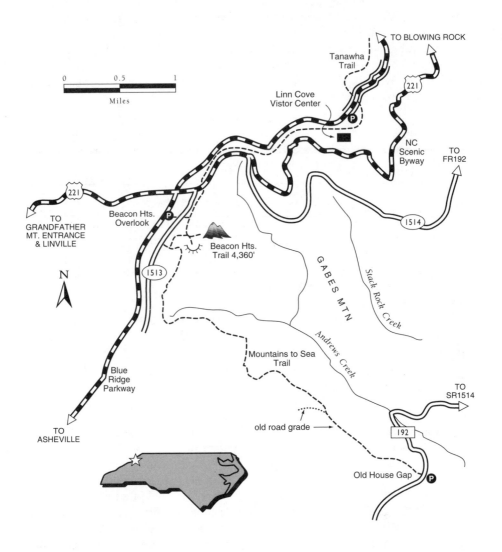

From the trailhead, hikers walk perpendicular to the Parkway, across the dirt road marked SR 1513, and enter the woods where the sign says "Tanawha Trail Beacon Heights 0.2". The path climbs gradually to a junction with the Tanawha Trail, a portion of the Mountains To Sea Trail. The trail turns right and passes an overhanging rock on the left, an excellent shelter to keep in mind during rainy weather. It then passes a bench on the right and continues up the steepest, rockiest part of the trail to a signed junction, where the Mountains To Sea Trail goes right.

The **Beacon Heights Trail** from the Parkway switchbacks left as it meanders to the crest (at 0.3 mile) and a bench. Side trails go in both directions amid galax, tall red spruce, fir, and rhododendron. A sign by the bench inspires the walker to get the most from the view: "The art of seeing nature is in essence the art of awareness. How much we see depends on what we bring to the encounter. - Unknown"

To the right, the path emerges on the top of a south-facing exfoliated dome with great views to the high peaks along the Parkway, Mount Mitchell, Linville Gorge, and the Piedmont. Left from the bench (as you approach from the bottom), the path wanders to a rustic flight of stone steps that emerge onto another dome. Here are spectacular views of the eastern flank of Grandfather Mountain and the Parkway north toward Blowing Rock. To the east, the mountain plummets into Pisgah National Forest's Wilson Creek drainage, a rippled, waterfall-filled area of scenic dirt roads. On the skyline, parts of Grandfather Mountain's visitor facilities are visible, but the overall view is of wilderness.

Hikers can retrace their steps to the bottom (0.7 mile) or, to extend the walk, take a left at the first junction with the Mountains To Sea Trail on the way down. This nice old logging grade, marked with white blazes, is grown close with mountain laurel. Not far down the trail, a subtle path goes left to the top of a crag for a view. The main trail then bears right and back left before eventually bearing back right again to join with SR 1513, the dirt road you crossed at the trailhead.

Blooming rhododendron and Grandfather Mountain flank Beacon Heights.

Just before reaching the road, turn left into the woods on the white-marked **Mountains To Sea Trail** as it descends to Old House Gap on the way to Linville Gorge. The trail slabs easily through an intimate forest of lichen-covered outcrops, galax, oak, pine, and rhododendron. This is a spongy, needle-covered trail that hasn't been excavated. It artfully bisects two boulders, meanders down a large outcrop, then exits and re-enters the woods across a nice ledge. This is a quiet, private view of the valley, perfect for a picnic.

The quickest route back to the trailhead retraces steps to the old logging grade portion of the Mountains To Sea Trail, then goes left to SR 1513. Turn right and walk on the road back to the Parkway. Total distance for this hike is 1.1 miles; hikers can also return up the Mountains To Sea Trail and descend the Beacon Heights Trail, slightly farther.

4   BLACK MOUNTAIN CREST

Overview

The serrated Black Mountains dominate the western skyline of North Carolina. The long range includes six of the ten highest peaks in eastern North America. Unlike the massive Great Smoky Mountains, which are nearly as high, the Blacks are relatively compact. But they tower loftily 15 miles from the Blue Ridge. The summits march across the sky, dipping into gaps and capping out as a black line. Often above the clouds, the mighty Blacks are cut by rockslides that appear as snow- and ice-covered chutes in winter.

The Black Mountains beg comparison to that contrastingly named northeastern range, the White Mountains of New Hampshire. The Blacks, despite being the highest in the East, would have to be nearly 8,000 feet in height before they reached a climate cold enough to create the treeline found in the north; the New Hampshire mountains nudge their summits into alpine climate at just under 5,000 feet. But the Black Mountains reign supreme. Mount Mitchell reaches closer to 7,000 feet than any peak east of the Mississippi.

High winds, deep snow (104 inches annually), and a surprisingly cold climate clothe Mount Mitchell's crags in evergreens. At one time, this Canadian-zone forest was dense and verdant, but now a decades-long attack by the balsam woolly aphid, a pest that preys on Fraser firs, and increasing airborne pollutants, ozone, and acid rain have quickly and alarmingly robbed this spectacular ridge of its red spruces and firs (see Hike 24, Mount Mitchell State Park). Low vegetation, including a remarkable thornless blackberry, clings to the cliffs and crags.

A hike here is not like a wheezing walk down a city street, but ozone and pollutant levels can be high in the summer. That notwithstanding, the

Black Mountain Crest Trail is a wonderful way to savor this legendary mountain area. It is possible to start atop Mount Mitchell for adventurous day hikes without expeditionary exertion. Hikers intent on arduous ascents should climb from adjacent valleys on the many taxing trails with an elevation gain of about 4,000 feet. Assuming that most hikers will start on Mount Mitchell and return to the peak or descend in a single overnight to Bowlens Creek, the following trail description reads in that direction.

General description: An inspiring overnight backpack or shorter day hike across the Black Mountains, with summits all well above 6,000 feet. Views are astounding along this sparsely vegetated ridge, plummeting 4,000 feet into adjacent valleys.

General location: Mount Mitchell, Burnsville, and the Blue Ridge Parkway.

Length: The entire ridge hike runs just under 12 miles. The best day hikes are from the Mount Mitchell summit to Mount Craig, 2 miles round-trip, and to Deep Gap, a round-trip of just under 8 miles from the Mount Mitchell summit and from the Carolina Hemlocks Recreation Area.

Degree of difficulty: Moderate for a day hike to Mount Craig, the closest neighboring peak; moderately strenuous for a longer day trip to Deep Gap; strenuous from the valley. The entire ridge walk and overnight trips are very strenuous.

Maps: USGS Celo, Mount Mitchell, Burnsville quads. Handiest map is the Forest Service South Toe River Trail Map, available from the addresses below. However, the quads add detail, even though the Mount Mitchell and Celo quads maddeningly are joined right along the ridgecrest.

Elevation gain and loss: About 5,799 feet from Mount Mitchell down to Bowlens Creek, and just under 6,000 feet for a Deep Gap day hike from the valley on the Colbert Ridge Trail.

Trailhead elevations: 6,620 feet atop Mount Mitchell, the high point; 3,040 feet at Bowlens Creek trailhead, the low point.

Water availability: Visitor facilities atop Mount Mitchell provide water from May to October. There is a spring 0.2 mile below Deep Gap. The lower portion of the trail parallels Bowlens Creek.

For more information: Toecane Ranger District, Pisgah National Forest. Or contact Supervisor's Office, National Forests in North Carolina, Asheville. Also contact Mount Mitchell State Park, Burnsville. See Appendix C.

Finding the trailheads: The Mount Mitchell summit trailhead is reached via the Blue Ridge Parkway. Motorists follow North Carolina Highway 128, a 5-mile spur road, from the Parkway to Mount Mitchell State Park; turn at milepost 355. The junction is 38 miles south of U.S. Highway 221 at Linville Falls; 11 miles south of North Carolina Highway 80 at Buck Creek Gap (west of Marion); and 30 miles north of U.S. Highway 74 near Asheville. Turn into Mount Mitchell State Park. When you round the last curve into the summit parking area, the trail begins on the left between two log-cabin style shelters. You've gone too far if you swing into the lot and can see the development that flanks the path to the summit tower.

4 BLACK MOUNTAIN CREST TRAIL— PISGAH NF

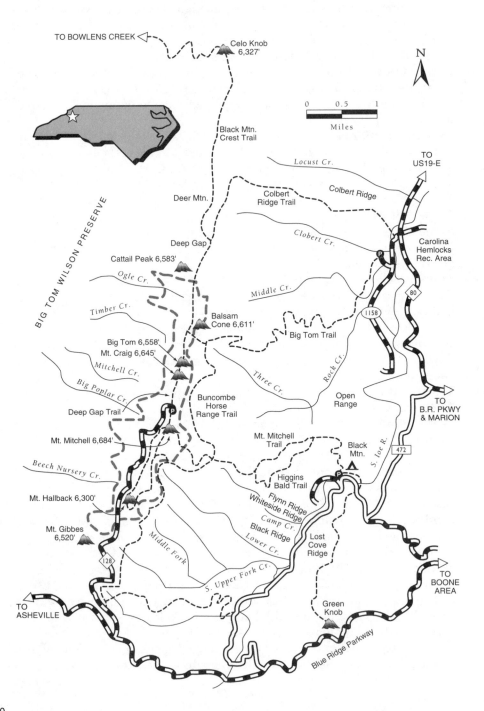

TO BOWLENS CREEK

Celo Knob 6,327'

Black Mtn. Crest Trail

N

0   0.5   1
Miles

TO US19-E

Locust Cr.

Colbert Ridge

Colbert Ridge Trail

Deer Mtn.

Clobert Cr.

Carolina Hemlocks Rec. Area

Deep Gap

P

Cattail Peak 6,583'

Middle Cr.

Ogle Cr.

BIG TOM WILSON PRESERVE

Timber Cr.

Balsam Cone 6,611'

Big Tom Trail

80

1158

Big Tom 6,558'
Mt. Craig 6,645'

Mitchell Cr.

Rock Cr.

Big Poplar Cr.

Three Cr.

Deep Gap Trail

P

Buncombe Horse Range Trail

Open Range

TO B.R. PKWY & MARION

Mt. Mitchell 6,684'

Mt. Mitchell Trail

Black Mtn.

S. Toe R.

472

Beech Nursery Cr.

Higgins Bald Trail

P

Mt. Hallback 6,300'

Flynn Ridge
Whiteside Ridge

Camp Cr.

Black Ridge

Lost Cove Ridge

TO BOONE AREA

Mt. Gibbes 6,520'

128

Middle Fork

Lower Cr.

S. Upper Fork Cr.

TO ASHEVILLE

Green Knob

Blue Ridge Parkway

The Bowlens Creek trailhead is near Burnsville, North Carolina. Turn south from U.S. Highway 19-E in Burnsville on NC 197. In 0.7 mile, turn left on the Bowlens Creek Road, (SR 1109). Go 2.4 miles to a road left in a hairpin curve. The trailhead is 0.2 mile up the road but park beyond the curve by a small cemetery on the right.

Trailheads for the Buncombe Horse Range Trail and the Colbert Ridge Trail are located near Carolina Hemlocks Recreation Area, reached from US 19-E, or the Blue Ridge Parkway, via NC 80. From US 19-E, about 4.5 miles north of Burnsville, turn right onto NC 80. Then in 10 miles, turn right before reaching Carolina Hemlocks Recreation Area on the Colbert Creek Road (SR 1158) in Hamrick. The trailhead for the Colbert Ridge Trail is on the right, in less than 0.5 mile. To reach the trailhead for the Buncombe Horse Range Trail, turn onto Colbert Creek Road and go 0.8 mile, then turn right and park on the left in 0.25 mile.

The hike: The orange-blazed **Black Mountain Crest Trail** leaves the north end of the parking lot, passes the picnic shelters, and descends through spruces. Its first segment, a wonderful out-and-back day hike, is a 2-mile round-trip walk to Mount Craig, where a plaque memorializes the peak's namesake, Locke Craig, the governor who helped secure the creation of this first North Carolina state park. The rugged route offers great views in all directions.

The gap between the peaks is about 0.5 mile from the start, and involves a descent to 6,330 feet. To the west the land drops away to Mitchell Creek and Mitchell Falls (4,400 feet), where Thomas "Big Tom" Wilson found the body of Mount Mitchell's namesake, Elisha Mitchell, in the pool at the base of the cataract (see Hike 24). To the east one of the more prominent slides on the Black Mountain Range is located, at the head of the Middle Fork of Rock Creek, covering almost 1,500 vertical feet.

From the gap, the climb to Mount Craig (6,645 feet) rebounds to the Blacks' second highest summit. There is a spectacular view back to the tower on Mount Mitchell. After descending briefly to another gap, the trail ascends to the summit of Big Tom (6,593 feet) at 1.2 miles, an elevation virtually identical to Mount LeConte, a noteworthy peak in the Great Smokies. A plaque memorializes Thomas Wilson.

The Black Mountain Crest Trail descends to the **Big Tom Trail** in about 0.4 mile. From that junction, the Big Tom Trail drops east abruptly down the mountain 0.5 mile, linking the Crest Trail to the 15-mile Buncombe Horse Range Trail. The white-blazed horse trail parallels the ridge crest south, but it also continues east 5.5 miles down the mountain from its junction with the Big Tom Trail, creating a 5.9-mile direct route to the Carolina Hemlocks Recreation Area. Used as a way up, this graded ascent is one of the easiest routes to the Black Mountain peaks.

Ascending beyond the Black Mountain Crest Trail's junction with the Big Tom Trail, the path climbs the west side of Balsam Cone and reaches the peak (6,611 feet) at about 2 miles. The trail reaches 6,583 feet as it

The Black Mountains dominate this snowy winter view from Banner Elk. Mount Mitchell (left) is the East's highest, and Deep Gap is on the right.

crosses Cattail Peak and leaves the state park for national forest. The Crest Trail drops 200 feet into a gap, then climbs again briefly to Potato Hill (6,440 feet) before dropping somewhat dramatically into Deep Gap at just under 4 miles. This is the more than 700-foot cleft visible for miles in the ridge of the Blacks (see photo above).

After crossing peaks named with such mundane names, and with Horse Rock, Deer Mountain, and Gibbs Mountain yet to come, it's interesting to note that the names for peaks in this range have been particularly controversial. Charlton Ogburn, in his 1975 book *The Southern Appala-chians*, complains bitterly that most of the summits on the range should still have their old names: Black Dome for Mount Mitchell, the Black Brothers, Hairy Bear, and others. Most hikers traversing the Blacks would agree to some extent; they may not like the old names, but they don't care for the current ones either. Of them all, Winter Star Mountain seems the most evocative.

Deep Gap's shelter was torn down in 1995, though in recent years the Crest Trail itself has been dramatically improved with the help of a youth program. A spring is 300 yards down the mountain in front of the shelter site. The white-blazed Colbert Ridge Trail leaves the gap to the east at about 4 miles, and drops just less than 3,000 feet in 3.6 miles to the vicinity of Carolina Hemlocks Recreation Area. This is a nice, easier approach for backpackers who want to gain the peaks the old-fashioned way and a good day hike, too, at just under 8 miles round-trip.

Climbing out of the gap, the Crest Trail rises at 4.5 miles to Deer Moun-tain (6,120 feet), then jogs right to higher Winter Star Mountain (6,203 feet). With this peak the trail gains the ridge of the northern Blacks, which are lower and have less varied elevation than the southern range. There are spectacular views on this section of the trail. The trail jogs left of the ridge at about 6 miles, passing Gibbs Mountain and Horse Rock. At just over 7 miles, the trail pitches up and follows slabs west of the final and most lofty of the northern Black Mountain peaks, Celo Knob (6,327 feet) at 7.5 miles.

The next 4.5 miles go downhill. After a switchbacking descent, the trail follows a prominent northwesterly ridge parallel with Bowlens Creek, the drainage to the southwest. At just under 11 miles, the trail switchbacks to the creek and follows its cascades and pools to a timber road and the dirt access road, at just under 12 miles.

5   BOONE GREENWAY

Overview

The Boone Greenway was sparked by the town of Boone's comprehen-sive planning process in 1986. The $100,000 path was built with money from the town and the federal Land and Water Conservation Fund. It was dedicated in 1991 as the Lee and Vivian Reynolds Greenway, in honor of the couple's work toward the beautification of Boone. Since then, the town and its citizen greenway committee have put together an impressive list of donated land. That, together with town and state property, will permit the path to be extended to Deerfield Road and other areas, perhaps in the next few years.

5 BOONE GREENWAY

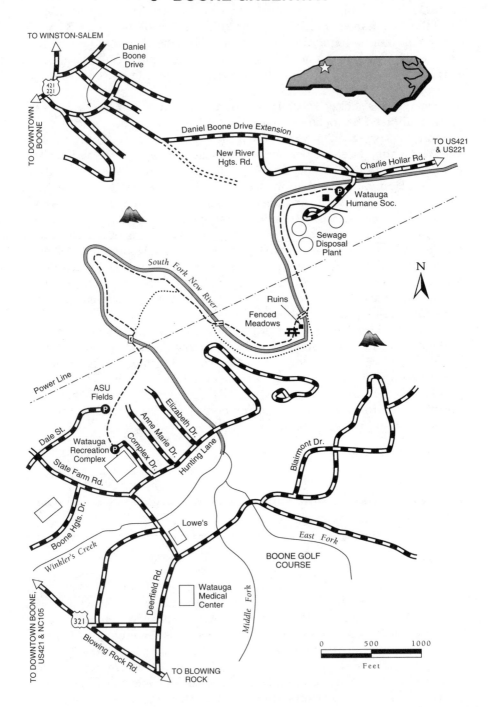

TO WINSTON-SALEM

Daniel Boone Drive

421 221

TO DOWNTOWN BOONE

Daniel Boone Drive Extension

New River Hgts. Rd.

TO US421 & US221

Charlie Hollar Rd.

P Watauga Humane Soc.

Sewage Disposal Plant

South Fork New River

Ruins

Fenced Meadows

N

Power Line

ASU Fields

P

Dale St.

Watauga Recreation Complex

P

Complex Dr.

Anne Marie Dr.

Elizabeth Dr.

Hunting Lane

Blairmont Dr.

State Farm Rd.

Boone Hgts. Dr.

Winkler's Creek

Lowe's

East Fork

BOONE GOLF COURSE

Deerfield Rd.

Middle Fork

Watauga Medical Center

TO DOWNTOWN BOONE, US421 & NC105

321

Blowing Rock Rd.

TO BLOWING ROCK

0   500   1000

Feet

General description: This pea gravel-surfaced trail follows a stretch of the South Fork of the New River between two neighborhoods in the town of Boone. The path has an almost backcountry feel, and is perfect for walking, jogging, biking, and cross-country skiing.

General location: Boone.

Length: 1.9 miles

Degree of difficulty: Easy.

Maps: USGS Boone quad.

Elevation gain and loss: Negligible.

Trailhead elevation: 3,100 feet.

Water availability: There is a warm-weather water fountain at the northern end of the trail. Water is also available at the Watauga County Recreation Complex, the southern terminus of the trail.

For more information: To receive a map of Boone that shows the greenway trailheads, send $2 (checks okay) to: Boone Area Chamber of Commerce. See Appendix C.

Finding the trailheads: The main trailhead is at the Watauga County Recreation Complex, just off State Farm Road, on Hunting Lane, with a left onto Complex Drive. Access is near Lowe's Building Supply store. The hike leaves the northwest side of the building and follows signs along the southeast side of Appalachian State University's intramural athletics fields. Parking is nearby.

The other trailhead is beside the Watauga County Humane Society Animal Shelter, just off Daniel Boone Drive. Access is marked by signs from U.S. Highway 421, opposite the New Market Shopping Center near the US 421/North Carolina Highway 194 intersection. Heading east from New Market Shopping Center on US 421, turn right onto Daniel Boone Drive, right on Daniel Boone Drive Extension, right onto New River Heights Road, and then take another right across a low water bridge at the junction with Charlie Hollar Road. Parking is on the right.

The hike: This isn't your average urban linear park. The Boone Greenway follows undeveloped land along the South Fork of the New River that belongs to Appalachian State University. The property is an almost backcountry watershed tucked between neighborhoods. From many places along the greenway, you wouldn't imagine that the town exists. All you see from some spots is forest, green summits, and a remarkably clean mountain stream.

The trail, with three bridges, provides a wonderful barrier-free route through open fields blooming with goldenrod in late summer, past cattle grazing in meadows, and along shady stream banks near the sound of rippling water. There is ample evidence of wildlife. Animal tracks are often seen by the river, and birds are plentiful, so consider the trail an ideal birding location.

Walkers will like this greenway, but the surface also makes jogging a breeze, and Boone's snowfall (about 3 feet, mostly December through February) makes it a great beginner trail for cross-country skiers.

The Boone Greenway passes grazing cattle in fenced fields and the ruins of a power station—the first in northwestern North Carolina.

There are benches along the trail, and two picnic areas. The largest, with two picnic tables, one with a small roof, surrounds a historic site at about the 1-mile mark. In this scenic bend in the river at the middle point of the trail, an open glade of trees surrounds the stone ruins of a hydroelectric generation station that served Appalachian State Teachers College, now Appalachian State University. The plank ruins of an old dam lie in the river, and another stone structure stands on the opposite bank. This electrical generation system, built in the early 1900s, was the first to serve any residence or institution in the northwestern mountains of North Carolina. The station provided electricity to the college and later served as the basis for the New River Power and Light Company. The ruin is frail, so climbing or even walking under the structure is discouraged until it is stabilized. Picnickers will note that wire mesh encircles the trunks of shade trees to discourage beavers. This picnic area is reached most quickly from the Daniel Boone Drive trailhead (about 2 miles round-trip).

The historical angle is enhanced when, in the warm months, hikers occasionally hear the pleasant train whistle of Tweetsie Railroad wafting over from Blowing Rock. The tourist attraction preserves the old steam trains that first connected this isolated area to the outside world between the 1890s and 1940s. Before a flood ended the old East Tennessee & Western North Carolina Railroad trips from Johnson City to Boone, no doubt that same whistle was a mainstay for early workers at the dam.

The trail makes a nice out-and-back hike of almost 4 miles, so only one car is necessary. I prefer starting at the Watauga Recreation Complex, but parking at the ASU lot. The trail skirts the athletic fields, bears left, crosses a covered bridge, then goes left along the river bank. There's a picnic table just across the bridge. By taking a right here and crossing the open field, often used by ASU employees as garden space, you can shortcut the looping route along the stream and more quickly get to the heart of the trail. This option is nice on the return since it follows the edge of the woods.

The main trail ambles along a big bend in the river, with open fields on the right and the river on the left. There are benches at intervals, and in summer the vegetation keeps the focus on the river. In winter, views reach to town. As the path bears right around the bend, you notice some power lines ahead, but the vista is one of green ridges dipping into a quiet little valley. Hikers reach the first bridge at 0.8 mile from the complex and notice the raised manhole covers that mark this as a sewage line right-of-way. Vegetation obscures much of the evidence of these in summer.

On the other side of the river, a fence often encloses cattle and the trail hugs the tree-lined bank to the next bend and the picnic area, about a mile from the complex. The trail bears left and dips through scenic open views to another bridge. The greenway again crosses the stream and goes left on a wooded road grade. A right turn here will take you along an informal path that reaches the ruin opposite the picnic area and eventually rejoins the greenway at the first bridge, after a little bushwhacking. The main trail continues through rhododendron and white pine to an opening below power lines where crags tower above.

Then you reach . . . the town sewage treatment plant! Obviously few people would choose to place a trail beside such a public facility, but there was no choice. There is indeed an odor (though not much of one), so if you've started from the complex, you might want to turn around here. Don't get the wrong impression. A fence blocks much of the view of the plant, and the trail itself is pretty here, winding among white pine. After this short stretch hikers reach the Watauga County Humane Society Shelter. If you start there, the walk beside the plant is only a minor drawback. And if you can flirt with the heartbreak of having to return a homeless pet, the society will permit responsible hikers to borrow a dog, and a leash, for some welcome exercise.

6   CHIMNEY ROCK PARK

Overview

Chimney Rock Park is a privately owned, commercial natural area. It isn't tax-supported, so expect to pay a fee when you enter the gate. Also expect scrupulously maintained facilities and trails. Indeed, after sampling the downright spectacular natural wonders accessible to casual tourists, hikers will want to venture over the bulk of the Chimney Rock property, more rightfully referred to as Hickory Nut Gorge. This "tourist attraction" refreshingly assumes that you will hike to appreciate it.

Visitors enter the park from the picturesque summer town of Chimney Rock, site of the Esmeralda Inn, a landmark since 1890. Cross the Rocky Broad River and take the Three Mile Road, which rises through a mature forest with several nice picnic spots along the way. At The Meadows, about 1,400 feet, is a nature museum that makes a worthwhile stop; there also are restrooms and picnic sites. Farther up, the Forest Stroll Trail begins in the last turn before the parking lot at the top.

Elsewhere in the park visitors can take an elevator that ascends through solid rock, 550 million-year-old Henderson Augen gneiss. Emerging from the shaft, they step up to awesome views atop a monolithic granite pillar that juts from the side of Chimney Rock Mountain. Lake Lure, a jewel-like summer vacation site, glistens in the valley, and views reach to King's Mountain, 75 miles distant.

After riding the 258-foot elevator to the Sky Lounge snack bar and gift shop, tourists climb forty-three steps to the top of Chimney Rock, elevation 2,280. They can then descend steps and walkways through a garden of rock formations and viewpoints. These are also reached from the northern end of the parking lot, as is Chimney Rock, in a 10- to 15-minute walk that passes attractions such as the Moonshiner's Cave, Pulpit Rock, the Needle's

Eye, the Subway, the Grotto, and others. Above Chimney Rock, a few noteworthy viewpoints such as the Devil's Head and the Opera Box are easily reached. These are on what is the start of the Skyline Trail. The Cliff Trail begins among the boulder garden at the base of Chimney Rock, and both join at the top of Hickory Nut Falls, a spectacular 45-minute walk from either location.

Chimney Rock's trails were featured in the 1992 film *The Last of the Mohicans*, of which the park is particularly proud. The entire film was made in North Carolina, and some of the most spectacular scenes were made at Chimney Rock Park along the Cliff Trail. The movie produced a surge of visitation here, unsurprising considering the dramatic vistas. To prepare for your visit, you may find it fun to rent the video.

The park got its start at the turn of the century when travelers spotted the cool, scenic Carolina mountains. A St. Louis physician, Lucius Morse, came to the area "seeking a more favorable climate" where he could recover from tuberculosis. He paid $5,000 in 1902 to buy 64 acres of Chimney Rock Mountain; his heirs still own the park today, now more than 1,000 acres.

The park was widely known as the site of the Chimney Rock Hill Climb, a wild foot race billed as the country's most challenging climb on asphalt. The spectacle ended fifty years of fame in spring 1995. Even purists among Chimney Rock hikers would do well to request a copy of the park's special events brochure before visiting, because it includes an impressive schedule of guided nature and bird walks led by the park's naturalist and ornithologist at this designated North Carolina Natural Heritage Area. These walks feature bird migrations, seasonal plant and flower bloomings, and spring and fall foliage shows, at no additional cost to visitors. There are also nature photography clinics, rock- and rope-climbing demonstrations, and a variety of educational programs that complement a visit to the park.

General description: Three trails—the Forest Stroll Nature Trail to the base of 404-foot Hickory Nut Falls, and the Skyline and the Cliff trails to the top—creating a spectacular circuit.
General location: Southeast of Asheville.
Length: 1.4 miles round-trip for the Forest Stroll Nature Trail; 0.7 mile for the Skyline Trail and 0.8 mile for the Cliff Trail, or 1.5 miles combined.
Degree of difficulty: Easy for the Forest Stroll Nature Trail; moderate for the combination of the Skyline and Cliff trails.
Maps: USGS quads Bat Cave, Lake Lure. The park issues a free pictorial map that is serviceable for hikers.
Elevation gain and loss: 120 feet on the Forest Stroll Nature Trail; 550 feet for the Skyline and Cliff trails combined.
Trailhead elevation: 1,910 feet for the Forest Stroll trail; 2,175 for the Skyline and Cliff trails.
High point: 2,480 feet on the Skyline Trail; 2,450 on the Cliff Trail.

6 CHIMNEY ROCK PARK TRAILS

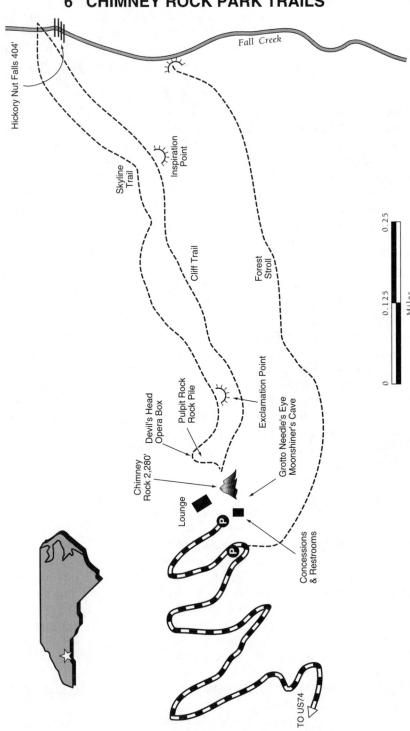

Fall Creek

Hickory Nut Falls 404'

Skyline Trail

Inspiration Point

Cliff Trail

Forest Stroll

Chimney Rock 2,280'

Devil's Head Opera Box

Pulpit Rock Rock Pile

Exclamation Point

Grotto Needle's Eye Moonshiner's Cave

Lounge

Concessions & Restrooms

TO US74

0   0.125   0.25

Miles

Low point: 1,850 on the Forest Stroll Trail.

Water availability: Whenever the park is open and trails are accessible, water is available from developed visitor service areas.

Finding the trailhead: Chimney Rock Park is 25 miles southeast of Asheville, just east of the intersection of U.S. Highways 64 and 74 in the town of Chimney Rock. It is a particularly easy and scenic trip from Charlotte, North Carolina, on Interstate Highway 85/US 74.

For more information: Chimney Rock Park. See Appendix C. The park has a pictorial trail map and informative brochures on special events, the park's birds, wildflowers, and more. The 1996 admission fees are $9.50 for adults, $5 for kids ages 6-15, 5 and under free. Annual passes also are available.

The hikes: The **Forest Stroll Nature Trail** is a 0.7-mile (1.4-mile round-trip) walk, an easy 45-minute stroll to a vantage point at the base of one of North Carolina's most impressive waterfalls.

The trail begins at the last turn below the park's uppermost parking lot. Hikers walk back down the road about 200 feet to where the path departs under an overhead sign resembling a gate. It is easy walking on an old road grade through a hardwood forest of hickory, oak, basswood, and maple. The path was originally built in 1963 as a jeep trail with tours offered to the base of the falls. Those were discontinued in 1977. The easy grade was then turned into a trail that climbs only 200 feet on the way to the falls. It is a bona fide beginner trail, perfect for families.

Along the way, there are seventeen lettered interpretive stops keyed to a trail brochure. There's also a developed viewing area and a picnic table at the base of the falls. Vistas reach across the town of Chimney Rock and up the towering rock face. If it's a rainy day, or a sunny day after a good rain, this can be a dramatic spot.

Combined, the **Skyline-Cliff trails** make a circuit that is one of the state's most scenic. It will astound hikers who have wondered what it must be like to be a rock climber on the way up a sheer cliff. But don't worry—the railings and well-kept trail make it a safe family hike. This 1.5-mile trail, about a 2-hour hike, is best tackled from the park's Sky Lounge. The first landmark leaving the Chimney is the Opera Box, an overhanging, sheltered viewpoint with theaterlike views of the entire valley. Next, after a climb up a stair structure, is Devil's Head, a fissure-filled piece of rock that seems to have teetered to a stop over the valley.

Leaving the cliff face, the trail enters the woods and switchbacks to the top of the cliffs at Exclamation Point. This 2,480-foot perch is a windy spot perfect for a pause. The trail wanders gradually along the crest of the gorge, often surrounded by Carolina rhododendrons, which blossom red here in late April and early May. Nearer the waterfall, the taller surrounding species is *Rhododendron maximum*, which has white blossoms and blooms in mid-June. Towering overhead are Carolina hemlocks.

The trail crosses Fall Creek at about 0.7 mile from the start, then on the way back to the parking lot becomes the Cliff Trail. From here on, the trail

"Hickory Nut Falls" Forest Stroll Trail. *Photo by Charles Goforth.*

follows a spectacular ledge that descends across the most dramatic faces of Hickory Nut Gorge. Nature's Showerbath comes first. This trickling, sprinkling spot is doused by a seepage that you crossed on the Skyline Trail. It's also where Hickory Nut Falls is seen in the background in the film *The Last of the Mohicans* as the Hurons traverse the trail. Stuntpersons jumped from above to a large, inflated bag below the trail. Then comes Inspiration Point, a scenic vista with Lake Lure to the right and Hickory Nut Falls to the left, where Daniel Day-Lewis and co-star Madeleine Stowe shared a rocky and romantic interlude. Next comes Groundhog Slide. Not far beyond, you'll squeeze behind Wildcat Trap. In many places along this portion of the trail, it is easy to imagine how rock climbers feel when they reach a major ledge.

Toward the bottom of the hike, you can climb back to the elevator and descend to your car, or choose a route through a labyrinth of developed paths, staircases, and walkways that lead to named passages and vistas on the way back to the parking lot. By the time you wander these, you may have walked just a bit farther than the 1.5-mile round-trip.

7 CLOUDLAND TRAIL

General description: A high-altitude family hike through spruce-fir forest to Roan High Bluff. The addition of a historic stretch of the Appalachian Trail (AT) takes hikers across the crest of Roan Mountain.

General location: Carvers Gap.

Length: The Cloudland Trail is 1.5 miles, a 3-mile round-trip, and includes a shorter option of 1 mile. Adding the AT section creates a 7.5-mile round-trip hike.

Degree of difficulty: Easy for the Cloudland Trail; strenuous for the AT addition.

Maps: USGS Carvers Gap quad. No detailed hiker's map to the summit is offered, but the ranger district will supply a photocopied brochure depicting trails.

Elevation gain and loss: About 600 feet overall, with approximately 100 feet gained between the summit road and Roan High Bluff. Overall gain and loss is about 1,700 feet for AT addition.

Trailhead elevation: 6,000 feet for Cloudland Trail; 5,512 feet for Appalachian Trail at Carvers Gap.

High point: 6,267 feet at Roan High Bluff; 6,286 feet at Roan High Knob on AT addition.

Water availability: There is a water fountain adjacent to the trail at a nearby Forest Service trailhead contact station, where there is also a restroom; open late spring through early fall. Water is also available from neighboring communities and Roan Mountain State Park.

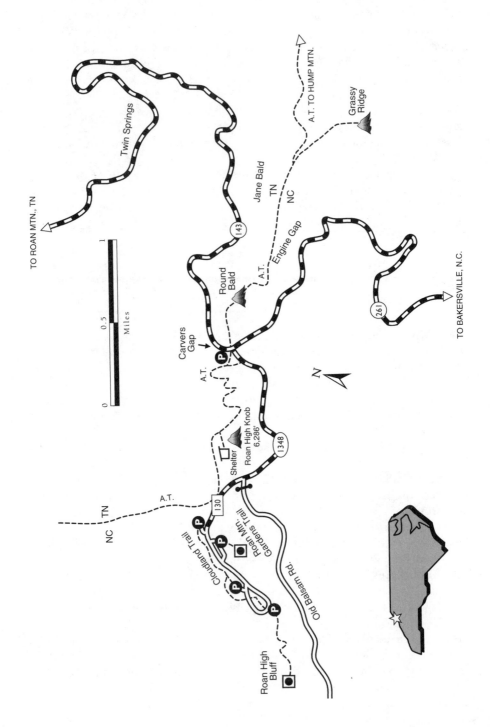

For more information: Toecane Ranger District, Pisgah National Forest, Burnsville. Or contact Supervisor's Office, National Forests in North Carolina. See Appendix C.

Finding the trailhead: The trail is reached from Carvers Gap, a high Appalachian crest on the North Carolina/Tennessee state line. From Boone, go west into Tennessee on U.S. Highway 19-E, then left on Tennessee Highway 143 in the town of Roan Mountain. From Asheville and more southerly areas, take North Carolina Highway 261 to Carvers Gap from Bakersville. For AT access, park along the fence line in the gap or in the tiny, picnic table-flanked parking lot. For the Cloudland Trail, take the paved summit road up the mountain (SR 1348) from Carvers Gap and go right at 1.7 miles into parking lot 1. This is the main trailhead; there are several others.

A left at parking lot 1 on the gravel Forest Road 130 meanders across the crest to other parking areas with trail access. Parking lot 2 comes after 1.8 miles, on the left; the Roan Mountain Gardens Trail begins here. Continue past parking lot 3 on the right, then bear right as the road makes its final loop. Pass a second entrance to parking lot 3 and the Cloudland Trail crossing. The road reaches its end and another Cloudland Trail crossing at 2.3 miles. From here, the second most popular trailhead, the path quickly reaches Roan High Bluff.

Roan High Bluff observation deck on the Cloudland Trail overlooks, east Tennessee.

The hike: The walks—or cross-country ski trips—described here, explore some of the South's lushest evergreen forests. In summer, cool breezes hiss through the spruces and mists roll across the meadows. In fall, evergreens contrast with electric mountain ash and yellow birch. Winter at these heights is a fairyland of frost-feathered trees and deep drifts.

Start the **Cloudland Trail** at parking lot 1, where there is a wonderful view into east Tennessee. The wide, at times carriage-width, trail enters the trees and climbs while meandering past a side trail to a viewpoint on the right. The unblazed trail levels out, exits the woods opposite parking lot 2, and gradually descends along Forest Road 130. Veering away from the road, the trail winds among rhododendron in a grassy bald spot, then descends directly to parking lot 3. Turn right just before reaching the lot. The trail crosses scenic wooden bridges as it parallels the edge of the lot to the road (about 0.7 mile).

The trail bisects the end loop of FR 130. The path continues beyond FR 130 bound for Roan High Bluff. This last stretch, about 0.5 mile, is a short, steep walk of moderate strenuousness, and makes a nice 1-mile hike for those who park at the end of the road. Along the way, the wide trail winds through the trees, offering intermediate to advanced cross-country skiers a dose of excitement.

The trail ends at a wooden observation deck that offers a spectacular vista over east Tennessee valleys, Bald Mountain, and the Unakas. Views back toward the trail reveal glimpses of the summit road and Roan High Knob (6,286 feet), the mountain's highest summit, reached best by the **Appalachian Trail**.

To lengthen the hike another 4.5 miles (for a 7.5-mile round-trip), take the white-blazed AT into the woods at Carvers Gap. The trail becomes a road-width carriage path used in the last century to ferry guests up to the Cloudland Hotel. It climbs gradually and makes a series of major switchbacks. This is the heart of the verdant evergreen forest motorists see as they near Carvers Gap from the Tennessee side. The trail crests at 1.5 miles. Here a routed trail sign marks the point where a side trail bears left 0.1 mile to Roan High Knob shelter, an enclosed cabin that sleeps about eight. The sign, and many others now missing or destroyed by the elements, is the work of Clyde Smith, a former Blue Ridge Parkway ranger who divided his time and passion for trails between New Hampshire and North Carolina. An AT shelter on the state line 5.4 miles south (about 2.1 miles south of the next AT road crossing in Hughes Gap), is named after him. The AT dips beyond this crest near the Roan High Knob cabin and descends to SR 1348 in about 2 miles. Walk the roadside uphill to parking lot 1, about 0.2 mile, and the start of the Cloudland Trail.

In winter, skiers reach the Cloudland trailhead at parking lot 1 by skiing up SR 1348 or the AT from Carvers Gap, where a gate blocks vehicular traffic when snow is likely to make travel on the mountain dangerous. If you choose to ski up the Appalachian Trail, the start of the path is unskiable from the Carvers Gap parking lot, so ski up beyond the gate 0.1 mile to a right turn. This old carriage road becomes the Appalachian Trail when the two join in about 0.2 mile. The Cloudland Trail and this part of the AT, together or separately, constitute one of the best cross-country ski tours in the South.

8   CRAGGY GARDENS

Overview

How can names like Craggy Gardens, Craggy Dome, and Craggy Pinnacle not be magnets for hikers? Visible from almost any corner of northwest North Carolina, these barren crags offer awesome views. Although this area lies beside the Blue Ridge Parkway and has roadside accessibility, it nevertheless is one of the Southern Appalachians' most scenic areas. Anyone driving this part of the Parkway will agree: this may be the high road's most dramatic scenery.

The high road starts in sunny lowlands around Asheville. As the Parkway climbs, visitors' eyes are drawn ahead, and the sun often disappears behind a microclimatic weather event caused by the Craggies; summits and clouds coalesce. The dramatic elevation change often lends the area the feel of much higher mountains. The sunny warmth of Asheville yields to shade and chill breeze.

The peaks in the area appear treeless, much like balds elsewhere in the state. But these are not the grass balds of Roan Mountain or Andrews Bald; these are heath balds, consisting of rhododendron, mountain laurel, blueberries, and other plants. The mountaineers called them "slicks" because they looked smooth from a distance. Atop the Craggies, the two kinds of balds alternate as huge whaleback ridges that crop out to crags and grassy meadows.

Craggy Gardens is known for wildflowers. It is one of the top spots in the region to appreciate the rhododendron bloom, often at its best the third week in June. A visitor center (no phone) sits on the Parkway beside the start of the Craggy Gardens Trail, and a nearby picnic area has facilities and a trailhead. Hikers here should remember that the balds are fragile and confine their walks to existing trails. A new section of North Carolina's Mountains To Sea Trail permits more hikes in the area.

General description: A more than mile-high area of crags and bald mountains with a variety of hikes, easy to moderate, with spectacular vistas and a waterfall.

General location: Blue Ridge Parkway.

Length: There are out-and-back summit view hikes of 0.7, 1.1 (Craggy Gardens), and 1.4 miles (Craggy Pinnacle). A longer, Mountains To Sea Trail hike to Craggy Gardens is 6.2 miles, and an adjoining waterfall walk can be 8 or 9 miles.

Degree of difficulty: Easy to moderate for the short view hikes; Mountains To Sea Trail hikes are moderately strenuous (Craggy Gardens) to strenuous (the waterfall walks).

Maps: USGS Craggy Pinnacle quad. A Blue Ridge Parkway trail map is available from the addresses below or from the trailhead visitor center.

Elevation gain and loss: 240 feet for Craggy Gardens Trail; 444 feet for Craggy Pinnacle; about 2,240 feet for the Douglas Falls Trail.

Trailhead elevations: Craggy Gardens Visitor Center, 5,520 feet; Craggy Dome parking overlook, 5,670 feet; picnic area, 5,240 feet; Graybeard parking area, 5,620 feet.

High point: Craggy Gardens, 5,640 feet; Craggy Pinnacle, 5,892 feet.

Water availability: From May to October, a trailhead visitor center and nearby picnic area dispense water for hikers.

For more information: The Blue Ridge Parkway, Asheville. Call for recorded information on weather, road closures, mailing requests, etc. The trail is in the Asheville Ranger District. See Appendix C.

Finding the trailhead: Craggy Gardens Visitor Center is on the Blue Ridge Parkway at milepost 364.5, about 20 miles north of Asheville, about 20.4 miles south of North Carolina Highway 80, and 73 miles south of U.S. Highway 321 between Boone and Blowing Rock.

The Craggy Gardens Trail begins beside the Craggy Gardens Visitor Center. A second trailhead is located south of the visitor center in the Craggy Gardens Picnic Area. To reach it, turn from the Parkway on the unpaved Stoney Fork Road at milepost 367.6. Take the next right into the picnic area and go to the end of the parking area.

The Craggy Pinnacle Trail begins in the Craggy Dome parking area, north of the visitor center and the Craggy Pinnacle Tunnel, at milepost 364.

The longest hikes start on the Mountains To Sea Trail from the picnic area (see above) and the Parkway's Graybeard Mountain parking overlook at milepost 363.4, 1 mile north of the visitor center.

The hike: From the Craggy Gardens Visitor Center, the **Craggy Gardens Trail** climbs gradually for 0.3 mile to a rustic trail shelter. This first section of the hike is a self-guiding nature trail with resting benches and signs identifying plants. Before the shelter, a side trail to the left leads up the balds to dramatic views of valleys in the east and the Black Mountains to the north. The round-trip is about 0.7 mile.

The same area can be reached from the Craggy Gardens Picnic area for a 1-mile round-trip hike. Leaving the picnic area, the trail climbs gradually past a short loop trail that leads left to a view from a gazebo shelter at about 0.3 mile. From this direction, the rustic old trail shelter is next at about 0.5 mile; and the round-trip about 1.1 miles. Hikers and picnickers might keep either of these shelters in mind if the weather threatens.

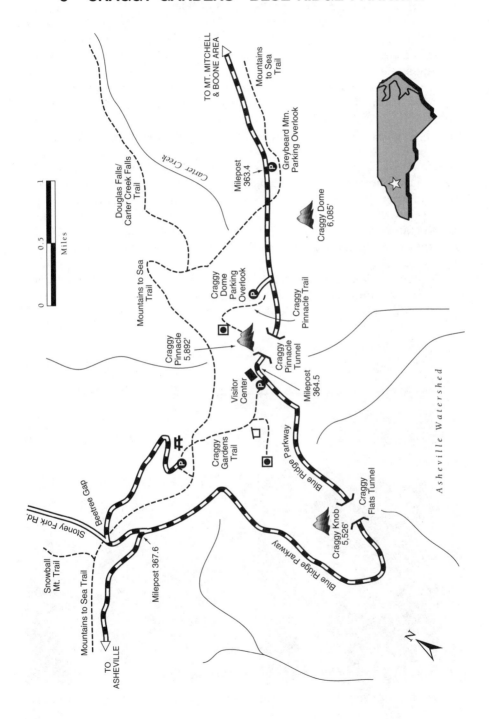

From the Parkway, the **Craggy Pinnacle Trail** climbs in 0.7 mile past resting benches to great views at 5,892 feet atop Craggy Pinnacle. Views from the easily reached summit circle 360 degrees. Just before the top, a side trail to the right leads to a rocky viewpoint. You'll note increased efforts to get hikers to stay on the trails and within the designated viewing spots. Please do your part.

Hikers who want longer walks can drive a short distance and use the new **Mountains To Sea Trail** to get just that: hikes of 6.2, 8, and 9 miles. From the Graybeard Mountain overlook, take the white dot-blazed trail back south and across the road. About 1 mile from the parking area a trail heads right. After 3 miles of rough, sometimes steep travel, this trail reaches a waterfall for a 4-mile hike (8 miles round-trip) beyond the overlook. Before reaching the impressive 70-foot cataract, the trail passes smaller cascades and groves of virgin hemlock. This alternately is called the **Douglas Falls Trail** or the **Carter Creek Falls Trail**. Whichever name you call it, the scenery near the falls is well worth the effort. (A Forest Service trail also reaches the falls from a parking area on nearby Forest Road 74, but the trailhead can be difficult to find.)

An even longer hike to the falls is possible from the picnic area. Starting there, the Mountains To Sea Trail takes 1.5 miles to reach the junction with the falls trail. The 4.5-mile hike makes a 9-mile round-trip.

Craggy Gardens summit view of Craggy Gardens visitor center, Craggy Pinnacle and tunnel.

To reach Craggy Gardens from the Graybeard Mountain Overlook, pass the waterfall turnoff at 1 mile and go to the picnic area at 2.5 miles. From there, take the Craggy Gardens Trail another 0.6 mile to the peak. The round-trip is about 6.2 miles.

9   ELK RIVER FALLS TRAIL

General description: A hike to a spectacular 50-foot waterfall. Big Falls, more often called Elk River Falls, drops directly to a large, cliff-encircled pool.
General location: Elk Park.
Length: 0.5 mile.
Degree of difficulty: Easy for distance; moderate for steepness.
Maps: USGS Elk Park quad.
Elevation gain and loss: 100 feet.
Trailhead elevation: 2,830 feet.
Low point: 2,780 feet.
Water availability: No water at the trailhead, but hikers access the trail through the town of Elk Park and can find water there. Hikers may also find water at the private Elk River Campground, on the way to the trailhead.
For more information: Toecane Ranger District, USDA Forest Service. Or contact Supervisor's Office, National Forests in North Carolina. See Appendix C.
Finding the trailhead: The trail is reached via back roads from the town of Elk Park, on U.S. Highway 19-E at the North Carolina–Tennessee border. From Tennessee, Elk Park is best reached from the town of Roan Mountain. From North Carolina, reach Elk Park via Newland or Banner Elk. From Newland, via North Carolina Highway 194, then US 19-E, it is 8.3 miles through Elk Park to a right turn onto SR 1303 (at an Elk River Falls sign). Measuring from this turn, go left at 0.3 mile, signed for Elk River Campground, onto the Elk River Road, SR 1305. At 2.5 miles continue straight on SR 1305, now a dirt road, as SR 1306 goes left across a bridge. Cross a bridge at 3.8 miles, enter the national forest at 4.1 miles, and reach the parking area at 4.3 miles from US 19-E.

The hike: This short waterfall hike is tucked into an isolated tract of Pisgah National Forest near the border with Tennessee. The entire trail has recently been upgraded by the Forest Service, so it is no longer the remote place it once was. On weekends, the trail gets sufficient use to feel like an ordinary

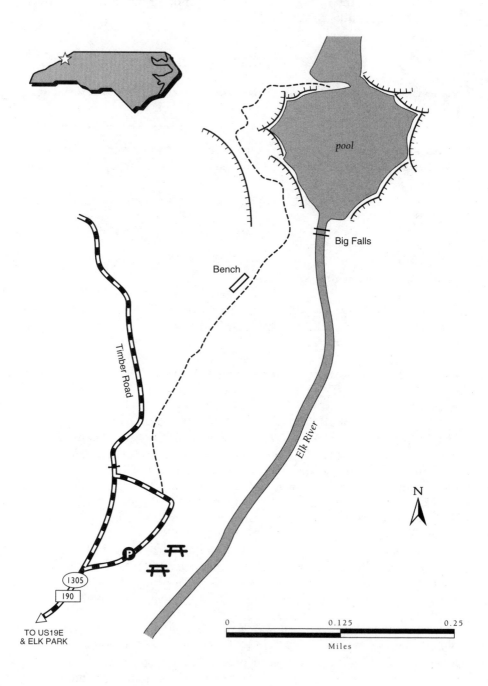

pool

Big Falls

Bench

Timber Road

Elk River

P

1305

190

TO US19E
& ELK PARK

N

| 0 | | 0.125 | | 0.25 |

Miles

public access site. Nevertheless, some visitors could feel uneasy if they happen upon a group of rough-hewn locals hanging out in the parking lot. Use good judgment; most locals are genuinely friendly. Still, nearby trailheads have had vehicle break-ins, so don't leave anything of value in your car. Despite that, the trail is so nice that the round-trip 0.5-mile hike is a popular saunter on Sunday for families after church. The parking lot is lined with grills and picnic tables (no camping), and a scenic, fishable river flows by.

The **Elk River Falls Trail** leaves the north end of the parking lot, ascends a flight of steps, swings close to a gated timber access road, then dips into a tall streamside forest of hemlock and rhododendron along the Elk River. This is a level walk that passes a bench before reaching the head of the falls.

A single log on the right barely creates a barrier that suggests hikers not step out onto the cliffs atop the waterfall. From here, daring, perhaps stupid students from local colleges occasionally leap into the pool, a heart-stopping, body-thumping 50 feet below. I bring this up only because the practice is common enough that you could see people taking the plunge during the warmer months. Don't do it. A slip near the falls, without the right momentum, could kill you. And even a forceful leap has seriously injured those who landed in the wrong area.

There isn't much of a view from up top, so stay off the rocks and descend the flights of steps; one parallels a cliff face. (The steps on this section of trail have been nicely upgraded, so most people will find it possible to descend to the falls if they take their time.) At the bottom, the path leads out of the woods onto a rocky bar with a great view of the large pool. The horseshoe-shaped canyon is hemmed in by sheer cliffs. The waterfall plummets straight down, a spectacular one even during relatively dry periods.

To the north, the Elk River tumbles on into Tennessee, not far away.

10   GLEN BURNEY TRAIL

Overview

The Glen Burney Trail represents the best, and worst, of North Carolina trails in the 1990s. This historic waterfall trail is open, thanks to an enlightened town government and the dedicated work of many volunteers and private landowners. Most hikers will dwell on the wonderful experience of wandering away from a quaint, wooded village and bustling residential area into a virgin, forested chasm.

But evidence of less-enlightened attitudes is harshly apparent. One lovely, huge home, built since the reopening of the trail in 1991, is plopped so directly over the stream that many nature lovers call it an eyesore. A privacy fence and plantings fail to insulate it from the trail. Its sewage connection soars across the pristine stream and a particularly good example of early Civilian Conservation Corps (CCC) trail construction, is now off-limits. Farther on, the trail once crossed two stone bridges built over rushing side streams during 1991, but the trail was forced to reroute downstream; the landowner refused to permit this poetic path to traverse even a corner of private property. The new path has been gouged into the steep streamcourse and routed over a less-than-scenic wooden bridge.

For all the positive things the Glen Burney Trail says about civic-mindedness in the mountain town of Blowing Rock, widely traveled hikers will be troubled when they contrast such antagonism with the European experience of following a public trail past the back door of a Swiss farmer's house. But don't let that discourage you. The cascades of New Year's Creek are so appealing that continued public access more than justifies the comprises made to achieve it. In fact, a fairer comparison between Blowing Rock and Switzerland reveals that it is possible in this North Carolina mountain town, as it is in many Alpine villages, to wander from one's lodging through quaint streets to virgin timber and tumbling waterfalls. Bravo, Blowing Rock.

The Glen Burney Trail has been in use since the earliest days of human habitation in the North Carolina mountains. Loggers used the path to commute between their homes on the heights and timber-harvesting operations at towns such as Edgemont in the Globe Valley. Formal trails were built in the late 1800s when tourists from the baked flatlands of the South first ventured to high mountain towns to escape the heat. Early guests at century-old hotels such as the Green Park Inn, Blowing Rock's landmark hostelry, picnicked at Glen Burney Falls.

These falls and a few others on the trail mark the start of the Johns River Gorge, a dramatic drop to the Piedmont that in the vicinity of Blowing Rock represents the greatest relief of the Blue Ridge escarpment: about 4,000 feet. The town's namesake attraction, the Blowing Rock, is a massive projection over that drop where Native American legend states that a maiden was returned to her lover by a dramatic updraft.

The scenic waterfall area that the trail explores was donated to the town in the early part of the century. Portions of the trail were rebuilt by the CCC during the 1930s, with beautiful stonework. Reopening the trail more recently, the town chose to complement this earlier artistry with additional rock work. One stone bridge at the start of the trail completely spans the creek.

As Blowing Rock developed into a modern resort town, public use was interrupted where portions of the trail passed over subdivided private land. Owners of recently built homes objected to the hikers, and the town, which owned the waterfall, was worried about its liability for injuries at the dramatic cascades.

In the mid-1980s a Sierra Club-coordinated group of trail volunteers upgraded the path, but poor access still deterred all but a few hikers. In 1989 the town received a Land and Water Conservation Fund grant from

Stone bridge spans New Year's Creek at the start of the Glen Burney Trail. The path to the falls wanders into the background.

10 GLEN BURNEY TRAIL—BLOWING ROCK

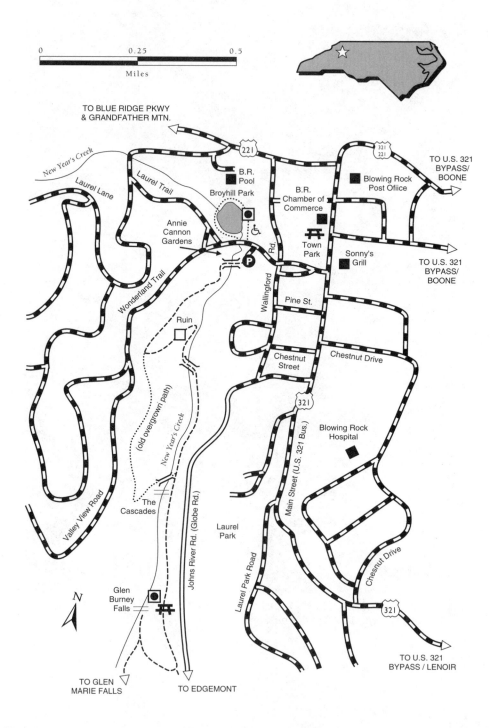

0   0.25   0.5

Miles

TO BLUE RIDGE PKWY
& GRANDFATHER MTN.

New Year's Creek

Laurel Lane

Laurel Trail

221

B.R.
Pool

Broyhill Park

Annie
Cannon
Gardens

Wonderland Trail

P

Ruin

(old overgrown path)

New Year's Creek

Valley View Road

The
Cascades

Johns River Rd. (Globe Rd.)

N

Glen
Burney
Falls

TO GLEN
MARIE FALLS

TO EDGEMONT

Laurel
Park

Laurel Park Road

B.R.
Chamber of
Commerce

Town
Park

Wallingford Rd.

Pine St.

Chestnut
Street

Chestnut Drive

321

Blowing Rock
Hospital

Main Street (U.S. 321 Bus.)

321
221

Blowing Rock
Post Ofiice

Sonny's
Grill

TO U.S. 321
BYPASS/
BOONE

TO U.S. 321
BYPASS/
BOONE

Chestnut Drive

321

TO U.S. 321
BYPASS / LENOIR

4/28/97

Dear Tim & Betty,
    Here is the book I mentioned
for planning your North Carolina.
If you have internet access, there
is a great bookshop on line which
also happens to be run by
one of my clients. It is called
World Traveller Books & Maps
and is found at www.travelbookshop.
com. They will ship books & you
can order on line or by phone
or fax.
        Looking forward to your visit.
                        Love,
                        Lila

the Department of the Interior and, by 1991, reopened the historic trail to the falls using a section of town-owned sewer line right-of-way.

The trail starts beside a beautiful new downtown park complex that includes scenic lake and shoreline jogging and barrier-free trails. Former town manager Chris May said plans include linking the parks to nearby Moses Cone Park on the Blue Ridge Parkway. "When that happens," May said, "you may be able to hike from downtown Blowing Rock all the way to the top of Grandfather Mountain on the Mountains To Sea Trail."

General description: A historic hike from a gentrified mountain village into a forest-filled cleft with three scenic waterfalls.

General location: Blowing Rock.

Length: 3 miles round-trip.

Degree of difficulty: Moderately strenuous.

Maps: USGS Globe quad. The Blowing Rock Chamber of Commerce offers a rudimentary trail map pamphlet.

Elevation gain and loss: 800 feet.

Trailhead elevation: 3,560 feet.

Low point: 3,160 feet.

Water availability: None on trail; various places in town.

For more information: Blowing Rock Chamber of Commerce. See Appendix C. The chamber's Main Street visitor center, beside Blowing Rock Park, is open Monday through Saturday, year-round.

Finding the trailhead: Blowing Rock is 8 miles south of Boone on U.S. Highway 321, about 30 miles northwest of Lenoir. From the US 321 bypass, turn at the traffic light onto Sunset Drive toward downtown Blowing Rock. At the traffic light facing the town park, turn left on Main Street. In 0.1 mile, turn right onto Laurel Lane. At the Wallingford Lane stop sign, in 0.2 mile, go straight and immediately turn left into the parking area for the trail at 0.3 mile.

The hike: The new section of the venerable old **Glen Burney Trail** leaves the landscaped parking area and veers right to avoid a gated road to a sewer line pump station. The trail drops into rhododendron and crosses New Year's Creek on a large boulder spanning the stream, then follows the stream amid towering beech and hemlock.

You do get a glimpse of the pump station across the stream, but the vegetation largely obscures the signs of municipal use. Side trails to the right lead to nearby homes, and in one case, a popular Blowing Rock seafood restaurant. The trail becomes a road-width, level path (along the sewage line), passes a privacy fence on the left, then wanders into the natural setting.

On the left and below, the stream drops into the beginnings of a gorge while hikers stay level above it, with views of massive, virgin hemlocks. The trail enters an open area; homes are subtly visible in the woods just as the trail dips left from the grade and descends a series of switchbacks. The switchbacks reverse the direction of the trail, which begins a descent into the gorge below the grade. Just as that happens, if you look ahead at where you'd go if you didn't make the turn, you can see an old trail grade across the way that is itself a route that you can return on (more on that later).

The trail, lined with benches, eases down and hikers soon notice an elaborate concrete and stone structure, one of the most offbeat interpretive sites to be found on a hiking trail. Built in the 1920s, this is one of the first modern sewage treatment plants erected in the North Carolina mountains. Given that you hiked in on a sewer right-of-way, where else would a trailside sewage treatment plant be more appropriate? This plant served the Mayview Manor, a resort hotel razed in the 1970s. A deck may be built atop the trailside structure, creating a formal viewpoint.

The trail dips among towering hemlocks at streamside, reverses direction again, and finally heads downstream, now beneath "the ruin," as the town trail map euphemistically calls the sewage plant. The trail reaches a shallow spot in the stream once intended to be spanned by stepping stones. But the trail continues a short distance to a wooden bridge which skirts this corner of private property.

Across the stream, enter the historic route of the Glen Burney Trail as it descends through tall, mixed evergreen and deciduous forest along a graded, not very rocky treadway above the rushing stream. Massive waterbars cross the trail, insuring that the path will shed torrential runoff from the Globe Road, just out of sight above. After a steeper section of trail, hikers emerge at a wooden bridge that crosses the stream atop The Cascades, about 0.8 mile from the parking area (a 1.6-mile round-trip hike). To the right and across the bridge an unmaintained trail climbs along the opposite bank and loops back to the spot where the new trail descends from the sewer line. The town may eventually formally clear and reopen this route.

Heading left down the stone steps the trail skirts the drop of The Cascades, with nice views back at the waterfall as the path rounds the next bend high above the stream. The trail dips again, leaving the streamside cleft for the broad, often sunny floor of the forest. At the next junction (where the sound of Glen Burney Falls is audible on the right), a right leads past a trickling spring box and picnic table to an observation deck perched atop the falls. Here the water spritzes from the shade of the hemlocks into the sunlight, splashing down the 50-foot face into a pool. (People have died here, so stay within the railing to avoid slipping on the top of the treacherous falls.) This is a premier place to have a picnic, about 1.2 miles from the parking area.

Back at the junction, go right (or keep left if you pass the side trail to Glen Burney Falls on the way down) to the base of the falls. The trail bears left away from the stream and a trail goes left to a private home just as the main trail switchbacks right toward the base of the falls. After a steep descent, the trail again becomes level across a rocky treadway and reaches a T-junction. To the right a short distance is the pool at the base of Glen Burney Falls. To the left, Glen Marie Falls is reached at 1.6 miles. For those inclined, the primitive path of old continues in various forms, down in elevation, and back in time.

GRANDFATHER MOUNTAIN (11-14)

Overview

In the years since young Hugh Morton, a World War II combat photographer, returned to his family's private lands on Grandfather Mountain, this spectacular North Carolina area has evolved from a tourist attraction to an International Biosphere Reserve. Morton's stewardship has preserved one of the Southern Appalachians' most significant natural heritage sites, setting a new standard in preservation and public use of private land.

Grandfather Mountain is a rocky, spectacular summit known to tourists for great views from its privately owned road and Mile-High Swinging Bridge. The peak is one of the region's premier natural areas with a wonderful network of trails. Grandfather Mountain's 4,000 acres boast forty-three species of rare or endangered plants and animals, more than Great Smoky Mountains National Park.

As part of a private conservation park, the mountain's summit road has been open since the 1930s. After World War II, Morton extended the road to "the top," actually one of the mountain's lower though spectacular summits. In 1951 the Mile-High Swinging Bridge was christened; a summit visitor center later opened beside it. Habitat animal exhibits debuted in 1973, and annual events were scheduled. Morton's promotional genius, and his gift for scenic photography, made the mountain a high point of North Carolina tourism.

Not everything went smoothly for Morton. Public-spirited people lobbied hard to remove Grandfather Mountain from private ownership. A 1950s effort by the National Park Service intended to complete the Blue Ridge Parkway using what came to be called "the high route," which would have ridden high on the mountain's flank. But Morton marshaled public opinion against a route that would have destroyed wilderness. The irony of a private landowner defending wildlands against the nation's principal conservation agency was a potent marketing tool.

Meanwhile, Grandfather Mountain's undeveloped backcountry, a nearly 5,000-acre parcel of jagged, evergreen-clothed cliffs and nearly 6,000-foot summits slumbered. An early book about the area described the wonderful hiking on the mountain, and at times during the development of the travel attraction new trails were cut, signed, and occasionally mowed by park maintenance employees.

Rhododendron blooms below Grandfather Mountain in late June, seen here from the Blue Ridge Parkway's Flatrock Trail.

In 1978 Morton's Grandfather Mountain park successfully implemented the mountain's fledgling hiker fee system, establishing a pay-for-use trail preservation program that over the years became a significant example of wilderness management. The program attracted the country's leading researchers, who did backcountry studies on a variety of topics. Among these were peregrine falcons; the first to be reintroduced into the wild Southern Appalachians were released here.

Eventually the Parkway battle came to a close. A lower route for the high road was agreed upon. And a state-of-the-art, computer-designed span that would lift the road above the fragile mountainside became technologically feasible. The National Park Service embraced the concept, and the road opened in 1987 to worldwide acclaim.

Spurred by the amicable resolution of the Parkway controversy and the success of the trail management program, Grandfather Mountain's status as a natural area soared. More than 3,000 acres of its backcountry is preserved in perpetuity through conservation easements granted to the North Carolina Nature Conservancy. In 1994 it became the nation's only privately owned Biosphere Reserve, one of 311 outstanding natural areas designated in 81 countries by UNESCO, the United Nations Educational, Cultural, and Scientific Organization.

Halfway up the auto road, adjacent to habitats for deer, bears, cougars, and eagles, a first-class nature museum contains natural history exhibits. Daily nature films and educational events, such as a free June outdoor photography clinic, are often held in the museum theater.

The mountain's innovative trail program is funded through a hiking permit system. All day and overnight trail use requires a permit ($4.50 adults, $2.50 4-12 years, free under 4; single person season pass $20, group pass for up to six hikers, $45). Campers pay the permit fee for each calendar day they are on the mountain. Permit outlets are plentiful and usually adjacent to trailheads. Motor entrance fees to the mountain are double the permit fee and include hiking.

Hikers should be alert to weather conditions at Grandfather Mountain. Others have died there from exposure, lightning strikes, falls, and heart attacks. The mountain is known for snowy winters and year-round high winds. A U.S. Weather Station caps the summit visitor center.

11 BLACK ROCK TRAIL

General description: This mostly level, day-use-only trail is an out-and-back hike to spectacular views on the eastern side of Grandfather Mountain, a superb vantage point on the nearly vertical-mile plummet to the Piedmont, the greatest relief of the Blue Ridge escarpment.
Length: 1.8 miles round-trip.

Black Rock Trail viewpoint—far above the Piedmont.

Degree of difficulty: Easy to moderate.
Maps: USGS Grandfather Mountain quad. Grandfather Mountain park has a free trail map, the best for this hike, available from the address below.
Elevation gain and loss: 320 feet.
Trailhead elevation: 5,040 feet.
High point: Trailhead.
Low point: 4,880.
Water availability: Water is available above the trailhead at the summit visitor center and on the way up to the trail at the Grandfather Mountain Nature Museum.
For more information: Grandfather Mountain. See Appendix C.
Finding the trailhead: The motor entrance to Grandfather Mountain is on U.S. Highway 221, 2 miles east of Linville and 17 miles south of Boone on North Carolina Highway 105. The entrance to the mountain is 1 mile west of the Blue Ridge Parkway's US 221 exit at milepost 305, 14 miles south of the U.S. Highways 321/221 junction between Boone and Blowing Rock.

The Black Rock trailhead is the first right past the 5,000 feet elevation sign near the top of the mountain.

The hike: Were the yellow-blazed **Black Rock Trail** smoothly level, it would be one of the best mass-appeal interpretive trails in the state. Though mostly flat, it is rocky, which limits its appeal for elderly people and young children. Nevertheless, many families make the hike. And because the path isn't heavily trafficked, serious hikers will also enjoy it.

Its biggest drawing point is the northern forest, but the view from the short scenic loop also recommends it. Hikers on this trail view the drop from Grandfather Mountain's jagged summits, at nearly 6,000 feet, to the Piedmont, at about 800 feet. This is the greatest relief of the Blue Ridge escarpment, roughly equal to that from the Front Range peaks of the Rockies to Denver.

The trail meanders onto the lofty side of the mountain, known for its northern climate and vegetation. The forest is a mix of evergreens, among them hemlocks, Fraser fir, and red spruce, and deciduous trees such as mountain ash, yellow birch, red and striped maples, and serviceberry. The feel of the forest is straight out of New England, an experience heightened by massive peaks and low surrounding valleys.

The rocky, shallow soil supports an understory of mountain laurel and galax, a shiny green ground plant that turns red in the fall and is so intensely pungent that often city dwellers wonder what a bear might have done in the woods. Rhododendron also flourishes here, principally the longleaf *Rhododendron maximum* that blooms white in early to mid-July. This is the Southern Appalachians' opposite to Catawba rhododendron, the shortleaf, red-blooming bush that flowers so spectacularly on the peaks and bald ridges in late June. In places, *Rhododendron maximum* makes a tunnel of the Black Rock Trail, an impressive sight on a damp, misty day.

At just under 0.5 mile, the trail reaches Arch Rock, a huge overhanging boulder on the left that offers shelter from showers. This was once the gateway to the Arch Rock Trail, now closed, which used to link this point to MacRae Gap on the Grandfather Trail. Large leathery patches of smooth rock tripe cover the upper reaches of the rock.

The trail continues, dipping across wet-weather streamcourses and through areas of blackberries. Then it descends to an area of rhododendron and spruce and, at about 0.8 mile, reaching a junction on the right where the end loop comes back in. Head left to start the loop. At a huge boulder, the trail goes right. (To the left, and now blocked, the old trail descends to a gated and locked cave in the jumbled crags of Black Rock Cliffs, namesake of the trail's former moniker, The Black Rock Cliffs Cave Trail. More on this later.)

Continuing, the path ambles among boulders that project above the dense rhododendron and high bush blueberries (ripe in late-August). The latter is profuse enough to have once attracted bears up out of the Daniel Boone Wildlife Sanctuary, a Pisgah National Forest area far below. A few designated crags provide dynamite views of the peaks towering above; below lay the Blue Ridge Parkway and descending scenery. Views reach to Tablerock, Hawksbill Mountain, the Linville Gorge, Lake James, Mount Mitchell, and other summits. On many rocks Allegheny sand myrtle blooms in tiny spring flowers of white and pink. The trail loop rejoins itself at about 1 mile, and hikers go left to retrace their steps, ending at the parking lot at about 1.8 miles.

Like the rest of the mountain, easements for the perpetual preservation of this area are held by the Nature Conservancy. That took place in the early 1990s and the trail to the cave was closed at that time. The entire Black Rock Cliffs area above the Parkway was simultaneously made a no-hiking area, due mostly to abuse by hikers from the Parkway who bushwhacked into the pristine area creating eroding trails. The cave was gated in the mid-1980s to block human access but permit the comings and goings of a small population of Virginia big-eared bats, an endangered species known to reside in North Carolina only on Grandfather Mountain. The bats were often overlooked by tourists who visited the four-room fissure cave in the 1950s.

Since then the Black Rock Trail has been substantially smoothed and nicely rerouted, greatly improving its hikeability. Numbered posts are keyed to an interpretive brochure, available free at the trailhead sign, which does a nice job of explaining this complex scenic area.

12 DANIEL BOONE SCOUT TRAIL AND PARKWAY AREA PATHS

General description: Tracking up the back side of Grandfather Mountain, the Daniel Boone Scout Trail climbs to Calloway Peak, the highest summit in the Blue Ridge Range. Two other view-packed trails, one a nice beginner backpacking trip, also start on the Tanawha Trail from the Blue Ridge Parkway.

Length: 5.8- or 4.9-mile hikes on the Boone Trail to Calloway Peak; 3.2 miles on the Nuwati Trail; a 3.6 mile-hike on the Cragway Trail.

Degree of difficulty: Strenuous for the Boone Trail to Calloway Peak; moderately easy for the Nuwati Trail; moderately strenuous for the Cragway circuit.

Maps: USGS Grandfather Mountain quad; the free trail map of Grandfather Mountain available at the park.

Elevation gains and losses: 4,088 feet for the climb to Calloway Peak; 1,160 for the Nuwati Trail; 1,840 feet for the Cragway circuit.

Trailhead elevations: 3,880 feet at the Boone trailhead on U.S. Highway 221; 3,920 feet at the Boone Fork parking area.

High points: 4,500 feet for the Nuwati Trail; 4,840 feet for Cragway, 5,964 feet for the Daniel Boone Scout Boone Trail.

Water availability: Near the trailhead, Boone Fork stream tumbles under the trail bridge out of the largely pristine watershed under Calloway Peak. Boone Fork and tributaries are again encountered higher up on the Nuwati Trail, with water easily reached from many campsites. On the Boone Trail, a marked spring is located 100 yards from a campsite at the junction of the Cragway Trail. No reliable water is available above this point or at Hi-Balsam Shelter.

For more information: Grandfather Mountain. See Appendix C.

Finding the trailhead: The Boone Trail's year-round trailhead is on U.S. Highway 221, 8.5 miles north of the Grandfather Mountain entrance and 1.5 miles south of the U.S. Highway 221/Holloway Mountain Road junction south of Blowing Rock. The best starting point for all these hikes is the Boone Fork parking area on the Blue Ridge Parkway, 5.1 miles north of the US 221/Parkway junction near Linville (1 mile from the Grandfather Mountain entrance) and 8.2 miles south of the Blue Ridge Parkway junction with U.S. Highways 321/221, between Blowing Rock and Boone.

Hiking permits for the trail are available at the Grandfather Mountain entrance and close to the trail at the Grandfather Mountain Country Store. The store is 3.6 miles from the Boone Fork parking area. To reach the store go north on the Parkway 2.6 miles and exit at Holloway Mountain Road. Go left under the Parkway on the paved road and in 1 mile reach the store at the junction with US 221. The store is 1.5 miles north of the US 221 Boone Trail parking area.

The hikes: The now-popular Blue Ridge Parkway side of Grandfather Mountain was once the least-visited part of the peak. U.S. Highway 221 quietly snaked its way around the mountain's convoluted ridges, leading Parkway motorists around the last link of this national scenic road, completed in the late 1980s.

But since the early days of World War II, a winding and primitive trail up this wild side of the mountain has been in existence, the dream of a part-time Parkway ranger named Clyde Smith and a Blowing Rock troop of Boy Scouts. Smith moved back and forth between New England and North Carolina, pursuing his dedication to trails, building new ones, maintaining old ones such as the Appalachian Trail, and hand-crafting trail route signs, many of which he installed on his favorite Southern summit: Grandfather Mountain. Smith's **Daniel Boone Scout Trail**, named to acknowledge the Blowing Rock Boy Scouts who'd helped construct it, was only a memory a decade before the Parkway opened.

Grandfather Mountain's trail fee program reclaimed it in early 1979. The route was pieced together from the remains of tin can-top trail markers bearing painted arrowheads. Also discovered was a decaying, half-century-old backpacking shelter felled by a wind-flattened grove of evergreens. By the early 1980s, the old backpacking shelter, Hi-Balsam, had been rebuilt. A few years after the Boone Trail was reclaimed and two new trails were added: the Nuwati Trail to the heart of the bowl beneath the nearby peak, and Cragway, a clifftop connector to the Boone Trail. Two Appalachian State University professors had guessed in the 1970s that the bowl-shaped valley under the peak had been gouged by a glacier. Though their conclusion was based on glacial grooves later discovered to have been made by logging cables, the valley is nevertheless spectacularly reminiscent of glacial bowls in New England and elsewhere.

In winter, when snow closes the Parkway, the Daniel Boone Trail hike can begin on US 221, from which a 0.4-mile connector leads under a Blue

12 — GRANDFATHER MOUNTAIN
DANIEL BOONE SCOUT-NUWATI-CRAGWAY

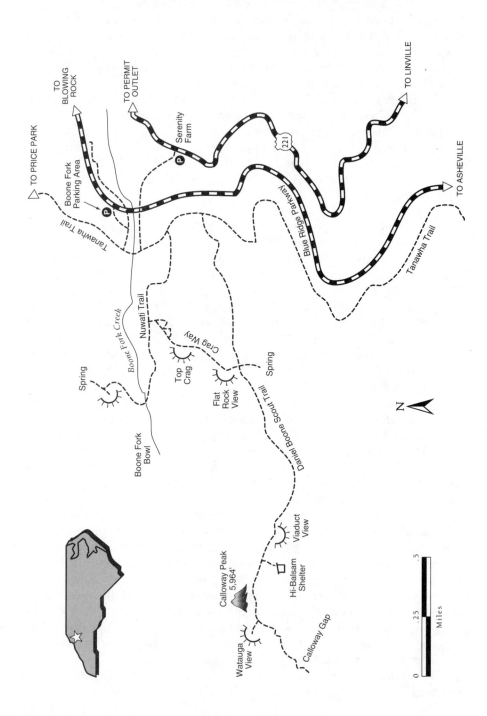

Ridge Parkway bridge to a junction with the Tanawha Trail beside the Boone Fork trail bridge.(Otherwise, this graded connector path just adds distance to the hike.) Starting at the Boone Fork Parking Area, leave the lot and go right at the first junction (a streamside trail that connects north to the Calloway Peak Overlook). The next junction is the Tanawha Trail. Go left and cross the elaborate laminated bridge spanning the creek. The connector to US 221 branches left just over the bridge, and the Tanawha Trail wanders along, gaining elevation with moderate climbs to a junction on the right at about 0.4 mile with the Nuwati Trail.

The **Nuwati Trail**, formerly the Grandfather Trail Extension, was renamed in the early 1990s with a Cherokee word meaning "good medicine," a reference to the healing power of the wilderness experience, complementing the nearby Tanawha Trail, which means "great hawk or eagle." Take a right on the blue-blazed trail, pass a trailhead signboard, and follow the level but rocky trail up an old logging railroad grade. A spring gushes under the trail at 0.7 mile. The trail winds along, gaining elevation until the bowl-like shape of the valley, and your progress into it, becomes noticeable. The sounds of the stream become audible far below on the right, and the old grade becomes a scenic rhododendron tunnel fringed by lacelike ferns. At 1.1 miles, the Cragway Trail goes left.

Within a few hundred feet is a designated campsite on the left beside a stream. From here to its end, the trail crosses numerous tributaries of Boone Fork, all of them easy hops except in very high water. Another campsite appears on the left, where a large logging cable is held firm in the V of a tree (apparently unnoticed by the geologists who walked by here on their way to discovering the ice-carved grooves of the "glacial cirque").

Cross Boone Fork at 1 mile and continue on the level path. A left fork leads steeply to a prominent tooth of rock projecting above the valley floor at 4,500 feet, 1.6 miles from the trailhead. A campsite lies below the rock. Continuing, the path terminates at other campsites. The 360-degree panorama from the pinnacle surveys one of the craggiest high mountain valleys in the state. The view rises southwest through the upper bowl, past the headwall of the "cirque," to nearly 6,000 feet at Calloway Peak. The cliffs of White Rock Ridge soar above, and rocky pinnacles on the Cragway Trail lie to the south on the opposite side of the valley. East, the view stretches along the Blue Ridge Parkway to Blowing Rock and Piedmont cities.

The Nuwati Trail gains only about 600 feet in 1.6 miles, so it is a good beginning backpacking trip with moderate elevation gain, a number of trailside campsites, and spectacular scenery. The lowest crags on Cragway, and the bowl view at the end of the trail, make nice evening viewpoints for campers.

The best way to hike the **Cragway Trail** is down, and that involves hiking up the lower part of the Daniel Boone Scout Trail. Cragway is steep in many places, though nice switchbacks are being constructed by a paid Grandfather Mountain trail crew that didn't exist early in the hiking permit program when the new path was opened largely by volunteers. One can hike up, and it is a spectacular, though strenuous climb.

Where the Nuwati Trail goes right, turn left and continue on the Tanawha Trail. The path ascends around a ridge, and just as it enters the drainage of Green Mountain Creek, 0.6 mile from the trailhead, the Daniel Boone Scout Trail goes right. Past the signboard and a flight of steps, the trail begins a long, gradual, switchbacking meander through terrain where the original trail went straight up a stream gully (crossed at 0.7 mile). Many of the earliest, volunteer-built sections of the trail were routed through wet-weather gullies under arching rhododendron to facilitate quick construction. Parts of the path are still located in the most stable, now better drained, sections of those gullies.

The trail reroutes and emerges between two rock outcroppings 1.6 miles from the trailhead. To the left, the Boone Scout Trail continues in 0.1 mile to the "middle campsite," a fine group of tent sites at about the center point on the trail. To the right, Cragway starts its trip down to the Nuwati Trail. Go right; immediately on the left, just steps from the trail, is Flat Rock View, a wonderful, table-flat vantage point in Boone Fork Bowl that makes a perfect lunch spot.

Going right, the trail skirts the outcropping of Flat Rock View and winds along open crags, entering the woods and artfully broaching a small line of cliffs. The trail winds through dense rhododendron then descends through occasional spruces. It emerges into an open meadow of blueberry bushes and rhododendron, then abruptly exits onto a spectacular view at Top Crag. Keep to the trail here to avoid further impacting the Allegheny sand myrtle, a low-growing alpine-like plant that covers the open area. This expansive view is one of the best on the mountain.

From Top Crag to the junction with the Nuwati Trail the path steeply descends rocky crags with many great views. From the lowest major view-point new switchbacks ease the descent, which ends after a level 100 yards at a signed junction (2.5 miles from the trailhead). Going right, the round-trip back to the Boone Fork parking area is 3.6 miles. If you go left and hike to the view at the end of the Nuwati Trail and back, the hike is 4.6 miles.

At about 1.6 miles from the trailhead, the Daniel Boone Scout Trail continues left near Flat Rock View and soon enters a small flat. A left reaches the middle campsite. A side trail from there continues through a mixed deciduous and spruce forest about 100 yards past the tent sites to a small, reliable spring.

Heading up, the trail climbs steeply, gradually encountering more and more spruces. When the trail finally gains the crest of Pilot Ridge, a nice campsite with a view appears on the left. Continuing, the trail enters the spruce–fir forest zone, a dark, cool, evergreen area carpeted with moss and wood sorrel. The trail climbs a rocky crag (with views left to the Piedmont). Then, at the top, a tiny view trail goes right onto the rock. This is a fine view from the top of Boone Bowl. The trail re-enters the woods and shortly reaches a signed trail on the left to Viaduct View, a rocky perch with a perspective on the dramatic eastern side of the mountain. The Parkway's Linn Cove Viaduct span is in view, too.

A hiker gazes from the cliff top in front of Hi-Balsam shelter atop Grandfather Mountain, Calloway Peak in background.

The Daniel Boone Scout Trail ascends another crag, then wanders to another side trail on the left, this one to Hi-Balsam Shelter, a tiny, low-lying leanto that sleeps four to six comfortably. The shelter, at about 2.6 miles, was built by Clyde Smith during World War II, and later rebuilt to the same style and dimensions. No tent camping or fires are permitted at the shelter site, but a designated campsite just 100 yards higher permits both. The shelter view is noteworthy, looking southeast over the Lost Cove area (see that entry), with spectacular nighttime views of distant cities out the front of the shelter and Calloway Peak, behind.

The Daniel Boone Scout Trail continues past a designated campsite on the left. Opposite the campsite, across the trail and off in the woods lie the remains of a single-engine plane that crashed in 1978. Past this point the trail suddenly stands on end, climbing steeply, with the aid of one large ladder, to Calloway Peak (5,964 feet; marked by a white X), 2.8 miles from the trailhead. The panoramic view takes in the dramatic drop to the Piedmont.

The Boone Trail terminates about 0.1 mile away at the Grandfather Trail's Watauga View, the best vantage point to the west. Between the peak and the junction the summit area is a rocky, evergreen-covered crest.

Retracing your steps, the entire hike is just under 6 miles; the route is just under 5 miles long if you follow the Cragway Trail on the way down.

General description: Grandfather Mountain's most rugged route, this trail traverses the summit ridge in one of the South's outstanding trail experiences. The route ascends peaks and scales ladders over cliffs to reach Calloway Peak, the highest summit in the Blue Ridge.

Length: 4.6-miles round-trip to Calloway Peak; a 2-mile circuit over the first major peak.

Degree of difficulty: Strenuous for both hikes.

Maps: USGS Grandfather Mountain quad. The best map for the hike is the free trail map of Grandfather Mountain.

Elevation gain and loss: 2,248 feet, assuming return on the Underwood Trail to avoid MacRae Peak.

Trailhead elevation: 5,260 feet.

High point: 5,964 feet.

Water availability: No reliable water is available at the trail's ridgetop location, so carry plenty from the summit visitor center. At the 2-mile mark, a steep, 0.3-mile descent to the left on the Calloway Trail reaches Shanty Spring, as old and pure a supply of water for hikers as exists on any North Carolina trail.

For more information: Grandfather Mountain. See Appendix C.

Finding the trailhead: The single motor access trailhead is at the highest parking lot atop Grandfather Mountain. The trail is reached on the road to the Linville Peak visitor center beside the Mile-High Swinging Bridge.

The hike: The **Grandfather Trail** starts opposite the visitor center with a steep, rocky pitch from the parking lot into the woods. In a flat reached in 200 feet, it turns right (going left, a view trail reaches clifftops, used in the past as a launch site for a hang-gliding exhibition program). Follow the fairly level, blue-blazed trail through open rhododendron areas and spruce forests. Crags afford occasional views to the left and right of the trail. Ascend past an overhanging rock (watch your head—it's called Head Bumpin' Rock) and attain a magnificent crag-top view that's a nice turnaround for a family stroll. Left, or west, is the resort development of Sugar Mountain and Linville Ridge. Right, or east, the land plummets to the Piedmont, a view that will get even better as you climb MacRae Peak (5,939 feet), the cliff-faced, evergreen-covered summit straight ahead. The trail ascends directly up that face, and if you peer closely at about 10 o'clock on the skyline, you might see hikers on a series of ladders.

Descend with cables intended for use when the trail is a river of ice. Ascend again and wander through a small meadow, under a rocky crag, and into a larger meadow to a junction on the left, at 0.5 mile, with the yellow-blazed Underwood Trail, just below the peak. The Underwood Trail is a convenient return route to the visitor center when the last thing you want

13 GRANDFATHER TRAIL

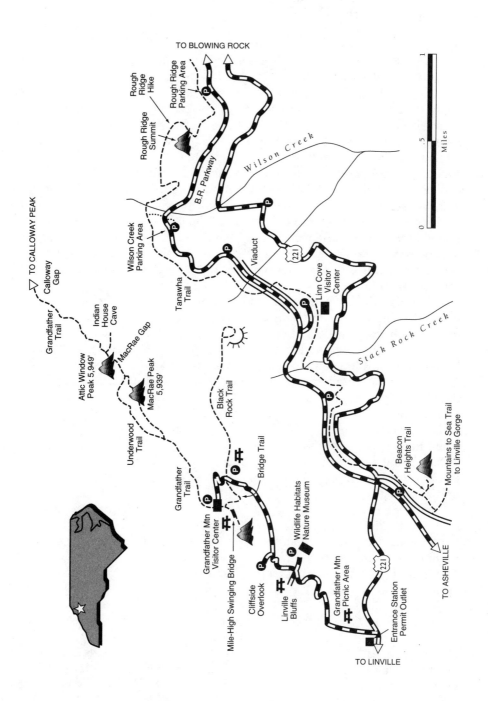

TO BLOWING ROCK

Rough Ridge Hike

Rough Ridge Parking Area

Rough Ridge Summit

Wilson Creek

B.R. Parkway

TO CALLOWAY PEAK

Calloway Gap

Grandfather Trail

Indian House Cave

MacRae Gap

Attic Window Peak 5,949'

MacRae Peak 5,939'

Underwood Trail

Wilson Creek Parking Area

Tanawha Trail

Viaduct

221

Linn Cove Visitor Center

Stack Rock Creek

Black Rock Trail

Grandfather Trail

Bridge Trail

Beacon Heights Trail

Mountains to Sea Trail to Linville Gorge

Grandfather Mtn Visitor Center

Mile-High Swinging Bridge

Wildlife Habitats Nature Museum

Cliffside Overlook

Linville Bluffs

Grandfather Mtn Picnic Area

221

TO ASHEVILLE

Entrance Station Permit Outlet

TO LINVILLE

1

.5

Miles

0

to do is climb over another peak. It's also a good route to the gap beyond MacRae Peak in severe weather when reaching the top of the peak would be dangerous. Perhaps the greatest value of the Underwood Trail is as a way to sample Grandfather Ridge without going all the way to Calloway Peak. Simply cross MacRae Peak, take a left on the Underwood Trail, and return to the visitor center for one of the truly spectacular short hikes in the state, 2 miles round-trip.

Back on the Grandfather Trail, turn right at the Underwood Trail junction and begin the climb to MacRae Peak. Ascend a cabled crag, then reach an overhanging cliff where the trail goes left. (A right around the cliff reveals a rock-reinforced shelter cave.) Ascending left, the trail veers right into a fissure where you'll encounter the first ladder. Ascend it, then climb a steep trail to where a glance left reveals a cliff that funnels in the summer breeze, or bitter wind in winter. Scramble up a few more rocks; above you, the steepest ladders reach to the clifftop overhead. An experienced hiker could scramble up the rocks around the ladders, but to most people, especially the inexperienced, this is as adventurous a section of trail as found in the South. Climb up and before the last ladder, consider pausing on the large ledge for a snack, a drink, or a few pictures. The visitor center is now far below.

Attaining the clifftop reveals ridge after rocky ridge of crags. Ascend to the right up the clifftop, climb another ladder, wander along a precipitous ridgeline, and emerge on a knife-edge with a house-size boulder perched atop it. That is MacRae Peak (5,939 feet). An unnerving ladder leans against it. Climb and have lunch; the eye-popping view is stupendous. To the east, the Blue Ridge escarpment plummets past the newest part of the Blue Ridge Parkway to the distant Carolina Piedmont. Farther along the ridge, the next summit, Attic Window Peak rises from the next gap, a deep cleft splitting its summit. The trail goes right through it. To the right of the peak, huge domes drop to the east. Beyond the boulder, the trail reaches a steep chute where cables aid the decent to another ladder. In winter, this is a frozen flow of ice: hikers should have instep crampons with them under snowy conditions.

At MacRae Gap, 1 mile from the visitor center, the **Underwood Trail** leads left. This is a nice alternate route back. The rocky 0.5-mile Underwood Trail leaves MacRae Gap through a beautiful evergreen forest reminiscent of the far north. Look right for views up to Attic Window Peak. The trail turns at a western viewpoint and scrambles down through crags, cliffs, and mossy defiles. It then levels, but stays very rocky to its junction with the Grandfather Trail.

Keep on the Grandfather Trail, winding through a wood sorrel-covered gap of evergreens to more ladders, this time scaling their way through a boulder cave called The Subway. Scramble higher, attain a ledge, and look up at the massive split in the peak. Then climb up into it. Two-thirds of the way to the top, step left out of the chute, around a bulging rock with a nice handhold on the far left, to a ledge. At that point, a crack leads into the rock, and emerges to a box seat view on the outside of the peak. Slide down (carefully) to the ledge, and enjoy. This is the Attic Window.

Retreat if the ledge, or even the exit view, is enough. But if you like the ledge, slip through the crack below it, drop into the fissure, and find an even-walled corridor of astounding perfection leading back down and out into the chute, about 15 feet below where you entered. You just missed it on the way up.

Continuing, reach the top of the couloir where a trail leading to the right reaches a campsite atop the domes. To the left, the trail emerges from between rocks to a stunning western view of Sugar Mountain, Beech Mountain, and the burg of Banner Elk. A left takes you out to more rocky perches, including a crag that dramatically overlooks MacRae Gap.

Following the Grandfather Trail to the right, drop to the next gap and a side trail on the right at 1.2 miles. A hundred yards down, a left turn reaches a massive overhanging rock called Indian House Cave. When discovered in the 1940s, the cave contained Indian artifacts suggesting it was a significant ritual site. This is a nice place to escape the rain.

Back at the gap, climb a small ladder and follow a clifftop with views on the left. The trail emerges at a viewpoint atop a dramatic cliff. Then the trail follows an evergreen-, rhododendron-, and mountain laurel-covered knife-edge above the cliff and emerges at a mirror-image viewpoint on the other side.

The trail then descends into a high, alpine-like meadow with a fine campsite accessible to nearby evening views. Farther on, the trail crosses another clifftop area and another tiny gap grown close with evergreens and wood-sorrel. Going over a whaleback of crags, the trail winds into Calloway

Backpackers pause on the Grandfather Trail high above the Blue Ridge Parkway on Attic Window Peak of Grandfather Mountain.

Gap at 1.9 miles, a traditional ridgetop campground with a number of campsites. The impact of firewood gathering at this site, now healing nicely, prompted the banning of all campfires on the Grandfather Trail. Campsite views are not far from Calloway Gap, but the closest is a crag reached by walking level out of the gap along the base of the crag that flanks the northwestern side. In the gap, the red-blazed Calloway Trail descends left to the Profile Trail. Following the Grandfather Trail, the path climbs again, through a tiny meadow and past a campsite with a spectacular view from a ledge just beyond the tentsite.

Farther up, a crag juts on the right and a campsite appears on the left as the trail veers into dense evergreens. Of all the summits in the state where the virgin forests were logged, Grandfather's Canadian-zone canopy of spruces and firs has grown back to the greatest extent. Almost immediately, the Grandfather Trail's last junction is reached at 2.3 miles. To the left, a short spur leads to Watauga (wa-TAW-ga) View, a west-facing ledge facing Banner Elk and overlooking the headwaters of the Watauga River. Just 0.1 mile away, on the white-blazed Daniel Boone Scout Trail, is Calloway Peak (5,964 feet), highest in the Blue Ridge.

The easiest way to gauge Grandfather Mountain's significance is to look east from Calloway, MacRae, or Attic Window peaks and realize that Andre Michaux, the earliest and most important botanical explorer of the New World, clawed his way there in the 1780s and completely lost all evidence of scientific objectivity. The result was perhaps the biggest error of Michaux's scientific career. In what biographer Henry Savage, Jr., says was an unprecedented burst of emotion, the botanist told his diary that he'd "reached the summit of the highest mountain in all of North America." He was so inspired he sang the Marseillaise and shouted "long live America and the Republic of France. Long live liberty, equality, and fraternity." Michaux's discovery of nearly 200 species of plants is a more fitting symbol of his achievements. He stayed in the new United States for seven years, diligently delving into the botanical richness of the New World for Louis XVI and then for the new French Republic.

The Grandfather Trail gives hikers the best glimpse of the kind of scenery that prompted Michaux's famous flub. They'll also observe many of the plants he found so interesting. On the high, rocky clifftops, hikers encounter reddish green, fuzzy leaves of Michaux's saxifrage, a delicate boreal plant that he might have first noticed here.

The masses don't reach this part of Grandfather Mountain, so it remains pristine. Some wilderness purists accurately compare Grandfather to the heart of the Great Smokies and say the mountain isn't a true wilderness experience; indeed, looking west, the Grandfather Mountain view is somewhat developed, with everything from ski slopes lit for night skiing to condos. But the mountain bulks against the intrusion, and campsites on the eastern side of the ridge along the Grandfather Trail overlook a stunning vista of Piedmont cities sprawling like distant pinwheels of light over the dark isolation of Pisgah National Forest.

14   *CALLOWAY PEAK*

General description: A hike up the western flank of Grandfather Mountain to Calloway Peak.
Length: 1.8 miles to Shanty Branch; 7 miles round-trip to Calloway Peak.
Difficulty: Strenuous.
Elevation gain and loss: 4,168 feet.
Trailhead elevation: 3,880 feet.
High point: 5,964 feet.
Maps: USGS Grandfather Mountain quad; the best map for the hike is the free Grandfather Mountain trail map, available at the park.
Water availability: A variety of streams and Shanty Spring provide ample water. Treatment is recommended, though Shanty Spring is an old and pure supply of water.
For more information: Grandfather Mountain. See Appendix C.
Finding the trailhead: The trailhead is 13 miles south of Boone on North Carolina Highway 105, 0.7 mile north of the North Carolina Highways 105/184 junction near Banner Elk. Hiking permits are available nearby at the Tynecastle development at the NC 105/184 junction. In the event this is closed, permits are also available at the Taylor Country Store (in the village of Foscoe, about 4 miles north of the trailhead) at the Grandfather Mountain entrance, and in Boone.

The hike: The **Profile Trail** was built in the mid- to late-1980s to replace the ancient Shanty Spring Trail, a steep and eroding trail dating from the latter half of the nineteenth century. The earliest tourists to visit northwestern North Carolina were attracted to cool climate venues like the Eseeola Lodge in Linville, the Green Park Inn in Blowing Rock (both still in existence), and the Grandfather Hotel, once located near the present-day Profile Trail parking area. A Mr. Calloway, proprietor of the hotel, is thought to be the namesake of Calloway Peak.

Some of those who hiked the Shanty Spring Trail arrived at the trailhead on the old E.T. & W.N.C. Railroad train that paused in Linville Gap on its way from Johnson City, Tennessee, to Boone. The early romance of that time in the surrounding mountains was eloquently told in the book *The Balsam Groves of the Grandfather Mountain*, by Shepherd Dugger, published in 1907.

Impending development of a small parcel of land adjacent to that trail prompted the creation of the Profile Trail. The new route shares the earlier route's dramatic views of the Profile, the multifaceted face of Grandfather Mountain looking west. The face, or faces, are best seen by hikers as they drive south through the Watauga River Valley town of Foscoe on the way toward the trailhead from Boone. The Profile Trail was the biggest trail-building project ever undertaken by the private park. The trail ranks as one of the most intensively developed paths in the state.

Don't take the trailbuilder's art for granted. As these trailblazers on Grandfather Mountain will tell, using pry bars and hand winches to manuever massive boulders into a paved appearance on the Profile Trail is no easy task.

14 PROFILE TRAIL / CALLOWAY PEAK

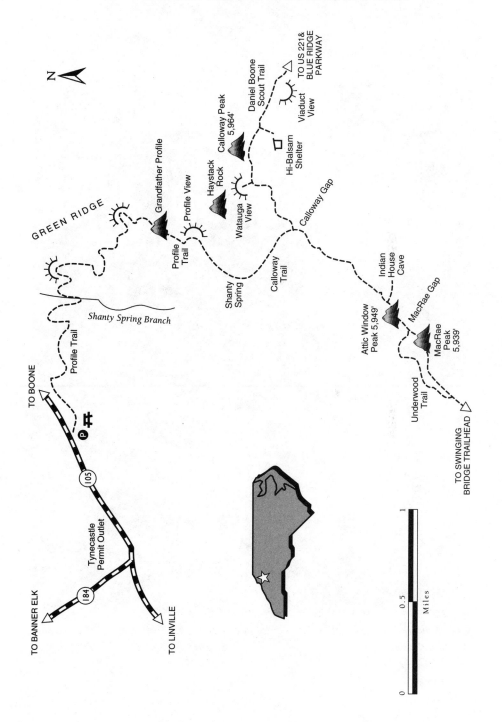

One of the namesake profiles on Grandfather Mountain's Profile Trail. *Photo by Jim Morton.*

The drive into the Profile Trail parking area is deceptive. Unless it's covered in snow or ice, don't let it intimidate you. The paved road's single steep switchback drops from busy North Carolina Highway 105 into an intimate spot beside the headwaters of the Watauga River. (During inclement weather, park in the gravel lot across NC 105 from the entrance.) A covered trailhead picnic table provides a place for backpackers to prepare packs.

The trail starts on the west side of the river, where snowlike fringe phacelia grows in April, then dips to cross the stream on huge boulders. With the exception of one steep section, this excavated and graded trail is quite level as it wanders for its first 0.8 mile along the beautiful stream. *Rhododendron maximum,* yellow birch, beech, and spruce populate a mature, New England-like forest.

The trail leaves the river, climbs steeply for 100 yards or so, and passes a mileage sign at 0.5 mile, the first of such reminders along the trail. The trail then levels out again as it winds in and out of scenic stream drainages. Just past the first such drainage, the large waxy evergreen-leafed ground plant is Fraser's sedge, on the endangered list. At about 0.9 mile, the trail dips across Shanty Branch, the source of which is Shanty Spring, 2 miles ahead. Stones bridge the stream, and places to sit suggest hikers pause in this scenic spot. Returning to the trailhead from here makes a nice kids' hike of 1.8 miles round-trip.

Past the stream, the trail dips, winds through a fissure in large rocks, then climbs steeply to another quiet drainage in a mixed evergreen and deciduous forest. It climbs again, winding higher up into and then back across the same drainage. Exiting the drainage, the trail climbs switchbacks, then straightens and climbs more gradually back across the top of the earlier drainage on its way around Green Ridge.

As the trail crosses over Green Ridge and levels on its way into the next drainage, immediately below the Grandfather Profile, it reaches a nice view at about 1.7 miles. It looks north over the Watauga River Valley and Foscoe, past Howard's Knob at Boone and the bald ridge of Snake Mountain, and on to White Top (with its crescent-shaped bald) and Mount Rogers (just visible), the second- and first-highest summits in Virginia respectively (See *Hiking Virginia*, Falcon Press).

Now below the lowest, most face-like of the Profiles, the trail switchbacks again to another crossing of Green Ridge at 2 miles, this time at a major campsite with numerous tentsites and a grandiose campfire pit. A small spring is on the left just beyond the spur trail to the campsite. From the campsite, the trail ascends south across the mountain over a jumbled boulder field spanned by outstanding pathways of natural stone. Looking back, the Profile is visible. A steep set of switchbacks reaches a huge boulder with a rock-paved shelter spot. A few hundred feet farther the trail turns a corner to Profile View, a dramatic view of the face that early mountaineers said looked like a grandfather when hoarfrost blasted the mountain.

Rising more gradually, the trail passes a spring, parallels a small cliff, then winds to a junction, now almost imperceptible, with the old Shanty

Spring Trail at 2.6 miles. At Shanty Spring, 2.8 miles from the start, water empties from below a cliff that is often spectacularly covered with ice in winter. In a typically Victorian claim, Dugger's *Balsam Groves* asserts that this is "the coldest water outside of perpetual snow in the United States."

Going right at the cliff, the red-blazed Calloway Trail rises on its historic, steep, and rocky route through increasing evergreens to Calloway Gap, at 3.1 miles. Dipping into the gap, the trail junctions with the Grandfather Trail at a historic campsite. Hikers can camp (no fires) at sites located out of sight of the trail.

Going left on the Grandfather Trail, hikers pass other campsites, tiny meadows, a jagged trailside crag, then head into a dense evergreen grove before reaching a junction at 3.5 miles. Left, a side trail leads onto the often windy western prow of the peak called Watauga View. Right, Calloway Peak is 0.1 mile away.

15 GRAVEYARD FIELDS

General description: A loop that reaches two waterfalls and explores a large, alpine-like valley.
General location: Between the Blue Ridge Parkway and the Shining Rock Wilderness.
Length: 3-mile loop.
Degree of difficulty: Easy to moderate. The area boasts easy backpacking for beginners.
Maps: USGS Shining Rock quad. The area is best covered by Pisgah National Forest's Shining Rock–Middle Prong Wilderness map.
Elevation gain and loss: 1,400 feet.
Trailhead elevation: 5,100 feet.
High point: 5,400 feet.
Low point: 4,800 feet.
Water availability: Water from the streams should be boiled or purified; better to bring your own.
For more information: Pisgah Ranger District. Or contact Supervisor's Office, National Forests in North Carolina, Asheville, NC. See Appendix C.
Finding the trailhead: The trail begins at Graveyard Fields Overlook, at milepost 418 on the Blue Ridge Parkway. The trailhead is a scenic 30-mile drive south of Asheville on the Parkway from U.S. Highway 25, a popular Parkway access a short distance from Interstate Highway 40. The trail is also easily reached from the southwest. From the vicinity of Brevard, reach the Parkway via U.S. Highway 276 or North Carolina Highway 215. Both

15 GRAVEYARD FIELDS

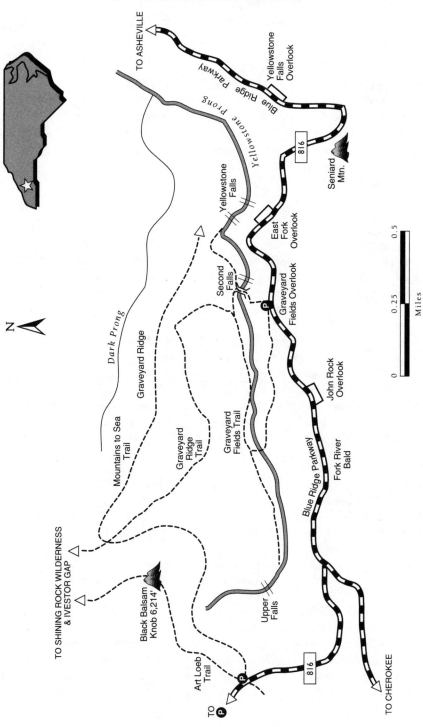

branch west from U.S. Highway 64 in the vicinity of Brevard, and both are segments of the popular Forest Heritage Scenic Byway, a loop that encircles Shining Rock Wilderness. The trail is about 7 miles south of the US 276 junction, and about 4.5 miles north of the NC 215 junction.

The hike: The **Graveyard Fields Loop** is an easy to moderate path that can range from a short out-and-back hike to a full-length streamside loop, with or without scenic waterfalls. The pool below the lower falls is a great summer spot to cool off, though this lofty area never gets very warm.

One caution: Probably the most daunting part of the entire hike is the steep descent from the Blue Ridge Parkway into the stream valley. It's short, only a few tenths of a mile. But it is steep on the way out if you return that way. Otherwise, the Graveyard Fields Loop is a relatively easy way to explore a lofty area near the Shining Rock Wilderness, one of the state's most scenic areas.

The open fields here were named following massive clearcutting early in the century. Thousands of stumps reminded some people of grave markers. The entire watershed was consumed by wildfires in the 1920s and again in the 1940s. These gave the Shining Rock area its above-treeline appearance; the results of the 25,000- and 50,000-acre conflagrations can still be seen in the largely treeless landscape. Few places in North Carolina have better views.

This gentle stream valley makes the perfect place for a day hike, picnic, or backpacking trip, especially for beginners or those who want scenic camping without arduous walking. The area is very popular in summer and fall, though, so campers in this fragile area should use scrupulous camping practices. Although accessible campsites may be filled during the busy seasons, it is easy to find out-of-the-way sites for low-impact camping.

Leaving the edge of the Parkway overlook, the trail descends the steep path, then crosses Yellowstone Prong on a bridge. Go right on a side trail down to Second Falls. The pool beneath the fall is deep enough for a cooling dip in summer. Retrace your steps to the bridge, at about 0.5 mile, and continue.

The **Graveyard Ridge Trail** branches right up a scenic ridge of open fields and forest. It is a nice day hike or backpack to the lofty summits found on a portion of the Art Loeb Trail (see the entry for Shining Rock Wilderness). The Graveyard Fields Loop continues along the stream through an open river valley. Fine campsites are located where evergreens intermingle with deciduous trees and blueberry bushes, just out of sight. Views reach up to the balds above, along the skyline of the Art Loeb Trail and Shining Rock Wilderness.

At the 1-mile mark, the return part of the loop heads left across the stream. Hikers may continue on the righthand trail, following a 0.7-mile trail to the Upper Falls, a less frequently visited, more precipitous cascade with impressive views down the valley. This section of trail, a side trip of about 1.4 miles, is steeper and rockier than the rest of the route.

Hikers visit these falls on Yellowstone Prong on the Graveyard Fields Loop. The bald ridges of Graveyard Ridge and Tennent Mountain rise above.

Retrace your steps downstream and take a right turn across Yellowstone Prong at about 2.7 miles. This return route gradually ascends through a boggy area with a high-altitude feel. You'll cross a log bridge on the way, and in about 0.5 mile, be back at the parking lot after a slightly more than 3 mile, moderate to moderately strenuous hike. Without taking in the Upper Falls, the entire loop is about 2 miles and rated easy, though some stream hopping makes it inadvisable for those who require absolutely flat and graded trails.

General description: A network of little-used, streamside trails in an area proposed for wilderness designation. These hikes, like those in the adjacent Lost Cove Wilderness Study Area (see Hike 21), include spectacular short walks and wilderness circuits that are among the best waterfall hikes in Western North Carolina.

General location: Near Lost Cove Wilderness Study Area, Pisgah National Forest.

Length: Hikes in the area include out-and-back walks of various lengths: 1.6 miles to South Harper Creek Falls; 2.4 miles to Bard Falls; 1.5 and 3 miles to North Harper Creek Falls; and circuits of 5.6, 8, and 9 miles.

Degree of difficulty: Easy to moderate, although the lengthier circuit hikes described here are moderately strenuous for seasoned hikers.

Maps: USGS Grandfather Mountain and Chestnut Mountain quads, but the Forest Service Wilson Creek Area map is the preferred trail map.

Elevation gains and losses: 960 feet to South Harper Creek Falls; 1,120 feet to Bard Falls; 350 and 1,360 feet to North Harper Creek Falls; 985, 2,440, and 1,440 feet respectively for the above three circuits.

Trailhead elevations: See low and high points.

Low points: Harper Creek Trail, 1,480 feet at SR 1328; Yellow Buck Trail, 1,800 feet at Harper Creek Trail; Raider Camp Trail, 1,560 feet at lower Harper Creek Trail; Persimmon Ridge Trail, 1,920 feet at Harper Creek, 2,200 feet at Forest Road 464; North Harper Creek Trail, 1,820 feet at Harper Creek Trail; North Harper Shortcut, 2,200 feet at North Harper Creek Trail; Harper Creek Falls Trail, 2,640 feet at North Harper Creek Falls Trail.

High points: Harper Creek Trail, 2,480 feet at Forest Road 58; Yellow Buck Trail, 2,200 feet at Persimmon Ridge Trail near FR 464 (but 2,400 feet near Yellow Buck summit); Raider Camp Trail, 2,200 feet at Upper Harper Creek Trail; Persimmon Ridge Trail, 2,600 feet at FR 58 (but 2,785 feet at peak near FR 58); North Harper Creek Trail, 3,175 feet at FR 58; North Harper Shortcut, 2,560 feet at FR 464; Harper Creek Falls Trail, 2,960 feet at FR 464.

Water availability: Though water is plentiful along these trails, bring water from outside the area to avoid having to boil drinking water.

For more information: Grandfather Ranger District, Pisgah National Forest. Or contact Supervisor's Office, National Forests in North Carolina, Asheville. See Appendix C.

Finding the trailheads: For hikers arriving from the south and west, the best way to reach the Lost Cove/Harper Creek area is from North Carolina Highway 181 near the Blue Ridge Parkway. About 24 miles north of Morganton on NC 181, turn right on Mortimer Road, SR 1401. Heading south on NC 181, turn left 0.9 mile from the NC 181/183 junction, 2.6 miles from the NC 181/Blue Ridge Parkway junction, and about 7.4 miles south of the U.S. Highway 221/NC 181 junction in Linville.

Once on SR 1401, the road becomes dirt at 1.7 miles. At 2.2 miles, turn right at a junction (a church is on the left) and in another 0.2 mile turn right at a junction opposite the Long Ridge Baptist Church. After turning, you'll see a Forest Road 464 sign on the right. At 4.3 miles, the unsigned trailhead for the Big Lost Cove Cliffs Trail is on the left. At 5.3 miles, a Forest Service picnic and primitive camping area is located at the junction with FR 58, on the right.

From the picnic area at the junction go south on FR 58 to reach trailheads on the west side of the Harper Creek area. From the junction, the signed start of the North Harper Creek Trail is 0.3 mile on the left. The signed start of the Persimmon Ridge Trail is on the left at 3.8 miles, and the Harper Creek Trail leaves the road with stone steps on the left at 4.4 miles. Only the Harper Creek Trail has an ample parking slip; the other trails have only roadside parking.

Trails on the north and east side of the Harper Creek Area are reached via FR 464 east of the junction with FR 58. From that junction, the signed upper and lower trailheads for the Little Lost Cove Cliffs Trail are on the right at 0.6 mile and 2.1 miles (in between, at 1.6 miles, FR 464A goes left with easy access to the middle of the Lost Cove Creek Trail; see Hike 21). The lower Little Lost Cove Cliffs trailhead is also where the signed North Harper Creek Falls Trail begins on the right. The unsigned Darkside Cliffs Trail starts on the left at 2.7 miles. The signed North Harper Shortcut starts on the right at 3.4 miles, with the Hunt Fish Falls Trail on the left at about 4 miles. The signed Persimmon Ridge Trail (with immediate access to the Yellow Buck Trail) begins on the right at about 4.9 miles.

To reach the easternmost trailhead for the Harper Creek Trail, continue to a junction with North Carolina Highway 90 at 7.1 miles. Go right, pass Mortimer Recreation Area, and at 1.8 miles, turn right on SR 1328. The signed Harper Creek Trail starts on the right, 1.3 miles south of the junction.

For hikers arriving from the east, the best way to reach the area is via scenic back roads between Lenoir and Morganton. Both towns are reached by major highways. From Morganton take NC 181 north about 10 miles, then turn right on the Brown Mountain Beach Road, SR 1405. Go about 5 miles and turn left onto SR 1328. To reach this point from Lenoir take NC 90 to Collettsville. Go left from NC 90 and continue south on SR 1337 just over 3 miles to a right turn onto SR 1328.

Once on SR 1328, which parallels beautiful Wilson Creek, go 4.7 miles and turn right at a T-junction. The Harper Creek Trail is on the left at 2.8 miles. Reach the SR 1328/NC 90 junction in another 1.3 miles and turn left on NC 90. Immediately pass the Mortimer Recreation Area and take another left in 1.9 miles on the Pineola Road, which is FR 464.

From the FR 464/NC 90 junction, trailheads are as follows: Persimmon Ridge Trail (and Yellow Buck Trail), 2.2 miles on left; Hunt Fish Falls Trail, 3.2 miles on right; North Harper Shortcut, 3.7 miles on left; Darkside Cliffs Trail, 4.4 miles on right; the North Harper Creek Falls Trail and the lower

16 HARPER CREEK

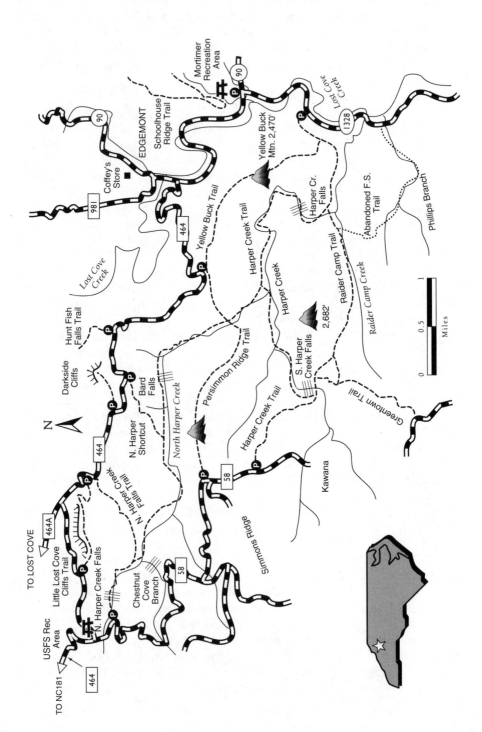

The Harper Creek area is a wealth of cascading streams perfect for trout fishing.

trailhead for the Little Lost Cove Cliffs Trail, 5.1 miles on the left; upper trailhead for the Little Lost Cove Cliffs Trail, 6.5 miles on left. Go left on FR 58 at 7.1 miles to reach the North Harper Creek Trail, 7.4 miles on the left; the Persimmon Ridge Trail, 10.9 miles on left; and the Harper Creek Trail, 11.5 miles on the left.

Also from this direction, the Big Lost Cove Cliffs Trail is 1 mile beyond the FR 58/FR 464 junction (8.1 miles from NC 90).

To reach the trailhead for the Lost Cove and Gragg Prong trails (see the Lost Cove entry) from either direction, go north from the FR 464/NC 90 junction 0.2 mile to Edgemont and take the next left onto Forest Road 981 (Coffey's General Store is just 100 yards farther on NC 90). Bear left at the first junction (Forest Road 451 goes right) and reach the trailhead on the left at about 4 miles.

From the north, there are routes into the area from Blowing Rock and Linville. The best is from Linville. Continue south of the US 221/NC 181 junction past the Eseeola Lodge and go left on a road marked SR 1511. At about 1 mile cross the Blue Ridge Parkway and descend on the Roseborough Road. At about 4.5 miles go right on FR 981. The Lost Cove trailhead is on the right in about 0.5 mile. Farther south is Edgemont and other trail access.

The hikes: The Harper Creek area is laced with nine trails. The main paths, the Harper Creek Trail and North Harper Creek Trail, connect and permit hikers to tour the two main waterfall-filled drainages that make up the tract. Other trails link these main paths to nearby roads and create circuit hikes. With two cars, top to bottom hikes of these spectacular streams are very easy—but positioning the two cars can take some time. Side trails come in handy, providing quick access from adjacent roads to scenic areas along the streams. That's especially nice for those who fish, since these are excellent trout streams. In the following description, the main trails are described first, with recommended circuit hikes and day hikes to waterfalls.

Above Harper Creek towers Grandfather Mountain.

The **Harper Creek Trail**, featuring Harper Creek Falls, the area's most spectacular cataract, leaves SR 1328 and climbs consistently to a junction with the Yellow Buck Trail (a return route for circuit hikers) at 0.5 mile. Continuing straight, the trail descends to nice campsites, Harper Creek, and a junction on the left with the **Raider Camp Trail** (also a return route for circuit hikers) at just over 1 mile. Turn right up Harper Creek and in 0.1 mile, a side trail leads to views of Harper Creek Falls and a large pool below. Continuing on Harper Creek Trail, it reaches the North Harper Creek Falls Trail at about 3.5 miles. After crossing a side stream at 4.5 miles, at just over 5 miles, the trail reaches views of South Harper Creek Falls, 200 feet high and a spectacular cascade, considered the ultimate waterfall in the Grandfather Ranger District.

Just above the waterfall, the Raider Camp Trail comes in on the left. The Harper Creek Trail continues above the falls, then winds away from the river gradually, reaching FR 58 at about 6 miles. Starting here, hiking to the falls makes a moderately strenuous out-and-back day hike of less than 2 miles.

A 9-mile circuit on the south side of Harper Creek can be formed by going left at the top of the falls on the Raider Camp Trail and descending about 2.6 miles back to the Harper Creek Trail (where it's another 1 mile back to your car). To do this, take the Raider Camp Trail left across the stream where a spur trail on the left leads to great views of the falls and Grandfather Mountain. The main trail continues, switchbacking steeply up to a trail junction on the right with the Greentown Trail, 0.2 mile from the Harper Creek Trail. (The Greentown Trail is another nice way into this area; look for it on the Wilson Creek Area map). Continue on the Raider Camp Trail, descending gradually then steeply dropping to Raider Camp Creek. The trail wanders past campsites through hemlocks and tulip poplars, then reaches an old junction with the Phillips Branch Trail. The Raider Camp Trail then veers left, away from the creek, to cross Harper Creek and join the Harper Creek Trail, from which it's just over 1 mile back to your car. Circuit hikers could also go up the Raider Camp Trail and down Harper Creek.

Another nice circuit hike, this one about 8 miles and on the north side of Harper Creek, can be created by leaving the Harper Creek Trail where North Harper Creek branches to the right (at about 3.5 miles) on the **North Harper Creek Trail**. Heading north, the easy trail is almost level for 4 miles, but circuit hikers should turn at the junction with the **Persimmon Ridge Trail**, at about 0.5 mile (4 miles from SR 1328). Hikers heading back to their car at the Harper Creek trailhead should go right, or east. The trail climbs steeply for 0.2 mile, then joins the Yellow Buck Trail (at 0.5 mile, about 4.5 from SR 1328). From there, a left of just 0.2 mile takes you to FR 464. Circuit hikers turn right, following the old logging grade of the Yellow Buck Trail down to the Harper Creek Trail at about 7.5 miles. Back at SR 1328, you have done an 8-mile circuit.

A less-traveled circuit in this area uses the western end of the Persimmon Ridge Trail and the Harper Creek Trail. From FR 58, hikers can create a 5.6-mile route that descends the steeper Persimmon Ridge Trail, goes right on the North Harper Creek Trail, and right again on the Harper Creek Trail for a gradual climb back to FR 58. This hike is possible with one car because it's only a 0.6-mile walk on FR 58 between the Harper Creek and Persimmon Ridge trailheads.

Above the Persimmon Ridge Trail, the North Harper Creek trail reaches beautiful Bard Falls at about 1.3 miles. The "hole-in-the-wall" waterfall here contains an arch. The trail is an old logging railroad grade; some moss-covered ties are visible. About 0.2 mile beyond the fall, the North Harper Shortcut heads right about 1 mile on a moderate and graded climb to a junction 1 mile away on FR 464. This trail permits a moderate, 2.4-mile day hike to Bard Falls from FR 464.

The North Harper Creek Trail continues with stream crossings. On the left at about 3.3 miles is a waterfall where Chestnut Cove Branch joins North Harper Creek. The Harper Creek Falls Trail branches right at about 3.4 miles, another access to the creek for casual day hikers and those who want to fish. The side trail leads right about 1.3 miles to FR 464, and makes a nice day hike to the falls on Chestnut Cove Branch (2.8 miles round-trip) or to North Harper Creek Falls, just 0.2 mile farther on the North Harper Creek Trail. From the base of the falls, the North Harper Creek Trail climbs steeply (the only steep section of the entire trail). There are good views of the falls and surrounding area from the top. The trail levels again and ends on FR 58 at 4.5 miles. From FR 58, the falls are an easy, 1.5-mile day hike with swimming possibilities.

For wilderness purists, a large part of the southern end of the Harper Creek WSA has no designated trails at all. However, a now-abandoned Forest Service trail leads into the area from Phillips Branch. The old path led up Phillips Branch and went right on the stream's north fork, climbing over the ridge to a junction with the Raider Camp Trail. It provides access to the heart of the now trail-less tract for map-and-compass explorers. The old trail leaves the west side of SR 1328, about 2 miles south of its junction with NC 90.

17 HAWKSBILL MOUNTAIN

General description: A tablerock on the rim of the Linville Gorge Wilderness, Hawksbill Mountain is a crag-capped peak with panoramic summit views of Linville Gorge, a dozen major summits, and the Carolina Piedmont.
General location: Near Morganton.
Lengths: 1.4 miles round-trip direct to the peak. A nearby trailhead yields a longer, more gradual hike of 1.8 miles round-trip.
Degree of difficulty: Moderately strenuous or moderate, depending on trailhead.
Maps: USGS Linville Falls quad, but the Forest Service Linville Gorge Wilderness map is better.

17 HAWSKBILL MOUNTAIN

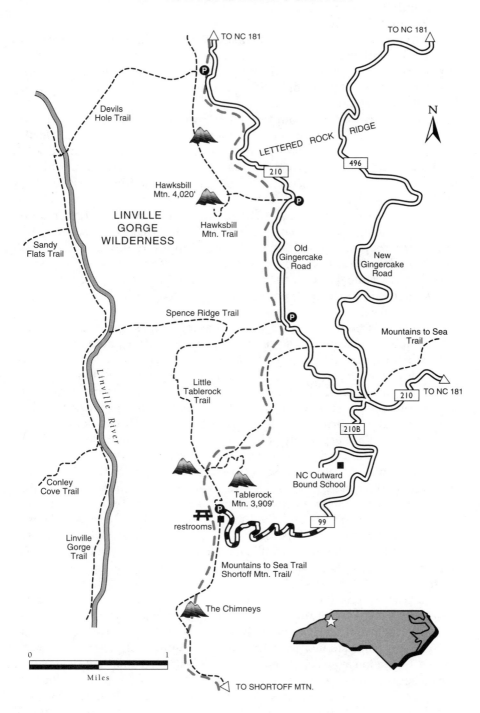

TO NC 181

TO NC 181

N

Devils
Hole Trail

LETTERED ROCK RIDGE

210

496

Hawksbill
Mtn. 4,020'

LINVILLE
GORGE
WILDERNESS

Hawksbill
Mtn. Trail

Sandy
Flats Trail

Old
Gingercake
Road

New
Gingercake
Road

Spence Ridge Trail

Mountains to Sea
Trail

Linville River

Little
Tablerock
Trail

210   TO NC 181

210B

NC Outward
Bound School

Conley
Cove Trail

Tablerock
Mtn. 3,909'

restrooms

99

Linville
Gorge
Trail

Mountains to Sea Trail
Shortoff Mtn. Trail/

0   1

The Chimneys

Miles

TO SHORTOFF MTN.

Elevation gain and loss: 1,400 feet.

Trailhead: 3,320 feet.

High point: 4,020 feet.

Water availability: No water is available at the trailhead and there are no commercial outlets nearby. Bring water.

For more information: Grandfather Ranger District, Pisgah National Forest. Or contact Supervisor's Office, National Forests in North Carolina, Asheville. See Appendix C.

Finding the trailhead: From the north, proceed south from the Boone area on North Carolina Highway 105, then U.S. Highway 221, then North Carolina Highway 181 toward Morganton. From the south, take NC 181 north from Morganton. A good marker, easily reached from either direction, is the NC 181/183 junction, just south of the Blue Ridge Parkway/NC 181 junction near Pineola.

Two miles south of that NC 181/183 intersection on NC 181, turn onto Gingercake Road, SR 1265. Turn right onto SR 1264 at 2.5 miles, at a junction marked with a sign to Tablerock. At 3.5 miles, the road, now Forest Road 210 (SR 1261), becomes gravel. At 5.1 miles pass the Sitting Bear Trail–Devil's Hole Trail on the right. At 6.2 miles, the Hawksbill Trail leaves the road on the right, with a parking area opposite it.

The hike: This hike is a scenic alternative for people who don't want to tackle Tablerock (see Hike 28), either due to its greater popularity or because reaching it requires another 5-mile drive on steep, winding, and dusty roads. Hawksbill is the less jagged summit in the prominent duo of peaks, Tablerock and Hawksbill, that dominate the skyline of Linville Gorge. It has a sloping, rocky crest and low vegetation that permits expansive views, and offers relative privacy, at least compared with Tablerock. Views of Tablerock itself are especially good here, and the vista includes adjoining cliffs and crags that are popular with many rock climbers.

The simple out-and-back walk to the peak begins at the Hawksbill Mountain parking area. The **Hawksbill Trail** enters the woods and climbs at a steady grade, then steepens. The climb is marked by big waterbars, designed to shed storm water from the trail and minimize erosion. These drainage bars are a step and half high, and the steep trail is covered in loose rock, so the first 0.25 mile of trail is not easy unless you take it slow. This is the sunny side of Letter Rock Ridge, so a summer sprint up this part of the trail can be a trudge.

The path flattens, then slips off the sunny side onto a fern-bordered grade through a shady forest of rhododendron, maple, mountain laurel, and chestnut oak. The trail descends gradually, and hikers should be alert: at about 0.5 mile, you'll need to make a sharp left to the summit. (If you miss it, you'll reach a T-junction at a signless post where trails go left and right. Just backtrack a short distance and take the first right. More on this junction later.)

After the turn, the trail gradually steepens. It's an undulating but decidedly uphill route through close vegetation and galax. After a shelter rock below the trail to the left, and just below the summit, the trail takes a hard right. It reaches the sandy soils and pines of the peak at 0.7 mile.

Here, near a large campfire area, views and trails fan out like spokes of a wheel, and trees give way to low vegetation such as Allegheny sand myrtle and sedges. Bear left on an obvious trail, and you'll wind down over prominent crags with fine views of Tablerock.

A longer, more gradual, less direct, and even less-trafficked hike starts 1.1 miles back on FR 210 at the **Sitting Bear Trailhead**. Ascend from the roadside parking spot to a large campsite at about 0.1 mile on the ridgecrest above the road. Go left on the obvious trail (a right leads to the distinctive Sitting Bear Rock; straight ahead, the primitive **Devils Hole Trail** drops 1.5 miles into Linville Gorge, fords the Linville River, and joins the Linville Gorge Trail 1.4 miles south of the Babel Tower Trail). Gradually ascend the ridge to Hawksbill Mountain. On the way, the trail climbs from the ridgecrest, (3,520 feet) and close to a summit (3,800 feet) before dipping to 3,600 feet as it slabs through the gap that marks the rise to Hawksbill.

Hikers will reach the intersection with the Hawksbill Trail at about 0.7 mile. It is marked by a signless post. Go left a short distance, then bear right to the summit, reached at 0.9 mile. If you go straight at the junction, the well-defined trail quickly disintegrates to a climber's trail under the crags that mark the summit. Go out the same way you came in for 1.8-mile round-trip.

---

18 JOYCE KILMER MEMORIAL FOREST–
POPLAR COVE LOOP

Overview

The Joyce Kilmer Memorial Forest is a 3,800-acre tract now combined with the Slickrock Wilderness to form a wild and wildly popular area in the extreme southwestern mountains of North Carolina not far from the Tennessee state line.

An easy figure-eight circuit comprises two trails through the mightily impressive forest of poplar, hemlock, oak, and beech, substantial portions of which are virgin. In all likelihood, there are trees here that were growing when Columbus landed in the New World. And many were flourishing before Europeans disturbed the comings and goings of the Cherokee Indians. Age estimates for the biggest of the trees range from 300 to 500 years. Many trees top 100 feet and are up to 20 feet around at the base.

The hike described here includes a memorial to poet Joyce Kilmer, author of the poem "Trees." The forest is massive, inspiring, and crowded on summer and fall weekends. Plan accordingly if you wish to use the potential silence of the tall trees for quiet contemplation.

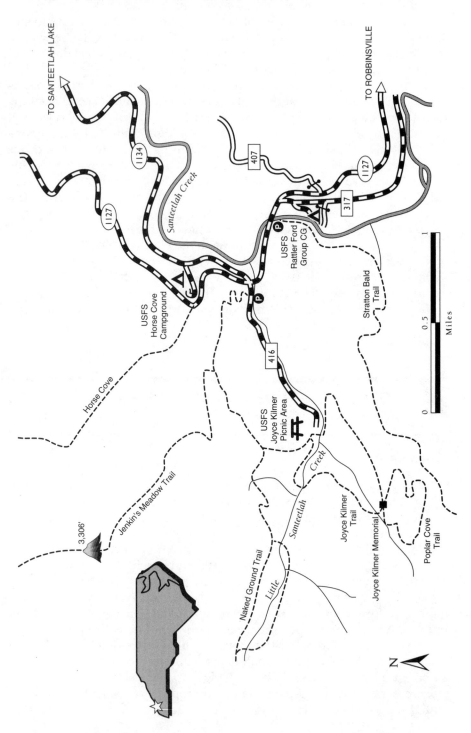

No other trail better typifies the towering virgin hardwood forest of the North Carolina mountains than the Joyce Kilmer Trail.

General description: A National Recreation Trail exploring one of the most stunning parcels of virgin hardwood forest left in the Southern Appalachians.
General location: Near Robbinsville.
Length: 1 mile for the Kilmer Memorial Trail; 2 miles for the Poplar Cove Loop.
Degree of difficulty: Easy.
Maps: USGS Santeetlah Creek quad. The preferred hiking map for this area is the Joyce Kilmer-Slickrock and Citico Creek Wilderness Map, available from the Forest Service.

Elevation gain and loss: 880 feet.

Trailhead elevation: 2,200 feet.

High point: 2,640 feet.

Water availability: Water is available in season at the trailhead Joyce Kilmer Picnic area.

For more information: Cheoah Ranger District, Nantahala National Forest. Or contact Supervisor's Office, National Forests in North Carolina, Asheville. See Appendix C.

Finding the trailhead: The trailhead is about 17 miles from Robbinsville. Leave Robbinsville on U.S. Highway 129. After about 2 mile, go left on SR 1116. The junction is well-marked with a sign directing visitors to the Joyce Kilmer area. In about 3 miles turn left from SR 1116 onto SR 1127. At about 12 miles turn left onto the access road (Forest Road 416), also well-marked. The trail starts behind the visitor shelter just off the parking area.

The hike: The **Joyce Kilmer Trail** leaves the parking area and climbs gradually along Little Santeetlah Creek. It crosses the stream and swings back to join the Poplar Cove Trail at a plaque memorializing poet and journalist Joyce Kilmer, who died during World War I combat in France and was buried there in 1918. Returning on the trail from here creates a 1-mile loop hike.

Take a right to enter the upper loop on the **Poplar Cove Trail**, which ventures through hardwood forest and plentiful yellow poplars, some truly huge. The deep soils of the fertile valley are well watered by the ridges above. The result is an internationally known grove of giant trees. The trail reaches its high point, then gradually descends back to the Kilmer Memorial. Take a right and the lower loop back to the parking lot to complete a 2-mile circuit.

19   LINVILLE FALLS RECREATION AREA

Overview

The Linville Falls Recreation Area is one of those periodic bulges in the narrow Blue Ridge Parkway. This National Park Service property runs to and includes the head of Linville Gorge, a canyon that below Linville Falls is a federal wilderness area managed by the Forest Service. The Parkway trails are relatively easy and give an insightful introduction to this wild chasm; trails leading hikers from the visitor center offer serious scenery.

The remoteness of the gorge kept loggers out of the area until John D. Rockefeller purchased the land and donated it to the National Park Service. Like the gorge itself, which has never been logged, the area explored by the falls trails contain an inspiring forest. Towering hemlocks give way to

Linville Falls from Erwins View. Hikers can descend to the base of the falls — but can't swim.

gnarled trees that cling to rocky viewpoints. Rhododendron blooms profusely here in June. From many viewpoints hikers can see Linville Falls, where the Linville River gushes 100 foaming feet into the gorge. One trail reaches the base of the falls, but no rock climbing or swimming is permitted anywhere in the area.

General description: A series of hikes exploring virgin forest and rugged scenery near Linville Falls.

General location: Blue Ridge Parkway near Linville Falls.

Length: 1 to 2 miles round-trip.

Degree of difficulty: Easy for Duggers Creek Trail and Upper Falls View; moderate for Erwins View; moderately strenuous for Chimney View; and strenuous for Plunge Basin Overlook and Linville Gorge Trail.

Maps: USGS Linville Falls quad. An adequate trail map/brochure is available from the addresses below or from the trailhead visitor center.

Elevation gain and loss: About 320 feet for both the descent below the falls and the hike to Erwins View.

Trailhead elevations: 3,200 feet at the Linville Falls visitor center; 3,280 at the trailhead on SR 1238.

High point: About 3,360 at Erwins View.

Low point: About 3,040 on the Linville River below the falls.

Water availability: From May to October, a trailhead visitor center, nearby campground, and picnic area dispense water for hikers. At other times, the town of Linville Falls community is only 1.5 miles away on U.S. Highway 221.

For more information: The Blue Ridge Parkway. Call for recorded information about weather road closures, mailing requests, etc. Or contact Blue Ridge Parkway's Gillespie Gap District. See Appendix C.

Finding the trailhead: The trailhead spur road leaves the Blue Ridge Parkway between mileposts 316 and 317, about 1 mile north of the US 221/ Blue Ridge Parkway junction at the town of Linville Falls. Leave the Parkway on the spur road heading southeast. The trail and visitor center parking is 1.4 miles from the Parkway.

To reach the Forest Service trailhead go south on the Parkway 1 mile from the Linville Falls spur road and take the US 221 exit. Go left to the community of Linville Falls and turn left on North Carolina Highway 183. In 0.7 mile from the US 221/NC 183 junction in Linville Falls, turn right on Wisemans View Road, SR 1238, where prominent signs direct hikers to the Linville Gorge. The trailhead is the first parking area on the left, and the national forest contact station is a short distance beyond on the right.

The hikes: Trails to the falls leave from both sides of the small visitor center and restroom complex. On the east side of the river, three trails make a nice hike. The **Duggers Creek Trail** starts with a left from the Plunge Basin Overlook Trail and ends north toward the Parkway near the entrance to the parking lot. Between that trailhead and the visitor center,

19 LINVILLE FALLS / BLUE RIDGE PARKWAY

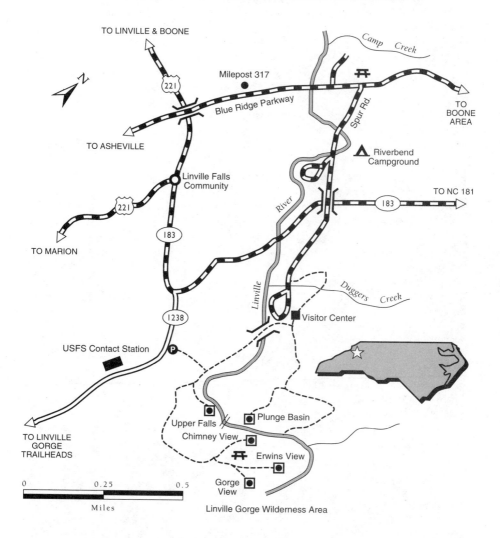

TO LINVILLE & BOONE

Camp Creek

Milepost 317

221

Blue Ridge Parkway

Spur Rd.

TO BOONE AREA

TO ASHEVILLE

Riverbend Campground

Linville Falls Community

River

TO NC 181

221

183

183

TO MARION

Linville

Duggers Creek

Visitor Center

1238

USFS Contact Station

P

TO LINVILLE GORGE TRAILHEADS

Upper Falls

Plunge Basin

Chimney View

Erwins View

Gorge View

Linville Gorge Wilderness Area

| 0 | 0.25 | 0.5 |

Miles

(about 0.3 mile) the path wanders along beautiful Duggers Creek past plaques with inspiring sayings.

From the visitor center, another trail descends to the plunge basin of Linville Falls, and a spur branches to the river below the falls. Leaving the visitor center, the trail forks at 0.2 mile. The leftward **Linville Gorge Trail** goes down 0.7 mile on steps through rocky cliffs to the thundering base of the falls and the large pool below craggy walls that mark the start of Linville Gorge. This is a wonderful place to enjoy a lingering lunch. To the right, the **Plunge Basin Overlook Trail** reaches a great view of the plunging water at 0.5 mile.

A bridge lets hikers explore both sides of the river at Linville Falls.

Across the river, various other viewpoints make nice hikes. Crossing the Linville River on a footbridge from the visitor center, the level, road-width **Linville Falls Trail** leads through a scenic forest paralleling the river. A junction on the right at 0.4 mile is a Forest Service spur trail from SR 1238, a short distance away. This route is a good choice for hikers heading to Linville Gorge trailheads, located all along SR 1238; a national forest information station is just down the road toward the gorge.

A side trail leads left to Upper Falls View, 0.5 mile from the visitor center with very little elevation change. Beyond it, the trail passes through impressive towering trees. This virgin hemlock forest is highlighted by white pine, oak, and birch trees. Here the trail starts a gradual rise to scrubbier vegetation associated with drier soils along the crags overlooking the gorge.

At 0.6 mile from the visitor center, another junction splits the trail at a rudimentary picnic/rain shelter. To the left, the trail descends steep steps and reaches Chimney View at 0.7 mile, where hikers get an oft-photographed view of the entire falls. Not far away is Gorge View Overlook, down the gorge.

Back at the shelter, hikers head away from the visitor center as the trail climbs through dry, piney forest. The gorge appears again on the right, and on the left at about 1 mile is Erwins View, where the falls and the gorge are both in sight.

Retrace your steps from here for a 2-mile round-trip hike.

20 *LINVILLE GORGE WILDERNESS*

Overview

An 11,000-acre tract of designated wilderness, Linville Gorge lies between Jonas Ridge on the east and Linville Mountain on the west. Peaks on the rim of the gorge tower over Morganton and Lake James. The wild canyon, up to 2,000 feet deep in places, was first protected as a primitive area by the Forest Service in 1951. It became an "instant wilderness" area with the passage of the 1964 Wilderness Act. A subsequent wilderness bill, in 1984, expanded the area.

The protection and expansion is appropriate, since this cleft is so rugged that no logging has ever taken place here. Towering virgin forest can be found in the gorge's isolated coves, and rugged, wild, tangles of primeval density in places where few people venture. For these reasons, Linville Gorge is the most popular of North Carolina's wilderness areas, and a limited number of permits are available for weekend camping between May 31 and October 31. Campers can only remain in the area for three days and two nights.

Ridgetop snow accentuates the cliffs and crags of the Linville Gorge.

It should come as no surprise that the shape of the gorge funnels traffic into a narrow area, concentrating trail use. Those who want solitude should pursue a rugged off-trail adventure, or go in late fall, winter, and spring—also the best times for cross-country hikers because the gorge contains timber rattlesnakes and copperheads.

If you must visit during peak season, go between Sunday and Thursday. Trail descriptions that follow include the Forest Service's assessment of how heavily each trail is used. Suffice it to say, the roughest, most strenuous, and primitive paths will be the best bet for seeing the fewest people. Several of these trails access trackless areas where the terrain invites bushwhacking. Consult the Linville Gorge Wilderness map to locate those places for yourself. Some are obvious and just off popular trails, which makes it relatively easy to find a secluded camp or lunch site. Others are large tracts just waiting for lightly packed, serious explorers.

Whether or not you leave existing trails, be prepared for primitive conditions. Except at trailheads, trails are unmarked, roughly maintained, and, in places, difficult to follow. Every year hikers get lost. Other precautions include practicing no-trace camping and wearing bright clothing during hunting season, late October to early January.

The gorge was named for William Linville, an explorer who along with his son John, was killed there by Indians in 1766.

General description: Hikes into a wilderness chasm, varying from a trip to the bottom of the gorge to many circuit hikes (requiring one or two vehicles).

General location: Near Linville Falls.

Length: 1.4-mile round-trip for the Pine Gap Trail; about 3 miles for a descent of Bynum Bluff and return on Pine Gap; a 9-mile circuit at the southern end of the gorge using the Pinch In, Conley Cove, and Rock Jock trails.

Degree of difficulty: Strenuous, with the exception of a few heavily used trails, since hikers plunge in and out of the gorge. Many trails are unmarked, except at trailheads, and the more primitive paths are notoriously hard to follow.

Maps: USGS Linville Falls and Ashford quads; the Forest Service Linville Gorge Wilderness map.

Elevation gain and loss: About 920 feet for the Pine Gap, Bynum Bluff hikes; 4,200 feet for the southern Linville Gorge circuit. The elevation change along the river on the Linville Gorge Trail, though rugged, is gradual, changing 2,000 feet during the trail's 11.5 miles.

Trailhead elevations: 3,300 feet for the Pine Gap Trail; 3,520 feet for the Bynum Bluff Trail; 3,785 feet for the Cabin Trail; 3,800 feet for the Babel Tower Trail; 3,500 feet for the Sandy Flats Trail; 2,980 feet for the Conley Cove Trail; and 3,220 feet for the Pinch In Trail.

Low point: 1,320 feet at the southernmost boundary of the wilderness.

High point: 4,020 feet atop Hawksbill Mountain.

Water availability: No water is available at the trailheads; the nearest commercial outlets are in the town of Linville Falls. Bring water, and boil all water taken from trailside water sources and the Linville River.

For more information: Weekend camping permits (required May 1 through October 31) and the Linville Gorge Wilderness from The Linville Gorge Information Cabin, open April through October, 9 a.m.-5 p.m., on the Kistler Memorial Highway, SR 1238, 0.5 mile from North Carolina Highway 183 near the town of Linville Falls. Grandfather Ranger District, Pisgah National Forest,. Or contact Supervisor's Office, National Forests in North Carolina, Asheville. See Appendix C.

Finding the trailheads: The easiest access to Linville Gorge is from the town of Linville Falls, located at the junction of the Blue Ridge Parkway and U.S. Highway 221 west of Marion. From US 221 in Linville Falls take NC 183, and shortly turn right onto SR 1238.

The trails that descend from SR 1238 into the gorge from the west are listed here according to their distance south of the NC 183 junction: Pine Gap, 0.9 mile; Bynum Bluff, 1.5 miles; Cabin Trail, 1.9 miles; Babel Tower Trail, 2.7 miles; Sandy Flats Trail, 3.7 miles; Conley Cove Trail, 5.3 miles; Pinch In Trail, 8.2 miles. On the east side of the gorge, the Devil's Hole Trail is near the Hawksbill Mountain Trail (see Hike 17); and the Shortoff Mountain Trail and Cambric Branch Trail start at the same parking area as the Tablerock Trail.

Unless you just hike to the river and back, which some people do to swim, fish, picnic, or camp, you'll need to have cars at two trailheads to avoid a walk along SR 1238. A walk along this dusty gravel road isn't the

20 LINVILLE GORGE WILDERNESS

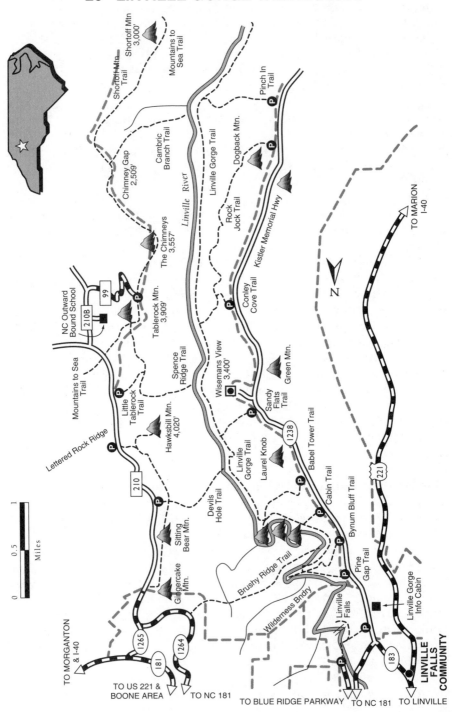

Shortoff Mtn 3,000'

Shortoff Mtn. Trail

Mountains to Sea Trail

Pinch In Trail

Cambric Branch Trail

Chimney Gap 2,509'

Linville Gorge Trail

Dogback Mtn.

Linville River

Rock Jock Trail

The Chimneys 3,557'

Kistler Memorial Hwy

99

Conley Cove Trail

NC Outward Bound School

210B

Tablerock Mtn. 3,909'

Spence Ridge Trail

Wisemans View 3,400'

Green Mtn.

N

TO MARION I-40

Mountains to Sea Trail

Little Tablerock Trail

Sandy Flats Trail

Hawksbill Mtn. 4,020'

1238

Babel Tower Trail

Lettered Rock Ridge

210

Linville Gorge Trail

Laurel Knob

Cabin Trail

221

Devils Hole Trail

Bynum Bluff Trail

Sitting Bear Mtn.

Pine Gap Trail

Gidgercake Mtn.

Brushy Ridge Trail

Wilderness Bndry

Linville Falls

Linville Gorge Info Cabin

1265

1264

LINVILLE FALLS COMMUNITY

TO MORGANTON & I-40

181

183

TO US 221 & BOONE AREA

TO NC 181

TO BLUE RIDGE PARKWAY

TO NC 181

TO LINVILLE

0   0.5   1
Miles

Wiseman's View overlooks the Linville Gorge.

best way to end a memorable wilderness experience. The trail description below suggests a few routes to minimize that inconvenience.

The hikes: Most hikers intent on a longer jaunt into Linville Gorge enter and exit two different western side trails and follow the river on the Linville Gorge Trail between them. The easiest of these trails into and out of the gorge is the 0.7-mile **Pine Gap Trail**. This trail drops on a rare gradual grade as it descends to the Bynum Bluff Trail on the right.

From its trailhead on SR 1238, the 1-mile **Bynum Bluff Trail** starts out gradually as it reaches the point of a long promontory, then plummets down a sharp ridge to the Pine Gap Trail. Just beyond this junction, the Linville Gorge Trail goes right downriver, and a short side trail descends left, then rises to a crag with spectacular views of a sharp bend in the river. This is an easy route for a 2-mile plus day hike. Leaving vehicles at both trailheads (only 0.5 mile apart), descend the Bynum Bluff Trail, and turn right for an out-and-back side trip on the Linville Gorge Trail. Check out the view near the junction of the three trails, then make the easy climb out of the gorge on the Pine Gap Trail. If you only have one car, this hike involves a brief 0.6 mile walk on the road.

The **Linville Gorge Trail** descends along the west side of the river for almost 11.5 miles. The trail goes south around a sharp bend in the river on sidehill terrain, close under the Kistler Memorial Highway. At just over 1 mile, the Linville Gorge Trail meets the **Cabin Trail**, a steep, strenuous, primitive trail that climbs to SR 1238 in just under 1 mile. On the left at the junction, a 3,090-foot promontory with trail juts into the river. Continuing along the river another 0.8 mile, the trail switchbacks down, then slabs to a junction with the Babel Tower Trail at 2 miles. A side trail goes left to another summit, this one 3,035 feet, encircled by an abrupt bend in the river. The popular Babel Tower Trail climbs a scenic ridge 1.2 miles to its trailhead on SR 1238.

From the junction, the Linville Gorge Trail switchbacks off a gap steeply down to the river. On the way to a junction with the obscure **Devils Hole Trail**, on the left at 3.4 miles, there are great views of the gorge as it rises east nearly 2,000 feet to Hawksbill Mountain. The Devil's Hole Trail climbs 1.5 miles to Forest Road 210. At 3.9 miles on the Gorge Trail, the terrain flattens and there are plentiful campsites and a spring near the very primitive Sandy Flats Trail. This side trail goes steeply right about 1 mile to SR 1238, not far from Wiseman's View, a large promontory on the rim of the canyon, provides the best auto-accessible perspective of the gorge.

The trail continues under Wisemans View and intersects the **Spence Ridge Trail** at 4.5 miles. Spence Ridge is the most popular trail into the gorge from the east side. It leaves the Linville Gorge Trail, fords the river, and climbs relatively gradually in 1.7 miles to FR 210.

Lacking the convolutions at the head of the gorge, the river flows directly down, the Linville Gorge Trail with it, to a junction on the right with the **Conley Cove Trail** at about 5.5 miles. This is a heavily used route, due largely to its lesser slope. From the junction, the Cove Trail rises on a graded tread to a spring, a junction on the left with the primitive, canyon rim-running **Rock Jock Trail** at about 1 mile. It finally meets SR 1238 at 1.3 miles.

The Gorge Trail passes this junction and runs for its greatest uninterrupted length along the river, about 3.5 miles. There are plentiful places to swim and nice views across the river at popular rock climbing areas. The bulk of this section of trail flattens out. (Along the way, on the opposite side of the Gorge, the **Cambric Branch Trail** descends from the Shortoff Mountain Trail to a dead end at the river)

At just over 9 miles, the junction on the right is **Pinch In Trail**, a ruggedly steep, view-packed 1.4 mile route to SR 1238. Below this trail junction, the Linville Gorge Trail gradually runs the next 2.4 miles beside the river, then fords it, to terminate at private property.

An out-and-back hike on this portion of the lesser-used lower Gorge Trail is nice, and a southern gorge circuit exists for the experienced hiker/ backpacker. Parking at the Pinch In Trail, descend into the gorge and hike up the canyon, exiting at the Conley Cove Trail. Go left on the Rock Jock Trail. When it exits onto SR 1238, it's about 0.5 mile downhill south to the Pinch In trailhead. This is a rugged 9-mile hike in either direction, exploring an area that the Forest Service says is among the least used in the gorge.

21 *LOST COVE WILDERNESS STUDY AREA*

Overview

The 5,710-acre Lost Cove and 7,140-acre Harper Creek wilderness study areas are part of a larger portion of Pisgah National Forest often identified as the Wilson Creek drainage. Lying below Grandfather Mountain, between U.S. Highway 321 to the north, North Carolina Highway 181 to the south, and North Carolina Highway 90 to the east, this vast area is perhaps North Carolina's largest contiguous area of unpaved roads. Just the drive to the trailhead is one of the best mountain experiences a visitor can have in North Carolina.

This huge watershed—the prominent gulf south of Blowing Rock and east of the Blue Ridge Parkway near Grandfather Mountain—is cut by dozens of streams, many with spectacular waterfalls. The region seems an endless ripple of ridges, laced with miles of dirt roads. There are tiny settlements, such as Gragg and Edgemont, where small cabins cluster in the woods beside rushing rivers. Early in the twentieth century, Lost Cove and Harper Creek formed the heart of a tract including Grandfather Mountain and Linville Gorge that was seriously proposed as a major Southern Appalachian national park. The Great Smokies were chosen instead.

To appreciate the lifestyle and history of this isolated region, visit Coffey's General Store in Edgemont. You'll find rudimentary last-minute supplies or post-hike refreshments and an eccentric collection of antiques and knickknacks. A sign says this is the store of three wonders: "You wonder if we have it, we wonder where it is, and everybody wonders how we find it." The store has been in operation for decades, since Edgemont and nearby Mortimer were bustling early century logging communities of thousands. (Mortimer is the site of a CCC-constructed national forest recreation/camping area: a good base of operations for hikers). For more on the area, take the time to talk to proprietor Bonnie Coffey Rash, former wife of the late Archie Coffey, the colorful, longtime operator of the store.

Photographs in Coffey's Store show the massive timber-harvesting operations and forest fires in 1916 and 1925. The 1916 fire, and a flood that followed, gave impetus to the effort to make these lands part of Pisgah National Forest. Another major flood occurred in 1940, and periodic deluges are not uncommon (a fact that hikers should not forget, since trails here are largely in stream drainages). During a flood in January 1995, three Boy Scouts were swept to their deaths from a cable bridge across the stream in front of the store.

Though logged, forests have come back, and two large tracts, in Lost Cove and Harper Creek, have been proposed as wilderness areas. The Forest Service and many Wilson Creek area residents support these proposals. But North Carolina's Senator Jesse Helms has led opposition to legislation that would designate the areas wilderness.

Both tracts have ample streams, waterfalls, and plentiful wildlife, which make hunting and fly fishing (artificial lures) popular here. And the surrounding area, also covered in the Forest Service's Wilson Creek Area Trail Map, is full of little-used trails to wild destinations. Other recommended routes in the area include the 4.3-mile **Schoolhouse Ridge Trail** loop at Mortimer Recreation Area (with a nice waterfall just 0.2 mile from the campground and views of Grandfather Mountain from the ridge), and the **Wilson Creek Trail**, a 6-mile hike between Forest Roads 192 and 45 (the latter trailhead is just north of Edgemont on NC 90) that follows one of the best trout streams in the state.

Trailheads in the area can be hard to find. Roadside camping isn't advised, nor is leaving valuables in your unattended vehicle. Also realize that at the relatively low elevations of the watershed, summer days can reach into the high 80s; that's one reason the waterfalls are such popular spots to cool off. Not far south of Mortimer is Brown Mountain Beach, the ultimate mountain summer scene. The sandy strip of Wilson Creek attracts hundreds on hot summer weekends.

In general, trails in this area have plenty of stream crossings, most accomplished with rock hopping. In times of high water, use extreme caution. Hikers here might consider carrying a pair of sport sandals or aqua shoes for water crossings.

The Lost Cove and Harper Creek wilderness proposals lie among the stream-laced lower ridges east of the Blue Ridge Parkway — seen here from the Beacon Heights Trail. *Photo by Hugh Morton.*

General description: Several trails in an area proposed for wilderness designation, including short walks to clifftop views, waterfalls, and wilderness circuit hikes that are among the best in North Carolina.

General location: Wilson Creek watershed, Pisgah National Forest.

Length: Out-and-back walks of 1.4 miles on Darkside Cliffs Trail; 1.5 miles for the Little Lost Cove Cliffs Trail; 1.6 miles for the Hunt Fish Falls Trail; 2.4 miles to pools on the Lost Cove Trail; 3 miles for the Big Lost Cove Cliffs Trail. Circuit trails of 4.7 and 7.5 miles on the Lost Cove Trail.

Degree of difficulty: Easy to moderate for Darkside Cliffs Trail, Big and Little Lost Cove Cliffs trails, and a day hike to Gragg Prong pools on the Lost Cove Trail. Moderate for Hunt Fish Falls Trail; strenuous for two Lost Cove loop hikes.

Maps: USGS Grandfather Mountain quad; the Forest Service Wilson Creek Area Trail Map.

Elevation gains and losses: 300 feet for Darkside Cliffs Trail; 800 feet for Little Lost Cove Cliffs Trail; 1,200 feet for Hunt Fish Falls Trail; 320 feet for the Lost Cove pools hike; 1,280 feet for Big Lost Cove Cliffs; 1,600 and 2,560 feet respectively for the short and long Lost Cove circuit hikes.

Trailhead elevations: Big Lost Cove Cliffs Trail, 3,480 feet; Little Lost Cove Cliffs, 3,000 feet for both trailheads; Darkside Cliffs Trail, 2,750 feet; Hunt Fish Falls Trail, 2,440 feet; Lost Cove Trail, 2,120 feet at Forest Road 981.

Low points: Big Lost Cove Cliffs Trail, 3,400 feet; Darkside Cliffs Trail, 2,600 feet; Hunt Fish Falls Trail, 1,840 feet; Lost Cove Trail, 1,720 feet at Lost Cove Creek; Timber Ridge Trail, 2,960 feet at Lost Cove Creek near junction with Lost Cove Trail.

High points: Big Lost Cove Cliffs Trail, 3,760 feet; Little Lost Cove Cliffs, 3,400 feet; Lost Cove Trail, 2,920 feet on Bee Mountain; Timber Ridge Trail, 2,600 feet atop Timber Ridge near junction with Lost Cove Trail.

Water availability: Although water is plentiful along these trails, bring water from outside the area to avoid having to boil drinking water.

For more information: Grandfather Ranger District, Pisgah National Forest. Or contact Supervisor's Office, National Forests in North Carolina, Asheville. See Appendix C.

Finding the trailheads: See Hike 16. Many trailheads in the Lost Cove area are the same as those in the adjacent Harper Creek area.

The hikes: Three hikes to the cliffs that clog the head of the Lost Cove valley make wonderful introductions to the area. Each is easy to moderate in difficulty and offers wonderful views that can orient you to the terrain. Also, each is short (less than 1.5 miles), so you have time to motor into and out of the region leisurely, which is a plus in so scenic and obscure an area.

The **Big Lost Cove Cliffs Trail** is a good backpack trip for beginners. It's a short out-and-back walk to the top of the cliffs above Lost Cove, a high, wild area under the Blue Ridge Parkway. Vistas extend in many directions, but the predominant landmark is Grandfather Mountain. This trail leads to the northernmost of the area's clifftop vantage points;

21 LOST COVE – PISGAH NF

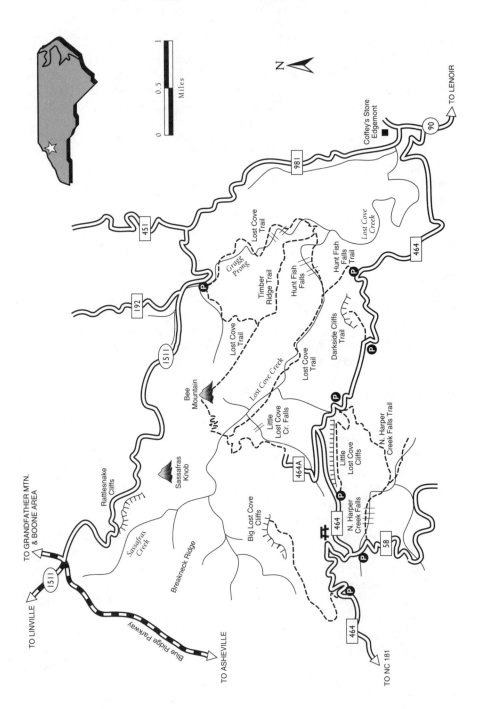

The falls of Little Lost Cove Creek — a trailless diversion from the Lost Cove Trail.

it is also the one located deepest in the would-be wilderness. From it, you look directly into the trailless amphitheater bordered by the crest of the Blue Ridge and the Parkway. The cliffs of Breakneck Ridge drop into the center of the vista.

The trail departs the north side of Forest Road 464 at an unsigned trailhead. A nice grassy parking area is just across the road, with open views south across a clearcut (which not far west on FR 464 permits a view of Little Lost Cove Cliffs). The unblazed, road-width trail surmounts some "tank trap" earthworks that deter vehicles and enters the woods framed by hemlocks. It immediately bears left, ascends steeply for a very short distance, then flattens to a gradual grade. It crests the broad top of Lost Cove Ridge at about 3,700 feet and follows it. For about 0.3 mile the trail drops steeply from 3,600 feet to the 3,400-foot elevation, then runs gradually again to the viewpoints, at about 1.5 miles. This is an easy to moderate, 3-mile day hike that could also be a novice backpacking trip.

Not very far east down FR 464, the **Little Lost Cove Cliffs Trail** provides a similar hike, but between two trailheads. This view of Lost Cove is on the south side of FR 464, which places it in the Harper Creek WSA. (The old CCC-built road bisects the two WSAs.)

For hikers in only one vehicle, both trailheads are at virtually the same elevation, so hiking the 1.5 miles in either direction is equally appealing. From the easternmost trailhead (beside the start of the North Harper Creek Falls Trail), the road-width path climbs through an old orchard, reaches

Lunching hikers gaze up at Grandfather Mountain from Darkside Cliffs, and look down into Lost Cove.

side trails north to various views of Grandfather Mountain and Lost Cove, then climbs the undulating ridge to a 3,400-foot peak with outstanding, nearly 360-degree views.

Not far down FR 464, the **Darkside Cliffs Trail** provides a one-third-length version of the Big Lost Cove Cliffs Trail. The 0.5-mile path leaves the north side of the road from a grassy parking area on the south side. It descends to a gap, then emerges dramatically onto the top of Darkside Cliffs. The view looks down the entire length of Lost Cove, and almost straight down on Hunt Fish Falls, the next trail into Lost Cove along FR 464.

The **Hunt Fish Falls Trail** begins at a formalized, rail-bordered parking area similar to those found at Linville Gorge. In 0.8 mile, the trail drops, steeply at times, from 2,400 feet to about 1,800 feet at Lost Cove Creek. This trail is often busy because it's short, only moderately strenuous, and reaches one of the area's best-known waterfalls. Hunt Fish Falls was no doubt named for what may be the two primary activities pursued in the area: It's not unusual to see people fishing above the falls or in the huge pool below. Pools downstream are favorite spots to sun and swim in warmer weather, popular on weekends.

Hikers can start a loop of the Lost Cove area from Hunt Fish Falls, but the best access for enjoying the entire 7.5-mile loop or a 4.7-mile circuit hike is from the trailhead on Forest Road 981 north of Edgemont. From that trailhead, start the lengthiest loop of the **Lost Cove Trail** by taking the trail to the right and begin a 1.1-mile climb to Timber Ridge. This is a lush, scenic walk, particularly near the top where the trail skirts the head of a high, open drainage. Emerging on Timber Ridge, the **Timber Ridge Trail** descends left to the Lost Cove Creek near Gragg Prong. Go right on the Lost Cove Trail as it artfully and almost effortlessly glides among the peaks of Timber Ridge with outstanding views of Grandfather Mountain. From Bee Mountain, at the end of Timber Ridge and about 2.1 miles from the start, the trail plummets to Lost Cove Creek.

Reaching the creek at just under 3 miles, the trail crosses a log bridge to the southwest side. The Lost Cove Trail goes left here. To the right, the bank rises to a Forest Service road that is closed to traffic and is itself an easy access to this area (it veers sharply off FR 464 between the two trailheads of the Little Lost Cove Cliffs Trail, 1.6 miles east of the FR 58/FR 464 junction).

It is here that serious hikers have their best options for trailless exploring. Upstream from the Lost Cove Trail lies a third of the area's acreage. Streams split into two main drainages, offering level streamside campsites hemmed in by the towering crags of Big Lost Cove Cliffs and Breakneck Ridge. With two cars, one at the Big Lost Cove Cliffs Trail and the other on FR 464A, hikers could start high, follow gradual terrain away from the Big Lost Cove Cliffs Trail, and dip down into Lost Cove Creek at many points, eventually coming out on the trail portion of FR 464A.

Continuing down the Lost Cove Creek, the rocky, boulder-strewn stream is consistently wide with nice campsites for almost 2 miles. In bright

A cairn marks a less than obvious trail in the Lost Cove area.

sun, the icy water gurgles between moss-covered banks. This is a prized trout-fishing location, with sandy soil on the banks and an open forest of hemlock, birch, and hardwoods.

At about 3.3 miles, Little Lost Cove Creek goes right. A short diversion here to Little Lost Cove Creek Falls is worthwhile. For the next 1.3 miles, the trail follows the stream with occasional crossings (which can be avoided; the trail eventually passes Hunt Fish Falls on the southwest side of the stream). At about 4.5 miles, the Hunt Fish Falls Trail goes right to FR 464. The Lost Cove Trail continues downstream past pools and falls and crosses Lost Cove Creek. Climbing from the creek, the Timber Ridge Trail goes left at just over 5 miles. The Lost Cove Trail skirts a parcel of private land where Lost Cove Creek meets Gragg Prong, then descends to Gragg Prong. From here to the trailhead, the path crosses the stream several times and passes waterfalls and cascades in mixed evergreen and deciduous forest.

At about 6 miles, you approach Gragg Prong's major waterfall from below, one of the best reasons for hiking the loop in this direction. Though the climb up Gragg Prong is gradual, you've just hiked a long loop; on a hot day consider taking a dip among the cascades and pools at about 6.8 miles. One pool can only be described as a cold-water Jacuzzi. A sharp outer rim is a perfect support as you bob in a straight-walled tub 15 feet wide. Cold water swirls from above, circulating and bubbling out over the lower side. As a day hike, this enticing waterfall is an easy 2.4-mile round trip, and there are nice campsites in the area. The last 1.2 miles make a gradual return to the parking lot at about 7.5 miles.

A shorter hike, in the same direction, involves taking the Lost Cove Trail to a left turn atop Timber Ridge on the Timber Ridge Trail at 1.1 miles. At 2.3 miles leave the Timber Ridge Trail, turning left on the Gragg Prong portion of the Lost Cove Trail and head back to the trailhead. This circuit hike is just under 5 miles.

---

22 MOUNTAINS TO SEA—
The Backway to Beacon Heights

Overview

Beacon Heights is a summit on the Blue Ridge Parkway reached by a popular leg-stretcher trail. It provides a fine perch from which to view Grandfather Mountain, Mount Mitchell, and the Blue Ridge escarpment as it drops dramatically to the Piedmont. Hike 3 describes a popular trail to Beacon Heights, but its appeal to serious hikers is limited. But you can reach Beacon Heights "the back way" on a new and little-used portion of the Mountains To Sea Trail.

Galax, green in summer, crimson in fall and winter, is a common ground cover at upper elevations in North Carolina mountains. *Photo by Hugh Morton.*

More than solitude recommends this route to a spectacular knob. The trail climbs, steeply at times, through scenic cove forests with occasional views of the skyline where you're bound. You may have to share the summit at Beacon Heights, but you won't run into Parkway walkers until the last 0.1 mile. If you choose not to join the Parkway trail, a ledge view near the top resembles the summit view but is more private.

General description: A new, little-traveled segment of the Mountains To Sea Trail to the open summit of Beacon Heights for serious hikers.
General location: East of Blue Ridge Parkway near Linville.
Length: 6.6 miles round-trip.
Degree of difficulty: Strenuous.
Maps: USGS Grandfather quad (best map, although this part of the Mountains To Sea Trail isn't marked on it); Wilson Creek Area Trail Map. The Grandfather Mountain hiking map shows the upper end of the trail.
Elevation gain and loss: 2,720 feet.
Trailhead elevation: 3,000 feet.
High point: 4,360.
Water availability: The trail crosses a few streams, but no designated springs are available. Carry water, or treat what you take from streams. The Grandfather Mountain park entrance, 1 mile away, has water year-round.

For more information: Blue Ridge Parkway. Or contact Grandfather Ranger District, Pisgah National Forest. Or write or call Supervisor's Office, National Forests in North Carolina, Asheville. See Appendix C.

Finding the trailhead: The easiest access is from the Blue Ridge Parkway south of Blowing Rock. From the U.S. Highway 321/ Blue Ridge Parkway junction between Boone and Blowing Rock, go south 13 miles and exit onto U.S. Highway 221. Go left under the Parkway, immediately passing SR 1513 on the right. About 0.4 mile from there, take the next right on SR 1514, the larger dirt road going downhill from US 221. At 0.5 mile on SR 1514 there is a spectacular view of Grandfather Mountain. At about 4.2 miles from US 221, turn right onto Forest Road 192. The road winds past

22 MOUNTAINS TO SEA

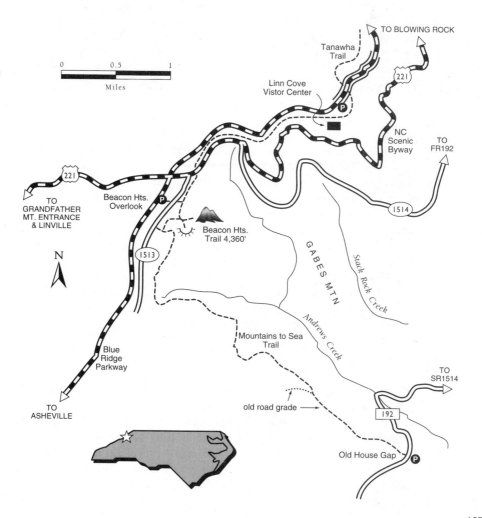

a nice roadside campsite at 0.8 mile, and reaches Old House Gap at 3.5 miles. The Mountains To Sea Trail enters the woods on the right. Its first white dot blazes are not visible from the parking area.

The hike: Leave the secluded, leafy parking area at Old House Gap (where there are roadside campsites) and go northwest on the white-blazed **Mountains to Sea Trail**. You'll cross eroded earth berms designed to deter four-wheel-drive traffic and follow an eroded, then sandy and pleasant old logging grade bordered by mountain laurel, pine, oak, and Catawba rhododendron. Where the path bears left, a level pine grove sits off to the right, suitable for camping.

The path rises gradually at first, then steeply, through close vegetation to a level area marked with various orange boundary blazes. The trail rises again and levels off at more orange blazes: Here, about 0.3 mile from the gap, the more obvious road grade goes left; the Mountains To Sea Trail goes right.

For a short distance the grassy grade is bordered by ferns. Then the path exits the old grade and wanders through tighter vegetation, slabbing northeast around the bulge of the ridge before swinging into the upper drainage of Andrews Creek, a multipronged stream that empties Grandmother Gap. The trail alternates between steeper and more gradual ascents, and between sections of newly benched trail and portions of path that are obviously very old.

The most memorable sections of this trail are when the path leaves the ridge and wanders close to a branch of Andrews Creek, climbing through towering hemlock and rhododendron beside the stream. Then it exits the side stream and slabs the ridge again on the way higher.

At the uppermost end of the drainage, actually quite near Grandmother Gap, the trail slabs into the rhododendron-lined stream, crosses it for the last time, then ascends steeply through an area of fallen hemlocks. The path shifts back to the left side of the drainage and wanders up a wet-weather runoff trough. Here the trail bears right, out of the high end of the drainage, and ascends a few switchbacks.

The path slides around an outcrop at the head of the drainage and bears north and northeast on a steady grade toward Beacon Heights. One major switchback breaks this general direction, but the trail again heads northeast through sparser, drier vegetation (oak and mountain laurel). A meandering, steeper section of vegetation-lined switchbacks marks the ascent of Beacon Heights' steeper southern slope.

The first major ledge offers a private view for picnickers who'd rather not go any farther. Grandmother Mountain and the rippled descent back to Old House Gap are closest, with distant views of the Piedmont. From here, the trail slabs again, going west through an intimate forest of lichen-covered outcrops, galax, oak, pine, and rhododendron. This spongy needle-covered trail hasn't been dug out by volunteers. It bisects two boulders and crests the ridge to intersect an old logging grade about 2 miles from Old House Gap.

To the left, the road-width grade reaches SR 1513 in a few hundred feet. A right on the dirt road takes you to the Beacon Heights Parkway Overlook in 0.1 mile. Hikers bound for the summit should go right on the white-blazed Mountains To Sea Trail. You're still on the grade, but it closes in to a scenic laurel tunnel that, except for one little jog, rises easily to meet the **Beacon Heights Trail**. At the signed junction, the Mountains To Sea Trail descends left with the Beacon Heights Trail, back to SR 1513 and to the Parkway parking area, and north along the flank of Grandfather Mountain. Turn right and follow the Beacon Heights Trail uphill as it meanders to the crest and a bench, about 3.3 miles from Old House Gap. Short side trails go right and left to great views amid galax, tall red spruce, fir, and rhododendron.

23 *MOUNT JEFFERSON STATE PARK*

Overview

Though not a lengthy hike, Mount Jefferson's Rhododendron Trail is noteworthy for its location and elevation. The bulking, rounded summit, at almost 5,000 feet, towers above pastoral farms and lesser ranges in a decidedly untouristed part of North Carolina. The big wilderness and ski resort summits of the Boone area, Grandfather, Beech, and Sugar mountains tower to the south as Virginia's Mount Rogers (5,729 feet) dominates the northern horizon. Scattered below are the working farms of a county known for the state's only cheese factory, noteworthy religious frescoes on the walls of two quaint mountain churches (a pastoral part of the Blue Ridge Parkway) and canoe routes on the New River, a National Wild and Scenic River (New River State Park is nearby).

Rising 1,600 feet above this terrain, dramatic Mount Jefferson boasts a diversity of vegetation that earned it a 1975 designation as a National Natural Landmark. The mountain was renamed Mount Jefferson in 1955, ostensibly in honor of Thomas Jefferson's father, who surveyed the nearby state line and owned land in the area. The new name was preferable to an older one, dating from 1810, with racial overtones that a state park is better off without. It's said the overhanging crags of Mount Jefferson, obvious along the Rhododendron Trail, sheltered runaway slaves traveling to Ohio on the Underground Railroad. A nearby mountain is named Mulatto Mountain.

Like so many others in North Carolina's park system, 541-acre Mount Jefferson State Park was proposed and secured for park status by citizens raising their own funds. The park has few developed facilities, with picnicking and hiking being its primary recreational activities. The summit picnic area, an easy stroll even for the elderly from the upper parking area, is a real treat. Water, restrooms, and picnic tables and grills are located in a beautiful summit forest.

The town of Jefferson nestles in the valley below Mt. Jefferson State Park in this view from Luther Rock. Mt Jefferson rises on the left.

The drive to the park's upper parking area is worth the trip even if you don't hike, with impressive overlooks at 2.2 and 3.2 miles. The first viewpoint scans Boone High Country, a name given by travel promoters; Grandfather Mountain is the dominant summit. The vista at 3.2 miles displays a raised-relief topographical map; to the north, Phoenix Mountain just blocks the view of Mount Rogers. Above the upper parking lot, at 3.6 miles, the trails provide the best views.

General description: A scenic interpretive trail in Mount Jefferson State Park, capping a nearly 5,000-foot peak. The park has a fine motor road with views of many high peaks, including Virginia's highest summit, Mount Rogers.

General location: Rural Ashe County near Jefferson.

Length: 1.5-mile circuit.

Difficulty: Easy to moderate.

Maps: USGS Jefferson quad; a state park map/brochure is available at the park office.

Elevation gain and loss: 400 feet.

Trailhead elevation: 4,500 feet.

High point: 4,683 feet.

Water availability: Water is available from summit picnic area restrooms and water fountains during warm months, and from surrounding communities during winter.

For more information: Mount Jefferson State Park, Jefferson. See Appendix C.

Finding the trailhead: The park is easily reached from U.S. Highway 221, the Robert G. Barr Expressway, a few minutes north of the US 221/North Carolina Highway 163/North Carolina Highway 16 junction at West Jefferson. This area is reached from Boone, or points east, including Winston-Salem, from U.S. Highway 421 in Deep Gap. Head north of the West Jefferson junction on US 221 and turn right at the first junction, on the Mount Jefferson State Park Road, SR 1152. Go straight through a stop sign and begin a winding ascent that enters the park 1.4 miles from US 221, and reaches the summit parking area, and trailhead, at 3.6 miles.

The hike: The 1.5-mile **Rhododendron Trail** leaves the picnic area at the upper parking lot, ascends to the Mount Jefferson summit, then branches right and descends back to the picnic area past spectacular Luther Rock. Leaving the lot, the day-use-only trail ascends through a picnic area on a rocky road grade that bears up and to the right. Spotlessly clean picnic tables and grills beckon from surrounding trees, often "ahiss" with high-elevation breezes. At 0.1 mile, side trails go right 50 feet to restrooms. In another 150 feet, the return of the Rhododendron Trail comes in on the right. (This junction is unmarked. Hikers wanting a more wilderness-like climb to the peak, or just to scenic Luther Rock, might go right here.)

The next part of the path will get your heart rate going. The road climbs, switchbacking left and reaching a trail junction on the right. An

23 JEFFERSON STATE PARK

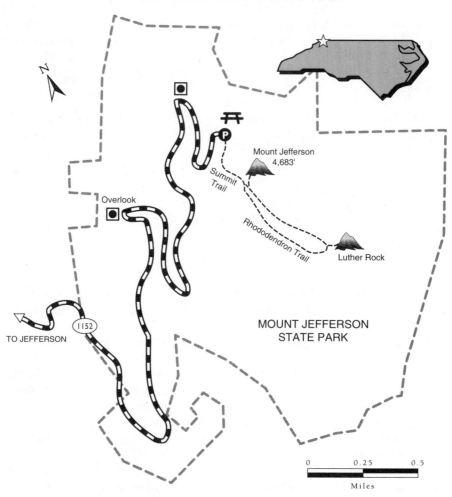

Mount Jefferson
4,683'

Overlook

Summit
Trail

Rhododendron Trail

Luther Rock

1152

TO JEFFERSON

MOUNT JEFFERSON
STATE PARK

0   0.25   0.5

Miles

interpretive sign shows how important dates in human history relate to a tree's annual rings. Here, the Rhododendron Trail goes right. Heading left, the road grade terminates at the base of a North Carolina Forest Service fire tower. The ladder is gone, and the tower may be too, someday. Just to its right, a sign on the uppermost crag says the peak is 4,683 feet above sea level. Behind the tower is a short, informal path to a view, but the summit is essentially tree-covered.

Luckily, there are fine views at Luther Rock. Head back down to where the Rhododendron Trail branches right and immediately note one of those interesting "shelter rock" overhangs below the trail on the left. Imagine what it might have been like 140 years ago to be a slave, ill-clothed and huddled up here. In all but the warmest weather, the experience must have been traumatic. This is easy, undulating ridgetop walking, with some rocky spots. Mount Jefferson has been praised for its unusually diverse tree species, and this section of trail wanders through a rich forest. An interpretive brochure available at the trailhead is keyed to numbered posts that line the trail. Northern red oak, sugar and mountain maples, and yellow birch are all found along this section of trail. You'll also see the rotting remains of huge American chestnuts that used to dominate this mountaintop before the Chestnut blight in 1910.

Take the left to Luther Rock and in a short distance emerge to open views, mostly to the north and east. To the left, the summit of Mount Jefferson is obvious. Just below is the town of Jefferson. Its classic county courthouse, built in the early 1900s, is discernible on clear days. Just above and to the right of town, Virginia's highest peaks tower on the horizon. Whitetop is on the left, and Mount Rogers, the Old Dominion's highest at 5,729 feet, is on the right. Farther out on the point, a vista to the right ripples to the edge of the Blue Ridge, over pastoral terrain that includes a sweeping curve of the South Fork of the New River. This outcrop of mica gneiss offers a pleasant place for a picnic.

Backtracking, take a left and descend the Rhododendron Trail. The trails dips steeply onto the sunny side of the mountain, amid mountain ash, white ash, and basswood. The trail levels out and slabs through forest openings that include wildflowers such as white bee balm and jack-in-the-pulpit. There's also an unusual three-level forest here. The forest floor is relatively open, and above towers a nice canopy of mature trees. Between them is a beautiful midstory of Catawba rhododendron. The effect is quite dramatic, especially between June 10 and July 1, a very good time to see many of the mountain's shrubs and flowers in bloom.

After a brief rise, the tunnel-like trail re-emerges on the now descending road from the fire tower, just above the restrooms.

24   MOUNT MITCHELL STATE PARK

Overview

Mount Mitchell State Park was North Carolina's first state park. The 1,700-acre parcel along the crest of the Black Mountains was established in 1915 through the efforts of then Governor Locke Craig (1913-1917) and Theodore Roosevelt, among others. The park was created at a time when massive logging of the state's western mountains threatened to destroy what had been virgin forest. Much of the grandeur of that old-growth forest is gone, but this mountaintop preserve is a wonderful glimpse at a Canada-like forest in the American South.

It is also a microcosm of the environmental problems that are destroying high-elevation forests throughout Eastern America and Europe. Significant research on the peak's environmental problems has been conducted over the last decade by Robert Bruck of North Carolina State University. Earlier research had ascribed much of the defoliation and destruction of the mountain's evergreen zone to an infestation by the balsam woolly aphid, a pest introduced into the United States around 1900. But the aphid only attacks Fraser fir, so the infestation doesn't account for the decline of the red spruce forests on the peaks. Bruck's studies suggested other factors. One of those, of course, is acid rain, highly acidic precipitation that upsets the pH balance of the soil, freeing heavy metals that inhibit the forest's ability to get nutrients.

Bruck discovered another significant factor: ozone. Like the smog trapped in cities, Bruck's measurements suggest that airborne pollution from major upwind utilities and industries lead to startlingly high ozone levels on Southern summits. His research discovered that such pollution, often contained in cloud caps as acidic as vinegar, burns the needles of firs, dramatically inhibiting the growth and survival of evergreens already fighting a severe climate. The result is that stark tree skeletons stand tall and gray in ghostlike groves here. The Balsam Nature Trail is an introduction to this ongoing ecological catastrophe.

The story of the peak's listing as the East's loftiest, and its naming, includes historic controversy. Although Elisha Mitchell, a Connecticut native, is acknowledged as the first to measure the preeminent peak, that distinction was also claimed by Thomas Clingman, a North Carolinian and congressman, senator, and Confederate brigadier general. In 1835 Mitchell

Acid rain interpretive sign, Mt. Mitchell, North Carolina.

was intrigued by the claim of early botanist Andre Michaux that a peak in the Black Mountains was the highest in the United States. Mitchell began measuring summits in the Black Mountains barometrically and arrived at the conclusion that one of the summits, then called Black Dome, was 6,476 feet high. As a result, the mountain was listed in an 1839 atlas as the East's highest peak.

Clingman vaulted into what was apparently already a controversy in 1855 stating that Mitchell had not measured the loftiest peak and that he had; Clingman claimed 6,941 feet for the summit. Perhaps wishing to consolidate his advantage, the elderly Mitchell returned to the mountain in 1857. Stopping his work near the end of June, Mitchell left his party to visit the homes of former guides, including Thomas "Big Tom" Wilson. Five days later, Mitchell's son reached Wilson's cabin to learn his father had never arrived. Wilson remembered an obscure route over the mountain that he'd shown Mitchell years before. Following that route to the base of a 40-foot waterfall, the party found Mitchell, who had apparently stumbled in the fading light and drowned in a large pool.

Needless to say, the public immediately flocked to Mitchell's side in the debate, and a year after his burial in Asheville he was laid to vindicated rest on the mountaintop. Thus, the peak officially became Mount Mitchell in 1858. The summit became, and still is, the site of his grave. It sits below a geometrical stone tower erected in the mid-1960s. Ultimately, Mitchell's claim to the peak is enhanced by the fact that his final measurement of 6,672 feet is only 12 feet shy of the peak's true elevation, remarkable in that much later measurements were even further off; Clingman's measurement was off by almost 300 feet.

If they were still alive, none of the protagonists in this story could complain about their place in history. Mitchell may have the East's highest peak, but Clingman's name adorns Clingmans Dome (6,643 feet), the Great Smokies' highest summit, which he is said to have measured. And Thomas "Big Tom" Wilson has his own summit; Big Tom (6,558 feet) is 1.1 miles north of Mount Mitchell on the Black Mountain Crest Trail.

Mount Mitchell State Park has a variety of public facilities. The ranger office is on the right immediately after the park entrance, and a restaurant (open mid-May to late-October) is next. The park's small, nine-site tent campground (open May through October) is accessible beside the park maintenance area. The summit facilities include a snack bar (open June 1 through Labor Day, and weekends through October) and restrooms beside the parking lot, and a visitor center/nature museum on the wide trail that leads to a panoramic view from the summit tower.

Backpackers must register their vehicles on trailhead forms before camping.

General description: The Balsam Nature Trail gives a startling introduction to acid rain deforestation. A summit circuit hike is also available, as is an out-and-back hike on the Black Mountain Crest Trail to Mount Craig.

General location: Mount Mitchell State Park, on the Blue Ridge Parkway.

Lengths: 0.8 mile for the Balsam Nature Trail; a 6.6-mile summit circuit; a 5.7-mile climb from the base on the Mount Mitchell Trail for almost 12 miles round-trip.

Degree of difficulty: Easy for the Balsam Nature Trail; strenuous for the circuit hike; extremely strenuous for the Mount Mitchell Trail.

Maps: USGS Mount Mitchell quad. A rudimentary state park map is available, but the best map, especially for a hike to Mount Craig, is the Forest Service South Toe River Trail map.

Elevation gain and loss: Negligible for the nature trail; about 7,200 feet for the Mount Mitchell Trail.

Trailhead elevation: 6,660 feet for the summit parking lot start of the Balsam Trail, Black Mountain Crest Trail, and summit circuit hike; about 3,100 feet for the start of the Mount Mitchell Trail at Black Mountain Campground.

High point: 6,684 feet at the summit tower.

Water availability: Visitor facilities atop Mount Mitchell provide water from May to October.

For more information: Mount Mitchell State Park, Burnsville. Also, the Toecane Ranger District, Pisgah National Forest. Or contact Supervisor's Office, National Forests in North Carolina, Asheville. See Appendix C.

Finding the trailhead: The Mount Mitchell summit trailhead is reached via the Blue Ridge Parkway. Motorists should follow North Carolina Highway 128, a 5-mile spur road from the Parkway, to the state park, from Parkway milepost 355. That junction is 11 miles south of the North Carolina Highway 80 junction at Buck Creek Gap (west of Marion). It is 30 miles north of the U.S. Highway 74 junction near Asheville.

Turn into the state park and drive to the summit parking area. The trail begins at the parking lot development on the path to the summit tower.

To reach Black Mountain Campground and the Mount Mitchell Trail, leave U.S. Highway 19-E, a major north-south highway west of the Blue Ridge, and turn onto NC 80, about 4.5 miles east of Burnsville. In about 14 miles, turn at the Mount Mitchell Golf Course onto Forest Road 472, the South Toe River Road. The campground is in just over 3 miles. Using NC 80 from the east (easily accessible from Interstate Highway 40 in the Marion/Old Fort area via U.S. Highways 70 or 221), cross the Blue Ridge Parkway, and in 2.2 miles, turn left onto FR 472.

In winter, motor access to the park is problematical. The Blue Ridge Parkway closes during snowfall. Though the road to the summit, including the Parkway, is plowed for park personnel, the road often isn't safe for public use. When the road is plowed and stable weather permits, public access is allowed from the NC 80/Blue Ridge Parkway junction. In winter, call ahead, either to the state park or the Blue Ridge Parkway, before making the drive.

The hikes: The **Balsam Nature Trail** is an 0.8-mile interpretive trail with numbered stations keyed to a brochure produced by the Mitchell Chapter of the National Audubon Society. To reach the trail hike toward the summit tower from the concession stand. Go left when the Old Mitchell Trail branches right and pass the nature museum on the left. Take the next left (a right leads to the summit tower) and follow the Balsam Trail as it gradually wanders through a landscape of evergreen or skeletal trees.

This is the highest, most northern climate in the South. The first station on the trail discusses the pollution-induced dieback of the forest. The guide brochure observes that dying trees have returned this forest to the early stages of succession one might discover after a forest fire or other catastrophe.

Besides Fraser fir and red spruce, mountain ash is the most prevalent deciduous species at this elevation. Among other plants growing here are those prevalent in New England, hobblebush and mountain wood sorrel or oxalis, a clover-like ground covering associated with boreal forests. It blooms here in late May and early June. Rhododendron is another prevalent species, blooming in late June. Yellow birch is found from these North Carolina peaks all the way north to Quebec and Minnesota. About 0.25 mile from the yellow birch found at stop 10 on the trail is a grove of mountain paper birch, similar to the white-barked birches so often associated with New Hampshire and Vermont. The small heart-shaped leaves are the giveaway. If, as some scientists speculate, this grove is actually a separate species of birch, then only about four hundred exist, all within this state park.

Stop 5 on the first leg of the trail is Camp Rock, an east-facing shelter ledge used by explorers as early as 1850. The damp seeps at similar outcrops along the trail are favored growing sites for the purple turtlehead, a snapdragon-like flower that tempts lethargic bumblebees on late summer mornings. Stop 6 is a nice view north along the Black Mountain range. Mount Craig is the dominant, nearer summit.

The Balsam Trail turns back left just past stop 10. Straight ahead, the Mount Mitchell Trail descends Commissary Ridge to Black Mountain Campground. Stop 21 recounts the forest impact of severe winter weather here, noting that the mountain received a record 50 inches of snow in two days in March 1993.

Stop 22 turns to the right. The trail leads to a nearby stream that is likely the highest spring in Eastern America. Its average temperature (when not frozen in winter) is 36 degrees Fahrenheit. About 100 yards beyond the turnoff, the Balsam Trail ends at the summit parking lot.

A circuit hike of the summit permits a 6.6-mile loop around the crest of Mount Mitchell. The only drawback is that most hikers like to start at the bottom, hike to a summit, and return, getting most of the work out of the way early. But from the summit of the East's highest peak, everywhere else you can go is downhill. To return on the most gradual route and savor the views of approaching this magnificent mountain, leave the summit parking area on the tower trail, then veer off on the Balsam Nature Trail. When that bears left, continue straight down Commissary Ridge to the

24 MT. MITCHELL STATE PARK

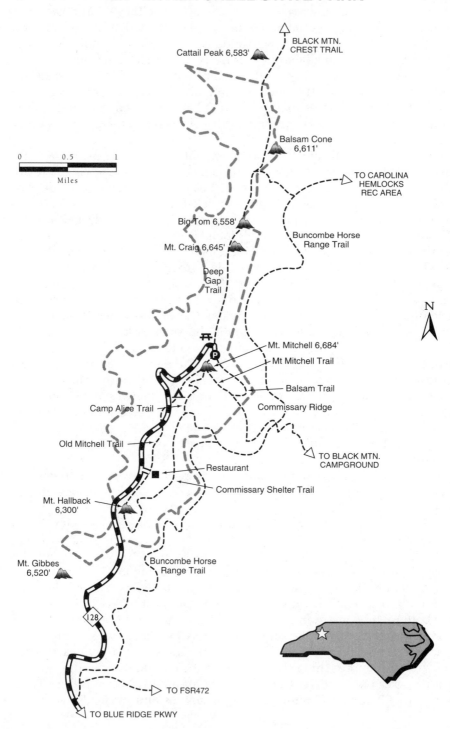

BLACK MTN.
CREST TRAIL

Cattail Peak 6,583'

0   0.5   1
Miles

Balsam Cone
6,611'

TO CAROLINA
HEMLOCKS
REC AREA

Big Tom 6,558'

Buncombe Horse
Range Trail

Mt. Craig 6,645'

Deep
Gap
Trail

N

Mt. Mitchell 6,684'

Mt Mitchell Trail

Balsam Trail

Camp Alice Trail

Commissary Ridge

Old Mitchell Trail

TO BLACK MTN.
CAMPGROUND

Restaurant

Commissary Shelter Trail

Mt. Hallback
6,300'

Mt. Gibbes
6,520'

Buncombe Horse
Range Trail

128

TO FSR472

TO BLUE RIDGE PKWY

Hiking toward Mt. Craig on the Black Mountain Crest Trail in Mt. Mitchell State Park.

Elisha Mitchell interpretive historical marker on trail to Mt. Mitchell observation tower.

Buncombe Horse Range Trail. Go left here, on the white-blazed old logging road, at about 1.6 miles from the summit. In 0.1 mile you'll reach the former site of the Camp Alice shelter on the right. Follow the rocky but level trail north 3 miles to a junction with the Big Tom Gap Trail. The horse trail goes right, to descend, but hikers should go left to make a steep 0.5-mile climb of about 560 feet to the crest of the Black Mountains.

Go left on the orange-blazed **Black Mountain Crest Trail** at about 5 miles and prepare for a spectacular return to Mount Mitchell. The trail dips into a gap, then climbs Big Tom (6,593 feet), and Mount Craig. From here, the return path is a leg of the 2-mile round-trip day hike to Mount Craig from Mount Mitchell (see Hike 4, the Black Mountain Crest Trail). The prospect of climbing to Mount Mitchell is suitably impressive from the open summit of Mount Craig. The size of the subburb development shrinks, and the mountain gains in stature. The final 1 mile back dips into a gap between the peaks, then reaches the summit parking area at the mountaintop picnic area, about 6.6 miles from the start.

If only climbing a mountain makes you feel like you've earned the summit, try the **Mount Mitchell Trail**. Its nearly 3,700 feet of elevation gain is a major trail challenge. The blue-blazed trail begins in the Black Mountain Campground, on the upper loop past the campground host's residence. The trail leaves the campground and quickly skirts a small nature trail loop, then crosses some small streams and climbs through impressive stands of virgin hardwoods and evergreens.

Continue on the Mount Mitchell Trail past its junction at 1.5 miles with the Higgins Bald Trail. The trail crosses Setrock Creek at about 2.5 miles, passes another junction with the Higgins Bald Trail at 2.7 miles, and climbs through more virgin forest, this time of red spruce and Fraser fir. At about 3.9 miles, join the Buncombe Horse Range Trail, and at 4 miles, pass the Camp Alice Shelter site. Continuing on, the trail turns right in about 0.1 mile and ascends a rocky section to a junction with the Balsam Nature Trail. A left on the Mount Mitchell tower trail reaches the peak in about 5.7 miles.

On the way down take a right on the white-blazed **Higgins Bald Trail**. The scenery is worth it, and it's only 0.3 mile farther than the section of the Mount Mitchell Trail you've already hiked. About 0.7 mile from the start of the trail pass through an open area where a chimney marks the site of a Forest Service cabin. The trail continues to descend gradually then slabs across Setrock Creek at a scenic waterfall.

This entire hike is about 12 miles and takes about 8 hours round-trip.

25 ROAN MOUNTAIN—RHODODENDRON GARDENS NATIONAL RECREATION TRAIL

Overview

Roan Mountain is more than a mountain; it is a massif. Though the bulking peak has two major summits, both just under 6,290 feet, the massive ridge that extends to the northeast comprises a region known as the Roan Highlands. (For more detail on a wonderful traverse of that area, see Hike 1, the Southern Balds section of the Appalachian Trail.) This is an area of immense natural significance. In fact, Roan Mountain and adjacent ridges contain the Southern Appalachians' greatest concentrations of rare and endangered species, among them sedges that add to the alpine look of the extensive, crag-capped meadows. Roan Mountain itself is a mottled mix of dark green Canadian-zone forests of red spruce and Fraser fir, and open grasslands and heath balds bulging with Catawba rhododendron that blooms spectacularly during the third week of June.

The mountain has long attracted hikers. Early explorer and botanist Asa Gray called it "the most beautiful mountain east of the Rockies." In 1877 the first tourist accommodation was built on the peak: Between 1885 and 1915 the 166-room Cloudland Hotel attracted visitors who rode trains to nearby stations, then took stagecoaches up the last 4 miles on a road now part of the Appalachian Trail (see Hike 7, the Cloudland Trail).

The mountain was logged, but its evergreen forests have recovered more than those on any other summit in the state. The Forest Service protects the mountain's scenery with roadside spraying for the balsam woolly aphid, the pest that, along with air pollution and acid rain is decimating stands of Fraser fir on many nearby summits. Pruning has preserved the gardenlike appearance of the rhododendron balds.

In late June, festivals in communities on both sides of the state line celebrate the rhododendron bloom. Roan Mountain State Park lies in a Tennessee valley to the north of the mountain, and the Tennessee town of Roan Mountain throws the biggest festival. But the vast bulk of Roan Mountain lies in North Carolina, including the famous rhododendron gardens, the road to the top, the national recreation trail, and indeed most trails.

Roan Mountain State Park is a wonderful resource for hikers. The park has a tent/RV campground, rustic cabins, a pool, a restaurant, picnic sites, and natural history programming that culminates during the rhododendron festivals and naturalists' rallies held in spring and fall. Through the 1980s, the park maintained a cross-country ski center that closed after a string of poor winters. Nevertheless, Roan averages about 100 inches of annual snowfall and easily offers the Deep South's best cross-country skiing and snow camping. With an eye on the weather, it isn't too difficult to find great ski conditions.

General description: An easy, paved National Recreation Trail that wanders through rhododendron gardens. A third of this three-loop, interpretive path is suitable for the wheelchair-bound.
General location: Roan Mountain, near Carvers Gap on the North Carolina–Tennessee border.
Length: 1-mile circuit.
Degree of difficulty: Easy, partly barrier-free.
Maps: USGS Bakersville quad.
Elevation gain and loss: Negligible.
Trailhead elevation: About 6,000 feet.
Low point: 5,950 feet.
Water availability: There is a water fountain at the trailhead contact station, also a trailhead restroom open late spring through early fall. Neighboring communities, and a state park on the Tennessee side, are other water sources nearby.
For more information: Toecane Ranger District, Pisgah National Forest. Or contact Supervisor's Office, National Forests in North Carolina, Asheville. Also, Roan Mountain State Park. See Appendix C.
Finding the trailhead: The trail is reached from Carvers Gap on the North Carolina/Tennessee state line. From the Boone, North Carolina, area, go west into Tennessee on U.S. Highway 19-E, then left on Tennessee Highway 143 in the town of Roan Mountain. From Asheville and more southerly areas, take North Carolina Highway 261 to Carvers Gap from Bakersville. Take the paved summit road up the mountain (SR 1348) from Carvers Gap and go left on a gravel road (Forest Road 130) at 1.7 miles to parking lot 2, on the left.

The hike: The 1-mile **Rhododendron Gardens National Recreation Trail** forms three loops. The uppermost loop is a flat, barrier-free, paved interpretive trail marked by sixteen stations keyed to a brochure. One stop is an observation deck with spectacular views, but most of the trail wanders through deep Canadian-zone forest. Branching from the upper loop is a lower figure-eight trail that is also easy, mostly gradual with a few brief sets of stone steps. The entire hike is suitable for elderly people and families with toddlers. The upper loop may be the best spruce/fir forest wheelchair-accessible trail in the Southern Appalachians.

The trail leaves parking lot 2 beside picnic tables and a small log cabin contact station staffed by volunteers during periods of peak visitation (especially during late June's rhododendron bloom). The trail heads away from the lot in an open area and passes a restroom building on the left. Turn right on the interpretive trail and wind through the whispering cool of the Canadian-zone forest. It is rarely warm at this elevation, and often quite chilly, even in summer. By mid-August bees cling sluggishly to goldenrod swaying in chill breezes.

25 ROAN MOUNTAIN — RHODODENDRON GARDENS NATIONAL RECREATION TRAIL

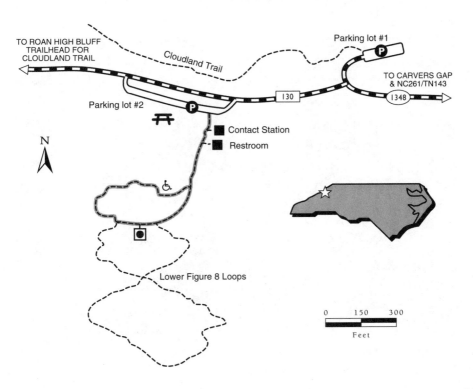

Signposts are keyed to a brochure that emphasizes the northern climate and species found here. There are many low-growing rare plants such as three-tooth cinquefoil, spreading avens, hair cap moss, and Allegheny sand myrtle. The latter resembles tundra azalea, which grows above timberline on New England's highest peak, Mount Washington, only 2 feet loftier than Roan Mountain. Elderberry, blueberry, and gooseberry bushes, mountain ash, red spruce, and Fraser fir round out a forest that drips with the feel of the far north. On foggy days, mist and clouds ebb and flow in surges.

The interpretive path passes a downhill junction on the right with the lower loops. Go left, then take a right onto the boardwalk to the observation deck. On a clear day, the view reaches to the serrated major ridge of the Black Mountains, of which Mount Mitchell is the loftiest. Beyond Mount Mitchell lie the Craggies, reached via the Blue Ridge Parkway. In winter, when this is a popular cross-country ski site, a frozen sea of summits stretches all around.

Take a right from the deck, then turn on the next right and descend to the upper of the two lower loops. The pavement narrows and becomes a little lumpier. There are gradual flights of stone steps, mostly at switchbacks. Much of the lower loops sojourn through a rich world of evergreens and overarching rhododendron. Mosses and ferns encroach on the trail. At the four-way junction go straight across and continue down the lower loop, switchbacking left, emerging from the trees, and crossing through a meadow area with bulging mounds of rhododendron accented

The late June rhododendron bloom is stunning on Roan Mountain's meadows.
Photo by Hugh Morton.

by soaring black spikes of red spruce. From here views reach to Grand-father Mountain.

Looping up to the left, go straight across the four-way junction and rise on the final leg back to the wheelchair-accessible trail. Enter the barrier free trail at the junction you encountered on the right just before the observation deck. Past the deck, go left at the right turn down into the lower loops, then go right at the beginning of the wheelchair-accessible trail on the left. Pass the restroom trail and contact station on the right to reach your car.

In winter this deeply drifted area is awesome. But skiers who reach it will have already skied nearly 2 miles up the road from the gate at Carvers Gap. A round-trip ski-tour is about 5 miles from Carvers Gap. The upper loop is suitable for beginning skiers, but the lower two require ample snow to insulate your skis from the shallow steps, and intermediate to advanced turning ability.

26 SHINING ROCK WILDERNESS

Overview

The Graveyard Ridge Trail and a new portion of the Mountains To Sea Trail create a relatively easy and less-crowded way to explore both the Shining Rock Wilderness and a lofty, alpinelike area between it and the Blue Ridge Parkway. These trails permit out-and-back and loop hikes over the spectacular open vistas of the Art Loeb Trail.

From the valley starting point to alpinelike summits, the hikes described here pass through a watershed that was consumed by wildfires in the 1920s and 1940s. Some North Carolina bald summits are assumed to be natural, but fires gave the grasslands of the Art Loeb Trail its barren appearance. Few areas in North Carolina offer better views. The area now called the Shining Rock Wilderness was not as impacted by fire. The bulk of the 19,000-acre evergreen tract lies north of the balds on the Art Loeb Trail. In the middle of the wilderness, Shining Rock Mountain (5,940 feet) thrusts its white, quartz-covered summit above the trees. A more distant and appropriately named peak, Cold Mountain, rises to 6,030 feet near the northern boundary of the wilderness area. The Shining Rock Wilderness is known for crowds, but many hikers feel the scenic appeal of the area is at its greatest on the balds of the Loeb Trail.

Starting at the Graveyard Fields Trail has other advantages. The Graveyard Ridge Trail and its access to the Mountains To Sea Trail create spectacular out-and-back hikes to peaks on the north and south ends of a particularly scenic stretch of the Art Loeb Trail. It also offers a circuit of those summits. Backpackers, regardless of where they're bound, will find that the less-used trails on the eastern side of this loop provide better access than parking areas on Forest Road 816. They also provide better camping alternatives than those on the western side of the ridge or to the north.

A hiker eyes the distant conical peak of Mt. Pisgah from the quartz summit of Shining Rock Mountain.

The best way to camp in popular Shining Rock is to get beyond the crowds into the vicinity of Cold Mountain. Other tips: Use access trails from valleys to the east and west of the wilderness, and focus on weekdays and less-popular seasons. If you decide to camp in this area, be aware that regulations prohibit groups of more than ten, and all campfires are banned.

General description: Hikes to bald summits and evergreen forests of the Shining Rock Wilderness. Most of these hikes begin on the Graveyard Ridge Trail, a less-used and scenic route.

General location: Blue Ridge Parkway.

Length: Out-and-back hikes of 6.4 miles to Black Balsam Knob and 8.8 miles to Tennent Mountain, and loop hikes of 5.2 and 9 miles, all of which include the Art Loeb Trail. Other trips include multiday hikes to Cold Mountain, the farthest point reached by trail in the Shining Rock Wilderness. One of those hikes is 10.6 miles from Daniel Boone Camp on the west via the Art Loeb and Cold Mountain Trails.

Degree of difficulty: Moderately strenuous to strenuous.

Maps: USGS Shining Rock quad. The recommended map is Pisgah National Forest's Shining Rock Wilderness and Middle Prong Wilderness map.

Elevation gain and loss: About 2,452 feet to and from Tennent Mountain; 2,788 for Black Balsam Knob; 3,120 feet for the entire loop. About 5,580 feet to Cold Mountain from the Art Loeb Trail on the west.

Trailhead elevation: About 5,100 feet for the Graveyard Ridge Trail; 3,240 feet for the Art Loeb Trail; 3,400 feet for the combined trailheads of the Old Butt Knob, Shining Creek, and Greasy Cove/Big East Cove Trails.
High points: About 5,700 feet for Graveyard Ridge Trail; 6,046 feet for Tennent Mountain; 6,214 for Black Balsam Knob; and 6,030 feet at Cold Mountain.
Low points: About 4,960 feet from Graveyard Fields Overlook; the trailheads for all others.
Water availability: Water from streams should be boiled or purified. Better to bring your own.
For more information: Pisgah Ranger District. Or contact Supervisor's Office, National Forests in North Carolina, Asheville. See Appendix C.
Finding the trailheads: To reach the starting point for hikes that begin at the Graveyard Fields Overlook, go to milepost 418 on the Blue Ridge Parkway. The trail is about 30 miles south of Asheville at the Parkway's junction with U.S. Highway 25, about 7 miles south of the U.S. Highway 276 junction, and about 4.5 miles north of the North Carolina Highway 215 junction.

The circuit of the Art Loeb Trail hike and the Ivestor Gap Trail, can also start from the trailhead on Forest Road 816, reached with a right turn 31.4 miles south of the US 25 entrance near Asheville. FR 816 is also a left turn from the Parkway about 3 miles north of NC 215, or a right turn about 8 miles south of US 276. The trailhead is the first formal parking area on FR 816, on the right about 0.8 mile from the Blue Ridge Parkway.

To reach other Shining Rock Wilderness trailheads go to US 276, 7 miles on the Parkway north of the Graveyard Fields Overlook, or NC 215, 4 miles south. The combined trailhead for the Old Butt Knob, Shining Creek, Greasy Cove/Big East Fork Trails is just under 3 miles north of the Parkway on US 276. The Daniel Boone Scout Camp trailhead for the Art Loeb and Little East Fork Trail is reached via NC 215. Go 13 miles north from the Parkway and turn right on the Little East Fork Road, SR 1129. Go 3.8 miles to parking at the Scout Camp.

The hikes: Start at the Blue Ridge Parkway's Graveyard Fields Overlook (see Hike 15). Anyone hiking the **Graveyard Fields Loop** is bound to look longingly up at the scenic mix of evergreens and hardwoods, fields, evergreen forests, and lofty summits and want to reach higher country. Descend from the trailhead, cross Yellowstone Prong and head left. At about 0.3 mile take a right onto the **Graveyard Ridge Trail**. Follow this gradual logging railroad grade to a trail junction in a gap between Black Balsam Knob (6,214 feet) on the left and an unnamed peak on the right. This is Dark Prong Gap, informally named such by Forest Service personnel and trail volunteers who recently built the new portion of the Mountains To Sea Trail that crosses the Graveyard Ridge Trail here. These first 1.8 miles are rich with campsites, especially out of sight of the trail.

Turn left where the newly cut **Mountains To Sea Trail** swings north out of the gap at about 5,400 feet, rises abruptly to the 5,600 foot level, then

26 SHINING ROCK WILDERNESS — PISGAH NF

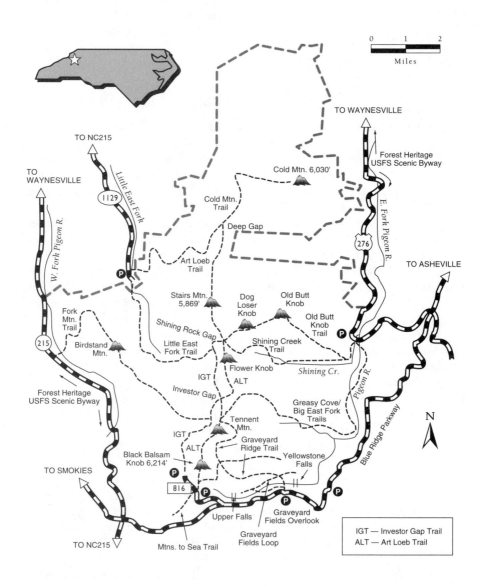

climbs gradually, at an average grade of 7 percent. On the way, the trail passes on the upper edge of the large flat, visible on the Forest Service map just above the 5,600-foot contour line. There are good campsites in this area, and the remains of an old railroad camp used during logging days are still visible. From there, the trail slides through the hollow holding the headwaters of Yellowstone Prong, follows an old railroad grade, and reaches FR

816 very close to where the Art Loeb Trail also exits the roadside. The trail reaches FR 816 in about 1 mile, just under 3 miles from the start.

From the road, hikers should take an immediate right and quickly rise into open vistas and waving grasses to Black Balsam Knob about 0.4 mile from the FR 816 trailhead (and 3.2 miles from your starting point). Retracing your steps from here creates an out-and-back hike of about 6.5 miles from the Parkway trailhead, and 0.8 mile from FR 816.

North, the **Art Loeb Trail** runs the open ridgetop, drops into a shrubby gap at about 5,880 feet, then climbs through eye-popping views to Tennent Mountain (6,046 feet) about 1.2 miles from Black Balsam Knob. Circuit hikers continue, but those wanting to reach Tennent Mountain more quickly should stay on the Graveyard Ridge Trail from Dark Prong Gap. From the gap, the road-width Graveyard Ridge Trail becomes a multipurpose route accessible to four-wheel-drive vehicles during hunting season. It crosses the upper reaches of Dark Prong, and passes a junction with the Greasy Cove/Big East Fork Trail (which descends right to US 276 in 6.6 miles). It then reaches Ivestor Gap and the Art Loeb Trail about 3.7 miles from the Parkway trailhead.

North, to the right, the Art Loeb and Ivestor Gap trails enter the Shining Rock Wilderness. To make the circuit, go left and take the Art Loeb Trail, a return to trail hiking after about 1.5 miles on the rocky four-wheel-drive surface. You can't miss the change. The trail immediately climbs to the spectacular balds of Tennent Mountain. The summit is only 0.7 mile from the gap, about 4.4 miles from the parking area, a round-trip of almost 9 miles from the Parkway. Of the two peaks accessible from the Parkway, the grade is easiest on the Graveyard Ridge Trail to Tennent Mountain, making it the more moderate hike, and therefore, the easiest direction in which to hike the circuit (that also applies for hikers starting on FR 816). Either direction, the circuit from the Parkway is just under 9 miles. Beginning from FR 816, the upper loop, following the Art Loeb Trail, and the connecting portions of the Graveyard Ridge and Mountains To Sea trails, is about 5.2 miles.

Farther north from Ivestor Gap, the Art Loeb Trail enters the Shining Rock Wilderness. At the gap, the **Ivestor Gap Trail** comes in from the west, having just intersected the Fork Mountain Trail, a 6.2-mile climb from the valley to the west on NC 215. From the gap, the Ivestor Gap Trail swings west of the main ridge, continuing its flat and popular route north. The Art Loeb heads that direction also, taking the high route over Grassy Cove Top to Flower Gap at 1.2 miles, then climbs around Flower Knob to Shining Rock Gap at 1.8 miles (5.5 miles from the trailhead).

At Shining Rock Gap, other trails access this heart of the wilderness. On the way to its termination here, the Ivestor Gap Trail intersected with another trail from the western valley: the **Little East Fork Trail**, a 5-mile climb from a trailhead at Daniel Boone Boy Scout Camp. From the east, two other trails join the Loeb Trail. The **Shining Creek Trail** is the most southerly and more popular. It climbs from US 276 in 4.1 miles. Just north of that

Art Loeb Trail on Tennent Mountain.

junction, the **Old Butt Trail** comes in on the right. This strenuous path with spectacular views is understandably the least used of the trails from the east, a hike of 3.6 miles. It leaves the Shining Creek Trail 0.7 mile above the trailhead on US 276. These trails permit circuits of various lengths up the east side of the wilderness (as do the Greasy Cove/Big East Fork Trails, though these are busy paths).

It should be obvious from the description of how many trails terminate in Shining Rock Gap that it has been one of the most popular campsites in any regional wilderness. The result is overuse. It's best not to camp here; any backpacking plans for this area should include time to find a secluded site. A better plan is to camp on any of the side trails that access the area, or go farther into the wilderness. The trails in that direction, especially the one to Cold Mountain, see much less use.

Beyond the gap and the namesake outcrops of quartz just above it, the Art Loeb Trail dips through Crawford Creek Gap and climbs over Stairs Mountain (5,869 feet). From this rocky peak and across a knife-edge ridge called The Narrows, the trail drops into Deep Gap, about 4.7 miles north of Ivestor Gap (8.4 miles north of the Parkway). The hike here from the Parkway, particularly for backpackers, is a long one. Overnighters bound for this area might be better off starting below Deep Gap where the Art Loeb Trail terminates at the Daniel Boone Scout Camp. That 3.8-mile trail is also a popular one, but those intent on solitude can continue north, on the **Cold Mountain Trail**. From Deep Gap, Cold Mountain is just 1.5

miles north, making that less-visited peak a 5.3-mile hike from the valley. That plan also puts Shining Rock within striking distance for day hikes. As on the east side, the Art Loeb Trail and the Little East Fork Trail provide a circuit from the west of 11.7 miles.

27 STONE MOUNTAIN STATE PARK

Overview

Stone Mountain State Park is a 13,000-acre parcel just below the Blue Ridge Parkway. Its namesake summit is a spectacular light gray granite dome that rises 600 feet above the surrounding forests. A variety of such domes are visible in the park, all part of a 25-square-mile pluton, a large blob of igneous rock formed underground. Over the 350 million years since its formation, erosion has exposed sections of the dome. Weathering has pockmarked the summits, and rain, snow, and ice have cracked and creased the face. The best example of this work is the Great Arch, a huge crack down the mountain's main dome that is a favorite climb for the thousands of rock climbers attracted to Stone Mountain.

Stone Mountain is indeed a world-class climbing destination, and casual visitors and hikers are among the people who pause to watch tiny figures inch their way up the steeply sloping domes. Unlike more vertical and crack-fractured types of rock, Stone Mountain's domes are home to friction climbing. Hikers here find great views from the peaks and streams that boast dramatic cascades, the biggest of which is Stone Mountain Falls, a 200-foot drop over— what else?—a dome.

Like most North Carolina state parks, Stone Mountain was preserved through citizen interest and purchase. Conservation efforts started in the 1960s and took a step toward fruition with the donation of 418 acres by the North Carolina Granite Corporation, owner of much of the surrounding land. A commission charged with creating the park acquired federal grants and more land, and the park was dedicated in 1969. Additional donations and purchases followed. Stone Mountain's natural significance was acknowledged in 1975 with its designation as a National Natural Landmark.

This park is a must see for the hiker who is seriously interested in the best North Carolina scenery. The area seems more modern and developed than most parks in North Carolina's decidedly rustic state park system, but in this case "developed" simply means adequate facilities, which most people expect at such a noteworthy landmark. Thirty-seven campsites serve tents and RVs, with amenities such as showers and laundry. Two group camping areas are available, and backpackers can amble down the scenic, 3-mile Widow's Creek Trail to six sites located between 1.5 and 3 miles from the trailhead. A main picnic area, with two grills and seven tables, is located

A dome-shaped granite mass rising 600 feet above its base identifies Stone Mountain State Park near Roaring Gap, North Carolina. This is a view from the observation area near the Stone Mountain Nature Trail. *Photo by William Russ.*

at the upper trailhead parking area, once the park's most popular but problematical trailhead due to its small size.

In the early 1990s, trail access at the park was reconfigured, a measure of the park's popularity and the problems created by a less-than-convenient parking situation. Trails once centered on the small upper parking area now reserved for picnickers and those using other developed facilities. The main summit trail has been rerouted down and across the road to a larger, lower parking area. The changes successfully permit hikers to avoid having to walk up, then down the entire dusty roadside to reach the trails from overflow lots.

Note, however, that because of the moved trails, some of the hikes described below do not include firm mileage figures. State park officials expect the trails to be completed by late 1995, but actual hiking mileage, especially for the Wolf Rock and Cedar Rock loops, will only be known when the project is finished. Nevertheless, the descriptions below, and the map of the park included here, are based on the final trail design. Hikers should compare this book with the park's newest map to quickly determine mileages and any name changes.

Trout fishing is another major attraction of the park. About 17 miles of streams are designated trout waters. This park is widely known for high-quality fishing. The park also offers naturalist's programs and invites program requests by groups.

General description: Trails in a world-class state park with a monolithic granite dome providing spectacular views. The strenuous Stone Mountain Trail climbs the peak and passes a 200-foot waterfall, but easier hikes lead to a nature trail, other dome-top views, and falls.

General location: Between the Blue Ridge Parkway and the town of Elkin.

Length: The Stone Mountain Trail is a 4.5-mile loop. Shorter hikes include the waterfall, at about 3 miles, a 2-mile hike to a nature trail below Stone Mountain face, and two circuit hikes of different lengths to Cedar Rock and Wolf Rock. Access trails were being built as this book was written, so consult the current park map for the latest mileages.

Degree of difficulty: Moderately strenuous for the Stone Mountain Trail; moderately easy for the nature trail; moderate to moderately strenuous for circuit hikes of Wolf and Cedar Rocks.

Elevation gain and loss: 1,492 feet.

Trailhead elevation: 1,560 feet.

High point: 2,306 feet.

Maps: USGS Glade Valley quad. A topographical hiking map is available at the state park.

Water availability: Water is available at the park visitor center, campground, and other trailhead facilities year-round. Do not drink from the streams without treating the water.

For more information: Stone Mountain State Park. See Appendix C.

Finding the trailhead: From Elkin, go north from Interstate Highway 77 about 11 miles on U.S. Highway 21, and turn left on SR 1002. Turn right at 4.6 miles on the John P. Frank Parkway to reach the Stone Mountain State Park entrance at 7 miles and the visitor center on the right at 7.8 miles. At the park entrance, SR 1100 comes in from the right. This is a good access route for hikers coming from the Blue Ridge Parkway; the road goes right from US 21 just below the crest of Roaring Gap.

Continuing on the park road, the main parking area for Stone Mountain trails is on the left at 10.3 miles. A left here leads to the upper lot and picnic area in about 0.4 mile. Continue on the main park road to trailhead parking for the Widow's Creek Trail, which leads to backcountry campsites, 1 mile beyond the main trailhead parking.

The hikes: From Stone Mountain State Park's main trailhead, serious hikers take the strenuous loop over the mountain's summit, descending past Stone Mountain Falls and back. Others just take the moderate hike up to the falls, or moderately strenuous loop hikes over the lower domes, which avoid the steep climb of Stone Mountain.

The premier hike here is the **Stone Mountain Loop**, a 4.5-mile circuit of the summit that takes in the top of the dome, a spectacular waterfall, and views of climbers scaling the rock face. To begin, leave the main trailhead parking lot on the main trail, a new and nicely graded path. The new path soon branches right, but go straight and at about 0.2 mile take a left turn. The trail switchbacks and crosses the road leading to the upper lot. Beyond

27 STONE MOUNTAIN STATE PARK

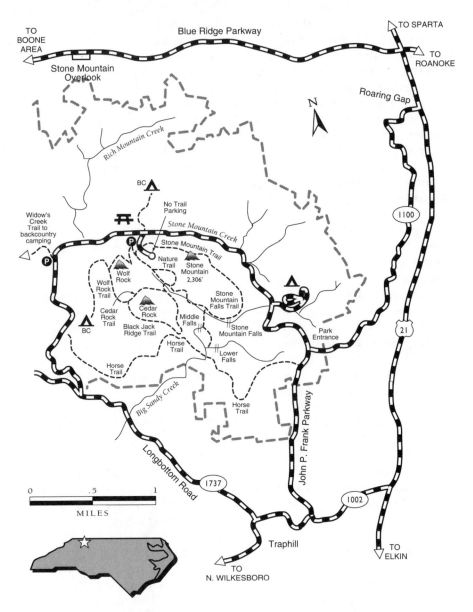

the road, the trail ascends over log and stone steps, approaching the edge of the domes, and, following yellow blazes, exits onto the lower domes. With great views on the left, the trail then tends up and right. At this steepest point, vegetation is close on the left of the trail.

As the steepness lessens near the top, views are accessible on the right, also. You can leave the main trail here, traverse along the top of the dome, and reach a tie-in to the main trail. But use caution: the vegetation is fragile, and the dome gets steeper the farther down you stray. At this point, it's not unusual to hear the jingle of rock-climbing gear wafting over from the face.

Entering the woods, the main trail ambles on a rocky tread in a spectacularly scenic forest. The slight arc of the larger summit dome is obvious, but the open understory of grasses and shrubs, and overstory of chestnut oak and pine gives little hint of the dropoffs that surround you. At the summit, just over 1 mile from the trailhead, an unmarked side trail bears right and reaches a great view of the valley to the southwest. Dead trees near the edge are twisted and weathered like driftwood, and the elements seem ready to rip the soil layer back from its tenuous toehold on the rock.

Yellow blazes lead the way down a road-width path. The trail dips, alternating between domes and woods. **CAUTION:** The first of these domes off the back of the summit is very steep. Its angle, and the steepness of the last pitch up to the summit on the other side, suggest that inexperienced hikers might avoid this trip in rainy weather.

Eventually the trail leaves the domes behind, curving right on a bull-dozed path through a grove of fallen trees. The chimney of a long-gone mountaineer's cabin is on the left at about 2.3 miles. The sounds of falling water announce the approach of Big Sandy Creek.

Fencing and warning signs mark Stone Mountain Falls, 200 feet, at about 2.6 miles. **CAUTION:** Fatalities have occurred here, so hikers should stay scrupulously within the elaborate enclosure of steps and railings. There's a viewing area halfway down. Toward the bottom of the steps, the left flight goes to the bottom of the falls (requiring a climb back up to continue the hike down). At the base of the steps, the trail becomes a wide amble above the stream. The irony is that as one follows the gradually rising trail, the stream becomes a small creek and can give the impression that the torrent that produced this impressive cataract has just dried up. Actually, the main stream went left, not obvious among the rhododendron.

Continuing down, the **Stone Mountain Nature Trail** enters from the right as the mountain's face also appears in that direction across a large open meadow; the nature trail makes a loop through the field. The Cedar Rock Trail soon comes in on the left, not far down which is the Blackjack Ridge Trail. Both are accessible from the trail that went to the right just above the parking lot on your way up the Stone Mountain Trail.

Farther on, a designated viewpoint appears on the right with a bench. This is a stunning view of the rock and climbers inching their way up the dome. A plaque here designates the park as a National Natural Landmark. The nature trail also officially starts here. It crosses the meadow and enters the woods below the cliffs, turns right and follows the base of the rock back to its junction with the Stone Mountain Trail that you just passed. This route across the meadow is the way climbers reach the face.

Massive steps descend past Stone Mountain Falls in Stone Mountain State Park.

About 0.9 mile below the falls, a new trail bound for the lower parking lot will pass the area of the upper parking lot at just under 4 miles. The new path passes a junction on the right (where you went left to climb Stone Mountain), then goes past a junction on the left (the route to Cedar and Wolf Rocks) before reaching the parking lot for a loop hike of about 4.5 miles.

Less energetic hikers can reach the base of the falls and the nature trail without crossing the summit. From the new parking area hike up the main trail (avoiding a left to Stone Mountain and a right to Cedar Rock) to the base of the falls, about 1.5 miles, for a moderate 3-mile round-trip. (Remember: Going down to the foot of the falls requires climbing up the wooden steps, then descending to the viewing area.) To reach the top of the falls this way, the steps can be called a formidable obstacle, making a round-trip hike of about 3.5 miles.

A hike to the viewing area in the meadow below the rock is a roundtrip of about 1.2 miles. Add the Stone Mountain Nature Trail to that and the hike is about 2.5 miles.

The newly designed trailhead scheme permits two other circuit hikes. Taking the route described above, and making a right turn on the **Cedar Rock Trail** in the vicinity of the nature trail, permits a big circuit that can include the summits of Cedar Rock and Wolf Rock. Both of these open domes are less visited than Stone Mountain. On the way up, go right on the Cedar Rock Trail to the junction with the Blackjack Ridge Trail. The shorter loop goes right on the Cedar Rock Trail to Cedar Rock summit and back to your car on the Wolf Rock Trail.

To take the longer circuit follow the **Blackjack Ridge Trail** left. The road grade trail dips to cross Cedar Rock Creek, then climbs steeply to intersect the Cedar Rock and Wolf Rock trails. Take a short side trip right on the Cedar Rock Trail to the peak, then backtrack to the junction and go right on the Wolf Rock Trail. A short spur reaches the open summit of Wolf Rock. A few tenths of a mile later, the side trail to group camping sites goes left. Continue down the new part of the Wolf Rock Trail to its junction with the main trail and go left to the parking lot. (Trail changes may have spawned changes in the names of these trails, though the routes described are accurate.)

Hikers bound for Wolf and Cedar Rocks can go right immediately above the trailhead and avoid what might be the more popular main trail.

28 TABLEROCK–SHORTOFF MOUNTAINS

General description: The most distinctive summit flanking the Linville Gorge Wilderness, Tablerock Mountain is a craggy peak popular with rock climbers. Hikers have panoramic views from the summit, and views from nearby Shortoff Mountain are even better. There is no better vista of the rugged chasm of Linville Gorge.

General location: Near Linville Gorge Wilderness and the town of Linville Falls.

Length: Tablerock Mountain is 2.2 miles round-trip; Shortoff Mountain is 11.2 miles round-trip.

Difficulty: Moderate for Tablerock; very strenuous for Shortoff Mountain.

Elevation gain and loss: 1,218 feet for Tablerock; about 3,750 feet for Shortoff.

Trailhead elevation: 3,400 feet for both.

High points: 3,909 feet for Tablerock; for Shortoff, 3,520 feet near the Chimneys and 3,000 feet at the summit.

Low point: 2,509 on the way to Shortoff Mountain.

Maps: USGS Linville Falls quad, but the Forest Service's Linville Gorge Wilderness map is preferred.

Water availability: No water at the trailhead and no nearby commercial outlets, so bring water. A side trail from the Tablerock Trail reaches a spring. On the Shortoff Mountain Trail there are usually reliable water sources at 2.3 miles, and just beyond the summit.

For more information: Grandfather Ranger District, Pisgah National Forest. Or contact Supervisor's Office, National Forests in North Carolina, Asheville. See Appendix C.

Finding the trailhead: Tablerock and Shortoff mountains lie between Linville Falls and Morganton. The peaks are rather isolated and require driving over gravel Forest Service roads. From the north, proceed south from the Boone area on North Carolina Highway 105, then U.S. Highway 221, then North Carolina 181 toward Morganton. (From the south, take NC 181 north from Morganton.) Just south of the Blue Ridge Parkway/NC 181 junction near Pineola is the NC 181/183 junction.

Two miles south of that intersection, toward Morganton on NC 181, turn onto Gingercake Road, SR 1265. Turn right onto SR 1264 at 2.5 miles, a junction marked with a sign to Tablerock. At 3.5 miles, the road, now Forest Road 210 (SR 1261), becomes gravel. At 7.2 miles pass parking for the Spence Ridge Trail (see Hike 20 for a description of that trail into the Gorge). At 8.2 miles turn right onto FR 210-B, following the sign to the Tablerock Picnic Area. At 8.9 miles pass the entrance to the North Carolina Outward Bound School. A paved, switchbacking ascent to the trailhead parking/picnic area starts at 9.8 miles. Reach the trailhead at 11.4 miles.

Other routes include the New Gingercake Road, Forest Road 496, just south of the Barkhouse Picnic Area on NC 181. That road is approximately 6 miles south of the NC 181/183 junction. The route then requires a right turn onto FR 210, then an immediate left onto FR 210-B for the climb to the trailhead.

From Morganton, hikers can also turn left onto the Simpson Creek Road (14.7 miles from Interstate Highway 40, exit 100, via Jamestown Road to NC 181). Once on Simpson Creek Road, take the right at the Table Rock sign at 0.3 mile and climb the Rose Mountain Road (also FR 210) to a left onto FR 210-B at 9.9 miles.

The hikes: The hike to Tablerock is far simpler than the auto route to the trailhead. The **Tablerock Trail**, here combined with the **Mountains To Sea Trail**, leaves the north end of the parking area through profuse ferns and switchbacks right, then left, to the bottom of a long flight of gradual steps. (These lower switchbacks, a barricade, and bulldozer-created tank traps deter hikers from taking the eroding straight route to the parking lot.)

Not far from the parking area, at the top of a long stretch of rocky steps, a climber's trail heads off to the right. The trail flattens, the footing gets easier, and at about 0.3 mile, the trail switchbacks right as a side trail dips left into a little gap. This is the unmarked **Little Tablerock Trail.** (Barely off the Tablerock Trail, in the gap on the Little Tablerock Trail, a trail goes right off the ridge to a spring.) Beyond, it joins Spence Ridge Trail.

Continuing on the Tablerock Trail, two white circle blazes announce an upcoming change of direction for the Mountains To Sea Trail. Soon thereafter, the white-blazed path goes left. The Tablerock Trail continues up and switchbacks left at the base of the first large crag. This indicates the summit isn't far. The trail squeezes between two boulders, then switchbacks twice before emerging into open, rocky terrain. There's a shelter rock on the right as you near the crest the peak.

A benchmark, its lettering illegible now from being struck with rocks, is on the left just as the views open up. This vista reaches the head of the gorge, toward Linville Falls. Gaining the crest, you're at the former site of a fire tower. A left quickly takes you north to a fine view of the upper gorge and Hawksbill Mountain, the rocky, gentle peak just north across the gap. Grandfather Mountain rises on the right. From out here, the gentle tinkling of rock-climbing hardware and the conversation of climbers drift up from Table Rock's North Ridge area. Summit vegetation is rooted in dry, almost sandy soil, and includes various sedges, Allegheny sand myrtle, mountain laurel, blueberries, and pine, all waving in the gusts of wind so typical of this cliff-edge environment.

If you're sure-footed, go south where the summit descends along a spectacular spine of rocks. Many trails wander over and among the boulders; all of these hiker routes eventually disintegrate into climber's paths, working their way to the cliffs and ending overlooking stomach-churning drops. There are dozens of spectacular and private crags on which to have lunch here.

This part of the Linville Gorge is one of Eastern America's premier rock climbing areas. Looking south, just past the Tablerock parking area (visible below), you can see the convoluted ridge called the Chimneys, another famous climbing site. Farther away, Shortoff Mountain drops off to Lake James and the blue distance of the Carolina Piedmont. Across the gorge, the prominent cliff is Wisemans View, a developed vista reached by road. Off to the right, the long crest of the Black Mountains includes Mount Mitchell.

The Tablerock Trail parking lot is a lightly developed recreation area with tables and grills for picnicking and modern pit toilets. But there's no

28 TABLEROCK–SHORTOFF MOUNTAINS

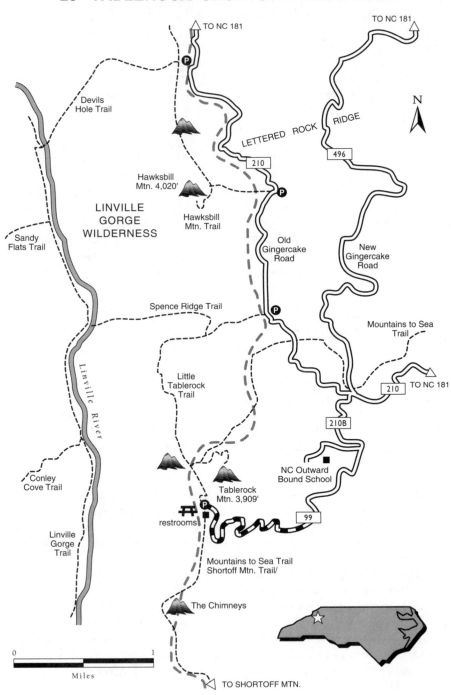

TO NC 181

TO NC 181

N

Devils
Hole Trail

LETTERED ROCK RIDGE

496

210

Hawksbill
Mtn. 4,020'

LINVILLE
GORGE
WILDERNESS

Hawksbill
Mtn. Trail

Old
Gingercake
Road

New
Gingercake
Road

Sandy
Flats Trail

Spence Ridge Trail

Mountains to Sea
Trail

210   TO NC 181

210B

Little
Tablerock
Trail

NC Outward
Bound School

Linville
River

Conley
Cove Trail

Tablerock
Mtn. 3,909'

restrooms

99

Linville
Gorge
Trail

Mountains to Sea Trail
Shortoff Mtn. Trail/

The Chimneys

0   1

Miles

TO SHORTOFF MTN.

Tablerock towers over the Linville River's winding route at the bottom of Linville Gorge.

water and no camping is allowed. There are, however, great views of Tablerock. Bring binoculars if you want to watch climbers scale the cliffs.

The **Shortoff Mountain Trail** leaves the same parking area but heads south. It follows a gradual ridgetop, then slabs to the west of The Chimneys (3,557) and their crags and cracks. The trail rejoins the ridge, then swings southeast and begins a descent of 900 feet, much of it steeply, into Chimney Gap (2,509 feet). At about 2 miles, the **Cambric Branch Trail** bears right along a rather level ridgetop, then drops down the ridge to a dead end at the Linville River.

Continuing along the Shortoff Mountain Trail (part of the Mountains To Sea Trail), a wet-weather spring is located 150 feet left of the trail at about 2.3 miles. The trail crosses a peak at about 3 miles and at 5.4 miles reaches the summit of Shortoff Mountain. Paths to the right reach clifftops with spectacular views directly up the deepest depths of the canyon, past all the highest summits along the rims. A spring is located beyond the summit in a small gap. Lake James sprawls below.

Overview

The Tanawha Trail is the crowning achievement of the Blue Ridge Parkway trail network. For thirty years the Department of the Interior wrangled with Grandfather Mountain owner Hugh Morton over where the Blue Ridge Parkway would cross his spectacular parcel of private land. Eventually precluded from condemning a high route for the road, the National Park Service finally built the lower road and the Tanawha Trail that lies above it, sparing no expense. Unbelievably costly trail- and road-building techniques were required to minimize impact on the fragile mountainside.

In one spot, visited on this hike, the road leaps away from the mountain on a multimillion-dollar, computer-designed, space-age span called the Linn Cove Viaduct. The segmented bridge was built with each ensuing section affixed to the one before it, over thin air. Views of the costly and curving bridge, now a fixture in televised car commercials, are plentiful from sections of the Tanawha Trail. Hikers also can't fail to notice an astounding number of intricate stone stairways, rock-paved treadways, and laminated wood bridges (lowered here by helicopter), all designed to minimize hiker damage to this scenic environment. The federal government

A Tanawha Trail view of the Linn Cove Viaduct from Rough Ridge.

spent almost $750,000 on the 13.5 miles of trail between Beacon Heights, near Linville, and Price Park Campground, near Blowing Rock.

Perhaps the best views on the Tanawha Trail are from Rough Ridge, a high outcrop where boardwalks and handrails were required to keep the public from trampling the low, alpine-like vegetation, some of it rare and endangered. To those familiar with the roadless grandeur of this area before the coming of the Parkway, the change speaks of how dramatically humankind dominates the wilds. Happily, a portion of human power has been devoted to preserving this wonderful area.

The hikes described below take in the grandest vistas on the trail, both of the scenery and of the technology employed to minimize the impact of human presence.

General description: A variety of hikes on the Tanawha Trail along the flank of Grandfather Mountain. Easy hikes, one accessible to wheelchairs, lead to great views, but the real foci are an end-to-end walk of the trail section, a hike to a viaduct view, and two ways to scale the peak of Rough Ridge.

General location: Blue Ridge Parkway, near Grandfather Mountain.

Length: 0.3-mile round-trip for barrier-free trail; 1 mile round-trip to views of the viaduct. Another 0.3-mile hike reaches boardwalk views. An end-to-end walk of the trail section is 2.7 miles, and round-trip hikes of 1.1 and 2 miles lead to the peak of Rough Ridge.

Degree of difficulty: Easy and barrier-free to moderately strenuous.

Elevation gain and loss: 960 feet from Rough Ridge Parking Area to peak; about 1,080 feet end-to-end.

Trailhead elevation: 4,320 feet at Linn Cove Parking Area; 4,200 feet at Rough Ridge Parking Area.

High point: 4,680 feet at Rough Ridge.

Maps: USGS Grandfather quad. The Grandfather Mountain hiking map shows the trail best, and is available free at the Grandfather Mountain park entrance, 1 mile away. A Parkway strip map and a Tanawha Trail map/brochure are available from Parkway headquarters.

Water availability: No water is available on the trail, but the Grandfather Mountain entrance has water year-round. Between May and September, the Linn Cove Information Station also has water and restrooms at the viaduct parking area.

For more information: The Blue Ridge Parkway. Call for recorded information, weather road closures, mailing requests, etc. The trail is in the Blue Ridge Parkway's Bluffs District. See Appendix C.

Finding the trailhead: The trailheads are located at mileposts 303 and 304 on the Blue Ridge Parkway, just north of the U.S. Highway 221 entrance to the Parkway, 2 miles east of Linville. The trailheads are located roughly 12 miles south of the US Highway 321 access between Boone and Blowing Rock, and 13 miles north of the US 221 access north of Marion.

The hikes: The easiest walk to a view of the **Linn Cove Viaduct** begins at the Linn Cove Information Station, just north of milepost 304. The small visitor center explains the technical and natural history behind this amazing portion of the Parkway. From here, a paved and barrier-free trail winds from the parking lot for 0.15 mile to a viewpoint underneath the Linn Cove Viaduct.

The next-easiest walk is for those who want to see more of the viaduct. Stay on the trail past the pavement as it wanders under the span to a picture-perfect, oft-photographed view back at the bridge. On the way, the trail climbs to the level of the bridge as it zigzags over impressive stone stairways, along the faces of huge boulder cliffs, and through towering rhododendron. Above it all soars the viaduct, with the occasional whoosh and thump of a passing car. The trail crosses over Linn Cove Branch and ascends out of the stream drainage to a ridgeline above the road. At the 0.5-mile mark take a right to the view of the bridge. Retrace your steps for a 1-mile round-trip hike.

End-to-end hikers will want to park another car at the Rough Ridge Parking Area. They will continue undulating across the flank of the mountain, eventually dipping to a junction at 1.2 miles. Right, a side trail runs 0.1 mile under the Parkway to Wilson Creek Overlook (milepost 303.7). This is another good starting point for a hike to the peak of **Rough Ridge,** and often less populated than the trail from Rough Ridge Parking Area.

Going left, cross Little Wilson Creek and drop around the prow of an outcrop that forces the trail down to within sight of the road. Then the climb begins, gradual and meandering, across boulder fields with towering trees and inspiring spring wildflowers. Climbing through mixed evergreens, hikers reach a saddle at 1.9 miles. Above is the crag-capped summit of Rough Ridge, about 1 mile from the Wilson Creek Parking Area (2 miles round-trip).

Follow the stone steps up and emerge on the flat, alpine-like summit of Rough Ridge. The clifftops here offer startling vistas and mark the start of a dramatic stone crag visible to Parkway motorists below. Climbers have named this Ship Rock, and it is one of the state's most challenging rock-climbing sites. (The National Park Service requires that climbers reach the rock from the Wilson Creek Parking Area.) Rough Ridge actually rises higher, meshing with Grandfather Mountain, but here are the best views. End-to-enders will descend from here to their other vehicle at Rough Ridge Parking Area, another 0.5 mile, for a 2.7-mile hike.

The most direct route to the summit of Rough Ridge is from the Parkway parking area of the same name, just north of milepost 303. Here the access trail ascends a muddy flight of log steps and bears left onto the **Tanawha Trail** to immediately cross an arching wooden bridge. A cascade slides down slippery rocks below and exits directly under the parking area.

The trail ascends through an often muddy area of evergreens, climbs a flight of stone steps, and levels across a rocky shelf amid low blueberry bushes and galax. Hikers then turn a corner and step onto the beginning

29 TANAWHA

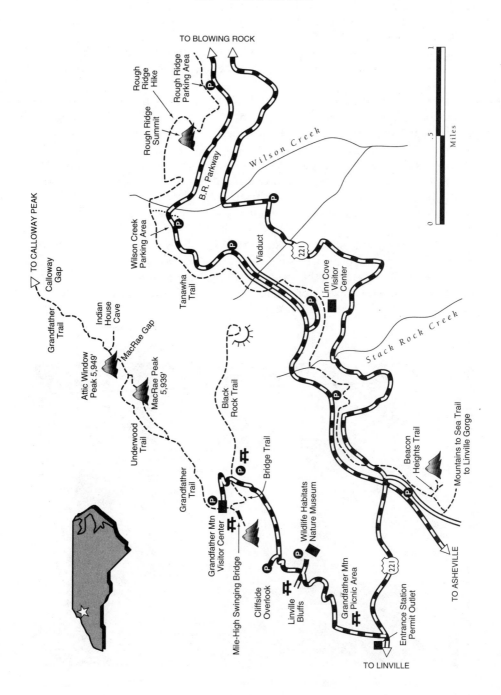

of 200 feet of ascending boardwalk, designed to keep hikers from trampling the low vegetation that explodes into view as you pass a stack rock formation on the right of the trail. This may be the easiest path along the entire Parkway to a great view. From this boardwalk, just a 0.3-mile round-trip from the parking area, the view is remarkably similar to that found on the summit, another 0.3 mile ahead up rocky, moderately strenuous switchbacks.

From either location, it is a nice spot to watch a sunset and get back to your car quickly; the vista seems to engulf you. Above, the three highest summits of Grandfather Mountain, all nearly 6,000 feet, reach a rocky, dramatic climax. From the highest, Calloway Peak (5,964 feet, farthest right), the Wilson Creek drainage drops like an expansive chute, past intervening pinnacles of Rough Ridge (where you're standing), Black Rock Cliffs (to the south, above the viaduct), and Pilot Knob (behind you). Mount Mitchell lies on the horizon. The Parkway and viaduct snake across this descending wave of rock.

This is the greatest single rise of the Blue Ridge escarpment. Below, across the rippling corduroy of the Wilson Creek area, the land continues to descend all the way to the first twinkling edge of the Piedmont. Add a crystal clear fall day, electric foliage, a summit dusting of snow and racing clouds, and . . . you get the picture.

Tanawha Trail view from Rough Ridge. The rippling ridges include the Harper Creek and Lost Cove areas. Rounded Grandmother Mountain at right.

General description: A spectacularly scenic loop trail with views from some of Eastern America's highest cliffs.

General location: Between the towns of Highlands and Cashiers.

Length: 2 miles round-trip.

Degree of difficulty: Moderately easy to moderate, depending on direction and length.

Maps: USGS Highlands quad.

Trailhead elevation: Approximately 4,400 feet.

High point: 4,930 feet.

Water availability: There is no drinkable water at the trailhead or on the trail, but ample opportunities exist to fill a canteen in the nearby towns of Highlands and Cashiers.

For more information: Highlands Ranger District Visitor Information Center. Open seven days per week during summer and fall, weekends before and after, and closed in winter. Highlands Ranger District. Or contact Supervisor's Office, National Forests in North Carolina, Asheville. See Appendix C.

Finding the trailhead: Take U.S. Highway 64 from Highlands or Cashiers, and turn left onto SR 1600 about 4 miles south of Cashiers, or turn right onto SR 1600, 5.7 miles north of the US 64/North Carolina Highway 28 junction in Highlands. The junction is marked by a Forest Service sign that reads "Vista Point/Whiteside Mountain." Take SR 1600 for 1 mile to a left turn into a parking area with pit toilets.

The hike: Whiteside Mountain's massive cliffs tower 400 to 750 feet along the southeastern side of the summit; only New Hampshire's Cannon Mountain compares for sheer grandeur. The **Whiteside Mountain Trail** boasts great views of the cliffs and from the clifftops. Rock climbers have flocked here since the first recorded face climb in 1971, which took two days. The faces are only for expert climbers, boasting "extreme exposure."

The mountain, composed of metamorphic gneiss commonly called Whiteside granite, has always been a landmark. Indians used the peak as a campsite, and early Spanish explorers under Hernando DeSoto also stopped at the mountain. The peak was reportedly named by Barak Norton, an early settler in the area. The summit was at one time a private tourist attraction. Shuttle buses ferried visitors to the top where a post office was located, a convenient place to mail raves about the view to the folks back home.

Today, a gradual hike to the summit follows that old road grade, grown into a forested route since the Forest Service acquired the property in 1974. That trail is relatively easy, leading to wonderful views without requiring

Whiteside Mountain reflects in a pond from the Whiteside Cove Road between Highlands and Cashiers.

30 WHITESIDE MOUNTAIN NATIONAL RECREATIONAL TRAIL

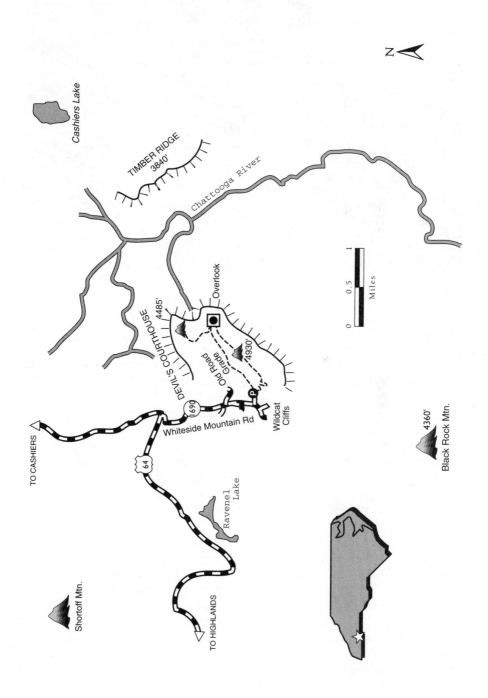

The view from the top of the cliffs on the Whiteside Mountain Trail.

hikers to use the rockier path that forms the loop. Up and back on the easiest route is a 2-mile, moderate hike.

Those who want a more strenuous walk can continue up the trail from the end of the old grade, making the loop; or reverse the loop, going right from the old road just above the parking lot and climbing the steeper switchbacks, then descending the old road grade. Either way, this is one of the scenic highlights of Nantahala National Forest's popular Highlands Ranger District. Starting at the parking area, enter the woods and ascend on steps until you bear left onto the old road grade. Major roadcuts on the right suggest this was once a well-used thoroughfare. The return of the loop goes right shortly after reaching the road grade. Keeping left, the grade and footing are easy except for a few rockier spots, one of which is just below roadcuts and natural cliffs on the right.

The path emerges into an open area as it rounds the end of the ridge at a grand vista to the south, east, and north, of dome-faced peaks. Looking east, the Chattooga River breaks out of the higher mountains to the left and flows right to a deep, broad valley more than 2,000 feet below the clifftops. Summits visible are Rock Mountain, Laurel Mountain, Chimneytop Mountain, and Timber Ridge. Head back to your car from here for an easy 2-mile hike.

Or bear right around the ridge and enter the woods along the clifftops. An observation slab appears on the left of the trail, with dramatic views of precipitous domes and cliffs. The trail continues beside an interesting rib of rock, encountering the first of six or seven long stretches of cliffside railings that extend for hundreds of yards along the face. Some of these can be seen down in the woods on the left, ready to deter the foolhardy from discovering that the vegetation abruptly gives way to air.

The railings are relatively low impact, in a visual sense, and they encompass some undulating rocky spots. Rails also encircle the summit crag (4,930 feet). There is rocky footing here, but it's gradual, so most people will find it an easy ramble. The farther you go, the more the view shifts south, into the pastoral valley of the Chattooga. (The best views of the cliffs can be had from that valley, via the gravel Whiteside Cove Road, SR 1107, between Highlands and Cashiers. Easiest access is south from Cashiers on North Carolina Highway 107, with a right turn onto the road just past the High Hampton Inn.)

As the clifftop trail crests and then descends, there are some less-developed viewpoints off to the left. But tread lightly around the fragile vegetation that clings in these areas, including Allegheny sand myrtle. From one of these, it's easy to see the new homes that are being built on the very edges of surrounding, privately owned cliffs.

The trail bears right into the woods and switchbacks on a steeper grade down to a flight of steps before emerging onto the old road grade. Head left to the parking lot to end the 2-mile loop.

For many more mountain hikes, see Appendix A: Appalachian Trail Day Hikes, Mileage Log, and Great Smoky Mountains National Park.

Overview

McAlpine Creek Park was the first of Mecklenburg County's greenway parks when it opened in 1979. The park stretches between Independence Boulevard and Sardis Road and encompasses 364 acres along McAlpine and Irwin creeks. A paved streamside greenway trail, suitable for walking, jogging, and bicycling, runs between the roads. This main path is buffered from neighborhoods (many of which have their own greenway access paths—see the map) by a varied landscape of marshes, meadows, and hardwood forests. Some of these surrounding woods, including some of the largest cottonwoods in the state, are explored by unpaved trails that wander away from the stream. A few of these climb to James Boyce Park, the best access point for hikers who want looping woods walks with some change in elevation.

James Boyce Park's 73 acres abut the greenway closer to Sardis Road. This was a unit of the city park system before the merger with the county in July 1992, and there is no office on premises. The park contains the foundation of the old Boyce homesite, two baseball fields, a nice playground for young children, a picnic shelter, and restrooms.

The McAlpine Creek Park office is located at the developed Monroe Road entrance and access area. Here also is a 3-acre lake, a nicely wooded, 5 kilometer cross-country jogging course, five soccer fields, and picnic facilities.

Together, the parks boast creekside hardwood and mixed pine forests, about 3 miles of streambanks on McAlpine Creek itself, and marshlands, all in a natural area large enough to offer habitat for opossum, raccoon, rabbit, squirrel, fox, muskrat, hawk, owl, pileated woodpecker, and a diverse assortment of migrating waterfowl and seasonal birds.

General description: A streamside greenway and adjoining hilltop forest that together offer miles of hiking on developed paved paths and woods trails. James Boyce Park, adjacent to the greenway, offers the best loops and out-and-back hikes on woodsy trails.

General location: The city of Charlotte.

Length: Hikes range from as short as you like to 3 or 4 miles.

Degree of difficulty: Easy to moderate, with some portions barrier-free.

Maps: USGS Charlotte East and Mint Hill quads. The Mecklenburg County Park and Recreation Department will send hikers free maps of the greenway and the cross-country running trail. A birders checklist is also available.

Elevation gain and loss: Negligible.

Trailhead elevation: Approximately 560 feet at streamside access points; about 650 feet at the James Boyce Park parking area.

Water availability: Water is available year-round at the McAlpine Greenway's main trailhead, and during the warmer months at the Boyce Park trailhead.

For more information: Mecklenburg County Park and Recreation Department, Hal Marshall County Services Center. McAlpine Greenway Park office. See Appendix C.

Finding the trailheads: To reach the park's main entrance from Interstates 85 or 77 north, take the Sugar Creek Road exit. Take Sugar Creek Road east to Eastway Drive (Charlotte Loop Highway 4) and bear right. Continue south on Eastway to Monroe Road and take a left. The park entrance is 4.5 miles on the right (8700 Monroe Road). From I-77 south, take the Woodlawn Road east exit. Go north for 7 miles on Woodlawn Road (again, part of Charlotte Loop Highway 4), and turn right on Monroe Road The park is again 4.5 miles, on the left, just before the Seaboard Railroad Overpass.

To reach Boyce Park continue on Monroe Road past the main entrance to the Greenway park, and go right onto Sardis Road North. When Sardis Road North intersects Sardis Road, go right on Sardis Road (On Sardis Road, the third street to the left is Old Bell Road, another McAlpine Park Greenway trailhead. A parking area is located on the corner at Sardis and Old Bell Road, and the trail exits the roadside across the street.) Continuing on Sardis, take a right in 0.9 mile on Boyce Road. Immediately past the Charlotte Montessori School, turn right into the park and proceed to the parking areas.

The hikes: The basic hike in **McAlpine Park** is the out-and-back greenway walk from any of the entrances. From the Old Bell Road parking area, east to the vicinity of the park office (and vice versa), the greenway trail is about 2 miles, or a 4-mile round-trip. East from the park office, the two loops of the cross-country trail total 5 kilometers, about 3 miles.

But the best hikes to be had here follow the woods paths north of McAlpine Creek between Monroe and Sardis roads. The dedicated woods walker can create everything from a short loop to a lengthy out-and-back walk in this area, solely on woods trails. The less pure can add segments of the paved greenway trail and create nice loops of varying lengths with diverse scenery. All of these hikes, except for the lengthiest, are suitable for older hikers and young children.

From **Boyce Park** the easiest woodsy walks involve loops that descend from the park's main parking area down to what is called the **Nature Trail**, McAlpine Park's forest trail that parallels the creek just below the heights of Boyce Park. From the parking area at Boyce Park three main trails enter the woods, all unsigned save for the openings in the trees through which they pass. All three pass portions of the ball fields, centered in large meadows around the parking lot, then enter the woods and loop back to each other. This permits a nice walk on the section of the Nature Trail closest to Boyce Park. During the transition from the ball field elevation of Boyce Park to the wooded floodplain of McAlpine Creek, each drops relatively

31 CHARLOTTE TRAILS –
MCALPINE GREENWAY / BOYCE PARK

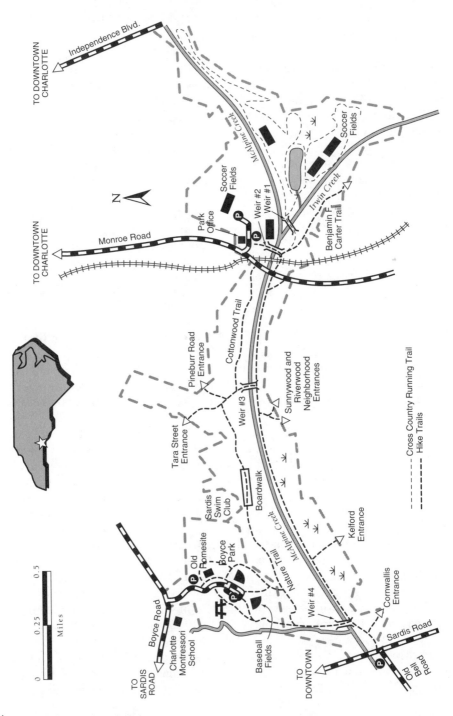

steeply at some point, through pleasant pines and leafy hardwoods. Just looping these trails together is a good leg-stretcher.

The best bet for a pleasant hour (or more) walk in this area is to descend from Boyce Park and make a nice long loop by combining the Nature Trail and the **McAlpine Greenway Trail**. Enter the woods directly behind the restrooms by following the edge of one of the ball fields; or, from the distantmost parking area, beside the small playground, strike out across the meadow along the right side of the ball field to where the trail enters the woods. Starting on this second route, enter the woods on the road-width trail and bear left at the first junction. (The trail to the right heads back through woods toward the parking area, a picnic shelter, and another trailhead on the road into Boyce Park.)

Going left, the trail descends through deciduous trees (a school athletic track is visible on the right) to a junction with a bench and a "No Horses" sign. Go to the right; to the left is the Nature Trail, which levels off and wanders through a pleasant forest that you'll see on your return. Going right, the trail levels at the elevation of McAlpine Creek through big beeches and oaks. You'll cross a small side stream on a bridge with a bench beside it, and then reach Weir 4, a low-water bridge. (If the water is high, don't cross; head back and take the Nature Trail.) If the weir is walkable, cross to the wide and developed greenway trail, about 0.4 mile from your start, and take a left.

After nearly 1 mile on the greenway (1.2 miles from the trailhead) take a left and cross Weir 3 on a paved neighborhood access trail. To the immediate right, the primitive Cottonwood Trail heads east along the creek, basically a less-used extension of the Nature Trail. Going straight, bear left where a paved side trail heads right to the Pineburr Road neighborhood entrance. The paved trail continues to the Tara Street neighborhood entrance, but go left at the next junction on the unpaved Nature Trail, about 1.3 miles from the start.

This next 0.5 mile or so back to Boyce Park is a pleasant walk through tunnel-like vegetation. Towering trees on the left separate the trail from McAlpine Creek; on the right, homes are visible in the surrounding neighborhood. You'll amble along a lengthy boardwalk (which can be slick in damp weather), past the Sardis Swim and Racquet Club, then into denser woods.

The next junction brings you to the first of the trails that climb the grade back up to Boyce Park. It's a bit eroded at first, splits on the way up, and the trail to the right splits again, but all arrive at or in the vicinity of the parking area and restrooms. All of these trails, one built in late 1993, rise through piney woods. Total distance is about 2 miles.

To lengthen the hike go straight along the last stretch of the Nature Trail and ascend up to the elevation of Boyce Park past the junction you passed earlier. Go left at the last junction and you'll skirt the playground and arrive at the picnic shelter near the parking area for a 2.4-mile hike.

You could avoid the climb to Boyce Park, or just vary your starting point, by parking at the Old Bell Road trailhead on Sardis Road and making this

A boardwalk carries McAlpine Park's Nature Trail past marshy, low-lying parts of Boyce Park.

circuit with a start on the greenway. This hike is about 2.4 miles.

The more primitive trail **Cottonwood Trail** is less used than the Nature Trail. It passes through an impressive cottonwood forest that rangers say may contain the largest tree of that species in the state. Hikers from either of the above trailheads can easily lengthen the circuit hikes just described by adding the Cottonwood Trail and the next section of the greenway trail that parallels it across the creek.

To just make a circuit hike of the Cottonwood Trail and the greenway, the best trailhead to use is the parking area at the McAlpine Park entrance/headquarters. The park entrance trailhead can also be a good starting point for the larger combined loop of the Cottonwood and Nature trails. The distance is about the same as the hike from Boyce Park.

To just hike the Cottonwood Trail leave the parking area at the park headquarters, follow the nicely landscaped paved path to Weir 2 and go right. At about 0.2 mile, you'll pass under a railroad bridge and Monroe Road emerging on the longest stretch of the Greenway (a side trail, which you'll use later, drops down from Monroe Road on the left).

Go right across Weir 3 at 0.9 mile and immediately go right onto the Cottonwood Trail. This is a wonderful wooded walk, with glimpses across the wide creek to the Greenway, through towering cottonwoods. After about 0.7 mile (1.6 miles from the start), the trail emerges onto Monroe Road, where hikers should walk to the right over the bridge that spans the Greenway. Once over the bridge, descend to the right onto the Greenway and go under the bridge for a return to the parking area. The round-trip hike is about 2 miles.

Adding the Cottonwood Trail loop onto the loop formed by the Nature and Greenway trails from Boyce Park (omitting the portion of the Cottonwood Loop from Monroe Road to the park office) adds about 1.5 miles to those hikes, creating walks of about 3.5 and 3.9 miles.

Omitting Boyce Park, and starting from the Old Bell Road trailhead, the Nature Trail/Cottonwood Trail loop is about 4 miles, about the same distance as starting from the Monroe Road park entrance.

32 *CROWDERS MOUNTAIN STATE PARK*

Overview

As the closest, most dramatic mountain park to Charlotte, Crowders just about says it all. The peak can indeed be crowded on weekends. It has a variety of trails, however, that make it well worth a visit. The park is composed of two major summits, Crowders Mountain (1,625 feet) and Kings Pinnacle (1,705 feet). Both are composed of kyanite-quartzite, very

Hikers hop across the crest of Crowders Mountain. *Charlotte Observer photo.*

hard rock that, like the volcanic material in the Uwharries at Morrow Mountain State Park, has resisted erosion and left isolated summits well out in the Piedmont and above the surrounding terrain; each summit rises as much as 800 feet above the land around it.

Crowders Mountain, a registered natural heritage area where cliffs soar 150 feet high, was not acquired as a state park until the early 1970s. Early in that decade, it became likely that Crowders and its adjoining peak would be mined. Kyanite had been stripmined in earlier days, and the area had been gripped by gold fever during the early 1800s when North Carolina was the nation's dominant source of gold. Local citizens opposed to the prospect of mining organized to save the mountain, state funds were appropriated, and much of the area was purchased. The park opened in 1974, but Kings Pinnacle didn't become public land until 1977. Crowders Mountain State Park currently claims about 2,000 acres.

Today the rock of Crowders is a major focus for climbers. The cliffs that surround the peak constitute one of the best rock-climbing sites in the state outside of the mountains. Guidelines are posted, but anyone interested in climbing should contact the part office in advance for information on which areas are open and how to register. There is no climbing permitted on Kings Pinnacle.

Besides climbers, the cliffs attract raptors. Black and turkey vultures are a common sight; they nest on the peaks. Like other monadnock parks, Crowders is a great place for birding, especially in the spring.

The park's facilities are modest. A 9-acre lake, with canoes available for rent at the park office (June through Labor Day), offers fishing for bass and bream. A picnic area is located near the lake. Secluded camping sites for groups and individual backpackers are about 1 mile from the park office. Group sites can be reserved in advance, and accommodate from 10 to 15 people. The individual backpacking sites are available on a first-come, first-served basis. Both types of sites have tent spots, a grill, and nearby water and pit toilets.

Visitors to Crowders Mountain would do well to include a stop at la Gastonia, the Schiele Museum of Natural History and Planetarium. This museum is easily North Carolina's best museum of natural history. It includes a 0.75-mile nature trail. On the way to or from Crowders Mountain from Charlotte, take the Gastonia exit south on New Hope Road (Exit 20/Route 279) to Garrison Boulevard. The free museum (closed Mondays, open weekends 1-5 p.m. and regular weekday hours) is located at 1500 E. Garrison Blvd.; (704) 866-6900.

General description: A monadnock state park with hikes ranging from circuits of Crowders Mountain and Kings Pinnacle to a short, steep summit hike popular with rock climbers. There's also an interpretive nature trail and a lake loop.
General location: Near Charlotte.
Length: Circuits of Crowders Mountain are 5 and 3.3 miles; it's 1.8 miles directly to the summit. A 3.7-mile circuit traverses Kings Pinnacle. Two interpretive trails are less than 1 mile each.
Degree of difficulty: Easy for the Fern and Lake trails; moderate to strenuous for Kings Pinnacle and Crowders Mountain hikes.
Maps: USGS Kings Mountain, Gastonia quads; state park map/brochure available at park office.
Elevation gain and loss: Negligible for the Fern and Lake trails; about 1,810 feet for the Pinnacle Trail; 1,870 for the Crowders/Rocktop trail circuit; and 1,450 for the Backside/Tower trail circuit.
Trailhead elevation: About 800 feet for the Pinnacle, Crowders, Turnback, Fern, and Lake trails; 900 feet or the Backside and Tower trails.
High point: 1,705 feet on Kings Pinnacle for the Pinnacle Trail; 1,625 feet atop Crowders Mountain for the Rocktop, Backside, and Tower trails.
Water availability: Water is available at the park's developed facilities.
For more information: Crowders Mountain State Park, Kings Mountain. See Appendix C.
Finding the trailheads: Take Interstate Highway 85 south of Charlotte to Exit 13 and turn left on Edgewood Road, SR 1307. In 0.8 mile, turn right on U.S. Highway 29/74. Go 1.9 miles and turn left on Sparrow Spring Road, SR 1125. In 2.7 miles turn right (this is where the Crowders Trail crosses the road) and continue on Sparrow Spring Road In another 0.6 mile, turn right into the park. Take the first right inside the park to reach the ranger office and parking area for many of the Pinnacle, Turnback, and Crowders trails. Go left inside the park and use the first lot on the left for the Lake Trail or the second lot on the left for the Fern Trail.

32 CROWDERS MOUNTAIN STATE PARK

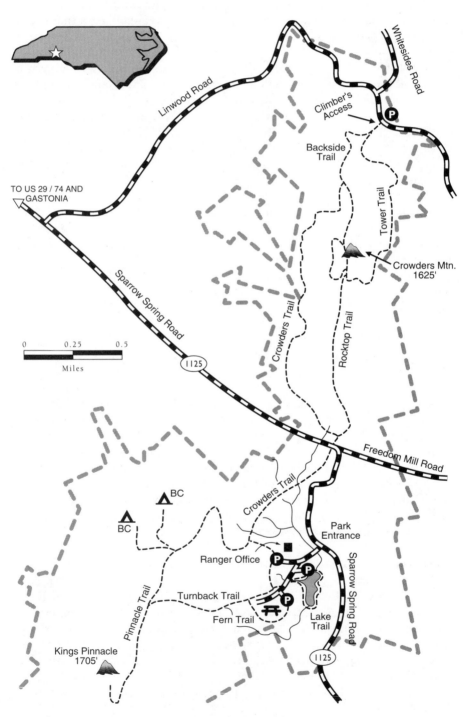

To reach the Backside and Tower trailheads, turn left from Sparrow Spring Road not far from US 29/74, on Linwood Road at a golf course. Go 1.6 miles to a junction and turn right. The trailhead parking area is 0.2 mile farther. From the park office, return toward US 29/74 and turn right at the golf course on Linwood Road.

The hikes: The yellow-blazed **Crowders Trail** and **Rocktop Trail** circuit hike scales Crowders Mountain from the vicinity of the park office. Together with the Backside and Rocktop trails, the Crowders Trail is the heart of a 5-mile hike over the summit.

Leave the park office on the road-width, pine-lined Pinnacle Trail, then turn right for Crowders Mountain; the Crowders Trail and the Rocktop Trail are combined for the first 0.8 mile through a beautiful hardwood forest. The trail crosses a few streams on the way to SR 1125, then goes across the road and up the embankment, where the trails split. The Crowders Trail slabs left and climbs through a forest that includes pine, along the northwest flank of the mountain. The trail intersects the Backside Trail (the quickest, most crowded route to the summit) on the left at 2.5 miles. Turn right on the Backside Trail. In 0.25 mile, you will climb steep steps to reach the summit at about 3 miles. Going left along the clifftops, you will get views reaching east all the way to the impressive skyline of Charlotte. Farther north, the clifftops become a scramble (care required). You may see rock climbers and rappelers on the faces.

To continue the circuit head southwest, taking the Rock Top Trail past the antennas on the Crowders summit and continue down the ridgetop where you might see Virginia pine, a dwarf tree only 3 to 6 feet high. The **Tower Trail** leads left at 3.4 miles, a connector to the Backside Trail, and the shortest loop over the summit. Continuing along the Rocktop Trail, hikers find the views are memorable. Large rocks and crags require scrambling. The trail descends the leading ridge of the mountain and winds to the junction with the Crowders Trail and SR 1125 at about 4.5 miles. Retracing your steps to the trailhead, the round-trip circuit hike is about 5 miles long.

The quickest way to the Crowders Mountain summit is up the backside—hence the **Backside Trail**'s status as the most heavily used path, especially on weekends. This is the preferred access for rock climbers. By adding the Tower Trail, hikers create the Backside and Tower Trail circuit, a more enjoyable way to see the summit than an up-and-down on the Backside Trail, but not as long or as time-consuming as the Crowders/Rocktop circuit.

From the new parking area ascend on the road-width, gated Tower Trail, which is actually the vehicle access route for the communications towers on the summit. Rising gradually through a pretty pine forest, turn right on the Backside Trail, site of rock climber information signs (neither trail is blazed). The building of the road-width Backside Trail in the late 1960s as part of a pre-mining mineral exploration project helped prompt local sentiment to preserve the area. It is steep in spots, so if you assume this shortest route is going to get you to the summit quickly, be prepared to huff and

A state park ranger enjoys autumn on the Tower Trail at Crowders Mountain State Park.

puff. The Backside Trail intersects the Crowders Trail at about 0.6 mile, just below the cliffs. Together they reach the summit and a junction with the Rocktop Trail. The round-trip on the Backside Trail is about 1.8 miles.

To lengthen the hike and make your return more interesting, head 0.4 mile southwest down the Rocktop Trail and turn left at 1.3 miles on the Tower Trail. The gradual, 2-mile descent takes you back to your car at 3.3 miles. Of course, you could reverse the direction of the above circuit for a gradual climb up the less-crowded Tower Trail and a quicker descent of the Backside Trail.

The less popular route to the park's highest peak, the **Pinnacle and Turnback Trail circuit**, is also worthwhile. Leave the park office on the Pinnacle Trail and bear left where the Crowders Trail goes right. The orange-blazed Pinnacle Trail winds then ascends the leading ridge of Kings Pinnacle. At just over 0.5 mile, a trail branches right to backpacker campsites. Continuing up a prominent ridge, the orange-blazed Turnback Trail heads left at about 1 mile. The Pinnacle Trail continues more steeply now, up to the first summit to good views at 1.5 miles, then descends between the peaks and climbs to the highest summit in the park (1,705 feet) at 1.7 miles. Fine views of Crowders Mountain and surrounding countryside are the reward.

On the descent turn right on the Turnback Trail and follow a portion of the **Fern Nature Trail** and a connector back to the office parking area for a 3.7-mile circuit hike. Or make the round-trip on the Pinnacle Trail, a little shorter at 3.4 miles.

The park's nature trail, The Fern Trail, starts in the picnic parking area on the left just past the lake. The easy 0.7-mile trail is keyed to red dots that describe points of interest along the route. Pick up a free copy of the interpretive brochure at a dispenser box just below a set of steps about 75 yards down the trail. The path loops around the picnic area, gaining its name from the ferns along the stream here. It eventually joins the Turnback Trail and turns right with it. The paths share a treadway for a short distance, then the Turnback Trail leads left to the park office and the Fern Trail goes right to terminate on the road between the lake and the nature trail parking area. Turn right on the road. At trail's end there's a box to return and recycle the guide brochure.

The 1-mile **Lake Trail** is a graveled and unblazed path that is perfect for a longer, easy walk. Park in the area on the left before the lake. A short access trail leads from the lot to the loop. The scenery often includes wildflowers, canoeists, and anglers. Wildlife is an attraction in the early morning.

Overview

Duke Forest was formed from farms and forest lands in the 1920s to buffer the developing campus of Duke University. The direction of Clarence F. Korstian led to the establishment of the university's school of forestry in 1938. The school's forest activities continue today, making the various tracts here an invaluable laboratory for students and scientists. More than 100 species of trees have been recorded. The predominant species is pine, of many varieties, with hardwoods mixed in. Forest maps available from the university denote the species composition by parcels, which makes it easy to take note of the type, and sometimes age, of trees you pass.

That kind of scientific precision explains why managers seem less than thrilled with public recreational use of the forest. Substantial effort has been expended to block hikers from what seem to be lightly impacted woods paths. Even popular foot trails here exhibit few trail construction techniques that might funnel use or minimize erosion. Nevertheless, responsible hikers will understand that, by necessity, many parts of the forest are closed for research purposes. And continued public access is contingent on recreationists' respect for the rules.

Duke Forest managers ask that hikers and mountain bikers stay strictly on road-width fire trails. That isn't much of an imposition, because the undulating roads are scenic. Do not bushwhack or hike cross-country, since many research plots and study areas lie throughout. Enter only at the gates designated for public access, and do not block them with vehicles. Developed picnic facilities, available for rent, are the only locations where open fires are permitted. No camping is allowed, and dogs should be leashed at all times.

Please read and heed the forest rules that are prominently posted at all access gates. Recent postings suggest that vehicle break-ins may be a problem at isolated locations.

General description: A handful of woodland tracts totaling 7,700 acres. Duke University conducts research and educational programs on the property, but permits public foot travel on road-width fire trails.
General location: Duke University, southwest of Durham.
Length: Hikes range from under 1 mile for an out-and-back walk to Laurel Hill Bluffs to 4 miles for the Cross-Country Trail and about 5 miles for a circuit of the Cement Bridge and Wooden Bridge Road Fire Trails.
Degree of difficulty: Easy for the Laurel Hill Bluffs; moderate for longer walks.
Maps: USGS Northwest Durham, Hillsborough, and Chapel Hill quads. The best maps of Duke Forest, which contain forest cover and topographic information, can be purchased from the address below.

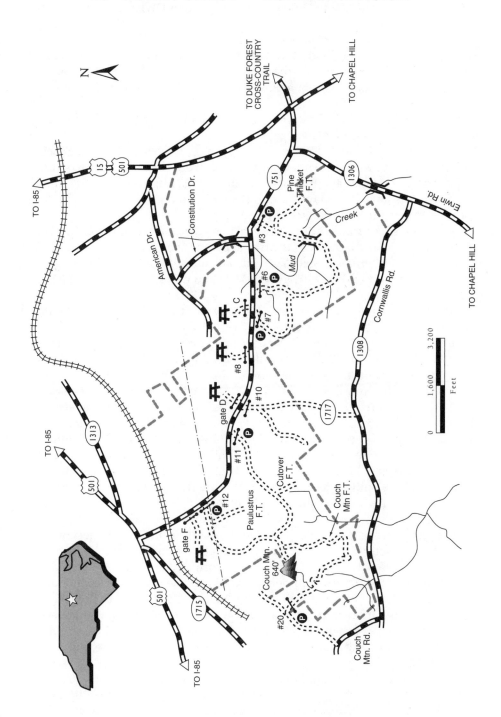

Elevation gain and loss: Generally negligible, though there are some pronounced ups and downs on trails in the Korstian Division of Duke Forest.

Trailhead elevation: 400 to 500 feet.

High point: 762 feet on Bald Mountain in the Blackwood Division; 640 feet on Couch Mountain on the Durham Division.

Water availability: No designated water sources in Duke Forest, so bring your own.

For more information: Duke Forest, Duke University School of the Environment. See Appendix C.

Finding the trailheads: To reach the Durham Division of Duke Forest and the trailhead for the Cross-Country Trail from the east, take Exit 175 from Interstate Highway 85 and go south on U.S. Highway 15/501. Take the North Carolina Highway 751 exit (Exit 107) and go left on NC 751. In 0.4 mile turn right into the gravel parking lot.

To reach other trailheads in this tract go right, or west on NC 751; all trailheads are on the left. From the traffic light at the NC 15/501 exit go 0.6 mile to gate 3, 1.2 miles to gate 7, 2 miles to gate 11, and 2.5 miles to gate 12. The T-junction with U.S. Highway 70 is at 3 miles; left there, to I-85 at 4.2 miles.

From the west leave Interstate Highway 40 at the NC 751/ University exit (Exit 170) and turn right onto NC 751 at 1.2 miles. The trailheads are on the right. From I-85, gate 12 is at 1.7 miles, gate 11 is at 2.2 miles, gate 7 is at 3 miles, and gate 3 is at 3.6 miles. A right turn onto Erwin Road (SR 1306) at 4.1 miles from I-85 takes you to the Korstian Division.

To reach the Korstian Division of Duke Forest and the Bluffs Trail, follow the same directions you would to reach the Durham Division above. After exiting US 15/501 go right on NC 751, then immediately left on Erwin Road (SR 1306). Go south past Mount Sinai Road (SR 1718) at 1.7 miles, cross New Hope Creek and gate 33 at 2.7 miles, and take the next right on Whitfield Road (SR 1731) at 3.1 miles. The start of the Bluffs Trail, gate 26, is on the right 0.7 mile after the turn to Whitfield Road. Gate 25 is reached at 1 mile and gate 24 is located at 1.5 miles.

The hikes: Duke Forest's 2,200-acre **Durham Division** is the largest of the Duke Forest tracts. Just across NC 751 south of the main Duke University campus, the **Cross-Country Trail** is its favorite hike. The trail starts at a gravel parking area on the south side of NC 751. Going west from the parking area, the 3-mile, gravel loop trail roughly follows Brownings Branch, then Sand Creek, in a triangular route around the Duke University golf course. Five emergency phones are located along its length. In the northeast corner of the loop, an approximately 1-mile fitness loop can be added to make the hike 4 miles total.

The bulk of the Durham Division acreage lies between NC 15/501 and NC 751's intersection with US 70 about 3 miles away. Two nice hikes are possible in this area. Going west from the Cross-Country Trail on NC 751,

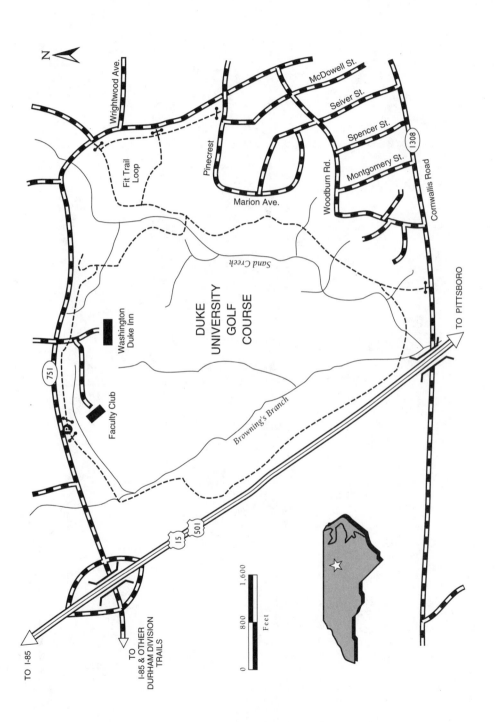

33 DUKE FOREST — KORSTIAN DIVISION

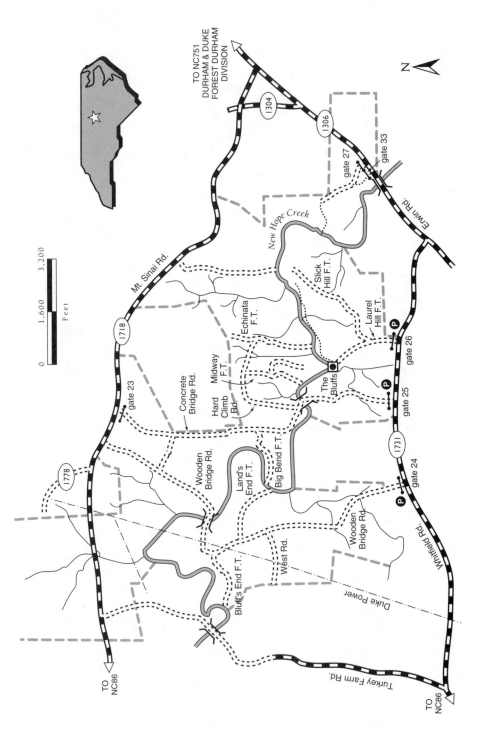

you'll pass forest access gates numbered 3 through 13 and various lettered gates on both sides of the road. Picnic tables are located at gate D and picnic shelters are accessible to those who've rented them via gates F and C.

Between gates 3 and 7, hikers have a 1.5-mile semicircular hike that requires two cars and could also be hiked as a 3-mile out-and-back walk from either trailhead. This hike winds through some of the forest's oldest stands of trees. Where the trail leaves gate 3 the loblolly and shortleaf pine forest on both sides of the trail is a century old. A side trail leads left not far from NC 751; this is the **Pine Thicket Fire Trail**. The main path continues to Mud Creek and crosses the stream on a scenic wooden bridge. Where the trail turns from south to north, the loblolly stands are sixty years old. A fire trail goes right to gate 6 and gate 7, where the pines to the left are again about 100 years old.

Farther west, Couch Mountain, the tract's highest prominence at 640 feet, is accessible from two trailheads. Starting on the fire trail at the first gate (11), hikers will pass two other fire trails that branch left. Go left on the third fire trail (to the right, the main trail leads back to NC 751 at gate 12). Keep straight past the next junction to reach the fire trail's end loop on the summit of Couch Mountain. The fire trail that branches left is part of the **Couch Mountain Fire Trail** and leads to gate 20. Retrace your steps to the main trail and go left. The trail turns sharply right along a powerline and reaches NC 751 at gate 12 for an approximately 2.5-mile hike.

Duke Forest's 2,000-acre **Korstian Division** is a scenic gem. The most appealing of the two major hikes here may be the best short walk on the forest. From gate 26 the **Laurel Hill Fire Trail** provides a 1-mile or less out-and-back walk to Laurel Hill Bluffs, an outcrop above New Hope Creek. The fire trail passes Slick Hill Fire Trail on the right (a 0.6-mile out-and-back hike that reaches an end loop). At the end loop of the Laurel Hill Fire Road a trail descends railroad tie steps and traffic flow fences to rock outcroppings overlooking New Hope Creek; rock climbing and bouldering are not allowed.

From the bank of the river one of the forest's most attractive woods paths wanders downstream. A rapid located about 200 yards east of the bluffs is a popular spot to cool off in summer. The trail winds along the bank, splitting occassionally into streamside and blufftop branches. Just beyond the first noticeable streamlet that comes in on the right is a scenic island. The rocky bluff just beyond is a turnaround point. The streamside trail continues along the river downstream to gate 33.

About 0.3 mile west of gate 26 is a 4-mile hike between gates 25 and 24. From gate 25, the next gate west of the Laurel Hill Fire Trail, the Concrete Bridge Road leads to and across New Hope Creek. The trail turns left just across the stream and **Hard Climb Fire Trail** branches right to a variety of side routes. Go left past where **Big Bend Fire Trail** heads left to the river. Continuing on the Concrete Bridge Road, turn left on the Wooden Bridge Road (straight ahead the Concrete Bridge Road soon reaches gate 23 on Mount Sinai Road).

Follow the Wooden Bridge Road and continue on that trail by going left at the next T-intersection. Now heading south on **Wooden Bridge Road**, the trail turns sharply northeast and crosses New Hope Creek on a wooden bridge. Across the creek the trail passes under a powerline, turns sharply south again, and passes the Bluff's End Fire Trail on the right. Continuing, the trail again goes under the powerline, passes **Land's End Road** on the left, **West Road** on the right, and makes its way to gate 24 at about 4 miles. Taking the trail from gate 25 out as far as the second bridge makes an out-and-back hike of about 5 miles that includes two points of contact with the creek. Though it would not be ideal hiking, visitors could make a loop by walking the 0.5-mile between trailheads along Whitfield Road.

34   ENO RIVER STATE PARK

Overview

Eno River State Park covers 2,304 acres in Durham and Orange counties. The rippling Eno River winds for 33 miles from its headwaters in Orange County to Falls Lake in Wake County, and the park protects a scenic 11-mile portion. The Eno's rapids cross the fall line, where the Piedmont descends to the coastal plain. Through the park, the Eno alternates between wide, slow-moving sections and sprightly whitewater. It is a popular canoeists' stream from Hillsborough all the way to Falls Lake.

Its fall-line location and the fact that the Eno is a clean river account for its diverse aquatic life. It contains ten species of freshwater mussels, five on the endangered species list. Eno mussels are a favorite food for muskrats, but they are protected by law from human consumption. The fifty-six species of fish found in the Eno represent a quarter of those recorded in the state and include largemouth bass, bluegill, chain pickerel, crappie, redbreasted sunfish, and catfish. The river is also home to the Neuse River waterdog, a rare aquatic salamander.

The park's 18 miles of red-blazed trails usually follow the river and its rocky bluffs, passing through forests of sycamore, river birch, ash, and musclewood. But the trails also wander away from the river up sizable, rocky hills where terrain and vegetation are remarkably similar to those found in the mountains. Prevalent plant species here are mountain laurel, rhododendron, pine, hickory, and oak. The last virgin timber to be harvested in the park was cut in 1941, but the woods have matured.

The park's noteworthy natural resources make it the perfect place to learn about nature. An educator's guide is available from the park head-quarters, and curriculum-based environmental education can be arranged. The leaders of school groups are encouraged to contact the park one month in advance for reservations and information.

Eno River in Durham, North Carolina.

The Eno is important for its human history as well. Long before European settlers arrived here, Eno and Shakori Indians built dams to trap fish in the small rapids. After white settlement, there were more than thirty grist, flour, and sawmills powered by the river. The earliest of these was built in the 1700s. A post-Civil War industrial revival in 1880 brought more mills, one every few miles. The modern industrial era dawned here with the creation of the Eno Cotton Mill in 1896. The sites of Few's Mill (1758-1908), and Holden's or Cole's Mill (1811-1908) are adjacent to hiking trails in the Few's Ford parcel of the park. Both mills included substantial structures, homes, and barns, few remains of which are visible from the trails.

The easiest way to appreciate some of the history of these early communities is to pause at the Piper-Dickson house, a late 1700s home beside the access road to the Buckquarter Creek and Holden's Mill trailhead (the first right past the park headquarters). The house is being restored and will one day be a museum. Until then, park headquarters has exhibits on various aspects of the park's human and natural history.

The park is a wonderful destination for novice backpackers. In the Few's Ford parcel, five numbered sites branch off the Fanny's Ford Trail about 1 mile from the parking area. Each site has a tent pad and a pit toilet nearby. No fires are permitted, and there is no water at the sites, but a water fountain is available during the warmer months at the day hiker trailhead. A group walk-in camping site is about 0.25 mile from the trailhead. A nightly fee is charged, and overnighters must leave a "camper" note visible in their vehicle.

General description: Several hikes exploring the Eno River's tumble over scenic ledges and deep pools on the fall line.

General location: Eno River State Park, northwest of Durham.

Lengths: 0.5 mile for Eno Trace nature trail; 2.8 miles for the Fanny's Ford Trail; 3.8 miles for Cox Mountain Trail, 1.5 miles for the Buckquarter Creek Trail; 4.1 for the Buckquarter Creek/Holden's Mill Trail circuit; about 3 miles for the Bobbit's Hole/Cole Mill Trail circuit; 1.3 miles for the Pea Creek Trail; 3.1 miles for Pea Creek/Dunnagan's Trail circuit; and 1.5 miles for the Pumpstation Trail.

Degree of difficulty: Easy for Eno Trace and Fanny's Ford Trails; moderate for everything else except the Cox Mountain Trail, which is moderately strenuous.

Maps: USGS Durham NW and Hillsborough quads. A hiking map is available from the state park office.

Elevation gain and loss: Negligible on most trails; about 620 feet on Cox Mountain Trail.

Trailhead elevations: About 450 feet at the main parking area at Few's Ford; about 410 feet for the start of the Buckquarter Creek Trail. The Cole Mill Parking area is about 400 feet.

High point: 680 feet on the Cox Mountain Trail; about 440 feet on Bobbit's Hole Trail.

Water availability: Though the Eno is a clean stream, hikers should bring water from home or use the park's facilities, including park headquarters. There are warm-weather water fountains beside the picnic area at the main trailhead in the Few's Ford parcel and beside the Cole Mill parking area.

For more information: Eno River State Park, Durham. See Appendix C.

Finding the trailheads: The park is located northwest of Durham and reached from Exit 170 on Interstate Highway 85. Going west, exit onto U.S. Highway 70 and turn right in 0.1 mile onto Pleasant Green Road, SR 1567. If coming east, exit and turn left onto US 70 west. Go back under the interstate 0.7 mile to a right onto SR 1567. Go 2.2 miles to a left turn onto Cole Mill Road, SR 1569. The park entrance to the Few's Ford parcel of the park is on the right in 0.8 mile, and the park headquarters is at 1 mile. The first turn to the right beyond the headquarters leads to the trailhead for the Buckquarter Creek and Holden's Mill trails. Beyond that turn, the road ends after 0.2 mile in a parking area that serves the Fanny's Ford, Cox Mountain, and Eno Trace trails. Campers heading to walk-in campsites on these trails should use the separate camper parking area on the left.

To reach the Cole Mill and Pumpstation parcels of the park, turn right from Pleasant Green Road onto Cole Mill Road instead of left to the park office. Go 1.15 miles and turn right into the trailhead parking area for the Cole Mill, Bobbit's Hole, Pea Creek, and Dunnagan's trails.

To reach the trailhead for the Pumpstation Trail go beyond the Cole Mill parking area and take the next left on Rivermont Road. Just past the bridge over Nancy Rhodes Creek, about 0.5 mile, park on the left side of the road by the park signs.

34 ENO RIVER STATE PARK

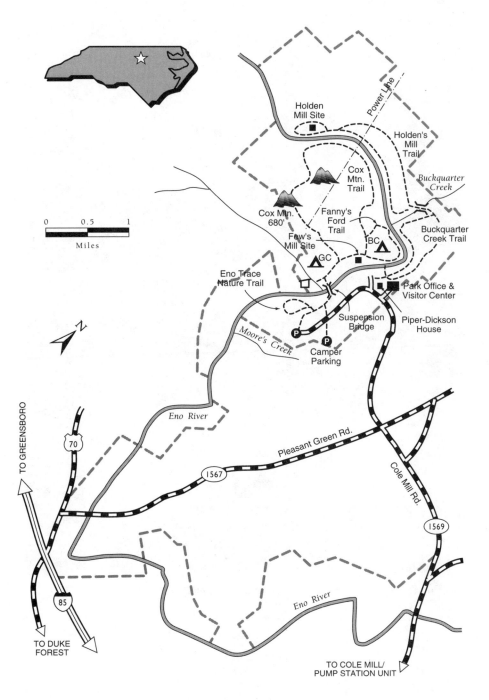

Holden Mill Site

Holden's Mill Trail

Power Line

Buckquarter Creek

Cox Mtn. Trail

Cox Mtn. 680'

Fanny's Ford Trail

Buckquarter Creek Trail

Few's Mill Site

BC

GC

Eno Trace Nature Trail

0   0.5   1
Miles

N

Park Office & Visitor Center

Piper-Dickson House

Suspension Bridge

P

Camper Parking

P

Moore's Creek

Eno River

TO GREENSBORO

70

Pleasant Green Rd.

1567

Cole Mill Rd.

1569

85

TO DUKE FOREST

Eno River

TO COLE MILL/ PUMP STATION UNIT

The Eno River tumbles over the fall line to the Coastal Plain.

The hikes: Currently, all trails in the park are blazed with red dots, though that may change in the next few years, say park officials.

The **Eno Trace** is a self-guided nature trail. Follow the trail from the main parking area of the Few's Ford area, past the water fountain and picnic tables. The trail turns and descends toward the river, and the signed Eno Trace Trail exits steeply to the left. The trail is level on the river (before rising back to the parking lot), but the steep descent and rooty, rocky treadway should deter people who require a perfectly flat walking surface. The 0.5-mile loop passes numbered stations keyed to a brochure available at the park office and at the trailhead. This is a nice spring wildflower hike.

Continuing past an intersection with the Eno Trace nature trail, the main trail descends, passes an access trail on the right (from a separate parking area for campers), and reaches the wood-and-cable suspension bridge across the Eno at about 0.2 mile. Take the bridge across the river and go 60 yards to a major trail junction. There, a left leads to a wilderness shelter and a group campsite (off to the right). A right at the junction leads to the Cox Mountain and Fanny's Ford trails.

Take a right on the old road grade of the **Cox Mountain Trail**. Pass the first left of the Cox Mountain Trail, then an old grade bears right (the route where the Fanny's Ford loop of the trail returns). Stay left and pass the second trail to the left, the other side of the Cox Mountain loop. The **Fanny's Ford Trail** turns east and follows the river back to rejoin the Cox Mountain Trail. There are five campsites in the end-loop area. The end loop of the trail is about 1 mile long, and the total round-trip is about 2.8 miles.

Following the same route over the suspension bridge, make a left onto the Cox Mountain Trail at the path closest to the river; the first trail immediately climbs the park's steepest, most sustained rise to the highest summit of Cox Mountain. The second trail wanders along the flat edge of the river on an old road grade. It crosses under a power line and continues on the bank where mature trees grow out to form a canopy over the river. At the streamside, you can see evidence of the dam that was once part of Holden's Mill.

The trail bears left away from the river along a small side stream, gradually climbing into a hardwood forest at the crest of Cox Mountain. A small dip separates the two hilltops, both about 680 feet. Piles of stone lie to one side of the trail. You again pass under the power line and start a steep descent through a pine forest. A bench is located about halfway down, useful for those who choose to climb this side of the trail. At the junction, go right and return across the suspension bridge. The entire hike is about 3.8 miles.

Probably the best hike in the Few's Ford parcel, for solitude and scenery, is a circuit of the Buckquarter Creek and Holden's Mill trails. The **Buckquarter Creek Trail** is 1.5 miles, but a combination of the three loops on both trails makes it possible to hike 4.1 miles without backtracking. By alternating which sides of the loop you take at each junction, the hike can be a constant combination of upland and riverside scenery. There is evidence of beaver activity on the river bank portions of both trails.

From the first parking area just past park headquarters, walk down to the river and go east along the bank. The Buckquarter Creek Trail immediately splits. The upland part of the 1.5-mile loop, the right fork, explores once-cleared land that was a farm a half century ago; you might catch glimpses from the trail of a few of the early homes that are still standing in this area. There are wintertime views from a ridge on this side of the trail. Both parts of the path rejoin near the river at a plank-topped steel bridge over the remarkably canal-like sidestream, Buckquarter Creek. A return from here is a 1.5-mile hike.

Cross the bridge to another trail split, this time for the **Holden's Mill Trail**, two loops totaling about 2.6 miles. The forest floor here is open except for Christmas fern. With the river gurgling on one side, birds call from the tall pines and hardwoods that tower overhead. Farther along, big outcrops and rocky crags line the river, creating a scene reminiscent of the mountains. Both branches of the trail pass beneath the same power line visible across the river on the Cox Mountain Trail. The trails again join at a tiny side stream amid an inspiring forest, and the shorter end loop of the Holden's Mill Trail branches out.

This loop explores the remains of Holden's Mill, actually looping below and then above the still visible stone wall. Not far from the end of the loop, on the upland side, an old road branches north. A side trip here leads past an old tobacco barn on the right, a startling two-story log cabin on the left, and an old collapsed hunting lodge on the right. Though not shown on the park map, this old road is visible on the USGS topographic quad.

Other good hikes are located in the Cole Mill and Pump Station parcels of the park. From the central trailhead on Cole Mill Road, the Cole Mill and Bobbit's Hole trails form an attractive figure-eight walk of about 2.6 miles. The highlight of this hike is Bobbit's Hole, a long-time swimming hole nearly 20 feet deep.

Leaving the middle of the parking lot at the water fountain, turn right on the **Cole Mill Trail** and go under a power line (the return end of the trail, with access to the Pea Creek Trail, leaves the corner of the parking area closest to the river). The quickest way to reach Bobbit's Hole is to turn left on the connector between the two trail loops, passing under a power line to go right on the Bobbit's Hole Trail. The trail follows the river through the park's typical riverside forest and crosses a bridge over Piper's Creek.

The trail reaches **Bobbit's Hole**, a deep pool at a major turn in the river. The main trail goes right to complete the loop, but a dead-end spur goes left to the end of the pool. Backtrack from there, continue on the loop, and go under a power line. Fewer people swim at Bobbit's Hole since the park ended vehicular access. The bottom is unchecked, so use caution if you're tempted to take a dip.

The trail rises away from the river to its high point in a mature hardwood forest of oak, hickory, and beech. Tiny Piper's Creek is again crossed, this time on stepping stones. At the junction with the connector between the Bobbit's Hole and Cole Mill trails, go left on the leg of the trail you

34 ENO RIVER –
COLE MILL / PUMPSTATION TRAILS

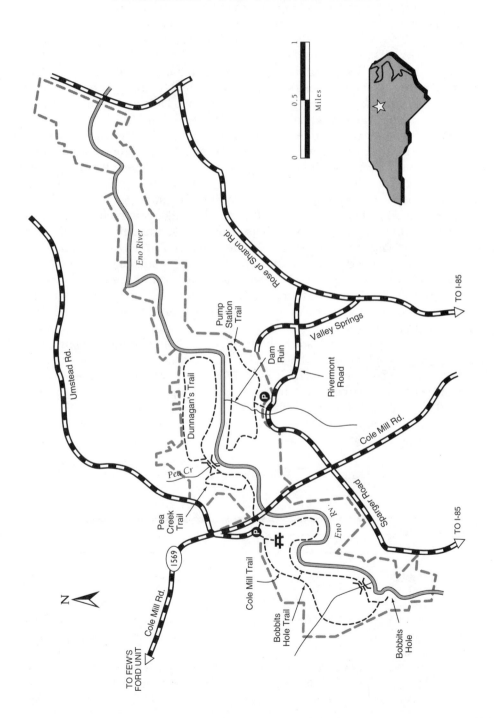

came in on to return quickly to the parking area for an approximately 2.5-mile hike. If you go right, the longest leg of the Cole Mill Trail follows a big bend in the river, creating a figure-eight circuit of about 3 miles.

That leg of the Cole Mill Trail returns to the end of the parking lot closest to the river. Just below the parking lot the Pea Creek Trail branches from the Cole Mill Trail and goes northeast under the bridge that carries Cole Mill Road over the Eno River. Heading downstream, the 1.3-mile Pea Creek Trail and the 1.8-mile Dunnagan's Trail form a 3.1-mile figure eight that is flatter and easier than the circuit formed by the Bobbit's Hole and Cole Mill trails.

The **Pea Creek Trail** passes under a power line. After it splits, the right branch follows the river. It then heads inland along scenic Pea Creek, a rocky stream that is particularly nice after rainfall. The trail reaches a bridge on the right that links it to Dunnagan's Trail. Above the bridge, the Pea Creek Trail continues to follow the creek, then turns left into the woods to rejoin itself on the way back to the parking area.

If you take **Dunnagan's Trail**, the easiest hike is to continue straight after crossing the bridge. The trail ascends a ridge gradually and follows it before dropping more steeply back to the river. Near the eastern end of the trail, there are good views of Durham's first city water plant on the other bank. Views of the old ruin are actually better from here than from the Pumpstation Trail across the river. The trail follows the river back to the bridge. Another obvious point of interest on the trail is an old homesite with a grave marker.

The **Pumpstation Trail** is the springtime choice for hikers wanting to see profuse displays of wildflowers. The 1.5-mile loop is bisected in opposite directions by a power line and Nancy Rhodes Creek. The eastern end of the trail passes the ruins of Durham's old drinking water treatment plant, in use from 1887 to 1927. The middle of the riverside leg of the trail passes an impressive stone dam. Now breached, it once impounded water for the pump station.

35   GREENSBORO TRAILS

Overview

Looking elsewhere in North Carolina, you might assume the state's reservoirs were built as subdivision sites for $500,000 mansions. A lack of such development and wonderful trails make Greensboro's Lake Brandt watershed unique.

Lake Brandt serves as a drinking water reservoir for the city of Greensboro. The 785-acre lake, named after mayor Leon Brandt (1907-1908), was built in 1925 and raised to its current level in 1958. Other lakes were constructed between the late 1970s and the early 1990s, and citizens said yes to purchasing a 750-foot buffer around them. About 30 miles of hiking paths have been built here, creating world-class, close-to-home places to enjoy nature.

Hikers can quickly be surrounded by silent, mature trees just minutes from the city. Sections of the trails wander through pine forests carpeted with running cedar. Other stretches explore deciduous woods; at times, the towering trees rise to impressive proportions. The trails view Lake Brandt's isolated coves, outstanding in fall when the shoreline forests are ablaze with color. Winter, so often mild in the Piedmont, is a wonderful time to watch seasonal migrations of waterfowl in the area's quiet, pearl gray days.

You might see people fishing, too. In Greensboro pleasure boaters are encouraged to use Lake Townsend, which helps keep Lake Brandt less developed. At Lake Brandt duck hunting is permitted; licenses are sold at the trailhead marina. No camping is allowed, though.

The trails are well maintained, so you needn't wear hiking boots. A sturdy pair of running shoes will do. Before hiking these trails consider sampling the nearby Greensboro Natural Science Center, a nature museum, planetarium, and zoo of regional significance.

General description: Extensive hiking in backcountry-like lakeshore natural areas.
General location: Greensboro, in the city's watershed at Lake Brandt and Bur-Mil Park.
Length: Lake Brandt's 3 trails total 10 miles. End-to-end trail walks average 3 miles, with out-and-back hikes of many lengths possible. Adjacent Bur-Mil Park has 4 miles of trails, arranged in 1- and 3-mile segments.
Degree of difficulty: Easy, except for the lengthiest circuit hikes.
Maps: USGS Lake Brandt quad. A map/brochure with mileage and trailhead location information and a map of Bur-Mil Park are available from the Greensboro Parks and Recreation Department.
Elevation gain and loss: Negligible.
Trailhead elevation: 740 feet at Lake Brandt Marina.
Water availability: At the Lake Brandt Marina, main trailhead for the Nat Greene Trail, a water fountain is located beside the main office and available from April through October. Water is available inside the building year-round when employees are present. Convenient stores are located at the junction of U.S. Highway 220 and Strawberry Road, and just south of the marina on Lake Brandt Road. At Bur-Mil Park, water and restrooms are available daily, year-round, at the clubhouse.
For more information: Greensboro Parks and Recreation Department. Or call the Lake Brandt Marina office or Bur-Mil Park. Also contact Greensboro Natural Science Center. See Appendix C.
Finding the trailheads: Access to trails in the Lake Brandt area is easiest via US Highway 220 (Battleground Avenue) in north Greensboro. To reach the trailheads for the Nat Greene and Piedmont Trails, turn right from US 220 onto New Garden Road at signs marking the Guilford Court-

house National Military Park. Take the next left onto Old Battleground Road. Measuring from that junction, turn right at 0.5 mile onto Lake Brandt Road, and at 1.75 mile, turn left onto Lake Brandt Road/Lawndale Drive. Turn left at 2.9 miles into the Lake Brandt Marina parking for the Nat Greene Trail (turn immediately left inside the marina onto a parking field), or go another 0.3 mile to parking for the Piedmont Trail on the other side of the dam spillway.

The other trailhead for the Nat Greene Trail is located on Old Battleground Road Take the original directions to Lake Brandt Marina, but pass Lake Brandt Road. The trail starts on the right side of Old Battleground Road 0.5 mile beyond that turn. The trailhead signboard is some distance from the road at the edge of the woods, so look carefully. Park in the gravel area at the gate, on the south side of the stream, closest to the power lines.

To reach this trailhead more conveniently from US 220 go north from New Garden Road 1.4 miles to a right onto Horse Pen Creek Road. That immediately enters Old Battleground Road, and the trail is on the left at about 0.9 mile.

To reach the main trailhead for the Owl's Roost Trail drive north on US 220. It becomes two lanes and passes the lake on the right. Take the next right on Strawberry Road, SR 2321. That turn is about 3.7 miles north of New Garden Road. The trail starts 0.1 mile on the right.

To reach Bur-Mil Park, an access for both the Bur-Mil Park Trail and the Owl's Roost Trail, drive north on US 220 from New Garden Road to a right onto Owl's Roost Road, at 2.5 miles, and make the next left into the park. The main trailhead for the Bur-Mil Park Trail is the major parking area on the left past the driving range. The trail starts beside the miniature golf course. To reach the start of the Bur-Mil Trail's smaller loop and another starting point for the Owl's Roost Trail, pass the main parking area, turn right at the clubhouse, then bear left down the gravel road by the barns to the last parking area beside the small pond. The trail begins near the lakeshore fishing pier.

The hikes: Three trails encircle Lake Brandt, but the paths fail to permit a true loop hike since two railroad trestle trail bridges that spanned arms of the lake were mysteriously burned in 1994 (one was rebuilt in 1995). The best hikes are out-and-back walks or end-to-enders arranged with two vehicles.

Named after General Nathanael Greene (see Hike 36), the **Nat Greene Trail** is a state historic trail that leads west from the Lake Brandt Marina and ends on Old Battleground Road in 3.2 miles. If the marina is closed, park at the gate; a formal access trail starts there, too, descending a gully to the preferred trailhead. The path enters the woods and immediately takes you through a tall pine and deciduous forest with open understory and a scenic green carpet of running cedar. In summer the lake shimmers through the vegetation, especially in the evening when the dipping sun casts this part of the trail in golden light. This is a great kids' walk.

35 GREENSBORO WATERSHED

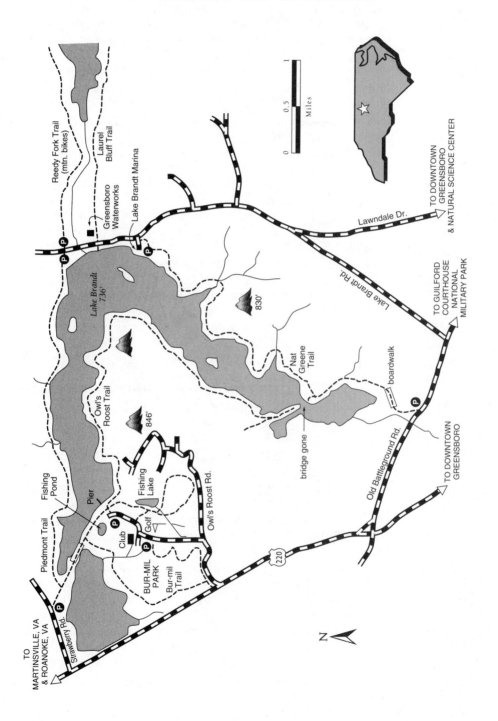

The trail splits just past a little bridge; the right fork wanders closest to the lakeshore where you can see freshwater mussels on the sandy bottom. The trails merge and cross a small stream in a cove and a larger stream at about the 1.5-mile mark. The trail slabs around a point covered in an unusual locust forest, then crosses a series of railroad tie bog logs (which can be slippery), before undulating through a mature pine and deciduous forest and joining a railroad grade at just under 3 miles. To the right the Owl's Roost Trail follows the railroad grade. The Nat Greene Trail jogs left on the grade then takes a right, marked the "General Greene Trail." The trail veers away from the railroad grade following the shoreline of the lake, then shows signs of having been an even older railroad grade. The trail trends away from the lakeshore and crosses a bridge in a marshy area, traversing a boardwalk and becoming very sandy along a stream just before exiting the woods beside Old Battleground Road at about 3.2 miles.

The **Owl's Roost Trail** bears right on the railroad grade from the Nat Greene Trail about 0.7 mile from Old Battleground Road. Unfortunately, the bridge that carried the trail across the lake and on to Strawberry Road in about 4.2 miles was one of two burned by vandals in 1994. This one may never be replaced and could force a reroute of the trail; check the latest trail maps. For now, this part of the Owl's Roost Trail is just a 0.2-mile side trip from the Nat Greene Trail for a view of the lake. It makes a particularly nice 1.8-mile round-trip evening hike from Old Battleground Road.

Lacking the bridge, the best starting points for a hike on the Owl's Roost Trail are Strawberry Road or Bur-Mil Park. From there the trail leads south into the lake's most isolated area. From Strawberry Road to the site of the missing bridge, it's a 3.5-mile hike one way. South from the tiny parking slip on Strawberry Road, the railroad grade trail parallels the lakeshore with kudzu-covered vegetation on the left. On the way, an opening on the right allows a fine view of the lake and US 220; the noise of the traffic fades at just about this point.

In a few tenths of a mile, the **Piedmont Trail** intersects your route on the left. The Owl's Roost Trail continues to a 300-foot bridge that spans the northern branch of Lake Brandt. This bridge, at about 0.3 mile, also burned in 1994 but sustained less damage and was rebuilt in 1995. (This initial out-and-back part of the hike is another great kids' walk.) Across the bridge, in Bur-Mil Park, the Bur-Mil Trail branches right along the shore of Lake Brandt. The wooded Owl's Roost Trail continues another 0.2 mile on the railroad grade to where steps lead to a parking area beside a fishing pond in Bur-Mil Park (about 0.5 mile from Strawberry Road). A fishing pier is on the left. The parking area here in Bur-Mil Park is another good place to start a hike on the Owl's Roost Trail.

Continue a short distance to a signed junction where the **Bur-Mil Trail** continues straight to a fishing lake. Go left on the Owl's Roost Trail as it follows the lakeshore and an even older railroad grade, then drops to cross a stream. It ascends around a cove close to some homes. Past the houses, the trail rises and falls with views back to the pier, and at about the 1-mile mark crosses a stream. The backcountry-like trail often leaves the lakeshore

The Nat Greene Trail combines lakeshore views and piney woods that glow as sunset bathes the lake.

as it winds around the peninsula that includes the area's highest elevation: 846 feet, more than 100 feet higher than the lake. Lake wardens call this large promontory The Horseshoe. At about 2.6 miles is a nice view down the lake to the marina. This is a good picnic/turnaround spot for a round-trip hike of just over 5 miles from Strawberry Road, or 4 miles from Bur-Mil Park.

The trail slabs below steep slopes along the south side of the promontory into a beautiful pine and deciduous forest, heavy with isolation and quiet. This area, once so convenient from the Nat Greene Trail before the bridge burned, is now about 3.5 miles from Strawberry Road, about 3 miles from Bur-Mil Park (a 7- or 6-mile round trip, respectively).

The last leg of the lakeshore circuit, the Piedmont Trail, can be hiked from Strawberry Road or Bur-Mil Park. From Strawberry Road go south. In about 0.2 mile turn left on the Piedmont Trail toward Lake Brandt Road 2.9 miles away. (From Bur-Mil Park go north, cross the bridge, and in 0.3 mile turn right.)

On its way along the northern shore of Lake Brandt the Piedmont Trail passes a broad, boggy area along the lake, crosses three streams, and at about the 1.5-mile mark traverses a boardwalk. The trail undulates through a scattering of cedars, then emerges to a lakeside view of the dam not far from Lake Brandt Road. The trail follows an old road grade to Lake Brandt Road, where Lake Brandt Marina is 0.2 mile south across the spillway.

Within Bur-Mil Park itself the 4-mile Bur-Mil Park Trail has two sections. A 3-mile segment, with mileage markers every 0.5 mile, circles the western side of the park. One leg follows the bank of Lake Brandt; another portion forms a 1-mile loop and passes the park's fishing lake. Parts of both trails coincide with the Owl's Roost Trail as described above.

To hike the 3-mile loop around the western portion of the park, a level trail popular with runners and mountain bikers, start at the miniature golf course and go left at the first junction. The trail flanks the driving range, swerves around soccer fields, and goes west to parallel Owl's Roost Road toward US 220. Go to the right with the trail as it turns north, avoiding a spur that goes left to a clearing by the highway.

The trail follows a stream drainage north, then heads east along the shore of Lake Brandt. A right turn onto the Owl's Roost Trail leads along the lake and past the second trailhead parking area beside the fishing pier. Just past the pier the Owl's Roost Trail goes left, and the Bur-Mil Trail continues into the loop portion of the path. The trail follows the right side of the fishing lake, and the 3-mile section of trail goes right to the gravel road, just up the hill from two barns that were erected when this was an estate of the Cone family, prominent Greensboro textile manufacturers. From there go left along the road past the clubhouse and left into the parking lot/trailhead at about 3 miles.

The smaller loop begins near the lakeshore and reaches the fishing lake as described above. When the main trail goes right, go left and continue along the lake. Near the head of the lake and picnic shelter 7 the trail branches into its forested end loop below Par 3 golf course. From the trailhead near the pier the total loop is about 1 mile.

36 *GUILFORD COURTHOUSE NATIONAL MILITARY PARK*

Overview

Serious hikers longing for the mountains will surely choose nearby state parks such as Pilot Mountain and Hanging Rock over this park, and even woods walkers may prefer the trails around nearby Lake Brandt. But this historic military park is nevertheless a jewel, especially for walkers and joggers on weekends or at the end of the workday (Pets must be on a leash, and in-line skating is not permitted). Guilford Courthouse National Military Park has a fine visitor center that tells the story of the pivotal Revolutionary War battle of Guilford Courthouse on March 15, 1781, and the American general, Nathanael Greene, who gave his name to Greensboro. An impressive visitor center and museum offers a slide program, historic dioramas, artifacts, a wealth of publications, and outdoor musket firings on weekends.

A 2.5-mile, one-way, paved road loops though the park, one lane of which is a designated bike path. Gated daily at 5 p.m., the entire road is turned over to cyclists, joggers, and walkers, some pushing baby carriages. That provides a lengthy, easy walk that is very nice, especially in summer, when daylight lasts until nearly 9 p.m. Paved paths branch from the road, creating loops, and a stretch of colonial road bisects the park. There are connections to other adjacent parks, too, all of which create options for walkers.

The park is most recommended for its forest. Whether you're hiking on the road or on a trail, its woods are mature and impressive. An almost manicured understory of evergreens and ornamental trees sprouts below a towering overstory of pines and massive hardwoods. Evening walks yield views of golden sidelight piercing deep shade. Bridges span streams that run through the undulating terrain. And forest gives way to hilly meadows, where heights of land overlook tight valleys reminiscent of a setting where a battle took place. Add the early morning curl of mist in swales below now silent cannons, and Guilford Courthouse National Military Park offers a startling feel for the lives and ideals of the men who fought here long ago.

Twenty-eight monuments dot the park, ranging from grave markers and obelisks to a massive equestrian statue of General Greene atop a marble plaza. Memorials crop up in the most remote locations. The park's interpretive signing provides a memorable account of the battle here, which the British barely won. Cornwallis's forces were pummeled by the daring Greene. The American army was still so strong following the battle that Cornwallis retreated to the coast, virtually abandoning the South to the Revolutionary Army and laying the groundwork for his defeat at Yorktown just seven months later. Three outdoor interpretive displays boast dramatic audio programs and maps detailing the action at the American lines, which are also explored by trail. Many other trailside signs narrate historical vignettes.

The old colonial road passes a cannon battery at Guilford Courthouse National Military Park. The fiercest fighting took place in these meadows.

Another plus for visitors is the City of Greensboro's adjacent Tannenbaum Park, opened in 1988. Only a block or so away at the corner of Battleground Avenue and New Garden Road, the park is centered on the Hoskins House, a restored home that was built on that site in 1778 and used as a residence during the battle. A relocated barn dates from 1820, and a blacksmith shed adds to a display that is the site of living history programs. There is also a large visitor center with many exhibits. In March, Tannenbaum hosts an annual recreation of the battle. Hundreds of uniformed participants stirringly re-enact the fight during a three-day encampment where the public can wander among tents and campfires.

General description: A fine urban hiking destination with paved and graveled forest paths including the remains of a colonial road. The park figured in one of the most significant Southern battles of the Revolutionary War.
General location: Guilford Courthouse National Military Park, in Greensboro.
Length: The roadside bike lane, often used by walkers, is a 2.5-mile loop. Other hikes range from loops of 0.3 and 0.5 mile to a 2-mile out-and-back hike on the park's wooded paths.
Degree of difficulty: Easy, and partly barrier-free.
Maps: The USGS Lake Brandt quad shows little detail of the park. The park's visitor map is preferable and available from the address below.
Elevation gain and loss: Negligible.
Trailhead elevation: 800 to 850 feet.
Water availability: Water is obtainable throughout the year at the visitor center. There is a water fountain at a satellite restroom facility open spring through fall.
For more information: Guilford Courthouse National Military Park, Greensboro. Also Tannenbaum Park. See Appendix C.
Finding the trailhead: The park is located between Old Battleground Road and Lawndale Drive in northwestern Greensboro, 0.5 mile off Battleground Road (U.S. Highway 220) on New Garden Road. The route to the park is marked from various interstate exits, including the Interstate Highway 40/85 Randleman Road exit (about 6 miles).

The hikes: The walks described below are just a few of the many in the park, and range from a short loop near the visitor center to a hike that encompasses virtually all of the park's woodsiest paths.

The easiest stroll involves crossing the parking lot from the visitor center and taking the paved path that departs in the direction of the loop road. Going straight across the off-road bike path at the first junction, hikers loop past the first stop on the road tour, the American first line. This is an easy jaunt through tall timber. Old-style timber fences stand in the woods, and squirrels chatter everywhere. The hike loops back to the visitor center in about 0.2 mile.

Another easy walk, and one that nicely extends the one above, leaves the visitor center parking lot at its farthest point from the building (about where the walk above ends), and heads across Old Battleground Road. Cross the next gravel road to the left and continue on the paved path paralleling the loop. At the second stop on the loop road, the American second line, the path wanders left through the woods to the Greene Monument, with its stirring, archaic wording. Pass the monument and go left onto the old colonial road to another crossing of Old Battleground Road. You can go left on a gravel path back to the trail you used to reach the monument, but go straight across Old Battleground Road to another group of monuments under tall trees. One honors the local Quaker women who tended to the wounded of both sides. Taking a left just beyond these monuments leads to the front of the visitor center and your car. The two connected loops total about 0.6 mile.

To create the lengthiest walk from the visitor center, link both loops as described above and reach the Greene Equestrian Monument. Turn right on the colonial road and immediately get a flavor of this tree-lined thoroughfare. Pass a trail junction on the left (part of a loop you'll take later that encircles the meadows where the fiercest fighting took place). The old road reaches a cannon and benches on a bluff overlooking the meadow where the battle raged. Across the meadow, cannons on the opposing bluff mark the American third line. From this high point, Cornwallis ordered grapeshot fired into his own ranks at the skirmish line to turn the tide of battle against the Americans, who seemed to be winning. As the road dips past the bluff into the meadow go right on the other side of the loop trail. Stop as you make the turn and listen to the third line program at the only off-road audio sign.

The loop trail winds to a bridge spanning a brook that could have carried the blood of the combatants. The trail climbs to another meadow-covered bluff at the edge of the loop road. Here, and visible across the meadow near the distant cannons, obelisks honor military units and individual British and American fighters. The parking area here is tour stop 4 on the loop road. On the opposite side of the meadows and out of sight beyond the cannons is the roadside parking area for tour stop 6. Either is a fine place to park for those who just want to hike this meadow circle of about 0.6 mile.

Continue on the loop hike to the colonial road and go right. You've hiked the right spur on the way out, and the left side of the loop remains for the way back. Keep on the colonial road, pass a trail that leaves to the left, and when you reach the paved road, walk the bicycle lane until the paved road veers right and you can again go straight onto the colonial road (passing a second trail on the left). Just ahead, restrooms, a water fountain, and another audio sign mark the site of Guilford Courthouse (tour stop 5 on the loop road).

From here head back the way you came, but take a right on the side trail instead of walking the paved bike lane. (In fact, many walkers might prefer to take the side trail coming and going). The trail dips to a scenic

36 GUILFORD COURTHOUSE
NATIONAL MILITARY PARK

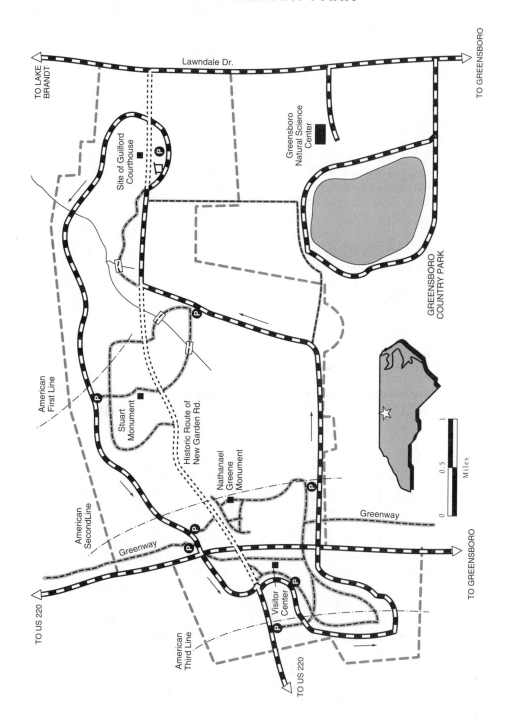

stream crossing. Back on the colonial road go right. When you reach the opposite side of the meadow loop, turn right and climb to the cannons and monuments along the bluff that marks the American first line at tour stop 6 on the loop road. The trail dips from there, then rises back to the colonial road. Go right and end your hike as you would the second easy walk described above: cross Old Battleground Road and pass the monuments to the visitor center for an approximately 2-mile walk.

A paved parking lot on Old Battleground Road (across from the visitor center and visible from the Greene Monument) is a favored parking area when the park's loop road is gated and can also be the start of the hike described above.

The park's longest walk is the 2.5-mile paved bike path, best walked after the park gate is closed and cyclists take to the auto side of the road. To add an interesting side trip to that hike, follow the path away from the loop road at the Winston Monument, loop tour stop 3, site of the last shots fired by American riflemen. Follow this into adjacent Greensboro Country Park, go left around the northern part of the lake, then go left again past the zoological exhibit area of the Greensboro Natural Science Center to re-enter the military park near stop 5 on the loop tour road. (See Hike 35, the Greensboro Watershed Trails, for more on the Natural Science Center.)

Hikers who combine parts of the tour road with the trails can greatly expand the shorter strolls into satisfying walks. A glance at the map will make these options obvious.

HANGING ROCK STATE PARK (37-38)

Overview

Easily accessible from the Piedmont cities of Winston-Salem and Greensboro, Hanging Rock State Park is an eyeful for flatland-weary hikers. The small collection of summits cluster together, forming a high bowl around a pristine lake. The peaks of Hanging Rock—Moore's Knob, Cook's Wall and others—jut up admirably to heights ranging from 2,100 to 2,500 feet above sea level, a sizable leap above surrounding 800-foot terrain. From the rural area around the park (an attraction for "shunpikers"), the summits soar remarkably. Hanging Rock State Park incorporates the bulk of the Sauratown Mountains, the state's most easterly range.

Local rock climbing, now principally focused on Cook's Wall and Moore's Wall, got its start here in the late 1950s and is now very popular. Hikers also will be pleased with this park. Although its summits aren't high enough to offer cooler summer temperatures than the surrounding Piedmont, its vegetation is similar to that found on the state's higher peaks. Mountain laurel, rhododendron, galax, oak, fern, and hemlock clothe the slopes and cling to the waterfall-filled drainages. Hikers may notice downed and broken trees from an ice storm that struck the park in March 1994; the park was closed for months until debris could be removed from roads and trails. You'll notice small lizards on the trail during most summer hikes, and you might see salamanders streamside.

Just getting to the park brings scenic rewards. You'll notice ancient log cabins in the area, and the quaint town of Danbury, the Stokes County seat, has a beautiful century-old courthouse that anchors a National Historic District.

Hanging Rock State Park recalls the role played by the Civilian Conservation Corps (CCC) in early park development. The park's roads, trails, 12-acre lake, and a stone bathhouse that's now on the National Register of Historic Places were all built by the CCC in seven years after the first 3,000 acres of land were donated to the state in the mid-1930s. By 1996 two barrier-free paths, one to a picnic site and another to a pier in the lake, will be added.

The park has many group camping and developed sites for tents and self-contained RVs, six rustic vacation cabins, and two picnic areas with sixty sites and fifteen grills each. Fishing for plentiful bass and bream is permitted in the clear, cold lake (state license required) and rowboats and canoes are available for rent in summer. A designated swimming beach has snack service and changing facilities.

The view from House Rock on the Cook's Wall Trail.

37 COOK'S AND MOORE'S WALLS TRAILS

General description: Two loop hikes north of Winston-Salem, with spectacular views from rocky cliffs that are popular with rock climbers, and an adjoining interpretive trail.

General location: Hanging Rock State Park.

Length: Cook's Wall Trail, 4 miles round-trip, with shorter hikes of 1.6, 2.4, and 3 miles; Moore's Wall Trail, just under 5 miles round-trip; Chestnut Oak Nature Trail, 0.7 mile.

Degree of difficulty: Moderate for nearby views; moderately strenuous for the Cook's Wall and Moore's Wall hikes; strenuous for a combination of the two. Easy for the nature trail.

Maps: USGS Hanging Rock quad. State park map/brochure available at park office and from address below.

Elevation gain and loss: Approximately 1,680 feet for Cook's Wall; 1,800 feet for Moore's Wall.

Trailhead elevation: 1,720.

High point: 2,480 feet at Cook's Wall; 2,579 at Moore's Wall.

Water availability: The park is open year-round, and water is available at a variety of facilities, primarily picnic areas, restrooms, a concession stand, campgrounds, and the park office. Streams are crossed on both hikes, but carry your water.

For more information: Hanging Rock State Park, Danbury. See Appendix C.

Finding the trailheads: From Winston-Salem, the fastest route to the park follows U.S. Highway 52 north, taking a right onto North Carolina Highway 65 into Rural Hall, then a left onto North Carolina Highway 66. About 0.5 mile beyond the tiny burg of Gap, go right onto SR 1001 to the park entrance. From Greensboro, go north on U.S. Highway 220 and turn left onto U.S. Highway 158, to Stokesdale. There, take a right onto NC 65 to Walnut Cove. Go north on North Carolina Highway 89/U.S. Highway 311 through Walnut Cove, then left on NC 89 to Danbury. Just over 2 miles past downtown Danbury, go left on SR 1001 to the park entrance at about 4 miles.

The Cook's Wall and Moore's Wall trails both begin in the upper, most distant parking area (just stay straight after entering the park). Leave the parking area at the corner closest to the lake on the wide path leading to the bathhouse and beach.

The hikes: The **Cook's Wall Trail** is probably the least traveled of the park's main trails; a great choice for a busy summer or fall weekend. The hike dead-ends at Devil's Chimney, a peak beyond Cook's Wall, for 3.8-mile round-trip, out-and-back hike. But you can choose a slightly different but equidistant route that gives this the feel of a loop hike. If you'd rather shorten the walk, you can omit Cook's Wall itself; there are great views at Wolf Rock and House Rock, both accessible on a 3-mile loop. The

37 AND 38 COOK'S AND MOORE'S WALLS TRAILS —
HANGING ROCK STATE PARK

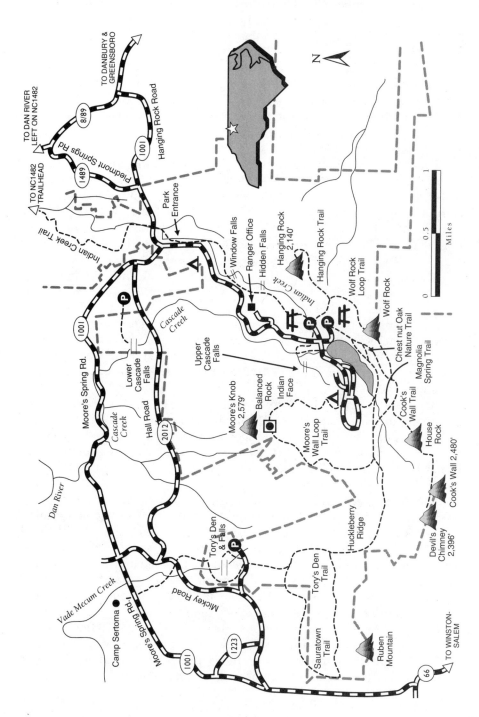

shortest hike on this trail is an out-and-back walk to a view at Wolf Gap, about 1.6 miles.

From the parking area take the road-width trail and make a sharp left. Do not go up the stone steps of the bathhouse, but up the trail steps even farther left. A sign then points to the right along the fenceline parallel to the building and the lakeshore. Take this busy trail with the knowledge you'll soon be on more solitary terrain.

Take the first left on the **Chestnut Oak Nature Trail**. You can pick up the guidebook to the numbered posts on this interpretive path here on the trail or, better, get one at the ranger station on the way in. The easy 0.7-mile loop nature trail from the parking area isn't particularly steep, but the footing is irregular and rocky.

Take the first left off the nature trail and follow the white dots up the scenic, graded Cook's Wall Trail as it climbs through galax and mountain laurel. From here on out, the trail has a character reminiscent of higher North Carolina mountains. At the ridgetop trail junction in Wolf Gap (about 0.8 mile from the parking area), the yellow-blazed Cook's Wall Trail goes right to Cook's Wall; left, the **Wolf Rock Trail** leads to a junction with the **Hanging Rock Trail** (see Hike 38).

Taking a left at the junction, you'll reach Wolf Rock in 0.4 mile. Going right at the junction, hikers will immediately reach a rock outcrop on the left, the shortest hike to a view on this trail, about 1.6 miles round-trip. Continuing along the ridgetop through summer vegetation or past winter views of Moore's Wall to the right, reach another junction about 1.3 miles from the trailhead. The white blazed, unsigned **Magnolia Spring Trail** drops right, a connection to the Moore's Wall Trail and your return route for a loop hike.

Stay left for now. The Cook's Wall Trail slabs gradually, then more steeply up to spectacular House Rock, about 1.5 miles from the trailhead. This flat-topped cliff is an inspiring spot with a perch and south-facing view of the Piedmont. Off to the left, Hanging Rock appears as a rock-capped bump on the next ridge. The clearest days bring Winston-Salem and Greensboro in the distance.

Continuing, the level trail climbs through rhododendron, chestnut oak, mountain laurel, pine, and maple trees. The trail crosses Cook's Wall, a wooded knob with a sheer cliff popular with rock climbers. Many little side paths, mostly climber's trails, head left to the cliffs, some with nice views.

The trail continues past Cook's Wall, losing elevation into Cool Gap then gaining it back across a grassy summit that gives way to good views from open crags. This is Devil's Chimney (2,396 feet), about 1.9 miles from the trailhead. From here, it's easy to see the rock faces that make Cook's Wall a favorite with climbers. Ravens often soar overhead. To the west, the graceful wave of the Sauratown Mountains crest toward the distinctive plug of Pilot Mountain. To the northwest, the rippled wall of the Blue Ridge juts up, surprisingly close, on its northeast-to-southwest march from Virginia into northwestern North Carolina. And north, Moore's Wall rises, a mix of rock and trees. This is the place for an isolated picnic.

Retracing your steps, you can return the way you hiked in, for a 3.8-mile round-trip. Or you can create a loop: Go left on the Magnolia Spring Trail instead. Its meandering 0.4-mile descent ends at a few small bridges over a stream and a junction with the red-blazed Moore's Wall Trail, about 2.9 miles from the trailhead. Here the most energetic hikers might go left and hike the Moore's Wall Loop (see below), finishing a nearly 8-mile trip that will make you feel like you've had a serious day hike.

To return to the parking lot more quickly go right, crossing a zigzagging boardwalk, and take a right at the next junction where the return loop of the Moore's Wall Trail comes in on the left at about 3.2 miles. This junction is marked poorly, and side trails make it confusing: just stay right. You'll cross a boardwalk over the lake's boggy inlet. The lakeside walk, which passes the return junction with the nature trail, is beautiful in fall. Back at the bathhouse parking area, the entire hike is 3.9 miles.

The **Moore's Wall Loop** is the park's most-traveled major trail. Its scenery makes that understandable. But it is about 5 miles long and strenuous, so unless it's the weekend of peak autumn color, you shouldn't find it crowded. Begin this hike in the same way as the Cook's Wall Trail, but keep right on the Moore's Wall Loop Trail at the Chestnut Oak Nature Trail (first left) and follow the scenic edge of the lake past the second connection to the nature trail and cross the boardwalk that bridges the feeder stream. Take the next left (about 0.7 mile from the trailhead), even though it's unmarked; you will soon reach a sign. The now level path crosses another boardwalk and passes a junction with the Magnolia Spring Trail at about 1 mile. Stay right, on the trail marked by red (Moore's Wall) and white (Sauratown Trail) plastic blazes.

The trail climbs gradually through hardwoods. It follows a short reroute (caused by the 1994 ice storm) up the hillside then heads back down to its streamside location. Branching right from the Sauratown Trail (also the blue-blazed route to Tory's Den Falls) at about 1.6 miles from the trailhead, the trail climbs steeply at times up the main ridge of Moore's Wall. This popular rock-climbing site, with cliffs up to 400 feet high, lies off to the left. The ridge then levels off for the meander to Moore's Knob, the highest peak in the Sauratown Mountains (2,579 feet). An old North Carolina Forest Service fire tower, reached at about 2.9 miles, provides great views.

The descent passes a balancing rock and a formation called Indian Face, then plummets to Cascade Creek, at about 4 miles. After a climb up from the creek turn left behind the park's amphitheater. Then, keeping right, reach the campground road. Follow the red dots on the road to the sign near site 39 directing hikers back toward the lake. At the junction with the Moore's Wall Trail go left, passing the lake and returning to the parking lot for a 5-mile loop.

General description: A popular and spectacular hike to the rock-capped vantage point of Hanging Rock. Other trails reach scenic waterfalls, and a few short paths are accessible to people in wheelchairs.

General location: Hanging Rock State Park.

Length: 2.2 miles round-trip for the Hanging Rock Trail. Hikes to Hidden Falls and Window Falls can range from 0.4 mile to 1 mile.

Degree of difficulty: Easy to moderately strenuous for waterfall trails; moderately strenuous for Hanging Rock Trail.

Maps: USGS Hanging Rock quad. State park map/brochure available at park office.

Elevation gain and loss: About 1,040 feet.

Trailhead elevation: About 1,700 feet.

High point: 2,140 feet.

Water availability: The park is open year-round, and water is available at a variety of facilities, primarily at picnic areas, restrooms, a concession stand, campgrounds, and in winter, at the park office.

For more information: Hanging Rock State Park, Danbury. See Appendix C.

Finding the trailheads: See directions to the park under Hike 37, above. The trail begins in the lower picnic area parking lot, the second road to the left after entering the park. (The first left is the ranger station, where maps are available outside.) Entering the parking area, the trail starts on the right, about halfway to the end of the lot. Continue and park at the end of the parking lot for the Window Falls and Hidden Falls Trail.

The hikes: The popular **Hanging Rock Trail** shows substantial recent signs of rerouting and grading, not to mention paving, all intended to cope with the large number of hikers who tackle the trail in summer and on weekends. For privacy the best time to hike here is in the spring, winter and on weekdays.

Starting on the right side of the lower picnic area parking lot, the road-width, paved trail descends to a swale before crossing a stream and beginning its climb to Hanging Rock. The trail climbs steeply and changes to a gravel/earthen surface. There are benches at intervals, and the Wolf Rock Trail branches off to the right before the steepest climb. (The narrow, little-used trail to Wolf Rock, and eventually to the Cook's Wall Trail, is an unsurfaced mountain path more suitable for people seeking solitude and a backcountry hiking experience.)

The Hanging Rock Trail gains a height of land, where there's a resting bench, then turns right and follows a ridgetop to the base of the prominent, 200-foot crag aptly named Hanging Rock. This is a nice place to rest. From here, the trail bears right and steepens, climbing over steps and roots to a

With surprising scenery for a Piedmont state park, Hanging Rock juts high above surrounding terrain. Hikers attain crags where pines and rhododendron cling to solid rock.

left turn onto the summit ridge. Viewpoints lie off to the right as you walk toward the craggy prow of Hanging Rock, itself a fine vista. Views stretch north across farmland, and swing west to south where the nearby summits of Moore's Knob and Cook's Wall appear, encircling the park's high bowl and lake, just out of sight.

Although Hanging Rock State Park is one of the South's best destinations for rock climbers and rappelers, and they are occasionally seen in this area, the park prohibits those activities on this particular peak. Do not climb here. The return route retraces your steps to the parking area.

The **Hidden Falls Trail** is an easy to moderate, 0.4-mile round-trip hike that delves into the park's more intimate scenery, reaching cascades in a scenic gorge. Starting at the end of the lower parking area by the water fountain, hike through the picnic shelter area past the restrooms, then turn on the signed side trail to the right at about 0.2 mile. Hidden Falls, in another 100 yards, cascades past rhododendron and mountain laurel. The descent to Hidden Falls is about 200 feet, making for a total elevation change of about 400 vertical feet.

Continuing beyond the turn off to Hidden Falls reaches a steeper, more rugged stretch of trail. At the bottom, another 100 vertical feet below Hidden Falls, a view through a water-carved picture frame highlights Window Falls. The trail then continues down to a second set of falls, and a view of the Giant Fireplace, if you walk behind the water. This hike is a moderately strenuous 0.8-mile round-trip, with a total elevation change of about 600 feet. Hikers who visit both Hidden and Window Falls could walk up to 1 mile.

Another fine trail at Hanging Rock is the **Upper Cascades Trail**. This nearly level trail reaches a beautiful waterfall after a gradual descent through a striking hemlock forest. It begins at the corner of the lower parking lot (the one shared by trailheads for the Hanging Rock Trail and the path to Hidden and Window Falls), at the part of the lot nearest the park's main road. The paved path crosses the park road and winds into the gorge of Cascade Creek. An observation deck presents a perspective on the falls. The round-trip is 0.4 mile. By 1996 a short barrier-free spur from this hike will provide a 0.2-mile round-trip trail for wheelchair users to a view of outcrops and the gorge.

39 MORROW MOUNTAIN STATE PARK

Overview

Unlike other Piedmont monadnock parks, where single or separated peaks have hiking trails, Morrow Mountain State Park is a wooded, hilly area where more than 30 miles of trails wander over and between modest mountains. The chance for solitude is therefore much greater on these forested summits than at a lone destination peak.

The 4,693-acre park is a southern part of the Uwharrie Mountains, north of Lake Tillery in the Uwharrie National Forest (see Hike 44). Morrow Mountain falls on the more developed side of the Uwharries, as visitors will notice when they discover the park's large network of paved roads. Diverse facilities include a 109-unit campground (for tents and RVs, with restrooms and showers), two picnic areas, a natural history museum, a boat ramp and lakeshore boat rental operation (rowboats and canoes), six cabins (available spring through fall), a swimming pool, and the Kron House, the restored home of a physician who served the isolated area in the mid-1800s. The park opened in 1939. Many of its facilities, among them the stone poolside bathhouse, were built by the Civilian Conservation Corps (CCC).

The ancient Uwharrie Mountains aren't high. Morrow Mountain, the highest, rises to only 936 feet above sea level. A motor road reaches the mountaintop's picnic area and view of Lake Tillery where it fuses with its three sources: the Yadkin, Uwharrie, and Pee Dee rivers. Hikers can walk to this crest but will prefer trails to the park's three other highest peaks: Sugarloaf, Hattaway, and Fall mountains. A spur from the Sugarloaf Mountain Trail leads to four backcountry camping sites where a pit toilet is available. A camping permit is required and costs $5 per night. If rangers aren't around to issue one, page them from the pay phone at the park office and one will return quickly from patrol.

Hikers will notice substantial downed timber in the park. Trees are toppled everywhere in some sections, with red clay clumped on their exposed root balls. This destruction is the result of Hurricane Hugo, in 1989.

Modest Morrow Mountain rises above Lake Tillery in Morrow Mountain State Park.
Photo by Wade E. Stubbs

Part of the appeal of the park for more serious hikers is that few of the trails are graded, flat paths. Instead, the hikes described below are largely blazed routes through little-disturbed woods. Sidehill sections tend to have roots, rocks, and leafy cover that makes them uneven, giving a nice primitive atmosphere for hikers who want to feel like they are in the mountains without a long drive. The experience is like walking freely in the woods but following dots on the trees. Switchbacks ease elevation gains, but there are some steeper sections.

The park is close to Charlotte, and thus popular, receiving almost 350,000 visitors a year. But relatively few backpackers camp here, and the trails, particularly those farthest from Morrow Mountain, are often deserted. That is especially true off season, when the panorama is a pleasant view of rolling flat-topped ridges and the lake seen through bare oaks and scattered pines.

The park also has 16 miles of popular, red-blazed bridle trails, mostly forest roads, that do not conflict with the hiking paths. These paths also may be used for hiking.

General description: Hikes in a moderately mountainous state park. A road reaches the crest of Morrow Mountain, and a variety of hikes explore scenic, hilly terrain reminiscent of the Blue Ridge.

General location: Northeast of Charlotte on the shore of Lake Tillery.

Length: 0.6 mile for the Three Rivers Nature Trail; 2 miles for the Hattaway Mountain Trail; 2.8 miles for the Sugarloaf Mountain Trail; 4.1 miles for the Fall Mountain Trail.

Degree of difficulty: Easy for the Three Rivers Nature Trail; moderate for Fall and Morrow mountains; strenuous for Hattaway and Sugarloaf mountains.

Maps: USGS Badin and Morrow Mountain quads. State park map/brochure is available at park office and from address below.

Elevation gain and loss: About 800 feet for Hattaway Mountain Trail; 820 feet for Fall Mountain Trail; and 640 feet for the Sugarloaf Mountain Trail.

Trailhead elevation: About 400 feet for Hattaway Mountain Trail; 290 feet for Fall Mountain Trail; and 540 feet for the Sugarloaf Mountain Trail.

High point: About 800 feet for Hattaway Mountain; 700 feet for Fall Mountain; and 860 feet for Sugarloaf Mountain.

Water availability: Water is available in season from trailhead restrooms and other visitor facilities.

For more information: Morrow Mountain State Park, Albemarle. See Appendix C.

Finding the trailhead: The park is about 40 miles or a 1-hour drive from Charlotte on North Carolina Highways 24/27. Turn right from NC 24/27 onto the Morrow Mountain Road, SR 1798. Measuring from the park entrance, Sugarloaf Trail parking is on the right at 0.6 mile. Go left at 0.8 mile (right leads to Morrow Mountain) for Hattaway Mountain Trail parking, reached by taking a left at 1.3 miles. To reach the Fall Mountain trailhead,

39 MORROW MOUNTAIN STATE PARK

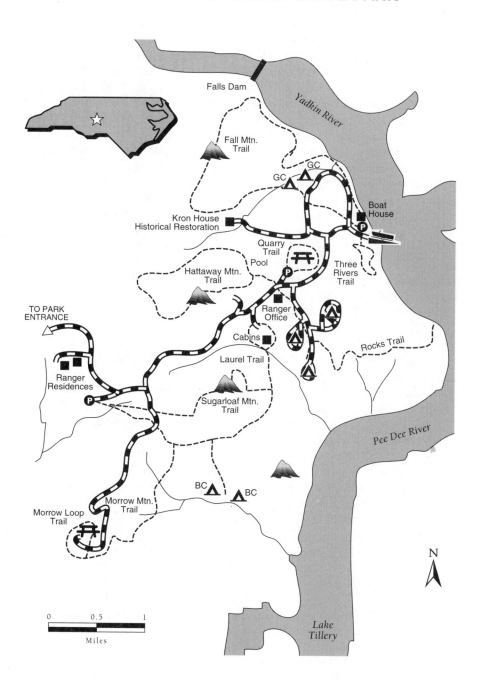

Falls Dam

Yadkin River

Fall Mtn. Trail

GC

GC

GC

Boat House

Kron House Historical Restoration

Quarry Trail

Pool

Three Rivers Trail

Hattaway Mtn. Trail

Ranger Office

Cabins

Rocks Trail

TO PARK ENTRANCE

Laurel Trail

Ranger Residences

Sugarloaf Mtn. Trail

Pee Dee River

BC

BC

Morrow Mtn. Trail

Morrow Loop Trail

N

0   0.5   1
Miles

Lake Tillery

go right at 1.3 miles and keep right at the next two lefts to reach the boat ramp parking on the left at about 1.6 miles.

The hikes: The **Hattaway Mountain Trail** is a 2-mile path that starts at the pool bathhouse. The trail starts gradually and soon reaches a junction where the loop splits left and right. Go right for the easiest ascent. The path slabs around the north side of Hattaway Mountain, gradually entering a stream drainage and then paralleling it within sound of the water. This is a nice flat section of trail lined with mountain laurel. You may notice a bridle trail across the stream. The path then turns from west to east as it starts a steep, rocky climb of Hattaway Mountain, the park's third highest summit. The trail gains a western summit, then follows a ridge to a flat, rocky traverse of the main peak, about 800 feet high. The trail then drops steeply down to the loop junction. A right quickly returns to the parking lot. An easy 0.6-mile **Quarry Trail** loop circles a quarried site near the picnic area and begins at the steps by the end of the parking lot.

Depending on the route you prefer, the 4.1-mile **Fall Mountain Trail** can either begin near the boathouse, on the northeastern end of the boat ramp parking area, or, along with the **Three Rivers Trail**, at the south-western corner of the lot. The latter route is the less steep.

Leave the parking area and pass a junction on the left with the Three Rivers Trail. You'll cross two road-width access paths to group campsites, then descend and cross a stream. At just more than 1 mile pass the Kron House and steeply ascend the southern end of Fall Mountain. The trail turns north and crosses the 700+-foot summit. The northern end of the mountain is extremely rugged, and many crags and outcrops have views of Falls Dam and the Yadkin River. At the base of the mountain, the trail slabs back southeast, navigating crags along the shore before veering away from the water. The trail again swings out to the lake, crossing a stream and paralleling the group camp access path before arriving at the boathouse.

The Three Rivers Trail is a pleasant add-on to this hike. The easy nature loop is 0.6 mile total. Go left from the Fall Mountain Trail just out of the parking lot and cross the boat ramp road. The self-guiding trail explores a marshy area and offers wildlife viewing opportunities. The trail's high point affords good views of the rivers that come together here to form Lake Tillery.

The **Sugarloaf Mountain Trail** leaves the bridle trail parking area just inside the park and enters a flat, rocky pine forest. It then splits and crosses a stream as it enters a more deciduous forest. Take the left fork through this scenic area and cross the motor road that leads right to Morrow Mountain. The trail then climbs up the northwestern slope of Sugarloaf Mountain, the park's second highest peak. On this next stretch of trail, it's easy to trace the geology of this typical volcanic monadnock, or isolated summit, so prevalent in mid-North Carolina. The trail ascends a leading ridge over volcanic slate, then snakes over volcanic ash tuff on the side of the mountain. The final conical cap is composed of volcanic flint, or rhyolite, and reaches about 860 feet altitude. The trail then winds steeply down the eastern side of the mountain.

Where the descent slackens, the **Laurel Trail** leads left to the cabin area and museum. The Sugarloaf Trail bears right and starts a level slab southwest around the mountain. A junction leads left to the backcountry campsites isolated in a stream drainage equidistant from the Morrow Mountain Road and Lake Tillery.

As the Sugarloaf Trail continues, the **Morrow Mountain Trail** branches left, reaching a scenic 0.8-mile summit loop hike (also accessible from the mountaintop parking area). Continuing, the Sugarloaf Trail ascends, then crosses the road to Morrow Mountain, continues to the junction of the loop (where you last went left), and reaches the trailhead at just under 3 miles.

Lake Tillery from the summit overlook of Morrow Mountain State Park. *Charlotte Observer photo.*

Overview

High Point City Lake was built in the early 1920s to serve as a water supply for the city of High Point. The Piedmont Environmental Center (PEC) was started on 936 acres of city lakeshore in 1972, and the Bicentennial Greenway (commemorating the ratification of the U.S. Constitution) became possible in 1989 when the citizens of Guilford County approved a $1.5 million bond issue. From the Piedmont Center Office Park, the PEC Trail is expected to be extended past the airport to Guilford Courthouse National Military Park in northern Greensboro.

Gibson Park, the major trailhead for the Bicentennial Greenway just north of the PEC parcels, started with a 1990 purchase of 200 acres by Guilford County.

High Point City Lake and its many trails are good, close-to-home places to enjoy nature. Sections of the trails wander through quiet pine forests carpeted with running cedar. Other stretches explore deciduous woods; at times, the towering trees rise to impressive proportions. The trails provide nice views of the lake's isolated coves, especially in fall when shoreline leaves are ablaze. Winter brings seasonal migrations of waterfowl. The area boasts more than thirty species of mushrooms.

Trails on PEC parcels are named for Bill Faver, the first director of the Piedmont Environmental Center, and Hollis Rogers, a biology professor at UNC-Greensboro who often brings students to the lake. Before hiking these and other area trails, sample the resources of the Piedmont Environmental Center, a great place to learn. The PEC has many exhibits, with more planned, including a 40 by 70-foot outdoor map of North Carolina that visitors walk across on their way to the trailhead. The PEC is not a museum but is a program-driven institution that offers educational classes and field trips.

Hiking boots are not necessary on these developed trails. A pair of sturdy running shoes will do.

General description: Extensive hiking in a lakeshore natural area is found on the paths of the Piedmont Environmental Center. The PEC trails connect with the paved Bicentennial Greenway.

General location: High Point, one city in the Piedmont Triad also including Greensboro and Winston-Salem.

Length: The PEC's elaborate trail networks total 11 miles and permit hikes of many lengths, including looping circuit walks that combine with the 6.5-mile Bicentennial Greenway. On PEC land, the Bill Faver Lakeshore Loop is about 2.5 miles. The greenway/Deep River Trail circuit is about 4.5 miles. Gibson Park's Twin Ponds Trail is about 0.8 mile, and a greenway walk to the park's wildlife observation deck is about 1.4 miles.

Floating bridge on Lakeshore Trail, Piedmont Environmental Center.

Degree of difficulty: Except for the lengthiest circuit hikes, all trails are easy.

Maps: For PEC trails and the Bicentennial Greenway, the USGS Guilford and High Point East quads. Serviceable hiking maps of PEC trails are available at the center, and a greenway map/brochure is available from the center and at Gibson Park.

Elevation gain and loss: Negligible.

Trailhead elevation: 850 feet at the PEC.

Low point: 757 feet at lakeshore.

Water availability: Water and restrooms are available at trailheads year-round at the PEC and Gibson Park, and during the warmer seasons at Jamestown Park golf course picnic area, just across East Fork Road (SR 1545) from the greenway trailhead.

For more information: Piedmont Environmental Center, High Point. The center is open Monday through Saturday, 9 a.m. to 5 p.m. For further information about local parks, contact High Point Parks and Recreation Department. See Appendix C.

Finding the trailheads: Access to trails at the Piedmont Environmental Center and Bicentennial Greenway is easiest from West Wendover Avenue and Interstate Highway 40 in Greensboro. From I-40 Exit 214, take Wendover Avenue west 3.6 miles to a left into Gibson Park (where the Twin Pond Trail starts on the right at 0.5 mile and the greenway access is at 0.5 mile). To reach the PEC, continue south on Wendover past Gibson Park and go left on Penny Road (SR 1536) at 4.4 miles and reset your odometer. To reach Jamestown Park go left at 0.8 mile onto East Fork Road (SR 1545). In a short distance turn right into the park and immediately right again into picnic area parking. To reach the PEC continue on Penny Road and turn left into the parking area at 2.1 miles.

The hikes: Piedmont Environmental Center trails focus on two lakeshore parcels. The southern parcel that surrounds the center is 151 acres between Penny Road, the lake, and Jamestown Park's golf course. The tract contains about 4 miles of trails bounded by the lake on the east and about 1.5 miles of the Bicentennial Greenway on the north and west.

The longest trail walk, a 2.5-mile loop, follows the white-blazed **Bill Faver Lakeshore Trail** from the south end of the PEC parking lot. The trail enters the woods and passes mini bleachers used in educational programs. Keep right and descend over boardwalk bridges to lake level where the trail goes left, then turns right across a floating bridge that spans the first cove. Go right at the junction just across the bridge and follow the lakeshore. Make a right onto the **Raccoon Run** Trail, a blue-blazed, 0.7-mile side trail that loops onto a promontory jutting out into the lake. Those who explore the peninsula may find the remains of an old structure here, one of many that remain on this once extensively farmed land.

Follow the Raccoon Run loop around the peninsula and go right again on the Bill Faver Trail. Keep right again along the shore when the **Dogwood Trail** goes left (and creates the second longest loop back to the center).

40 PIEDMONT ENVIRONMENTAL CENTER — BICENTENNIAL GREENWAY

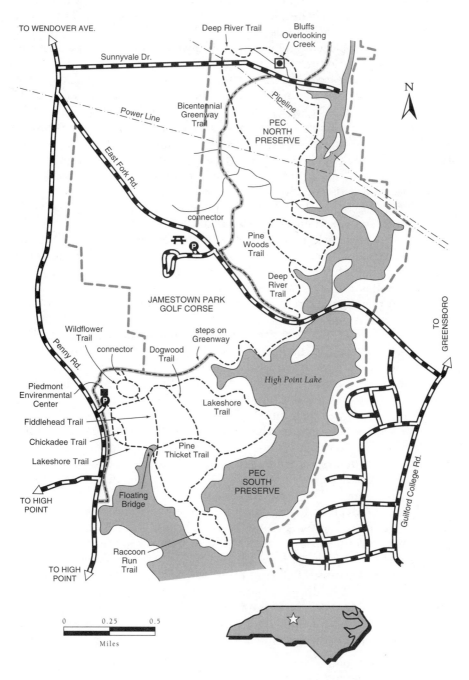

TO WENDOVER AVE.

Deep River Trail

Bluffs Overlooking Creek

Sunnyvale Dr.

Power Line

Pipeline

Bicentennial Greenway Trail

PEC NORTH PRESERVE

East Fork Rd.

connector

Pine Woods Trail

Deep River Trail

JAMESTOWN PARK GOLF CORSE

Wildflower Trail

connector

Dogwood Trail

steps on Greenway

Penny Rd.

Piedmont Enviromental Center

Fiddlehead Trail

Chickadee Trail

Lakeshore Trail

High Point Lake

Lakeshore Trail

Pine Thicket Trail

PEC SOUTH PRESERVE

Floating Bridge

TO HIGH POINT

Raccoon Run Trail

TO HIGH POINT

TO GREENSBORO

Guilford College Rd.

N

0   0.25   0.5
Miles

Remains of another old homesite are visible, and a now decrepit wildlife-viewing blind also sits near the lake. The trail winds away from the lake, parallels the greenway (a short trail to the right links them), then veers left to return past the PEC's Wildflower Trail to the trailhead.

Shorter loops are possible. The **Wildflower Trail** is only 0.2 mile, and even toddlers can navigate the tiny circuit created by the Bill Faver and green-blazed **Chickadee** trails. Kids would also enjoy a circuit of the Bill Faver and yellow-blazed Fiddlehead trails; just take the first left across the floating bridge and return to the center.

The northern parcel of PEC property contains the most backcountry hiking. A 1.5-mile section of the Bicentennial Greenway flanks the western side of this 225-acre tract bordered on the east by the lake.

The red/white-blazed **Deep River Trail** and orange/green-blazed **Hollis Rogers Pinewoods Trail** (opened in summer 1995) are the attractions here. From the picnic parking area at Jamestown Park, the greenway and Deep River Trail form a major circuit of about 4.5 miles, and a few other circuits are also possible.

To hike the biggest loop leave the Jamestown Park picnic area, walk to the park entrance on East Fork Road, and cross the street. Turn right on the paved greenway and parallel East Fork Road for about 0.4 mile through beautiful forest. Where the greenway crosses East Fork Road the Deep River Trail goes left into the woods. (There isn't much room on the roadside here, but a few cars could probably use this trailhead to create a Deep River/Pine Woods trail circuit with no greenway walking to mar an otherwise backwoodsy hike.)

From this point, the Deep River Trail goes north, following the distinctive blaze posts used in the northern PEC parcel (and eventually planned for installation in the southern parcel). The trail winds away from the lake into a deep cove, crosses a bridge, and does the same thing again. Just across the second bridge, the Hollis Rogers Pine Woods Trail goes left. The Deep River Trail goes right but stays away from the lakeshore and climbs to a high point with chunks of white quartz in the trail. The second leg of the Pine Woods Trail comes in on the left. Between these two trailheads the Pine Woods Trail explores a towering loblolly pine forest that is periodically burned. From Jamestown Park, or East Fork Road, this Pine Woods/Deep River Trail circuit is a short day hike.

The Deep River Trail continues north along the lake, staying high on hardwood-covered bluffs. The trail crosses a bridge, leads deep into a cove, then crosses a double bridge over a rocky, fern-bordered creek. As the trail approaches the head of the lake, the bluffs give way to flat lakeshore and the trail crosses swaths of cleared forest at a power line and gas pipeline. The trail swings away from the lake into a final cove, passes an extensive growth of running cedar, crosses a muddy area, and ascends wooden steps onto Sunnyvale Road and the greenway. To the right, the greenway immediately takes a left to the Gibson Park observation deck, 0.5 mile away, and

Piedmont Environmental Center – unpaved Bicentennial Greenway near East Fork Road.

Gibson Park trailhead, 1.2 miles. To the left, the greenway goes 0.8 mile back to the Jamestown Park picnic area.

If you'd like more woods walking, cross the road, descend wooden steps, and again take the Deep River Trail. Follow plentiful blaze posts north along bluffs that rise above the creek. The trail descends to creek level, crosses a bridge, then briefly and steeply climbs into and across the pipe-line swath and Sunnyvale Road. The trail re-enters the woods and joins the greenway again. To the right, the greenway shortly arrives at Jamestown Park. The Deep River Trail almost immediately re-enters the woods on the left of the greenway. This unsigned, less-used leg of the trail runs to the power line, then follows it left to the lakeshore part of the Deep River Trail. For those parked on East Fork Rd. that permits a return to the trailhead with virtually no greenway walking.

But the **Bicentennial Greenway** is not an unpleasant walk. At present the greenway is 6.5 miles long. North of Gibson Park, it is a typical urban paved trail, but between the PEC and Gibson Park, the greenway is often bordered by scenic forest. It also undulates, which makes it one of the more interesting greenways in the state. Indeed, it is a pleasant out-and-back walk from any of its most worthwhile trailheads: the PEC or Jamestown and Gibson parks.

One of the nicest stretches is south from Jamestown Park. At first, the paved greenway parallels the road through tall trees. After it crosses East Fork Rd., the path's surface becomes gravel, grass, and pine needles. It follows the fenceline at Jamestown Park golf course, but the trees are tall and the lakeside stroll is enjoyable. The second and biggest set of steps (which includes a novel ramp for bikes) is a nice turnaround point.

Immediately south from Gibson Park, the greenway is less wooded and a little sunnier (and hotter in the summer). The wildlife observation deck makes a good destination, 0.7 mile south of Gibson Park. A boardwalk view-point reaches into the cattail-covered wetland where High Point Lake be-comes the Deep River again. In morning and evening, there is excellent birding here.

In Gibson Park, the **Twin Ponds Trail** is a grassy, 0.8-mile hike that encircles two ponds in a wooded area known for profuse blackberries in summer. The path passes the ranger residence. From the park's main park-ing area, just past the Twin Ponds Trail, a connector reaches the greenway. A right leads to the observation deck described above.

A side trail to the left arrives at one of the few pre-Civil War cabins left in the area. Just a stroll from the parking lot, the Deep River Cabin was built in two sections between 1800 and 1830. A sizable community of people lived on the shores of Deep River before the Civil War, one reason why so many old homesites are visible today on nearby lakeshore trails. The community dwindled in the late 1800s with the waning of its primary industries, water-powered milling and the manufacture of flintlock rifles.

40 GIBSON PARK — BICENTENNIAL GREENWAY

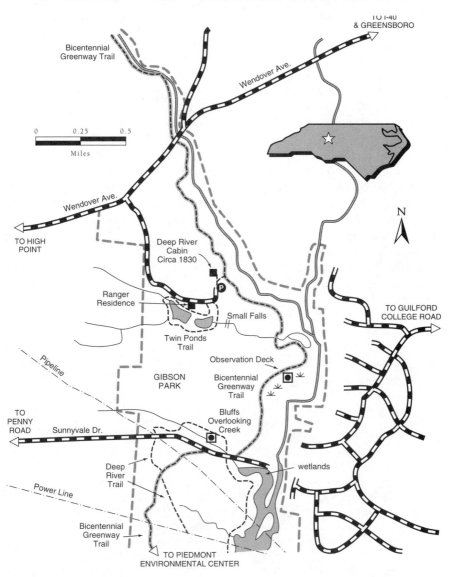

A sign on the greenway near the cabin pictures the Jamestown long rifle, many of which were used in the Civil War. The plaque, erected by the Sons of Confederate Veterans, lists eighty-two of the local gunsmiths and apprentices who made guns here.

41   *PILOT MOUNTAIN STATE PARK*

Overview

Pilot Mountain juts prominently above the northern Piedmont, perhaps the most distinctive monadnock in the state. The adjacent summits of the Sauratown Mountains, of which Pilot Mountain is a part, could also be called monadnocks, as could the peaks of Crowders Mountain State Park near Charlotte.

Hikers can't actually reach the Big Pinnacle summit of Pilot Mountain (2,420 feet). This quartzite plug has been so resistant to erosion that it is surrounded by an uninterrupted rampart of cliffs. At one time, prior to its 1968 establishment as North Carolina's fourteenth state park, the peak was a commercial tourist attraction; hikers could climb a system of ladders to the top. The ladders came down to preserve the many raven- and raptor-nesting sites on the summit. Nevertheless, there are excellent viewpoints on Little Pinnacle (a perfect perch from which to watch the September and October hawk migration), and a trail encircles the base of the Big Pinnacle cliffs.

Below the peak, acreage on the Yadkin River enlarges the park to almost 4,000 acres. The area encompasses two of the most scenic miles of the Yadkin and part of a 165-mile canoe trail. Two large islands in the river can be reached by wading, and trails along the river also require getting wet feet. Canoeists may camp at two wilderness sites on the larger island. A

View from the main viewpoint trail near the summit parking at Pilot Mountain State Park. The peaks of Hanging Rock State Park are visible in the distance on the left. *Photo by William Russ.*

nineteenth-century canal is visible on the riverside trails, built so that river transportation could circumvent shoals.

The summit area of the park is the most popular, due to the sentinel status of the mountain. The Saura Indians called it Jomeokee, which means "Great Guide" or "Pilot." Later settlers also used it as a beacon for navigation. A picture of the peak towering over U.S. Highway 52 served as a recent cover of the state highway map. Today, as in the past, Pilot Mountain is visible from all over northwestern North Carolina.

There are forty-nine tent and trailer campsites just inside the entrance of the park, and a youth group camping area in the river section. Picnic areas can be found adjacent to the summit parking area and on both sides of the Yadkin River.

Hikers should be aware that the trails close a half hour before the park does. Rangers ask that hikers return well before darkness.

General description: Various hikes in a western Piedmont state park dominated by a dramatic, rock-crowned summit. One route winds through a wooded corridor between the peak and a nearby park parcel on the Yadkin River, where an interpretive trail explores a restored, late-nineteenth-century farm.

General location: Pilot Mountain State Park, north of Winston-Salem.

Length: 0.5 mile for the Sassafras Trail; about 1 mile for the Jomeokee Trail around Pilot Mountain; just over 2 miles for the Ledge Spring circuit around the summit; and 8 miles for the park's premier hike, a climb to the Ledge Spring summit circuit on the Grindstone Trail. The Corridor Trail is 5.5 miles and the Horne Creek Trail interpretive loop is about 1 mile.

Degree of difficulty: Easy for the Sassafras and Horne Creek trails; moderate for the Jomeokee Trail; moderately strenuous for the Corridor Trail and Ledge Spring Trail; strenuous for the Grindstone/Ledge Spring Trail circuit.

Maps: USGS Pinnacle and Siloam quads. State park map/brochure available at park office and from address below.

Elevation gain and loss: 1,720 for the Grindstone Trail; under 200 feet for the Jomeokee Trail and Horne Creek Trails.

Trailhead elevation: 1,440 feet for the Grindstone Trail; 2,200 for the Jomeokee Trail; 880 feet for the Horne Creek Trail.

High point: About 2,300 feet.

Water availability: Water is available at trailhead restrooms during the warmer months at both the campground and the summit.

For more information: Pilot Mountain State Park. Horne Creek Farm Visitor Center. See Appendix C.

Finding the trailhead: The park is easily reached via U.S. Highway 52. Take the Pilot Mountain State Park exit 22 miles north of Business Interstate Highway 40 in Winston-Salem. Go left at the stop sign, then left into the state park less than 0.5 mile later. From the north, take the same exit and follow the signs, then turn right into the park. To reach the Horne Creek Farm/Yadkin River section of the park, exit US 52 at the Pinnacle exit, immediately south of the Pilot Mountain State Park exit. The 10-mile route is well-signed.

Corridor trail parking is available on the north end, near Pilot Mountain State Park proper, by exiting the park entrance and going right to a stop sign. Turn right on the Old Winston Highway, cross a railroad track and make a right on old US 52. Go about 0.25 mile and turn right on Surry Line Road. Go 1.2 miles to a left on Culler Road to parking by a Corridor Trail sign. To reach parking for the Corridor Trail on the south end, follow the directions above to Horne Creek Farm. Continue beyond the park entrance about 0.25 mile and park on the right.

The hikes: From the summit parking lot, the two most scenic alternatives are hikes to the Little and Big pinnacles of Pilot Mountain. There's also a short nature walk called the Sassafras Trail.

The hike to **Little Pinnacle** is really a stroll. This crag is a series of cliffs flanking the parking lot to the east, rising above the gap that separates it from Big Pinnacle. The hike thus provides great views. From the parking lot, and an adjacent restroom facility, a paved path arcs along the clifftops. Three right turns take walkers out to fenced viewpoints. Use caution here: don't imagine you are secure enough to step beyond the railings. The park's last fatality, in late summer 1994, occurred here when a hiker climbed over and held onto a clifftop tree limb—which broke.

The third of these right turns leads out a rocky access path to the park's main viewpoint. This is a spectacular view from the peak of Little Pinnacle across to the rock-ringed summit of Pilot Mountain. Beyond, to the east, one can see the Sauratown Mountains, including the summits of Hanging Rock State Park (see Hike 38). Views reach north and south too and are reminiscent of other Piedmont monadnock state parks; rolling flatlands, 1,400 feet below, stretch out dramatically on clear days.

Continuing past the Little Pinnacle view, and descending, the orange-blazed **Jomeokee Trail to Big Pinnacle** appears on the right. Turn here to descend the north side of Little Pinnacle on its way through the gap you were just looking over. The trail is wide and excavated, but has rocky sections. The side of Little Pinnacle recedes on the right as the trail enters the gap. Just as you pass this last edge of Little Pinnacle, the Ledge Spring Trail begins with a right turn and quick scramble onto a path that slabs a scenic route under Little Pinnacle to connections with the park's upper parking lot. Continuing, the Jomeokee Trail rises out of the gap and splits into a loop that circles but never climbs the Big Pinnacle. The trail to the right is less obvious to see, so bear left around the loop.

The true peak-bagger might assume there has to be a way to the summit, but there isn't. The peak presents an uninterrupted rampart against all but rock climbers, and climbing isn't permitted here. (Rock climbing in Pilot Mountain State Park is permitted from access points in the vicinity of the Ledge Spring Trail, and climbers must register.) A system of stairs was once in place, but it has been removed to encourage birds to nest on the crags.

41 PILOT MOUNTAIN STATE PARK

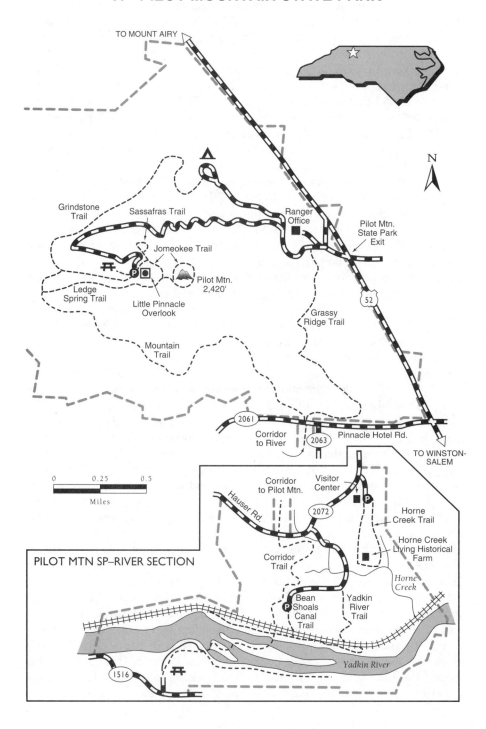

TO MOUNT AIRY

N

Grindstone Trail

Sassafras Trail

Ranger Office

Pilot Mtn. State Park Exit

Jomeokee Trail

Pilot Mtn. 2,420'

Ledge Spring Trail

Little Pinnacle Overlook

52

Grassy Ridge Trail

Mountain Trail

2061

Corridor to River

2063

Pinnacle Hotel Rd.

TO WINSTON-SALEM

0   0.25   0.5

Miles

PILOT MTN SP–RIVER SECTION

Corridor to Pilot Mtn.

Hauser Rd.

2072

Visitor Center

P

Horne Creek Trail

Horne Creek Living Historical Farm

Corridor Trail

Horne Creek

P

Bean Shoals Canal Trail

Yadkin River Trail

1516

Yadkin River

So circle the summit. The trail stays below the edge of the cliffs, but hiker traffic has created a variety of paths that follow the base of the rock. There are picnic spots in many nooks. You'll eventually rejoin the route you entered on. The total hike, out-and-back, is about 1 mile.

Back at the trailhead a right turn takes you out the Sassafras Trail. The gradual 0.5-mile path circles through summit forest and returns. This is a good place to appreciate the similarity between the vegetation in this Piedmont park and that of the distant, lofty Blue Ridge. Both the Sassafras and Jomeokee trailheads are just behind the restroom at the summit parking lot.

The **Ledge Spring Trail** is another enjoyable summit hike. The less than 2-mile trail, marked with yellow dots, permits a scenic hike from the southwestern corner of the summit parking area, under the cliffs of Little Pinnacle to the Jomeokee Trail, and back to the mountaintop parking. This trail is the best route for hikers who want to circle Pilot Mountain but want a longer, more rugged access route than the Jomeokee Trail.

The Ledge Spring Trail is reached from the summit parking area. If you start here, don't be funneled down into then out the bottom of the picnic area. That route, obviously the source of much confusion, seems plausible but it isn't a trail. If you walk down the steps toward the picnic area, go left on the road grade before reaching the woods and the picnic sites. Or walk to the southwestern corner of the parking area and leave on the Ledge Spring Trail as it wanders about 0.25 mile down to a junction with the Grindstone Trail (a nearly 2-mile route to the campground near the park entrance; see below).

Go left on the Ledge Spring Trail at the junction beyond the picnic area. The Ledge Spring Trail descends steeply southwest and reaches a junction with the red-blazed Mountain Trail (an old bridle trail that reaches the Corridor Trail in 2.5 miles). The Ledge Spring Trail turns east at the junction with the Mountain Trail, passes Ledge Spring, and heads back along the base of the cliffs, from which there are far-reaching views. At the junction with the Jomeokee Trail, about 1.5 miles, turn right. Circle the Pilot Mountain summit and return on the Jomeokee Trail to the mountaintop parking lot and your car for a hike of just over 2 miles; or for a slightly less than 5-mile, moderately strenuous hike retrace your Ledge Spring Trail route. Of course, the last loop of the peak on the Jomeokee Trail may be busy, but the out-and-back hike on the Ledge Spring Trail will be wild and quiet.

The **Grindstone Trail** is really the ultimate starting point for hikers who want a strenuous experience at Pilot Mountain. Starting between campsites 16 and 17 at the bottom of the park road, the rocky, cliff-bordered trail follows blue dots as it gains more than 500 feet in elevation in under 2 miles. At its junction with the Ledge Spring Trail go right, away from the summit parking area, and descend steeply. Where the Mountain Trail descends the south side of the peak, follow the Ledge Spring Trail. At this point, the hike is much like the Ledge Spring circuit over the summit described above. The trail passes Piedmont views on its way to the junction with the Jomeokee Trail. After a loop of the peak it crosses the summit parking areas, rejoins the Ledge Spring Trail, and retraces steps back down the mountain for a strenuous 8-mile hike. Hikers who don't want to cross the parking lot can also retrace their steps on the Ledge Spring Trail, but remember that there is a steep climb to the elevation of the parking lot before descending the Grindstone Trail.

The **Corridor Trail** runs from the upland portion of Pilot Mountain State Park to the Yadkin River and beyond at a trailhead south of the river. Along the way are views back to Pilot Mountain. The trail's 5.5 miles lead through pine and deciduous forests, fields, and the remnants of agricultural activities, and terminates at a living-history farm. Taking this trail end-to-end requires two cars.

The **Horne Creek Trail** is an easy loop through the historic farm site, reconstructed to appear as it did during the tenure of subsistence farmer Thomas Hauser. This 0.75-mile walk is one of the state's finest interpretive trails, but more for human than natural history. Pulling into the parking area, visitors will find the Horne Creek visitor center on the right and a large folklife demonstration area on the left. The signed trailhead is in the field near the woods.

Pick up an interpretive brochure and examine the exhibits at the visitor center before entering the woods. (The center is open six days a week, year-round, closed Mondays.) The trail descends as a woodland path southwest to Horne Creek and follows the stream. It swings away from the stream heading west, then turns north and passes through the Hauser family cemetery. The trail becomes an old farm road, which you'll follow back to the visitor center as it enters the farm.

The farm is fascinating. At any given time you'll find costumed interpreters on hand demonstrating turn-of-the-century farming technology. The tasks vary by season. The main structure is the Hauser home (1875), unfurnished at this point but about 50 percent restored. Other structures have yet to be rebuilt, but you will see an 1847 double-crib log barn, a smokehouse, and a fruit house (used to store foods canned on the premises).

Fields here were being reclaimed by nature, and the entire scene was slipping back into forest until the state acquired the land. Some of that is being reversed now, but only subtly, so that visitors sense what it must have been like to farm here in the late 1800s when there were few cash crops. Unlike today, when one or two crops can dictate an entire farm's focus, the Hauser farm was a collection of separate industries. From the farm, hike the road back to the parking area.

Overview

Raleigh has appropriately been called "the park with a city in it." Its impressive, ever expanding, 38-mile, 1,200-acre system of greenways is the largest in the state. Here, as in other North Carolina communities (see the entries for Boone, Charlotte, High Point, and Winston-Salem), greenways are seen as a way to enhance the value of property in both established neighborhoods and new suburban communities. The result is that open space, significant natural areas, and historic sites are being buffered from the pressures of urban sprawl.

North Carolina is a leader in the greenway movement, largely due to early greenway proponents in Raleigh. In 1974, the Raleigh Greenway Commission was formed and a demonstration greenway completed. A state-wide greenway conference first met in 1987, and in 1991, the state established a governor's advisory panel to help create more urban greenways.

Raleigh is nationally known for institutionalizing its trails as a community priority. City ordinances require developers to grant greenway easements in undeveloped areas targeted by the greenway master plan. Developers are compensated for the property, but they also pay a facility fee per residential unit that defrays a portion of the city's park expenses. Recently, the city contracted to enlarge its sewer system; when the project is completed, the contractor will build a greenway on top of the sewage line. Within the next decade, the lengthy greenway corridors of Walnut Creek and Crabtree Creek will be completed. Add the regular passage of park bond referendums by Raleigh residents, and it's no wonder this progressive, fast-growing community excites trail enthusiasts.

Today Raleigh's greenways connect neighborhoods to parks, shopping centers, schools, and other points of interest. Most are urban, but some portions are more like woodsy hiking trails. And then there are downright natural greenway trails such as Raleigh's Loblolly Trail and related circuit hikes between Carter Finley Stadium at North Carolina State University and William B. Umstead State Park (see Hikes 45 and 46). The **Neuse River Trail** is one of Raleigh's newest paths, highly recommended to serious hikers. The 4-mile woods trail follows the Neuse River just east of the city northward from Anderson Point Park.

The greenway paths described below are the cream of Raleigh's crop of wooded walks.

General description: Paved and unpaved, streamside and lakeshore greenway trails in the state's largest, most diverse system of linear urban parks.
General location: Raleigh.
Length: Greenway system hikes range from short to lengthy. The Neuse River Trail is 4 miles, one-way. There's a 4-mile, out-and-back viewpoint

Parts of the Shelley Lake Trail are wonderfully wooded.
Raleigh News & Observer photo.

walk on the Buckeye Trail. Lake Johnson has lakeshore loops of 2.3, 3.5, 4.4, and 5.5 miles. At Lake Lynn, loops are 2.2 and 3.2 miles. Shelley Lake's loop hike is 2.2 miles, and a 5.1-mile circuit of the lake is available from the Bent Creek and Sawmill trails (which without looping the lake are hikes of 2.2 and 3.3 miles). The Ironwood Trail is a 1.6-mile round-trip.

Degree of difficulty: Easy to moderate.

Maps: USGS Raleigh East quad for the Buckeye Trail; Raleigh West quad for Lake Johnson, Shelley Lake (Bent Creek and Sawmill trails), and Lake Lynn. Greenway users should buy a copy of Raleigh's greenway guide booklet (available from the address in Appendix C and on-line, see Appendix D) and request a copy of the free Raleigh Bike Map to aid in locating trailheads.

Elevation gain and loss: Negligible, with gradual grades.

Water availability: Many greenways have warm-weather water fountains on premises or at adjacent public parks. But it's better to bring your own.

For more information: Raleigh Parks and Recreation Department. See Appendix C.

Finding the trailheads: Use the directions below with the city's greenway guide and free bicycling map.

The Buckeye Trail, in southeast Raleigh, starts at the west end of the trail near the intersection of Crabtree and Raleigh boulevards off of Capital Boulevard.

The Lake Johnson Trail, in southwest Raleigh, lies adjacent to Interstate Highway 40/440, and is reached via Exit 295. Exiting there, go north on Gorman Street and turn left on Avent Ferry Road. The main trailhead parking area is easily visible beside the lake at the boathouse on Avent Ferry Road. The best trailhead may be beside the stadium at Athens Drive High School, however. To start there take a right from Avent Ferry Road onto Athens Drive before reaching the boathouse parking area. Turn left just after the high school toward the football stadium and Lake Johnson Pool. Continue to the large gravel parking area at the football stadium. An asphalt trail extends to the bark chip trail and a boardwalk located on the north side of Lake Johnson.

The Lake Lynn Trail, in northwest Raleigh, starts at the main parking area below the dam off Lynn Road between Leesville Road and Ray Road. Lake Lynn Park, just north of the lake, also has a trailhead and is reached from Ray Road to the east of the main parking area.

The Shelley Lake Trail, in north central Raleigh, can be started from the West Millbrook Road parking area below the Shelley Lake Dam (which is also the trailhead for the Ironwood Trail), or from the Sertoma Arts Center, both on Millbrook Road between Creedmore Road and Six Forks Road. Reach the Bent Creek Trail by taking Six Forks Rd. north from the vicinity of the lake to a left on Longstreet Drive. The trail leaves from the junction of Longstreet and Bent Creek drives. The Sawmill Trail starts on Sawmill Road. Following the directions above, pass Longstreet Drive and go left on Sawmill Drive. The trail begins on the left between Leadmine Road and Brandywine Court.

42 RALEIGH GREENWAYS —
LAKE JOHNSON TRAILS

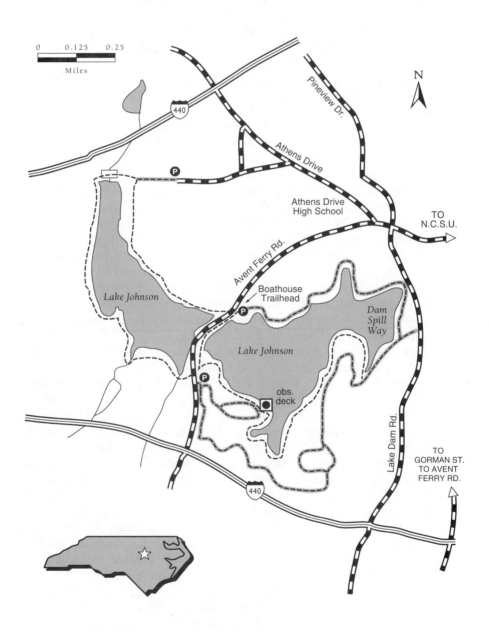

The hikes: Raleigh greenways are so varied that a handful of options illustrate the breadth of the system.

The paved **Buckeye Trail** leads hikers to some of the most unique scenery in the entire system. The trail is about 2.5 miles one-way. From Raleigh Boulevard, the main trailhead, the inspiring wooded trail heads east along the floodplain. The trail leaves the woods at about 1.4 miles to parallel Crabtree Boulevard past a playground and recreation fields. Back in the woods, the most interesting section of the trail passes through rich forest containing the namesake buckeye, as well as river birch and pine. A formal viewpoint atop bluffs provides panoramic views of the creek and surrounding forest. An out-and-back hike from the trailhead to here is about a 4-mile round-trip.

From the bluffs, it's about 0.5 mile east to Milburnie Road (no parking). A round-trip hike to there and back is about 5 miles.

The **Lake Johnson Trail** loops the lake with paved, bark chip-covered and woods trails. Avent Ferry Road splits the lake, and the trail circles each end, creating two small loops or one large one. Going east from the boathouse trailhead, the paved path winds along the lakeshore in mature forest, then turns with the lakeshore and passes the dam and spillway to a T-junction at about 0.8 mile. Going right (to the left, a side trail reaches Lake Dam Drive), the main trail parallels the shore to where, at about 1.1 miles, an unpaved woods trail goes right to follow the lakeshore. This trail eventually intersects the paved trail near the end of the loop, but takes a shorter route. Go left and the trail ascends a ridge to a T-junction. Here, go either way: the two trails meet after looping the top of a knob. At their junction, about 1.8 miles into the hike, continue as the trail descends south then turns west through stands of bigleaf magnolias at about 2 miles. Below this area, the woods trail follows the lakeshore.

The paved trail winds west to a parking area on the south side of the lake at about 2.5 miles. Near the parking area turn right at a junction on a paved side trail that splits into an end loop and, along with the woods trail, arrives at a lakeshore viewpoint. The woods trail continues along the lakeshore, and the paved trail loops back to the main trail, where the greenway and woods trails join again by the picnic area. To return to your car, cross the 700 feet of boardwalk bridge that reaches the boathouse side of the lake. The total hike is about 3.5 miles on the paved trail, or about 2.3 miles via the lakeshore trail (the choice for the most natural experience).

To loop the western side of the lake, cross Avent Ferry Road and take an unpaved woods path along the southern lakeshore. (You could just hike this side of the lake from the boathouse trailhead by crossing the boardwalk then crossing Avent Ferry Road) At the head of the lake, about 1.1 miles from the road, a 380-foot boardwalk crosses Walnut Creek. The trail from there is paved 0.2 mile to the parking area at Athens Drive High School. Just beyond the boardwalk, a bark chip-covered trail, surfaced with chips to appeal to runners, branches right and follows the northern side of the lake about 0.9 mile back to the boathouse across Avent Ferry Road, for a

42 RALEIGH GREENWAYS —
LAKE LYNN TRAILS

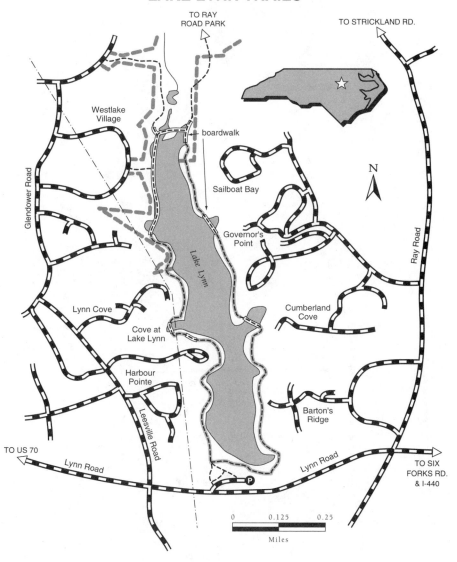

TO RAY
ROAD PARK

TO STRICKLAND RD.

Westlake
Village

boardwalk

Sailboat Bay

N

Governor's
Point

Lake Lynn

Lynn Cove

Cumberland
Cove

Cove at
Lake Lynn

Glendower Road

Ray Road

Harbour
Pointe

Leesville Road

Barton's
Ridge

TO US 70

Lynn Road

Lynn Road

P

TO SIX
FORKS RD.
& I-440

0   0.125   0.25

Miles

little more than 2-mile hike. The loop of the entire lake is just over 5.5 miles
via the paved trail on the eastern side of the lake, and about 4.4 miles if you
take the woods trail instead.

The **Lake Lynn Trail** is the newest jewel in Raleigh's greenway
crown. Unlike more circular lakes in the system, Lake Lynn is narrow and
its shore hike offers a wealth of coves. This paved trail provides a nature-
like experience, especially near the marshy head of the lake where 0.5 mile
of boardwalks skirt away from the steep banks and wander over the water.

42 RALEIGH GREENWAYS —
SHELLEY LAKE TRAILS

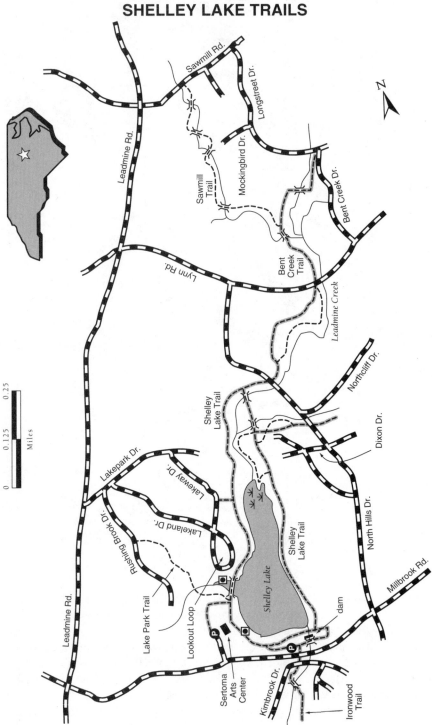

The elevated trail encloses coves, providing the opposite view you expect from lakeshore hikes.

The 2.2-mile hike starts from the parking area below the dam on Lynn Road, but another trailhead is available at Lake Lynn Park being developed on nearby Ray Road. A greenway trail from there follows a drainage from the south end of the park to the north end of the Lake Lynn loop trail. Leaving the main parking area on Lynn Road, take the feeder path to the greenway loop and go right, or east, across the dam. The trail swings north past Barton's Ridge, the first of many residential developments around the lake. Between Cumberland Cove and Governor's Point, the trail crosses a boardwalk bridge over a cove. The next boardwalk bridges the cove between Governor's Point and Sailboat Bay, another urban lakeshore development.

The trail leaves the city growth behind as it enters Lake Lynn Park near the head of the lake. It swings around the head of the lake on a lengthy and impressive boardwalk, at times over water, other times over marshland. The first section of boardwalk holds a trail junction. Left, the boardwalk continues the lakeshore loop, and straight, it reaches land and joins a paved path to the parking area at Lake Lynn Park on Ray Road, about 0.5 mile away (which makes the lake loop a hike of 3.2 miles for hikers starting there).

Go left and the boardwalk reaches another junction. Here a right turn on the boardwalk leads to an unpaved foot trail that reaches a nearby neighborhood. Go left and cross a long stretch of water. Again on the lakeshore, a paved side trail leads right to a neighborhood. Continuing, the trail again crosses a long lakeshore boardwalk that encloses a cove and reaches shore again. Just beyond that point, the trail leaves the park and passes other developments before crossing another brief boardwalk section beside The Cove At Lake Lynn. A short section of paved trail swings east then crosses the last section of boardwalk before turning south past Harbour Pointe and reaching the trailhead.

The paved **Shelley Lake Trail** loops the lake in about 2.2 miles. Greenway paths go three directions from the lake. One of those corridors, the Bent Creek/Sawmill Trail combination, is not heavily used and permits lake loops to start as far as 1.5 miles away (creating a 5.1-mile hike; see below). To start at the main trailhead, park at the Sertoma Arts Center. From there the access trail dips through a cultivated corridor of birch trees past fitness stations to the lakeshore trail junction at 0.1 mile. On the left, the unpaved Lake Park Trail comes in from the neighborhood along Rushing Brook Drive. Also to the left, the Shelley Lake Trail goes north over a small arm of the lake; the offset bridge has decks to accommodate fishing. An observation tower on the other side provides a panoramic view. A return from there is a short, scenic walk of about 0.3 mile.

Take the right turn on the Shelley Lake Trail and skirt the south side of the lake past another view tower, boathouse, and restrooms with an emergency phone. The trail turns around the end of the lake, and a side trail goes right to the West Millbrook Road parking area at about 0.3 mile.

The trail passes the dam/spillway and another trail branches right and swings wide to the parking lot. Before that trail reaches the lot, the Ironwood Trail branches left (a right if you start from this parking lot) and heads south under the Millbrook Road bridge along Leadmine Creek.

Staying straight past the Millbrook Road parking area and continuing around the lake, the Shelley Lake Trail turns north through fields and picnic sites east of the lake at about 0.5 mile and enters the woods. At about 1 mile, near the head of the lake, an unpaved trail to the left is part of a worthwhile side loop that includes a boardwalk over the marsh.

Going straight on the main trail, another unpaved short trail branches right, bound for the **Snelling Branch Trail**. The paved Snelling Branch Trail branches right just as the return route of the unpaved loop trail comes in on the left. A short distance farther the trail crosses Bent Creek to a junction where the **Bent Creek Trail** goes right at about 1.3 miles. Turn left on the Shelley Lake Trail and follow it west through tall trees past a paved side trail on the right to Lakeway Drive at about 1.7 miles. Pass the observation tower and bridge near the start of the hike. Back at the trailhead, you'll have made a round-trip of about 2.2 miles.

To make this hike longer—and woodsier—start at one of two distant trailheads reached via the Bent Creek Trail. From the junction of Longstreet and Bent Creek drives, the Bent Creek Trail reaches the Shelley Lake Trail in 1.1 miles (a 4.4-mile round-trip around the lake). From that direction the trail leads through impressive forest then crosses Leadmine Creek. The **Sawmill Trail** branches to the right at about 0.4 mile, and the Bent Creek Trail crosses the creek, turns south, and passes through an arching canopy of river birches. The trail goes under the Lynn Road bridge and a 0.2-mile, unpaved side trail branches left, definitely the choice for hikers who want to stay closer to the creek. The main trail passes under more river birch, then the woods trail rejoins on the left. Going under North Hills Drive via a tunnel, the main path joins the Shelley Lake Trail. Hikers not wanting to loop the lake could explore the marshy head of the lake by circling the unpaved side trail that includes a boardwalk along the edge of Shelley Lake. That shorter option would be about 2.5 miles.

The best way to lengthen and "naturalize" the Shelley Lake loop is to start on the Sawmill Trail. This 0.9-mile unpaved path leaves the south side of Sawmill Road and crosses numerous bridges as it follows a tributary of Leadmine Creek. You'll notice sections of mature forest and rock outcroppings in the creek. The trail intersects the paved Bent Creek Trail at 0.9 mile. Going right on that trail, you join the Shelley Lake loop at 1.5 miles for a round-trip circuit hike of 5 miles. Just circling the shorter boardwalk side trail at the lake makes for a 3.3-mile hike, much of it on unsurfaced paths.

From the parking area near the dam on Millbrook Road, the **Ironwood Trail** is also a worthwhile hike, as an out-and-back trip from the parking area or a prelude to circling the lake. The trail leaves the parking area and goes under the two roads, then crosses two bridges on the way to North

The offset bridge on the Shelley Lake Trail near the Sertoma Arts Center has "balconies" to permit fishing. *Raleigh News Observer photo.*

Hills Drive. (Along the way, a short unpaved path diverts west to Yorkgate Drive) The nicest section of this 1.6-mile round-trip hike is the stretch nearest North Hills Drive, where the trail drops steeply from the street into a picturesque area with a large rock outcropping beside the stream. The trail is wooded for most of its length.

43   *WINSTON – SALEM TRAILS*

Overview

Salem Lake, a 300-acre water impoundment for the city of Winston-Salem, is a multiple-use recreational facility built in 1919. Part of the 7-mile lake circle path, enclosed by 1,500 acres of wooded land, was built by the Civilian Conservation Corps (CCC) in the 1930s. Since then, the city and the Friends of Salem Lake, a citizens group, have expanded and formalized the network.

Fishing is a primary use of Salem Lake. The marina has a bait and tackle shop and thirty rowboats for rent. The lake is stocked with bass, crappie, white perch, brim, catfish, and carp, but fishing is not allowed from the shore.

The Salem Creek Trail was the first of Winston-Salem's greenway paths and was started in 1985. The route creates wonderful opportunities for residents to walk or bike between neighborhoods, recreational facilities, and shopping areas. The trail is also enjoyable because of the unpolluted water that courses beside the path in Salem Creek. With the lake so close by, it's no wonder the stream is so clean and inviting.

General description: An unpaved level path that meanders around scenic Salem Lake and connects to a paved greenway trail. Both paths are popular with hikers and bicyclists.
General location: Winston-Salem.
Length: A 7-mile lake loop on the Salem Lake Trail that can be extended to 9.6 miles from a nearby greenway trailhead for the Salem Creek Trail. That 4.5-mile greenway has numerous out-and-back possibilities for hikes of many lengths, including the 3.2-mile round-trip to Salem Lake from Reynolds Park Road and a 2-mile out-and-back walk from Marketplace Mall.
Degree of difficulty: Easy, in part barrier-free.
Maps: A trail map is available from the Winston-Salem Recreation and Parks Department.
Elevation gain and loss: Negligible on the greenway and lakeshore trails. There are only two ups and downs of less than 20 vertical feet on the lakeshore, but the trail steeply rises and falls about 50 feet as it passes the dam.
Trailhead elevation: 805 feet.

Salem Lake Trail.

Water availability: A water fountain is available in the trailhead picnic area of the Salem lake Trail during the warm months.

For more information: The Winston-Salem Recreation and Parks Department. See Appendix C.

Finding the trailhead: To reach the Salem Lake Trail and the two easternmost trailheads for the Salem Creek Trail, take U.S. Highway 52 north from Bypass Interstate Highway 40, or south from Business I-40 and exit on Stadium Drive. After exiting, turn left then immediately right at the stoplight onto M. L. King, Jr. Drive. Turn left onto Reynolds Park Road 0.4 mile from the stoplight. Measuring from that turn, cross a bridge over the Salem Creek Trail at 0.6 mile and pass the Reynolds Park Rd. greenway parking area on the left at 0.7 mile. Pass the Reynolds Park Golf Course, and at 1.8 miles turn left onto Salem Lake Road, where the Salem Lake Trail parking lot is 0.5 mile on the right, before the gate at the marina. To join the Salem Creek Trail from the Salem Lake Trail parking area, take a paved connector that leads west from the lake parking area, across the gated entrance to the marina.

To reach Marketplace Mall, the western end of the Salem Creek Trail, exit I-40 at the Peters Creek Parkway (Exit 192). Turn left to the next light, the junction with Silas Creek Parkway. Measuring from there, go straight on Peter's Creek Parkway 0.3 mile and turn right into Marketplace Mall on Hutton Street. Turn left immediately inside the mall parking area and follow the perimeter lane around to the left, back corner of the mall parking area at the greenway signs.

The hikes: The **Salem Lake Trail** starts in a parking lot by a picnic area that occupies a promontory near the Salem Lake Dam. Benches and picnic tables overlook the lake, marina, and playground. While bikers and hikers prepare for the trail, picnickers and sightseers toss snacks for seagulls, ducks, and geese.

The trail is a uniform single-lane road about 10 feet wide that leaves the lot to the east beside a signboard. The tread alternates between packed earth and gravel in areas that are prone to wetness, so mountain bikes are most appropriate for riders. Staying close to the banks, with frequent views, the trail passes periodic metal mileage markers, an occasional bench, and shoreline rocks suitable for rests and picnics. (There is no fishing from the banks.) Occasionally the trail edges farther away from the lake, but is never out of sight.

The trail at first winds very little, following wide arms of the lake. After the first few coves, the trail crosses a bridge at about 1.1 miles where a side stream enters the lake. The creek tumbles over scenic ledges and rocks just above the bridge and often attracts picnickers. At about 1.3 miles, the trail climbs its steepest ascent just beyond the bridge, then descends around a promontory and enters the longer, narrower part of the lake. In this area, about 1.5 miles into the hike, the hiker's eye is drawn down the lake.

43 SALEM LAKE

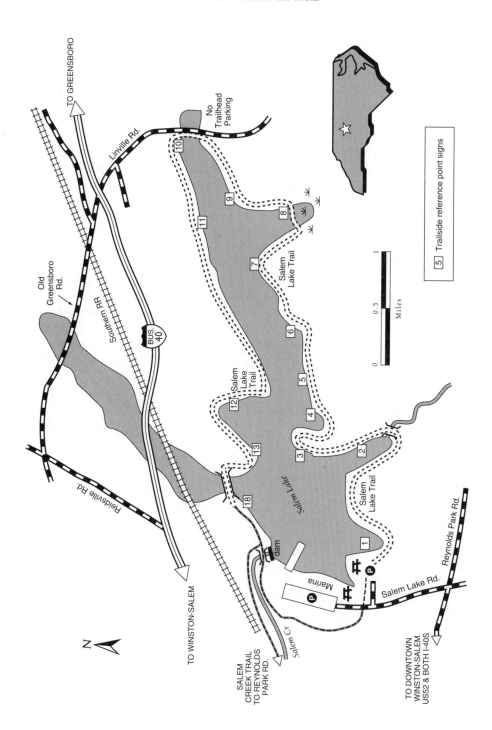

251

The trail continues to follow shallow coves through tall deciduous forest, then turns into a large cove at 2.6 miles. It crosses this arm of the lake on a reinforced, gravel treadway that separates the open cove on the left from a marshy area on the right, often resounding with frog sounds in warm weather. Soon after that, at about 3.6 miles, the path exits at a gate onto Linville Road. Go left using the well-worn trail on the lake side of the guardrail to traverse the 0.1-mile roadside. Go left again where the trail re-enters the woods and resumes its loop of the lake.

On the north side of the lake, the coves are smaller and the trail quickly winds in and out among denser, often pine-populated woods. That makes this section of the trail from Linville Road one of the best areas on Salem Lake for interesting out-and-back hikes. (Sadly, parking isn't permitted on Linville Road, so you'll have to arrange to be dropped off and hike back to a car in the lot.) You'll notice the blue-blazed beginnings of side trails on this side of the lake; these don't go far, just up through the woods and down to the next leg of the trail. At about 5 miles (1.3 miles from Linville Road), you round a cove near the broader head of the lake, and the picnic area, trailhead parking area, and marina become visible on the opposite shore.

The trail rounds the point of another promontory at 6 miles and swings right, again reaching a gravel treadway that turns left across the northern arm of the lake. (To the right, another gravel tread continues a short distance along the shore, part of what will eventually be a trail around this northern arm.) A bridge spans a gap in the causeway. From it, views to the right include a railroad bridge that also crosses the lake.

Re-entering the woods at about 6.2 miles, the trail winds along for a short distance, becomes paved, and rises over a hill and steeply drops to a T-junction below the dam at 6.5 miles. To the right, the paved Salem Creek Trail follows Salem Creek 4.5 miles, with numerous trailheads along the way. The closest, 1.3 miles west at Reynolds Park Road, is an alternate starting point, which turns the Salem Lake Trail into a 9.6-mile loop.

Going left at the greenway trail junction, the Salem Lake Trail immediately dips across a low-water bridge (weir) below the dam. **NOTE:** If this crossing is flooded you will have hiked almost 7 miles and be blocked from making the loop back to your car! Attempt to cross at low-water only. Beyond the bridge, the trail climbs steeply up and crests a hill above the fenced marina, then descends to a stop sign at the marina gate before re-entering the trailhead parking area at 6.9 miles.

The **Salem Creek Trail** is a paved path between Marketplace Mall and the Salem Lake Trail that passes occasional picnic tables and resting benches, with the most enjoyable section of the trail between Reynolds Park Road and Salem Lake. From the Salem Lake Trail parking area head west around the marina, down across the weir bridge to a junction with the Salem Creek Trail (which goes right and steeply uphill). This junction is about 0.4 mile from the parking area.

Going left, the Salem Creek Trail goes 1.3 miles to a short, uphill side path left to a parking area, picnic shelter, and playground on Reynolds Park Road. A recommended way to hike this section of trail is to go east from this parking area toward the lake (the direction you'd go if you used this hike to lengthen a lake loop). Hiking east, the wooded trail leaves the Reynolds Park Road trailhead, passes the green expanse of Reynolds Park Golf Course, crosses a weir, wanders through a scenic little gorge, and gradually parallels railroad tracks high on the north side of the creek. The nicest finish for a hike in this direction is to go left on the Salem Lake Trail for about 0.3 mile to the bridge, benches, and views near the northern arm of the lake. That's about a 1.6-mile (3.2-mile round-trip) hike from Reynolds Park Road.

West, the trail goes under Reynolds Park Road and keeps its secluded woods character. Then, eventually, the holding ponds of the Thomas Water Treatment Plant appear on the left and the trailside vegetation recedes to open fields where the trail goes under M. L. King, Jr. Drive, just south of Reynolds Park Road and Winston-Salem State University, and not far north of Bowman Gray Stadium (about 0.5 mile from the Reynolds Park Road trailhead). The path enters the Civitan Park section of the greenway, one of the nicer portions of the trail. It wanders past baseball diamonds and passes a pedestrian bridge on the right with access to Winston-Salem State University. Then comes Vargrave Street, and the trail goes under U.S. Highway 52 and a railway trestle about 0.9 mile from Reynolds Park Rd.

Passing a neighborhood on the left, the trail enters Happy Hills Park, then crosses a bridge into Central Park at about 0.6 mile from Vargrave Street (1.5 miles from the Reynolds Park Road trailhead). The Central Park area, where trailhead parking is available, is about 0.3 mile past the Happy Hills Park bridge (1.8 miles from the trailhead). Trailhead parking here is reached from Salem Avenue. From this trailhead, out-and-back round-trip hikes east (toward Salem Lake) reach Vargrave Street in 0.9 mile, M. L. King, Jr. Drive in 1.3 miles, and the Reynolds Park Road trailhead in 1.8 miles (3.6 miles round-trip). A hike from here all the way to the bridge turnaround point north of Salem Lake is 3.8 miles one-way.

The trail follows just under 0.3 mile of sidewalks from Central Park west to Broad Street, its next wooded section. On this urbanized interlude, the least natural segment of the path, you pass the Strollway, a 1.1-mile, lightly paved, urban rail trail that leads left to the North Carolina School of the Arts, right to Old Salem (a restored Moravian settlement), and beyond to downtown Winston-Salem.

Going west from Broad Street (where the only informal trailhead parking is available at the Duke Power building), the trail reaches its terminus at Marketplace Mall in 1 mile. From there hike away from the mall, passing a bench and the exercise stations of the Salem Creek Trail's fitness course. The trail rises to a power line, then dips along the right bank of Salem Creek as it enters Washington Park. The fitness stations continue, and Washington Park sprawls to the right, from a soccer and baseball field just

43 SALEM CREEK TRAIL

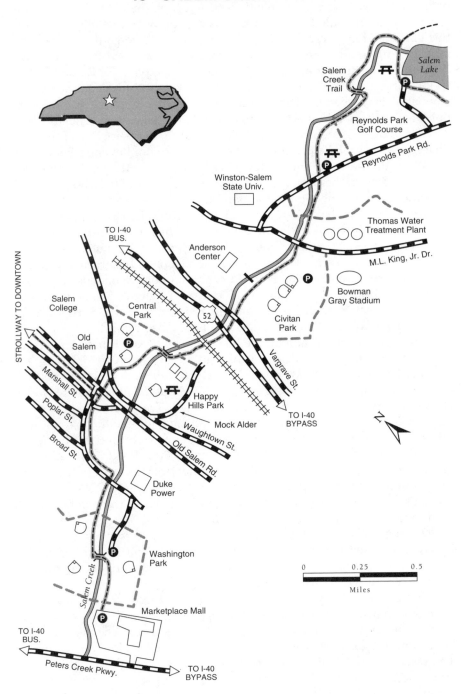

to the right of the trail to picnic shelters and basketball courts farther away. Left, the trail crosses a bridge over Salem Creek, at about 0.5 mile, avoiding a Washington Park trailhead parking area on the right side of the creek (accessible via a gravel road from the Duke Power building).

Across the bridge, the fitness stations continue east, with three more ballfields to the left of the trail. There are more fitness tasks for a short distance, then the trail re-enters the woods along the stream, eventually emerging at the Salem Creek bridge on Broad Street, just under 0.5 mile from the Washington Park trail bridge, about 1 mile from the mall trailhead. The round-trip from and to the mall is about 2 miles.

44 UWHARRIE NATIONAL FOREST

Overview

Uwharrie National Forest, the state's smallest and only Piedmont national forest, sprawls for nearly 47,000 acres over rolling summits between the Pee Dee River and Badin Lake, and between the small towns of Asheboro and Troy. These hills are the Uwharrie Mountains, but like the peaks across the river in Morrow Mountain State Park, they rise only modestly from stream valleys at 450 or so feet to round summits. The highest in the southern Uwharries, at 950 feet, is Cedar Rock Mountain, on the edge of the Birkhead Mountains Wilderness.

Uwharrie National Forest began with federal land acquisitions in the early 1930s. Later, President John F. Kennedy declared the 43,000-acre reserve Uwharrie National Forest in 1961. The nearly 5,000-acre Birkhead Mountains Wilderness, designated in 1984, is the only legislated wilderness in the Carolina Piedmont.

In the early 1980s, the Forest Service announced it was evaluating over 6 million acres of national forest land. North Carolinians were flabbergasted when the Reagan administration proposed selling 42,000 of Uwharrie's forested acres. Community outcry and support from legislators quashed those plans and, a decade later, the national forest is finishing its first major expansion. An improvement budget has consolidated the forest's holdings and thus preserved and enhanced public access to trails. The improvements also include a major campground on Badin Lake. With 3 million people living less than a 2-hour drive away, the new focus on recreation comes just as nearby residents are looking for outlets close to home. The forest's facilities appear well tended and well marked, suggesting that the national forest's employees and users take pride in it.

The area's geologic history leads scientists to speculate that the Uwharries are the oldest mountain range in North America. Indian habitation in these volcanic hills has been dated to twelve thousand years ago.

European explorers first penetrated the area in the 1600s, but agricultural settlers didn't inhabit the region until the 1760s. The Birkhead Mountains got their name from John Birkhead, born in 1858, who accumulated about 3,000 acres of land here by 1900, which he and tenant farmers tilled. Birkhead moved to nearby Asheboro when his farmhouse burned in 1914, and he lived there until 1933. His plantation, now covered in mature hardwoods, makes up the bulk of the area designated as wilderness.

In warmer months ticks, copperheads, and timber rattlesnakes are common in the Uwharrie, so winter is probably the best time to hike the area. Second best may be late fall and early spring. Hunting seasons threaten hikers in off-trail areas. Deer season prevails from mid-November to January 1; turkey season lasts from April to mid-May. Remember that wearing blaze orange is appropriate gear for deer season, but not for turkey season.

General description: Wonderful, woodsy circuit hikes in Uwharrie National Forest, some of substantial length. The Uwharrie and Dutchmans Creek trails form a figure eight that when linked with forest roads can create hikes of many lengths. There's also an interpretive walk beside the ranger station on the Denson's Creek Trail.

General location: Uwharrie National Forest, in the central Piedmont between Troy and Asheboro.

Length: The Birkhead Mountain Wilderness circuit is 7 miles. The Uwharrie–Dutchmans Creek figure eight is 20.1 miles. The southern half of the circuit is 11.6 miles; the northern circuit is 9.5 miles (though a forest road shortcut creates a hike of under 3 miles). The Denson's Creek Trail is 3 miles.

Degree of difficulty: Easy for the Densons Creek Trail; moderate to moderately strenuous for the Birkhead Mountain Wilderness circuit; moderately strenuous to strenuous for both Uwharrie–Dutchmans Creek circuits.

Maps: USGS Eleazer and Farmer quads for the Birkhead Mountain Wilderness; USGS Troy, Morrow Mountain, and Lovejoy quads for the Uwharrie Trail. The preferred map for the Birkhead Mountain Wilderness is the map of the same name published by the Forest Service. That map, USGS, and Forest Service quads that show current trails, are available from the district ranger. A topographical hiker's map of the Uwharrie Trail similar to the one available for the Birkhead Mountain Wilderness may soon be available, too.

Elevation gain and loss: Negligible for the Densons Creek Trail; about 1,480 feet for the Birkhead Mountain Wilderness circuit; 2,688 feet for the southern hike of Uwharrie/Dutchmans Creek circuit, and 2,200 feet for the northern hike.

Trailhead elevation: 580 feet for the Birkhead Mountain Wilderness parking area; 553 feet for the Uwharrie Trail parking area on North Carolina Highway 24/27; 770 feet at Yates Place Campground.

Low points: About 490 feet on the Hannah's Creek Trail in the Birkhead Mountain Wilderness; about 380 feet on the Uwharrie Trail at Island Creek (southern hike); about 440 feet on the Dutchmans Creek Trail at Little Island Creek (northern hike).

44 UWHARRIE NATIONAL FOREST —
UWHARRIE / DUTCHMANS CREEK TRAILS

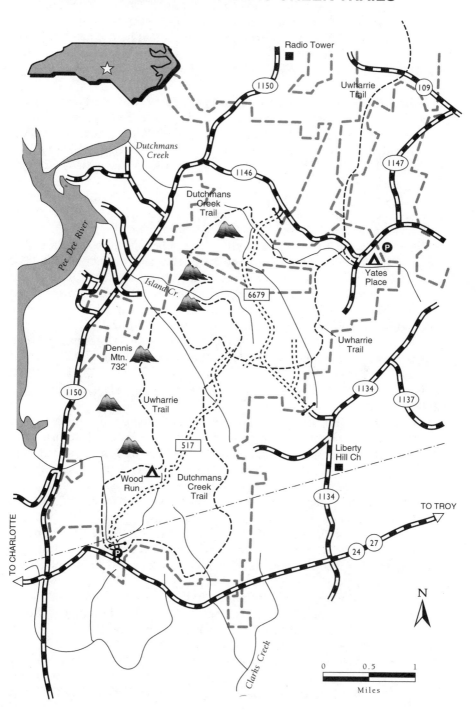

Radio Tower

Uwharrie
Trail

109

1150

1147

Dutchmans
Creek

1146

Dutchmans
Creek
Trail

Pee Dee River

Island Cr.

6679

P

Yates
Place

Uwharrie
Trail

Dennis
Mtn.
732'

Uwharrie
Trail

517

1134

1137

Wood
Run

Dutchmans
Creek
Trail

Liberty
Hill Ch

1134

TO TROY

TO CHARLOTTE

24 27

N

Clarks Creek

0   0.5   1
Miles

High points: About 910 feet on the Birkhead Mountain Trail along the crest of Coolers Knob Mountain; 768 feet on the Dutchmans Creek Trail; about 700 feet at two places on the Uwharrie Trail (one is Dennis Mountain).

Water availability: Water near the headwaters of streams in the Birkhead Wilderness is relatively clean, but it should be boiled before drinking. Day hikers will find it easier to bring water from nearby towns. A warm-weather water fountain and the Uwharrie Ranger Station are located immediately beside the Densons Creek trailhead.

For more information: Uwharrie National Forest,. Or contact Supervisor's Office, National Forests in North Carolina, Asheville. See Appendix C.

Finding the trailheads: The Birkhead Mountain Wilderness circuit is best started at the wilderness trailhead on SR 1107. From U.S. Highway 220, about 25 miles south of the Interstate Highway 85/U.S. Highway 220 exit in Greensboro (Exit 122A/NC Zoo), take the U.S. Highway 64/North Carolina Highway 49 exit in Asheboro and turn right. Measuring from there, turn left at 2.5 miles on SR 1170. Coming from Charlotte on NC 49, this turn, a right, is about 70 miles, about 4.3 miles past the little village of Martha, and about 2.7 miles past where the only four-lane section of NC 49 north of the Badin Lake Bridge turns to two lanes. Once on SR 1170 (Mechanic Road), turn right at 0.6 mile on SR 1107 (Lassiter Mill Road). At 3.2 miles (junction with SR 1174) bear left on SR 1107. At 5.1 miles turn left into the signed Birkhead Mountain Wilderness parking area. The trailhead is 0.6 mile away on a rough, unpaved FR 6532.

The southernmost trailhead for the Uwharrie and Dutchmans Creek trails is on the right side of NC 24/27, 10 miles west from where NC 134 meets NC 24/27 in the heart of Troy. From Charlotte, the trailhead is about 54 miles via NC 24/27, and 2.3 miles from the start of the Pee Dee River/Lake Tillery bridge.

The northern trailhead for the figure eight formed by the Uwharrie and Dutchmans Creek trails is on a spur trail from the Yates Place primitive campground. To reach that trailhead from Charlotte and the west, turn left from NC 24/27 on SR 1150, 1.3 miles from the Pee Dee River/Lake Tillery bridge. Measuring from there, turn right on the unpaved SR 1146 at 5.9 miles at the Forest Service sign for Yates Place Campground. The Uwharrie Trail crosses the road at 8.2 miles, and Yates Place is on the right at 8.5 miles.

To reach Yates Place from the north, east, and south, go west from the center of Troy on NC 24/27 and turn right at 0.5 mile on North Carolina Highway 109 Bypass, just past the McDonald's restaurant. At 5.4 miles turn left onto SR 1147. At 7.3 miles turn right onto unpaved SR 1146. Yates Place is on the left at 7.9 miles; the Uwharrie Trail crosses the road at 8.2 miles.

The Densons Creek Trail starts behind the Uwharrie Ranger Station, 1.7 miles east of where NC 24/27 meets NC 134 in Troy.

The hikes: Perhaps the forest's easiest, most interesting trail is the **Densons Creek Nature Trail**, built in 1974 by the Youth Conservation Corps. The white-blazed trail has seventeen designated stops keyed to an

44 BIRKHEAD WILDERNESS — UWHARRIE NATIONAL FOREST — BIRKHEAD MOUNTAIN

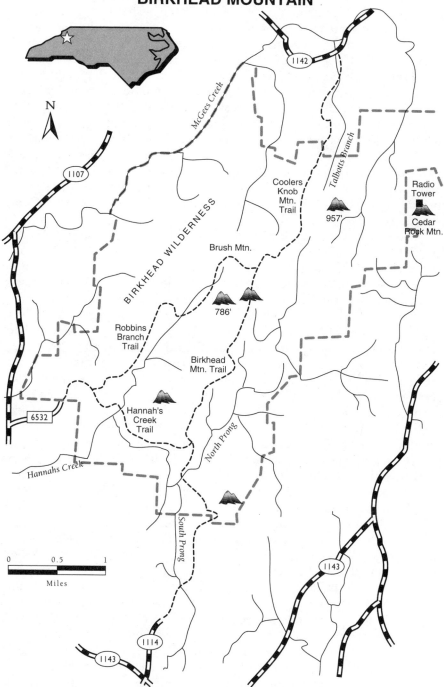

N

BIRKHEAD WILDERNESS

McGees Creek

Talbotts Branch

1142

1107

Coolers Knob Mtn. Trail

957'

Radio Tower

Cedar Rock Mtn.

Brush Mtn.

786'

Robbins Branch Trail

Birkhead Mtn. Trail

6532

Hannah's Creek Trail

North Prong

Hannahs Creek

South Prong

1143

1114

1143

0   0.5   1
Miles

interpretive brochure available at the information sign beside the Uwharrie Ranger Station. Plaques along the trail list the names of trees and plants.

The trail starts immediately behind the Uwharrie Ranger Station, beside a water fountain and a large, split millstone. The route is a two-loop trail that can permit a hike of up to 3 miles. It's designed so that the shortest loop, a 1-mile circle, is closest to the trailhead. Take the left fork at stop 1 to start the short loop and follow the brochure in order. The longer 2.2-mile loop branches off at stop 3. The larger loop goes left at the junction, and the short loop goes right. The long loop wanders out to Densons Creek and back, with each side of the loop crossing SR 1324 on the way.

The path at times explores half-century-old pine and hardwood forest noted for patches of running cedar, deer, and turkey. In fact, some portions of the trail are seeded to attract wildlife, so quiet morning or evening rests on the many trail benches may be rewarded with animal sightings. The trail leads to once-inhabited locations, among them a pre-1935 sawmill site and an old homestead used before 1910. Sizeable Densons Creek is visible from a clifftop.

The Birkhead Mountains Wilderness contains a 7-mile circuit consisting of the Birkhead Mountain, Hannah's Creek, and Robbins Branch trails. The **Birkhead Mountain Trail** runs 5.6 miles north to south through the wilderness, but its trailheads on SR 1114 (to the south) and SR 1142 (to the north) are poorly marked. Serious hikers, especially backpackers wanting solitude, might do well to get the wilderness map and investigate these alternate starting points. They substantially lengthen the loop hike and are far less traveled than the trails that begin at the wilderness parking area. But the Uwharrie's network of small local roads, many of them unpaved, aren't the easiest routes to find your way around. Therefore, the best access to the wilderness is via the Hannah's Creek or Robbins Branch trails, both of which begin at a well-marked, well-maintained parking area reached from SR 1107 on the western side of the wilderness. That makes Robbins Branch the area's busiest trail; if you're hoping to escape crowds, you should hike the loop by taking the first right out of the parking lot on the **Hannah's Creek Trail**.

Taking that advice, leave the parking lot on a level path through tall trees. At 0.4 mile go right on the Hannah's Creek Trail, an old logging road. The trail dips through tall oak and holly before crossing Robbins Branch at about 1 mile. The trail then parallels Hannah's Creek before crossing a drainage, passing the remains of an old house, and finally climbing to junction with the Birkhead Mountain Trail at 1.8 miles.

To the right, the trail goes about 2.2 miles to SR 1114 and the vicinity of Strieby Church, about 1 mile north of SR 1143. Backpackers can take a side trip in this direction to camp. The trail descends in 0.2 mile (2.2 miles from the wilderness trailhead) to North Prong, where campsites can be found, and then continues another 0.5 mile (at 2.7 miles) to a campsite near the wilderness boundary with water. This area might also be of interest to trailless hikers. Hikers heading north on the Birkhead Mountain Trail can easily bushwhack east of that trail (at almost any point) and follow the North Prong drainage south to where it crosses the Birkhead Mountain Trail. A right turn there leads back to the Hannah's Creek Trail and a circuit hike that includes a big dose of trailless solitude.

Go left from the Hannah's Creek Trail onto the Birkhead Mountain Trail (at about 1.8 miles) and start a climb of about 600 feet over the next few miles. This ascending ridge runs north past various campsites. You'll pass the remains of John Birkhead's early plantation at 2.8 miles. Farther along the ridge, at about 3.8 miles, the Robbins Branch Trail comes in from the left.

North of this junction, the Birkhead Mountain Trail runs 2.6 miles to SR 1132, the Tot Hill Farm Road. The trailhead is obscure, but backpackers might use this portion of trail as a side trip north. There are nice ridgetop campsites and a vista east to Cedar Rock Mountain at about 5.2 miles, about 1.5 miles north of the **Robbins Branch Trail** junction (just 0.1 mile from the national forest boundary). Going left on the Robbins Branch Trail, the trail dips into the headwaters of Robbins Branch and follows the stream to a final crossing at about 5 miles. The path passes evidence of early farming, then climbs 0.8 mile to a vista. The trail gradually descends to the Hannah's Creek Trail junction at 6.6 miles and returns to the parking area at 7 miles.

This wilderness is particularly approrpriate to trailless travel, especially in winter. If you're not in the mood for crowds, and are relatively skilled at map and compass, consider a bushwhacking trip in the Uwharrie. The area's elevation changes are gradual, and a variety of stream drainages make loops and alternate routes feasible from starting points along the main trails. For instance, the unnnamed 957-foot summit is a nice destination to the east from Cooler's Knob Mountain, and North Prong provides an enjoyable descending return route to Birkhead Mountain Trail. In fact, you could continue on North Prong past that trail, go right on Hannah's Creek to two spots where easy connections to the Hannah's Creek Trail can be made. A similar kind of bushwhack exists using Robbins Branch. Go south from the Robbins Branch Trail at the stream crossing and follow Robbins Branch south to Hannah's Creek Trail and right to the parking area. Also, hikes are possible from the Robbins Branch Trail north to trailless Brush Mountain and surroundings. And along all of these routes, various flats make attractive destinations and remote campsites.

The **Uwharrie Trail** is the area's jewel of long-distance hiking. It runs south to north from NC 24/27 to SR 1306. This National Recreation Trail is the most formal 20.5-mile section of a 33-mile path blazed between 1972 and 1975 by an Asheboro Boy Scout troop. Leader Joe Moffitt envisioned the trail as an Eagle Scout project for his troop and founded the Uwharrie Trail Club. Today the white-blazed Uwharrie Trail is almost entirely on national forest land, which has solved the problems of poor marking and a fluctuating route. Four primitive designated campsites line the way, and two other campsites, accessible by side trails, have pit toilets

Robbins Branch Trail, Uwharrie National Forest, Birkhead Wilderness.

but no drinking water. In addition, undesignated campsites are plentiful along the trail.

Perhaps the most attractive portion of the Uwharrie Trail is the section covered here, the 9 miles between the southernmost terminus on NC 24/27 and SR 1146. Here the trail plays tag with the yellow-blazed, 11.1-mile **Dutchmans Creek Trail**. This path was built specifically to create a figure-eight trail circuit, perfect for day hiking or backpacking for novice and expert alike. Streams, lush creekside vegetation, and areas of mature forest are big attractions. Also, many forest roads wind through the area, so experienced, topographic map-equipped hikers can create custom circuits of many lengths.

The trails begin on NC 24/27 at a marked and maintained trailhead. The Uwharrie Trail begins on the left side of the signboard through a gap in the fence, the gated, gravel Forest Road 517 starts to the right of the designated parking spaces, and the Dutchmans Creek Trail enters the woods to the right of that. This description covers each loop as a separate day hike from trailheads on the south and north, then discusses the lengthiest figure-eight loop.

From the Uwharrie Trail's southern terminus, the lower half of the figure eight formed by the Uwharrie and Dutchmans Creek trails creates an 11.6-mile circuit. But FR 517 wanders through this big circuit, touching the trails at various points, creating other circuit and figure-eight possibilities.

The Uwharrie Trail leaves NC 24/27 (briefly paralleling FR 517) and ducks under a power line at 0.3 mile. The trail descends along Wood Run Creek and crosses it at 1 mile. At 2 miles, a yellow-blazed spur leads 0.3 mile right to Wood Run Camp (a large field with no facilities beside FR 517, 1.5 miles on that road from the parking area). The Uwharrie Trail continues to FR 517 at 2.5 miles. This first section of the Uwharrie Trail and FR 517 form a nice 4- to 4.5-mile circuit, depending on whether you reach FR 517 via the spur to Wood Run Camp or continue. Either route, in either direction, is a nice hike or beginner backpacking trip, partially on a wooded road, with a designated campsite in the middle.

Continuing, the trail branches left down Upper Wood Run Creek, and FR 517 goes right to cross the Uwharrie Trail at the 5.5-mile mark. The trail leaves the creek and climbs steeply north to just below the summit of Dennis Mountain (732 feet) at 3.7 miles. Off to the east, you can see Morrow Mountain from here in the winter.

Dipping off the northern ridge of Dennis Mountain, the trail swings down to the lowest elevation on this circuit hike (about 380 feet on Island Creek) at about 4.5 miles. It crosses and follows Island Creek up the next drainage. At about 5.5 miles, the trail crosses FR 517.

From here FR 517 goes to the right, back toward the parking lot with two other connections to the Dutchmans Creek Trail. But go straight, and where the Uwharrie Trail continues on at 5.7 miles, turn right on the Dutchmans Creek Trail and cross FR 517 again at 6.1 miles. The Dutchmans Creek Trail crosses the road, then dips down into, crosses, and climbs out of the headwaters of Island Creek. At 6.7 miles, the trail again crosses FR 517. From here, a right on the road returns the flagging hiker to the parking lot in about 3 miles, compared with another 5 miles on the Dutchmans Creek Trail. That shortcut reduces the circuit to under 10 miles, but the road can be a hotter walk under a summer sun.

Taking the Dutchmans Creek Trail instead, hikers climb steeply for 0.5 mile to a ridgetop at 700 feet and stay there for 1 mile or so. Then, skirting east of a parcel of private land, the trail dips to a drainage and climbs to the high point of this hike, an unnamed peak at 768 feet. The trail swings south, crossing a stream at just over 9 miles, then goes north around another private holding. Skirting west along that boundary, the trail dips to another drainage at just over 10 miles and reaches the parking lot at 11.6 miles.

The northern trailhead for the Uwharrie Trail is on SR 1146. But at that little-used starting point, the trail just crosses the unpaved road with no public parking. The best place to start the northern half of the figure eight formed by the Uwharrie and Dutchmans Creek trails, a circuit of about 9.5 miles, is from the nearby and more frequented Yates Place primitive campground. From there take the spur from the west side of the campground not far from SR 1146 and descend along the north slope of a knob for about 0.5 mile to a junction with the Uwharrie Trail. Right, the Uwharrie Trail crosses SR 1146 in 0.1 mile. Go left at the junction on the Uwharrie Trail and slab the west side of the knob for another 0.5 mile to a junction with the Dutchmans Creek Trail on the right at about 1 mile. Go left on the Uwharrie Trail; it continues gradually south through the heads of three drainages before reaching the upper end of Dutchmans Creek at about 2.5 miles.

Climbing away from Dutchmans Creek, the trail crosses Forest Road 6678, dips into a swale, and rises to cross Forest Road 6679 (both of these are gated, untraveled roads). To the right FR 6679 bisects this northern circuit of the Dutchmans Creek–Uwharrie trails, cutting a few miles off the 9.5-mile circuit.

Continuing on the Uwharrie Trail, cross FR 6679 and shortly, at about 3.5 miles, pass a junction where Forest Road 6680 (to the right) intersects another forest road that crosses the trail route. Continue, and at 3.8 miles turn right on the Dutchmans Creek Trail.

The Dutchmans Creek Trail descends the east side of a knob, then drops to the low point of this hike, about 420 feet at Little Island Creek. The drop into and climb out of this steep notch, the portal through which Little Island Creek breaks out of the higher Uwharries, is one of the more dramatic elevation changes in the area. The path crosses this scenic stream, then climbs the rocky rise of the flanking peak and crosses the 700-foot summit at about 5.5 miles. The trail swings off the summit, passing an inholding of private land and a junction with Forest Road 518 at 6 miles. FR 518 goes left about 0.75 mile to SR 1150, creating a rarely used access to this part of the trail. (To reach the roadside start of FR 518, go west 1 mile from the NC 24/27 Uwharrie Trail parking area and turn right on SR 1150. The forest road begins on the right side, just over 4 miles north of NC 24/27.)

Passing FR 518, the trail climbs steeply to a peak at about 6.5 miles, with winter views of the lake to the west and nearby Lick Mountain to the east. The trail descends and exits the gap under Lick Mountain, then dips steeply to Dutchmans Creek and rises through a towering hardwood forest. The trail continues upstream, then veers left, climbing to the Uwharrie Trail at about 8.5 miles. Go left, and in 0.5 mile turn right (ahead the Uwharrie Trail crosses SR 1146 in 0.1 mile) on the spur to arrive at Yates Place Campground at about 9.5 miles.

Both the northern and southern circuits of the Dutchmans Creek and Uwharrie trails are long enough that most hikers will be challenged by hiking one circuit at a time. But for backpackers who don't hike fast, want to take their time, or are inclined to carry life's luxuries, the entire figure-eight circuit can be a wonderful three-day trip.

WILLIAM B. UMSTEAD STATE PARK (45-46)

Overview

William B. Umstead State Park includes 5,400 acres in two major tracts, Reedy Creek (the section emphasized here) and Crabtree Creek.

The bulk of the park was acquired in 1934 under a Resettlement Administration program that turned exhausted farmland into recreation areas. The Civilian Conservation Corps (CCC) went to work, and in 1937 the park opened. It was deeded to the state in 1943 for $1. In 1950, during the dark days of Jim Crow, a second parcel was added to create a separate park for blacks. The larger park was named William B. Umstead State Park after a former governor in 1955. The two parks merged in 1966.

With state park stewardship, the area is now reverting to towering deciduous forest, as it was prior to 1774, the year a land grant opened the area to settlement. An isolated 50-acre tract, the Piedmont Beech Natural Area, recalls such forest with a massive stand of virgin trees more than 300 years old.

The park holds 16 miles of hiking trails and 17 miles of bridle trails. Its three lakes allow fishing; rowboats are available in Big Lake, the park's largest at 55 acres. Two of the lakes permit swimming at remarkable cabin camps available for rent to youth groups and nonprofit organizations. Reservations at any of the park's four camps must be made in writing. The park also has a campground for tents and RVs, a lodge, and two primitive camping areas open year-round.

45 COMPANY MILL CIRCUITS

General description: A variety of hikes in a state park on the fall line.
General location: Reedy Creek section, William B. Umstead State Park, west of Raleigh.
Length: Two looping nature walks, 1.1 miles on the Inspiration Trail, and 2.1 miles on a circuit of the Company Mill, Beech, and Inspiration trails; also two longer circuit hikes of approximately 4.2 and 4.7 miles on parts of the Company Mill Trail. A side trip to views of the runways at Raleigh-Durham International Airport adds 2 miles.
Degree of difficulty: Easy for the two shortest circuits; moderate to moderately strenuous for the Company Mill Trail.
Maps: USGS Cary, Raleigh West, Bayleaf, and East Durham quads. State park map/brochure available at park office and from address below.
Elevation gain and loss: Undulating terrain, without sustained elevation changes.
Trailhead elevation: 450 feet.
Low point: 250 feet.
High point: 450 feet.
Water availability: The picnic area where all the trails start has restrooms and water year-round.
For more information: William B. Umstead State Park, Raleigh. See Appendix C.
Finding the trailhead: The Reedy Creek trails begin near Interstate Highway 40. Heading east on I-40, take Exit 287, the Cary-Harrison Avenue exit. Go left at the stoplight onto Harrison Avenue, which leads immediately into the park. After entering the state park, take a right at the first junction to reach the ranger office and pick up maps. Bear left to enter the large trailhead parking area. The path to the picnic area is the access trail for all of the hikes described here. It leaves on the left end of the distantmost parking area.

The hikes: In 1994, the reopening of the bridge across Crabtree Creek triggered name changes for a few small loop trails between the parking area and the Company Mill Trail. By now, trail signing and blazing should match the descriptions below.

The 1.1-mile **Inspiration Trail** is aptly named. It loops through an inspiring large forest in a designated natural area along Crabtree Creek. Like the other trails described here, this nature hike is marked by unusually open and mature forest. To take it, start on the main trail that links the picnic area with Crabtree Creek and the longest loop hike, the Company Mill Trail. The Company Mill Trail heads off on the right (formerly the Beech Trail) at the picnic shelter, but stay straight on the main trail. The next two leftward junctions are marked with Inspiration Trail signs, and the loop, marked with blue diamonds, can be taken in either direction. There are benches for quiet contemplation under the big trees.

45 WILLIAM B. UMSTEAD STATE PARK

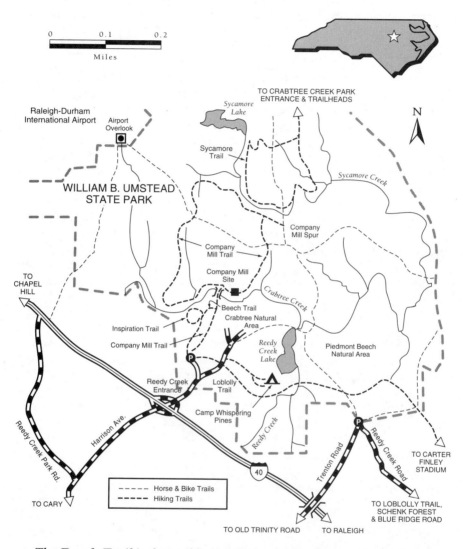

The **Beech Trail** is the trail links the Inspiration Trail with the Company Mill Trail. This means that the Beech Trail runs from the most distant Inspiration Trail loop and intersects the Company Mill Trail at the largest stream before Crabtree Creek. Total length is about 0.5 mile. The connector permits a few easy circuits, as noted below.

At about 4.8 miles, the orange square-blazed **Company Mill Trail** is the longest loop on this side of the park. It wanders through two major stream drainages, crosses a colonial road, and reaches a century-old dam at a historic mill site. This trail branches right at the picnic shelter and descends in a long curve to a small stream where it joins the Beech Trail, as noted. When the Company Mill Trail reaches its low point at the small stream, a path seems to cross the stream on the right, but hikers should ignore this and continue to the Beech Trail junction and a map sign. Go right here, descending and crossing the stream. The trail climbs gently to a ridge crest above Crabtree Creek, to the left. The lazy, brown stream is about 15 feet wide, and deep.

An unmarked trail switchbacks to the stream crossing, while the main trail continues right then drops abruptly left to a new metal stream bridge, about 0.8 mile from the parking area. The modern metal bridge, donated in 1993, replaces an old wooden structure that was washed away. The bridge is one of the more interesting destinations for a nice out-and-back hike of about 2 miles. Cross the bridge to a T-junction. Go right, and in 100 feet notice a pile of boulders on the opposite side of the stream. These rocks indicate the ruins of an old dam, in use here as early as 1810. The ruins are reached via an informal trail on the other side of the bridge. According to park historian Garth Hamilton, the dam and a grist mill beside it were economic focal points of the Raleigh area. Farmers flatboated or hauled grains and produce here for sale and processing; the community gathered for dances, and for swimming and boating in the pond behind the dam. About half of the dam structure remains and probably appears much as it did centuries ago. Its huge stones, quarried from adjacent ridges, are fitted.

Nearby, one of the mill's grindstones is displayed beside the trail. It had been assumed that the millstones, possibly manufactured in France, had washed away or been stolen. But in the winter of 1993-1994, park historian Hamilton began exploring the riverbed below the dam. He found the stone not 200 feet below the dam, standing upright against the northern bank. National guard helicopters lifted it out of the stream.

Continuing east, not far from the dam, an old eighteenth-century stage road bears left and uphill at a flexible strip sign. For those who wander up, a variety of ruins are visible. The old road skirts a rock outcrop. When you can see left through the trees to the metal trail bridge, keep a sharp eye out for a 5-by-10-foot pit that used to be a root cellar for the mill operator's house. Diagonally off in the woods on the same side of the trail, you'll find a few foundations, evidence that the operator's home occupied this promontory. Adjacent hollows once bore evidence of a still. The old stage road, lined with trees and carpeted in pine needles, eventually joins the bridle trail that bisects the Company Mill Trail, providing other loop options.

The main trail follows a side ravine and rises to the park's main bridle trail, the **Durham Road**, a centuries-old route between Raleigh and Durham. (A left here bisects the Company Mill Trail loop, and reaches the spot where the old stage road comes in on the left; this connector is about 0.7 mile.) This height of land is both the location of the Durham Road bridle trail and the buffer that separates the park's two stream drainages.

Dropping off the height of land, the Company Mill Trail meets the **Company Mill Spur**, a 0.2-mile link to a horse/bicycle trail that connects to the **Sycamore Trail**, a good loop hike from the other side of the park.

This is about 1.1 miles from the old dam, just under 2 miles from the parking area. Going left, the trail passes the George Linn Mill site, in use in 1870 but now difficult to identify. The trail then climbs gently along a stream, passing a lush patch of ferns just before reaching the bridle trail again, about 0.8 mile from the last junction and 2.7 miles from the parking area.

Hikers can take a side trip here. Going right on the Durham Road, it's about 1 mile to the Airport Overlook. Where the bike trail bends south toward a trailhead on Reedy Creek Park Road, the trail emerges onto airport authority land and provides a great view of the Raleigh-Durham International Airport. Runways are as close as 300 feet, and picnic tables and the easy bicycle access make this a great kids' destination for a hike or bike trip.

Back at the Company Mill Trail, the path descends to Crabtree Creek at 3.5 miles, then the small stream crossing is at about 3.9 miles. The entire hike back to the picnic area is approximately 4.7 miles.

There are other options. If you bisect the Company Mill Trail using the Durham Road, the loop is about 4.2 miles. Continuing to the Airport Overlook, the hike is about 6.7 miles, with 2.7 of that on an easy, unpaved horse/bike trail. A shorter hike, but the longest on the south side of Crabtree Creek, involves taking the Company Mill Trail from the picnic shelter and making a left onto the Beech Trail. Once there, go right on the Inspiration Trail, and right again on the Beech Trail, heading back to the picnic shelter and the parking area. This slightly more than 2-mile loop is undulating enough to be an active but untaxing outing.

46 SCHENCK FOREST — LOBLOLLY TRAIL

General description: The Loblolly Trail links William B. Umstead State Park with Carter Finley Stadium at North Carolina State University in two lakeside and streamside sections. The portion bordering the university's Schenck Forest connects with the Frances Liles Interpretive Trail, allowing highly scenic circuit hikes.

General location: William B. Umstead State Park, Raleigh.

Length: 6 miles one-way. When linked with the Frances Liles Interpretive Trail, hikes of 1.2, 2, and 3 miles are possible.

Degree of difficulty: Moderately strenuous for the 6-mile end-to-end hike, with easy to moderate out-and-back or loop hikes possible. The Frances Liles Trail and related loops are easy.

Maps: USGS Cary and Raleigh West quads. State park map/brochure available at park office and from address below. The city of Raleigh publishes the spiral-bound "Capital Area Greenway Trail System Maps," which includes a rough area map of the trail (See "Maps" under Hike 42).

Elevation gain and loss: Minimal, except for undulating terrain in Umstead State Park.

Trailhead elevation: 450 feet at Umstead State Park.

Water availability: Water is available year-round in the picnic area near the Umstead State Park trailhead.

For more information: William B. Umstead State Park, Raleigh. Raleigh Parks and Recreation Department. See Appendix C.

Finding the trailheads: To reach the Loblolly Trail's northern terminus in William B. Umstead State Park, see the directions for the Company Mill Trail, above.

To reach the southern terminus, or the Carter Finley Stadium trailhead, from I-40, take the Wade Avenue exit, Exit 289, and go south on Blue Ridge Road. Turn right in 0.3 mile on Trinity Road. In 1 mile turn into Gate D of Carter Finley Stadium and park at the trailhead.

To reach the Schenck Forest trailhead for the Frances Liles Interpretive Trail, also take the Wade Avenue exit, but go north. In about 0.3 mile turn left on Reedy Creek Park Road. The road becomes gravel at 0.7 mile. Go 1 mile and turn left on a gravel road. Park at (but not blocking) a gate on the right side of that road at 0.1 mile. Cross the gate and the Schenck Forest picnic area and trailhead is a few hundred feet on the right.

To reach the other Loblolly trailheads on Reedy Creek Park Road, pass the turn to the Liles trailhead and go another 0.8 mile to near the Wake County Flood Control Lake. On the right, about 0.1 of a mile before the bridge, the Loblolly Trail goes to its northern terminus in Umstead State Park. On the left at the bridge, the Loblolly Trail goes south at a Schenck Forest sign. To do the upper section of the Loblolly Trail, use the directions to the Schenck Forest area and leave a car at this Loblolly trailhead on Reedy Creek Road. Then backtrack to I-40 and start hiking at Umstead State Park.

To hike the lower Loblolly Trail, use the above directions and leave one car near the bridge on Reedy Creek Road. Then, in another car, continue straight across the bridge. Measuring from the bridge, take the sharp left onto Trenton Road at 0.5 mile (on the right at the turn, Umstead Park's bike/horse trails, and the Loblolly Trail, are accessible via dirt roads). Continuing, Trenton Road becomes paved at 0.7 mile and crosses I-40 at 1.4 miles. At 2.5 make a left onto Trinity Road and reach the trailhead on the left at stadium Gate D at 3.7 miles. From here, one can continue straight 1 mile to Blue Ridge Road, where a left reaches I-40.

The hikes: Given the length of the Loblolly Trail, you might consider hiking it in sections before attempting the whole thing. Both sections are very wild, but the planned mid-1990s extension of a nearby road will likely mean the southernmost section of trail will be temporarily closed and, unfortunately, further impacted by highway development (it already passes under I-40). Indeed, the Finley Stadium trailhead was closed in late 1994 while parking lots were under construction there. Improved trail parking is a priority, but it may be a few years before the new trailhead and completed construction renew interest in the southern section.

Beginning at Finley Stadium, the lower section of the trail runs parallel to but some distance away from Richland Creek and is part of Raleigh's

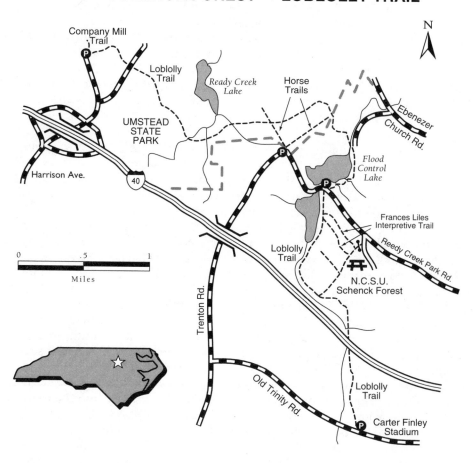

Richland Creek Greenway. The white-blazed **Loblolly Trail** crosses a small side stream and follows a concrete culvert under I-40 at about 0.6 mile. The footing can be wet if the stream is at flood stage; if that's the case, the upcoming lakeside portion of the trail will also be under water, so turn back.

North of I-40 the trail wanders along the streambank. At about 1.2 miles a road-width earth-surfaced grade goes right. This is part of the loop hike in Schenck Forest, described below. The sounds of I-40 diminish and disappear as the footpath continues along the scenic stream with blocks of quartz scattered in the woods. Eventually, it becomes obvious that you've entered the research lands of the North Carolina State University College of Forest Resources. Plots of trees, growing in crop-like rows, appear with signs that tell their type and when they were planted. Among these are loblolly pine, the species after which the trail was named. These plantings end as the trail dips into the forested wetland that surrounds the flood-prone, flatter section of the stream. At about 2 miles, multiple treadways carry the trail under a canopy of huge loblolly, river birch, red maple, and sweetgum. As you near where Richland Creek empties into the flood control lake, beavers have gnawed trees. Deer and wood ducks are often seen here.

As you reach the lake, the trail rises onto the dry bank and intersects two side-by-side junctions with the **Frances Liles Interpretive Trail**, on the right at just about 2.1 miles. The trail continues within sight of the lake under big trees, reaching Reedy Creek Park Road at the bridge over the lake at about 2.4 miles.

The upper section of the trail begins at Reedy Creek Road. Go about 0.1 mile east of the bridge, then take a left from the roadside onto the trail. The trail drops into a damp, shady young forest, then rises to drier ground. On this section, many side paths lead to lakeshore views popular with those who fish the lake: Some have left bait cups and drink cans in the woods.

The trail crosses a few side streams on its way to the route over the dam at about 0.7 mile (just over 3 miles from Carter Finley Stadium). At just over 1 mile from the trailhead, it crosses a bike/horse trail. To the right, this trail loops through the park, eventually coming back to the Loblolly Trail about 0.8 mile farther on. To the left, this trail reaches roadside parking where Reedy Creek Park Road and Trenton Road join.

Continuing on the Loblolly Trail, cross a stream and pass beside a small woodland lake at 1.3 miles (just under 4 miles from the stadium). A few tenths of a mile farther, again cross the park bike/horse trail. The next section of the trail passes through open, fern-filled forest as it undulates over ridges and heads down to three stream crossings, the lattermost being Reedy Creek. The trail then rises about 150 feet on its way into the more developed portion of the park. This open forest is popular with orienteers, hikers who use map and compass to go off trail. The Loblolly Trail crosses the ranger office access road at about 3.2 miles from the trailhead (5.7 miles from the stadium). The trail ends at the Reedy Creek Day Use Area parking lot, about 3.5 miles from the trailhead.

For those who like circuit hikes, the Schenck Forest's Frances Liles Interpretive Trail, the Loblolly Trail, and other forest roads make this area an ideal destination. The interpretive trail starts on the upland portion of the forest, dipping to a lakeshore junction with the Loblolly Trail. Its return leg rises from the lakeshore but takes a different route, creating a loop around a 108-acre watershed. Both sides of the loop follow streams through towering trees, and ten interpretive signs provide information about the forest. The trail's opening in the early 1980s was a fitting retirement tribute to Frances Liles, the longtime student services coordinator for the North Carolina State College of Forest Resources.

The simplest way to hike the trail is to cross the gate at the parking area, and in a few hundred feet reach the trailhead on the right at a grassy picnic area. A plaque dedicates the picnic area, and the forest, to C. A. Schenck, founder and director of the Biltmore Forest School, the birthplace of forestry in America.

The forest got its start in 1938 with the planting of 80 acres of loblolly pine by workers for the Depression-era Works Progress Administration.

Following the yellow blazes from the trailhead sign, just behind the picnic shelter, wander through the upland pine community. The trees get taller and the forest becomes a mixed woodland of pines and deciduous trees. An interpretive sign describes an infestation of the Southern pine beetle, and smaller markers tell the names of trees. The forest gets bigger as the trail flattens, providing a nice view on the left of a meandering stream. The trees reach impressive proportions, with open understory covered in Christmas ferns.

At about 0.5 mile, a T-junction is reached with the Loblolly Trail beside a North Carolina State-maintained weir and hydrology device that measures streamflow. Go left across the stream, then left again, back into the drainage you've just descended. Farther up, a side stream joins the trail, and after a climb, the path emerges into a tall grove of loblolly pines where the last of the interpretive signs describes the controlled burns that keeps the understory clear. The trail joins the main forest road at a T-junction. Go left to the picnic area, about 0.2 mile, and your car in a few hundred more feet, to complete a 1.2-mile hike.

To the right, the forest road also joins the Loblolly Trail, on its way in from Carter Finley Stadium, permitting a larger loop. A few other options permit the Liles Trail to be the centerpiece of longer loop hikes. Starting at the Loblolly trailhead on Reedy Creek Park Road, the loop follows the lakeshore and passes a plaque honoring Dr. Leon Goldberg; the sign is a

View on the Loblolly Trail beside the Wake County flood control lake.

reminder of the importance placed on nature by many of the more learned members of society. The Liles trail junctions are reached in just under 0.5 mile, and that loop, hiked in either direction, yields a round-trip of just over 2 miles. The picnic area is a place for a mid-hike lunch.

The longest loop of the Schenck Forest area can begin at either Reedy Creek Park Road, on the Loblolly Trail (about 3 miles), or at the gate, the closest trailhead for the Liles Trail (about 2 miles). From the Loblolly Trail hikers pass the two Liles Trail junctions, leave the lakeshore, and follow the Loblolly Trail along scenic Richland Creek. Past the tree plantings, when you reach the forest road that branches left at about 1 mile, take it. It climbs steeply for only a short distance. Other forest roads branch left, but continue straight past a large grassy area that contains the forestry school's arboretum, established in 1960. Pass another forest road on the left. Shortly, the first leg of the Liles Trail comes in from the left at about 1.5 miles. Descend to the Loblolly Trail here, or continue another 0.1 mile to a left at the picnic area and descend the other half of the Liles Trail. Backtrack on the Loblolly Trail to Reedy Creek Park Road for a 3-mile hike.

If you start at the Liles trailhead gate, the hike is about 2 miles, since the 0.5-mile hike in and out on the Loblolly Trail is omitted.

47   BALD HEAD ISLAND

Overview

Most environmentalists balk at being too positive about an upscale beach resort. But Bald Head Island is a rarity. It boasts an endangered loggerhead sea turtle preservation program, and its "newest" attraction is the oldest lighthouse on the North Carolina coast, restored and open to visitors. Exclusive homes, condos, fairways and greens, plaid pants, and country-club consciousness are also visible parts of Bald Head Island, along with park-like land of social and natural significance.

Visitors can spend the night here, since many of the island's villas, condos, and single family homes can be rented. Island guests have temporary membership in the Bald Head Island Club, so visitors can use the eighteen-hole championship golf course, driving range, putting green, four outdoor tennis courts, croquet lawns, swimming pool, marina, and all clubhouse facilities, including a fine dining room. There are no cars on Bald Head Island, so an electric shuttle meets the ferry. Thereafter you roam the island in the electric golf carts, jostling down narrow, Caribbean-style roads under forest abuzz with cicadas and heavy with the feel of the subtropics.

The living may be easy for residents and paying guests, but the preservation of this tangled web of wild forest is the best symbol of Bald

Head, once called Smith Island, and its rich history. The island's forest contains virgin trees up to 300 years old. Live oaks spread massive, wind-gnarled crowns. The forest holds sway here. Conservationists say the island's 800 acres of mature maritime forest are the state's best remaining example of such. The resort developers went so far as to deed 10,000 acres of land to the North Carolina Nature Conservancy as a wilderness preserve.

Bald Head Island's Cape Fear is a landmark. One of the most treacherous parts of the graveyard of the Atlantic, the area's name was first recorded in 1585 when a mariner wrote that "we were in great danger of a Wracke on a breache called the Cape of Feare." Today, Bald Head Islanders look down at this churning Cape of Fear from one of the state's most pristine bathing beaches. The beeline-straight Federal Road leads to this undeveloped side of the island.

On the way, you'll find the Kent Mitchell Nature Trail. A sandy side road leads to a channel through the marsh of Bald Head Creek, where a boathouse still stands from a century ago. The boathouse, like the road itself, was built to supply the island's only residents at the time: lighthouse keepers and lifesaving personnel. An outfitter uses this site as a put-in point for canoe trips that explore the marsh.

The oldest manmade structure on the island is Old Baldy, the state's oldest lighthouse. A foundation was established on the island in 1985 to preserve the old light, built in 1817, and in summer 1993 it opened to the public after extensive restoration. Visitors can climb to the top from dawn to dusk, seven days a week.

Though another light, the Cape Fear Lighthouse, was razed in 1958, the lighthouse keeper's residence and lifesaving structures are now restored and serve as housing for university students who keep track of the after-dark nesting habits of endangered loggerhead sea turtles. The students are employed by the Bald Head Island Conservancy, a nonprofit group responsible for the island's wild lands. The group operates a bookstore, Turtle Central, at the site of the razed lighthouse.

One of the local sandy summits, worn free of vegetation by river pilots looking for incoming ships, is the island's "bald head." Others are the remains of a Civil War fort that guarded the entrance to the Cape Fear River. Historic tours of the island are offered, the fee for which, about $30 for adults, includes parking, ferry, island transportation, interpretive tour, and lunch. Call (910) 457-5003 for details and reservations.

General description: A short nature trail on a spectacular but private barrier island. Public access is available for the ferry fee.
General location: Bald Head Island, near Southport.
Length: 0.6 mile.
Degree of difficulty: Easy.
Maps: USGS Cape Fear quad. The Bald Head Island Conservancy and the Bald Head Island resort can provide a free interpretive pamphlet with plant descriptions and a serviceable map.

Elevation gain and loss: Negligible.

Trailhead elevation: 10 feet.

Water availability: No water is available at the trailhead, but public facilities at the dock are open year-round.

For more information: Bald Head Island. The Bald Head Island Conservancy. Bald Head Island Ferry reservations. See Appendix C.

Finding the trailhead: Residents and guests take a passenger ferry from the Bald Head Island ferry terminal in Southport, about 3 hours south of Raleigh and 4 hours from Greensboro and Charlotte. Southport is about 40 minutes south of Wilmington, a city easily reached via Interstate Highway 40. Cross the Cape Fear Memorial Bridge, following the signs to U.S. Highway 17 South and Myrtle Beach. South of Wilmington, take a left onto North Carolina Highway 87 South. At NC 87's junction with North Carolina Highway 211, go left on Howe Street and proceed into Southport. Do not follow the signs to the North Carolina state ferry to Fort Fisher, but turn right on West Ninth Street to Indigo Plantation, 1.7 miles from NC 211. Take Indigo Plantation Drive to its dead end at the Bald Head Island ferry terminal. Day visitors are charged for parking, the ferry ride, and any cargo, such as a bicycle, surfboard, canoe, or whatever. Fees vary and no-frills tickets are available.

From the island ferry terminal hop on your bicycle—or golf cart if you're renting on the island—and ride along Federal Road past the historic Bald Head Island lighthouse. The trailhead is on the left, about 1.8 miles from the dock, just past the junction with Muscadine Wynd.

The hike: The **Kent Mitchell Nature Trail** leaves Federal Road at the trailhead signboard and immediately crosses the first boardwalk. This marshy stretch separates the main part of the island from the three tiny islets over which the trail wanders in its 0.5-mile loop back to the boardwalk.

The boardwalk presents a nice perspective: three small islands barely rise above the tidal ebb and flow that animates the thousands of acres of marshy wetlands visible all around. This is the preserved home of more than a third of the animal species listed as endangered in the United States. Its birdlife includes bald eagles and red-cockaded woodpeckers. There are also otters, raccoons, alligators, and minks. Though you won't necessarily see them all on a walk, you may notice signs of these residents.

Bring your binoculars. The islands sprout as clumps of maritime forest, quiet, warm, and semi-tropical amidst the eye-stretching expanse of marshes. Benches, perfect for birding, are located in a few spots on the trail; breezes will occasionally rustle in off the flat expanse of the marsh. And bring bug and insect repellent between May and October, not to mention sunscreen.

From the first boardwalk, the surrounding terrain is covered with black needlerush, the tubular rush that dominates the marsh where fresh water from the island mingles with saltwater. The plant's sharp tip was used as a needle during colonial times. The first dominating plant you'll notice when crossing onto Bayberry Island is the cabbage palmetto. The island is

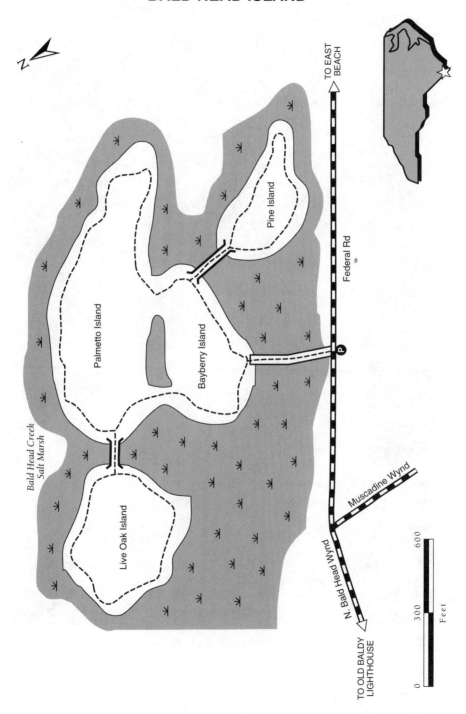

The Kent Mitchell Nature Trail is perfect for exploratory toddlers.

covered with it, the state tree of both Florida and South Carolina. Palmetto logs were used not far from here to reinforce Confederate army forts defending the entrance of the Cape Fear River. This is the northernmost limit of this subtropical tree. (A smaller plant at ground level is the palmetto, which never grows to tree size and reaches as far north as Cape Hatteras.)

Signs direct hikers counter-clockwise around the trail. Wander through low, subtropical vegetation and cross a boardwalk over to Palmetto Island. Take the next left and cross the boardwalk onto Live Oak Island. You'll recross the boardwalk after looping around the island, so head left. This island is named after one of the most prolific trees of the maritime forest, the live oak. These are the trees one sees arching over entrance roads in photos of plantation homes in South Carolina and Mississippi. The trees can grow to massive size; a tiny informal trail along Federal Road reaches the largest on the island. But here they are mostly small, as they often are in close proximity to salt spray and groundwater.

At the most distant end of Live Oak Island, a side trail leads left to a nice bench and a view of the distant boathouse, the historic resupply facility for the island's lighthouse keepers. From here, and just a short distance farther along the trail, the view stretches past Bald Head Creek to the expanse of Smith Island, the larger landmass of which Bald Head Island is the southernmost part. The farther east you look, the more you see Middle Island. From here, hundreds of acres of saltmeadow cordgrass and smooth cordgrass, the major species of marsh grasses, stretch before you.

Back on Palmetto Island, the trail goes left along the north shore to the end of the island. Beautiful red cedar predominates here, a species that often grows in the driest part of the maritime forest and tolerates salty water. You'll reach a third bench as you round the tip of the island. After crossing a small boardwalk onto Bayberry Island again, go left out to Pine Island for another loop. Here you'll find loblolly pine and see Spanish moss.

Back on Bayberry Island, go left to another left onto the first boardwalk and the return to Federal Road.

48 NATIONAL SEASHORE TRAILS — CAPE HATTERAS–PEA ISLAND

Overview

Most hikers reach this premier barrier island by heading south from the touristy northern Outer Banks, past signs that mark the entrance to federal lands. Here is the sudden end of condos and cotton candy. The two-lane road that bisects the narrow islands, North Carolina Highway 12, is embraced by oceanside dunes and marshes that mesh with the watery

Snow Geese wintering at Pea Island Wildlife Refuge on Hatteras Island. *Photo by Hugh Morton.*

horizon of the Pamlico Sound. Hatteras Island is rarely more than 1 mile wide. Cape Hatteras National Seashore, the first such seaside park in the nation, makes up the bulk of this 80-mile island chain.

South of the Cape Hatteras National Seashore boundary at the Whalebone Junction Visitor Center (just south of where U.S. Highway 64 meets NC 12 on Bodie Island), the road skips past tiny towns such as Waves and Avon. The farther south you go, the more quaint the towns become. One, Salvo, got its name (according to legend) during the Civil War, when a passing Union sea captain noticed no name for the village on the map and ordered, "Give it a salvo anyway." Salvo was scrawled on the chart, and a post office with that name opened in 1901. Between the villages, you'll revel in the refreshing seaside wilderness of the Cape Hatteras National Seashore or the Pea Island Wildlife Refuge. All along these barrier islands, you'll find campgrounds, nature trails, picnic areas, lighthouses, historic lifesaving stations, and shipwrecks. The area is rich in history and natural heritage.

The Buxton Woods Trail is located on Hatteras Island near the Cape Hatteras Lighthouse. Hatteras is probably a corruption of the Algonquin word meaning "area of sparse vegetation." During the Civil War, the town claimed to be the true capital of North Carolina. As in the mountains, Union sentiment was strong along the Banks. The result: post-war neglect by state government. Residents at either end of North Carolina are still skeptical of control from Raleigh.

Farther south, at the end of the island, a free ferry crosses over to isolated Ocracoke, the southernmost part of the national seashore. Under spreading live oaks, chickens wander from yard to yard. Mesmerized tourists watch the sun sink from a harborside pub flying the skull and crossbones, and North Carolina's oldest operating lighthouse caps the scene. Imagine Key West years ago; that's Ocracoke.

A 13-mile drive down the island passes more marsh grass-lined inlets and coastal dunes, and one of the East's highest-rated beaches. The Hammock Hills Trail is just across the island from the campground. From Ocracoke Village, a tiny settlement of sandy streets and only 700 residents, access is by toll ferry from the south. Two routes link this wonderful island with the mainland, each a more than 2-hour cruise. Ocracoke fishermen offer private shuttles across Ocracoke Inlet to the next island, Portsmouth, where the Portsmouth Island ghost town is a wonderful and wildly unique Outer Banks hiking experience in Cape Lookout National Seashore (see Hike 49).

Pea Island National Wildlife Refuge is a smaller, 6,000-acre parcel on the northernmost 13 miles of Hatteras Island. It includes a nearly 26,000-acre area of Pamlico Sound closed to hunting of migratory waterfowl. Until the 1930s, the Banks were a wide, flat area of sand that frequently was washed over by the sea. The Civilian Conservation Corps (CCC) changed that with artificial dune systems, and the Pea Island Refuge took shape as a series of manmade ponds. Today fields of annual grasses are sown in this area as waterfowl food, and many other active management efforts are made to support and monitor wild users of the refuge.

The area got its name because snow geese foraged there for beach pea, the seeds of pink or lavender flowers. They are among many birds sighted here, as are piping plovers, twenty-five species of ducks, tundra swans, peregrine falcons, and many more. Birding on the Atlantic Flyway is among the best in the nation. In Pea Island National Wildlife Refuge, the North Pond Trail is a birder's paradise. The total number of birds here exceeds 265 species. Other wildlife here: loggerhead sea turtles. Pea Island nests are thought to produce most of the males for the species because of the sand temperatures prevalent here at the turtle's northern range.

Some cautions are in order for hikers heading to the Outer Banks. Sunburn can come quickly here. Ocean breezes on the Banks may help keep you cool (and permit comfortable summer camping), but summertime highs can reach into the 90-degree range, so bring sunscreen and a hat. In addition, insects can be a challenge, on the beach as well as in marshy areas. If you plan to hike in the warmer seasons, definitely take repellent.

Though many sections of the beach are open to users of four-wheel drive vehicles, driving on the dunes is forbidden everywhere. Check with rangers to learn about seasonal beach driving regulations.

General description: Three trails on the spectacular barrier island chain of the Outer Banks, including two in Cape Hatteras National Seashore and one in Pea Island National Wildlife Refuge. The Buxton Woods Trail is a maritime forest trail that borders a freshwater marsh. Ocracoke Island's Hammock Hills Trail explores a diversity of terrain beside a saltwater marsh. And Pea Island's North Pond Wildlife Trail is perfect for observing waterfowl.

48 CAPE HATTERAS — PEA ISLAND

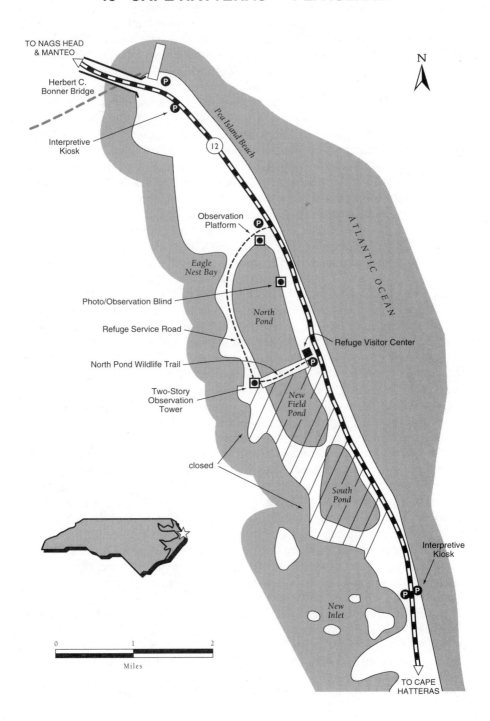

TO NAGS HEAD
& MANTEO

Herbert C.
Bonner Bridge

Interpretive
Kiosk

N

Pea Island Beach

12

Observation
Platform

Eagle
Nest Bay

Photo/Observation Blind

North
Pond

Refuge Service Road

North Pond Wildlife Trail

Refuge Visitor Center

Two-Story
Observation
Tower

New
Field
Pond

closed

South
Pond

Interpretive
Kiosk

New
Inlet

ATLANTIC OCEAN

0   1   2
Miles

TO CAPE
HATTERAS

Length: 0.6 mile for the Buxton Woods Trail; 0.8 mile for the Hammock Hills Trail. From 0.5 mile to about 4 miles for the North Pond Wildlife Trail.
Degree of difficulty: Easy.
Maps: USGS Oregon Inlet and Pea Island quads for Pea Island National Wildlife Refuge; USGS Buxton and Cape Hatteras quads for the Buxton Woods Trail; USGS Ocracoke and Howards Reef quads for Hammock Hills Trail.
Elevation gain and loss: Negligible.
Trailhead elevations: Just above sea level.
Water availability: No drinking water on the trails. Nearby restrooms and facilities run by the managing agencies are the best bet for water, as are businesses that line this popular beach vacation area.
For more information: Cape Hatteras National Seashore, Manteo. A seashore map and other information can be requested after business hours via recording. Or contact Hatteras Island Visitor Center; (919) 995-4474. For Pea Island National Wildlife Refuge information, contact Refuge Manager, Alligator River National Wildlife Refuge, Manteo. See Appendix C.
Finding the trailheads: The southernmost trailhead for the North Pond Trail in the Pea Island National Wildlife Refuge is located on the west side of North Carolina Highway 12, about 4.5 miles south of Oregon Inlet and the Herbert C. Bonner Bridge. To reach the Buxton Woods Trail leave NC 12 just north of Buxton on the National Park Service spur road to Hatteras Island Visitor Center and Cape Hatteras Lighthouse. Go right toward Cape Point Campground and the trail begins in the next picnic area parking lot on the right. The well-signed Hammock Hills Nature Trail, on Ocracoke Island, starts on the west side of NC 12, about 3 miles north of the village of Ocracoke.

The hikes: The **North Pond Trail** is the quintessential wildlife-viewing trail in the Pea Island National Wildlife Refuge. Numerous viewpoints and a two-level observation tower provide hikers with seven binocular spotting scopes. Just don't expect wilderness in the conventional sense. This is a highly managed environment where roads and dikes accommodate agency vehicles, and many areas are planted to provide food for waterfowl. No wonder it's a great place to watch birds: it's basically an avian eatery.

Start the North Pond Trail at the parking area on the side of NC 12 where the visitor center has year-round restrooms. The trail leads directly west and reaches an observation platform at about 0.1 mile. The path then follows a dike west between North Pond and New Field Pond (on the left). At about 0.5 mile, the trail terminates across the ponds on the western shore of the refuge at a two-story tower overlooking Pamlico Sound. Backtracking from here makes a nice 1.2-mile hike with many opportunities to watch waterfowl, even if you've forgotten your own binoculars.

You can turn north on an unpaved refuge road, follow the edge of North Pond for just over 1 mile until it reaches Eagle Nest Bay then turns east. There's another observation deck at 2.5 miles near where the road terminates at a more northerly parking area at about 2.7 miles (5.4 miles round-trip). If you walk the edge of the lake along NC 12, the total hike is about 4 miles.

The refuge visitor center, located at the main North Pond trailhead, has a year-round information kiosk, restrooms, and a small, visitor contact station and bookstore. The refuge and its volunteers offer weekend scheduled activities and bird watching tours, so call in advance for details.

The **Buxton Woods Trail** near the Cape Hatteras Lighthouse is another coastal foray into the maritime forest, the largest in the national seashore. The trail leaves the large picnic area parking lot and tables and ascends a dune as it undulates over a crest and down into the forest that surrounds a wonderfully secluded freshwater marsh. There are many plaques along the 0.6-mile trail that explain the forest's ecology.

On the right, marshside views offer opportunities to see wildlife, including many species of birds. You're likely to see coot, heron, white egret, ibis, duck, rail, and osprey. If you look far to the right, the top of the Cape Hatteras Lighthouse is also visible.

Some locals call these marshes "sedges," and in them, grasslike sedges grow. One is named Jennett's Sedge, for a local family. This forest and marsh burned all the way to the beach in 1954. Most trees survived, and now species include loblolly pine, American hornbeam, redbay, bald cypress, yaupon (an evergreen form of holly that yields a caffeine drink when cured), red mulberry, live oak (some hung with Spanish moss), and the dwarf palmetto (*Sabal minor*), a species that grows fan-like leaves from its ground level rootstock. In some places you'll notice fox grape, a favorite food for birds and mammals, and one that was developed into Concord and Chatauqua grapes.

Animals you may notice can include water moccasins. They like to swim and sun near water, so use caution near the banks of the marsh or the black water ponds that collect rain water between wooded dunes. You also might notice what locals call "Russian rats;" the coypu, or nutria. The web-footed, aquatic South American rodent, introduced by a hunting club in 1941, can be as big as a raccoon.

The **Hammock Hills Nature Trail**, on Ocracoke Island, wanders through a variety of habitats on its 0.8-mile journey from NC 12 to the marsh grass-lined edge of Pamlico Sound. Here you'll be able to see an earlier stage in the growth of a maritime forest than is visible nearby at Buxton Woods and Nags Head Woods, both established forests.

The trail begins in a scrub thicket woodland. It splits into its loop just past a small, freshwater branch of Island Creek that runs under NC 12. This is a rare surface accumulation of the fresh water table that sustains the salt wind-stunted forest you'll explore ahead. Go right, and the trail emerges from scrub thicket into an open dunescape as it parallels the highway. In sunnier, sandy spots, you'll notice low-growing prickly pear cactus. Leaving the dunes, the path swings left into a pine forest, then again enters scrub

48 CAPE HATTERAS NATIONAL SEASHORE — BUXTON WOODS TRAIL

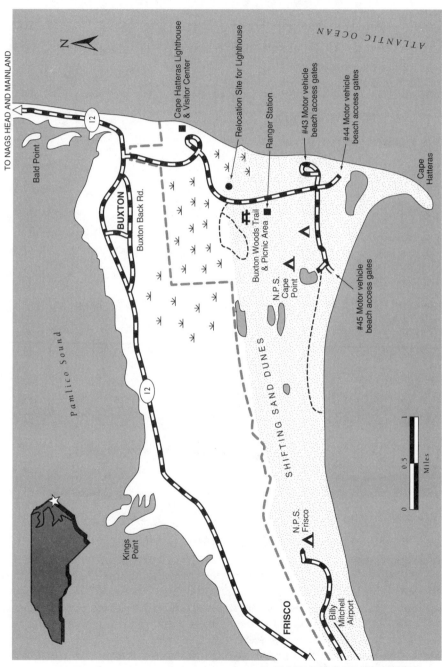

48 CAPE HATTERAS NATIONAL SEASHORE —
HAMMOCK HILLS TRAIL

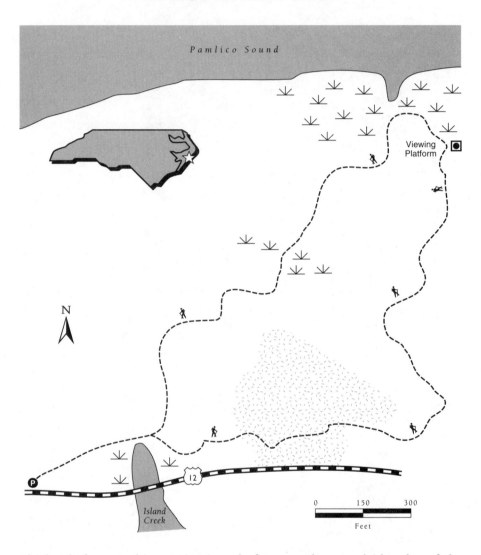

thicket before reaching a viewing platform on the soundside edge of the saltwater marsh.

Along the marsh, vegetation varies from the saltmeadow hay found above the highest tide lines, the supratidal zone, to black needlerush and saltmarsh cordgrass that grows in the intertidal zone. A rich organic mix of minerals, muck, saltwater, and decaying sea and plant life creates the perfect nursery for fish and crustaceans such as clams, crabs, and oysters. The black skimmer, a gull-like bird, swoops low to the water and uses a large lower bill to scoop fish and other food from this fertile marsh.

The trail swings back away from the marsh among thickets and then re-enters the pine forest. This low, protective cover is the key to survival for the forest's population of rabbits, black racers, skinks, mice, and tree frogs. It protects them from owls and the northern harriers often seen circling overhead.

The trail rejoins the loop in a scrub thicket. Go right to retrace your steps to the parking area.

49 CAPE LOOKOUT NATIONAL SEASHORE

Overview

The Cape Lookout National Seashore was established in 1966 to cover 28,000 acres in the southern Outer Banks, one of the few remaining natural barrier-island ecosystems in the world. The park comprises three islands that run 55 miles southeast from Beaufort Inlet to Cape Lookout and northeast to the deserted village of Portsmouth at Ocracoke Inlet (which marks the start of Cape Hatteras National Seashore; see Hike 48).

Southernmost Shackleford Banks, oriented east-west against wind, have a developed series of high dunes and the national seashore's only stand of maritime forest. The more northerly Core Banks and Portsmouth Island are a wild, low-lying landscape of shrub thickets, tidal flats, dunes, and, on the Core and Pamlico Sound side, saltwater marshlands. This ever-changing landscape is fragile and beautiful, requiring special care from those who come to see it. Ferries reach the Banks at three locations, and four-wheel-drive vehicles are an accepted and managed means to reach points of interest. Motorists must have a permit if their vehicle will be parked unattended for more than 24 hours. Drivers must also stick to approved routes to protect nesting threatened species, including loggerhead turtles and shorebirds, and sea oats, which are protected by law. No known venomous snakes populate the southernmost Banks.

Though isolated, the sparse public facilities that mark the handful of ferry-accessible sites on the Core Banks are visited by about 250,000 people a year. Rental cabins known as Morris' Kabin Kamps are situated on the Banks between Drum Inlet and Portsmouth Village. The cabins are available through Morris Marina in Atlantic, NC; (919) 225-4261. By vehicle, Portsmouth Village is 17 miles north of the ferry landing at Kabin Kamps.

Opportunities are excellent on these islands for all types of undeveloped recreation, from shellfishing to hiking, surf fishing, hunting, beachcombing, camping, and swimming. But the weather and elements can be unrelenting. High winds, heavy rain, flooding, voracious hordes of mosquitoes, not to mention withering sun, can make life miserable. Visitors can cope with these problems by being prepared (windproof tents with long sand stakes, fine-mesh mosquito netting, hats, sunscreen) or visiting when the weather and the bugs are at their least troublesome (October, March, and April).

Portsmouth Island is the northernmost of the Core Banks' islands and the location of a longtime and fascinating Outer Banks settlement. It is separated by 5-mile-wide Ocracoke Inlet from the tourist island of Ocracoke. Portsmouth was founded by the North Carolina colonial assembly in 1753, just thirty-five years after the pirate Blackbeard (Edward Teach) was slain by a raiding party sent by Virginia's governor. The battle took place just across the inlet on Ocracoke in an area still called Teach's Hole. Blackbeard and, later, enemy submarines during World War II, sheltered here just out of the way of bad weather and prying eyes.

Portsmouth village got its economic impetus as a trans-shipment point for goods through Ocracoke Inlet. To conduct commerce with North Carolina ports such as New Bern, Washington, and Bath, heavy seagoing vessels had to transfer goods to boats with shallower drafts. This "lightering" business led to the town's becoming the Banks' largest settlement by 1770. In 1842, 1,400 vessels and two-thirds of North Carolina's exports passed through.

In 1860, 685 people lived in the village. Then a storm dug a deeper channel through Hatteras Inlet in 1864, and Ocracoke Inlet became shallower. Trade shifted to other inlets. The hospital closed, then the Civil War drove most residents to the mainland. The customs office closed due to lack of trade. Fishing and helping those stranded in shipwrecks became dominant occupations. Federal legislation authorized three lifesaving stations for the Core Banks in 1888, and in 1894 the Portsmouth Island station opened. In 1915 the Lifesaving Service's merger with the Revenue Cutter Service made one station a Coast Guard Station, which was decommissioned in 1937, four years after a major hurricane did severe damage. The school closed in 1943, and the post office closed in 1959. The last resident residents moved out in 1971.

In 1976 the Cape Lookout National Seashore was established, and the 250-acre village was listed on the National Register of Historic Places in 1979. Luckily for us, and a quickly developing Outer Banks, it is still possible to experience the area's past in this startling ghost town. A walk through Portsmouth Village gives insight to the long-gone lifestyle of the "Bankers." The federal government protects what remains, in part by leasing these old structures to organizations and individuals who'll abide by agreements about maintenance and restoration. A few buildings in the community, the Dixon/Salter House and the church, are open to the public. The National Park Service asks that the privacy of other lessees be respected.

General description: A seaside walk through a barrier island ghost town listed on the National Register of Historic Places. Explore the village of Portsmouth, including its eerie, open buildings, or wander all the way to the ocean.
General location: Portsmouth Island, Outer Banks.
Length: About 1.5 miles for a hike through the village; about 3.4 miles for a trip through the village to the beach and back.

Degree of difficulty: Easy for walking; difficult for access, isolation, and possibility of challenging weather or insect conditions.

Maps: USGS Portsmouth quad is highly recommended, as are navigational charts and the national seashore's strip orientation map.

Elevation gain and loss: Little, if any.

Trailhead elevation: Just above sea level.

Water availability: None. Bring all needed drinking water.

For more information: Cape Lookout National Seashore, Harkers Island. See Appendix C.

Finding the trailhead: Undeveloped trailheads for beach walks on any of the three major islands of the national seashore can be reached via ferries that connect those islands to the mainland; contact address above for information and ferry schedules.

To reach Portsmouth Island, motorists with ATVs or four-wheel-drive vehicles may drive north on the Core Banks from the Morris' Kabin Kamps, accessible by ferry from the town of Atlantic and U.S. Highway 70 north of Beaufort. Easiest access to Portsmouth Island is from neighboring Ocracoke Island, itself reachable only via toll ferry from Cedar Island, north of Beaufort; from Swan Quarter, near Washington and Bath; or from Hatteras Island on the southern end of the popular Outer Banks vacation area of Dare County.

From Ocracoke boat access to Portsmouth Island is available from concession ferries operated by Rudy Austin, (919)-928-4361. The service usually costs $40 round-trip for two people, $15 round-trip ($20 with a big backpack) for each additional person (1996 rates).

The hike: Your hike starts about 1 mile offshore on the way over from Ocracoke. From there, Portsmouth appears as an immaculate handful of uninhabited buildings sprouting from the rich green reeds of the saltwater marsh. A National Park Service-maintained pier juts from the island between oceanside dunes and tidal flats (on the left) and the meandering saltwater channels (on the right) that "Bankers" call creeks, even though they carry no fresh water.

Land at the Haulover Point Dock and wander into "town." Perfectly preserved remnants of Outer Banks architecture stand eerily quiet. On this walk you'll notice remnants of rooftop rainwater storage systems that show how villagers trapped fresh water and funneled it into cisterns. You'll see small outbuildings that illustrate how islanders coped with cooking when the heating of cooking would have turned their homes into sweltering saunas. Beside these summer kitchens, you may a see tiny cool house, a dog house-size structure where fresh food stayed cool. No doubt these houses contained planks and provisions from dozens of ships lost off the coast.

You'll wander the main road and reach the first "mainland" of the village near the Dixon/Salter House, now a visitor center, open when volunteer care-takers or park staff are present. Bearing right behind and beyond the house brings you to a cemetery and ruins of another house. Obviously, not all of the island's structures are preserved or under the lease program. Those who lease the structures are the only people permitted to spend the night in the village; all camping is prohibited.

Continuing on the main road, the old U.S. Post Office is on the right. Past it, a right turn from the main path into town passes a cemetery, then crosses a bridge to the Jody Styron and Tom Bragg House. Around the house to the northwest and out toward the marsh is another ruin, but southwest from the house another path follows the edge of the marsh. It reaches a junction, and to the right a side trail leads to an isolated point and the T. T. Potter House. Straight beyond that junction is a cemetery and ruin.

Left in the vicinity of the post office takes you toward Ocracoke Inlet on the northwest side of Doctors Creek. The Robert Wallace or Old Grace Home is first, then the Tom Gilgo House. Next on the creekside, before the path wanders left or northwest, is the Henry Pigott House, home of the last male resident of Portsmouth, whose death in 1971 prompted the desertion of the island. Bearing northwest, the Carl Dixon House is on the left, and the path ends out by the inlet at the Frank Gaskill House.

Backtrack to the post office where the main trail turns left, continuing into town. In this area, a path also goes straight, crossing a bridge to the Cecil Gilgo House. A right leads past another ruin and on to the ruins of "the middle community." A path also leads straight from the Gilgo House to the Schoolhouse, with its big cylindrical cistern.

Back at the main trail, a small trail bears left before a cemetery and explores the Doctors Creek side of the Dixon/Salter and Gilgo Houses. Pass the cemetery and cross bridges to the central part of Portsmouth. On the way, the bridges offer views up Doctors Creek to the Henry Pigott House and into Ocracoke Inlet. The George Dixon House lies between the two bridges. Crossing the final bridge into the largest expanse of Portsmouth, the Methodist Church is on the left. The original church was destroyed in a 1913 hurricane, and this one was built the following year. Inside this open building, the church is set up as if a service were about to begin.

Beyond and set back on the left is the McWilliams/Dixon House, and then the Jesse Babb House. (Between the two, a path goes left passing the Ed Styron House and looping back out to the main path.) Beyond the Babb House on the left is the Dennis Mason House, now a Ranger Station. Beyond this house, the path from the Ed Styron House comes in on the left.

Opposite the church and the McWilliams/Dixon and Babb houses, on the right of the main trail, sit the Washington Roberts House and Roy Robinson House. Just beyond the Robinson House, the main path swings left or northeast, and winds out to the beautifully restored Lifesaving Service complex on Coast Guard Creek, with a grass landing strip. Opposite the complex, a brick cistern built in 1853 marks the site of the island hospital.

Continuing on the road beyond the Lifesaving Station complex, pass a gate that bars all but park service and lessee vehicles from the village. A path to the left leads to a cemetery. Continuing straight, a road goes left

49 CAPE LOOKOUT NATIONAL SEASHORE — PORTSMOUTH VILLAGE TRAIL

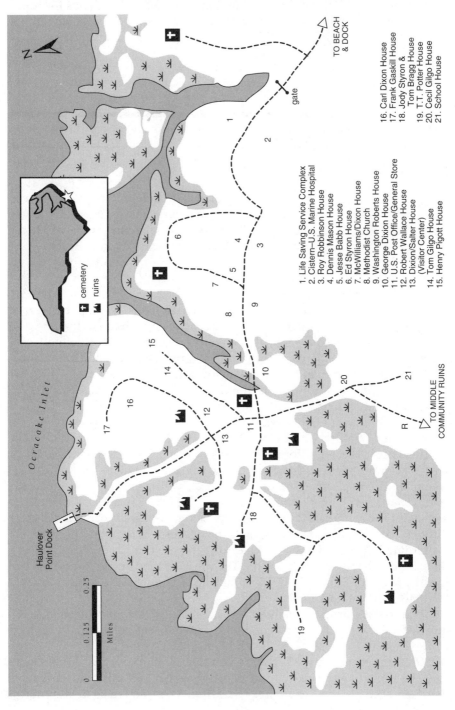

1. Life Saving Service Complex
2. Cistern—U.S. Marine Hospital
3. Roy Robbinson House
4. Dennis Mason House
5. Jesse Babb House
6. Ed Styron House
7. McWilliams/Dixon House
8. Methodist Church
9. Washington Roberts House
10. George Dixon House
11. U.S. Post Office/General Store
12. Robert Wallace House
13. Dixion/Salter House (Visitor Center)
14. Tom Gilgo House
15. Henry Pigott House
16. Carl Dixon House
17. Frank Gaskill House
18. Jody Styron & Tom Bragg House
19. T.T. Potter House
20. Cecil Gilgo House
21. School House

TO BEACH & DOCK

gate

TO MIDDLE COMMUNITY RUINS

Ocracoke Inlet

Haulover Point Dock

cemetery
ruins

0   0.125   0.25
Miles

(marked by posts across the tidal flats), leads to the Wallace Channel dock in 1 mile. Straight, the post-marked road crosses the flats to the dunes at the beach, about 1.2 miles away. Whether you walk to the dunes for lunch or to camp, or come to Portsmouth by vehicle from the south, remember that under a south wind, the tidal flats are dry. Under a north wind, they can be covered by 6 inches or more of water.

50   CROATAN NATIONAL FOREST

Overview

Croatan National Forest is made up of 159,102 acres of unique forest scattered south of New Bern, west of Beaufort, and north of the islands of the Bogue Banks. The forest's facilities, especially the two trails described here, add to the popular ocean vacation areas between Emerald Isle and Atlantic Beach.

The forest's summer regime is basically that of a baking piney woods ecosystem. But vast portions of the area are much more than that. Five large freshwater lakes (only two of which, Great Lake and Catfish Lake, are entirely on forest land) total 4,300 acres. These lakes, the highest part of the forest, are fed by rain and surrounding acres of *pocosin*, an Indian word that means "swamp on a hill." This poorly drained area of acidic freshwater bogs is home to unusual dwarf swamp vegetation. The serious, rubber-booted hiker can find challenging water-inundated trails in many parts of the forest, among them the **Sheep Ridge Trail**, which runs 3.5 miles, and the **Neusiok Trail**, a 20-mile end-to-end path.

Approximately 31,000 acres of the forest are designated as wilderness in chunks named Catfish Lake South, Pocosin, Pond Pine, and Sheep Ridge. The tracts cluster in the boggy forest and border three of the five freshwater lakes, where swamp cypress is often seen. These wild environments are home to the cottonmouth moccasin, eastern diamondback rattlesnake, and American alligator. They are also wonderful for birders. The lakes, swamps, and marshes are home or way station for bald eagles, ducks, geese, egrets, peregrine falcons, rare red-cockaded woodpeckers, owls, woodcocks, and more. The best spot for birding is the Catfish Lake Waterfowl Impoundment, especially during January, February, and early spring. The site is marked on the forest map and is easily reached. From SR 1004 just outside of Pollocksville, turn right onto SR 1110 (Bender Road).

The forest's primary recreational uses are fishing and hunting. Fresh and saltwater fishing is very good, and game species available to hunters run the gamut from deer and black bear to turkey and quail.

Cooler seasons are the best times for hikes in the Croatan. Summer can find the trails buggy, snaky, and hot. But spring and fall offer enjoyable days. And the nearby beach areas are often as attractive as in summer.

Boardwalk on Cedar Point Tideland Trail, Croatan National Forest.

General description: Two short nature trails in eastern North Carolina's only national forest. The Cedar Point Tideland Trail explores a tidal marsh, and the Island Creek Trail wanders through a rare, coastal virgin forest.
General location: Croatan National Forest, near Maysville.
Length: 1.5 miles for the Cedar Point Tideland Trail; 1 mile for the Island Creek Trail, with a second loop expected to be added by 1996 that could make the trail up to 2.5 miles in length.
Degree of difficulty: Easy.
Maps: USGS Swansboro quad for the Tideland Trail; USGS Pollocksville quad for the Island Creek Trail.
Elevation gain and loss: Negligible for Tideland Trail; 50 feet for Island Creek Trail.
Trailhead elevation: Just above sea level for Tideland Trail; 30 feet for Island Creek Trail.
Low point: 5 feet for Island Creek Trail.
Water availability: Water is available at the Cedar Point recreation area, which includes restrooms, a campground, boat landing, and picnic area, from mid-April through mid-October. For the Island Creek Trail, pick up water in nearby Pollocksville, or at the closest national forest facilities, Fisher's Landing picnic area, or Neuse River recreation area.
For more information: Croatan National Forest, New Bern Or contact Supervisor's Office, National Forests in North Carolina, Asheville. See Appendix C.

Finding the trailheads: The Tideland Trail is about 17 miles south of Maysville and 22 miles from Morehead City. From North Carolina Highway 58 (0.7 mile north of North Carolina Highway 24), turn onto SR 1114. Go 0.5 mile to a left on gravel Forest Road 153A and park on the right at 0.8 mile where the road terminates at a boat landing.

The Island Creek Forest Walk starts in a parking area on the north side of Island Creek Road (SR 1004), between Pollocksville (where the road is signed as Beaufort Road), to the west, and New Bern, to the northeast. The road branches east from U.S. Highway 17 in Pollocksville, and west from a junction with U.S. Highway 70, about 1 mile south of New Bern. The trailhead is 5.6 miles from Pollocksville, and about 10 miles from New Bern. From New Bern go south on US 70 to a right at the Burger King restaurant. At the next stop sign, take a left on SR 1004. Measuring from there, the trailhead is on the right at 7 miles.

The hikes: The best Croatan National Forest offerings are explored by the two nature trails described here.

The **Cedar Point Tideland Trail** juts into the White Oak River where it joins Bogue Sound. It is this mixing of fresh and saltwater that nurtures

50 CROATAN NATIONAL FOREST — CEDAR POINT TIDELAND TRAIL

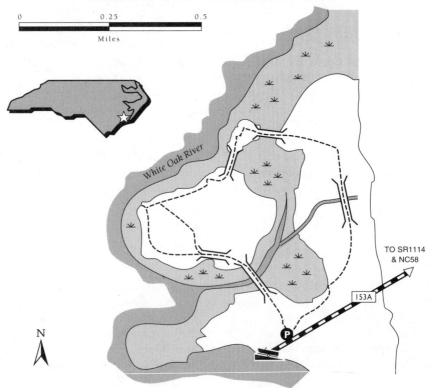

50 CROATAN NATIONAL FOREST —
ISLAND CREEK TRAIL

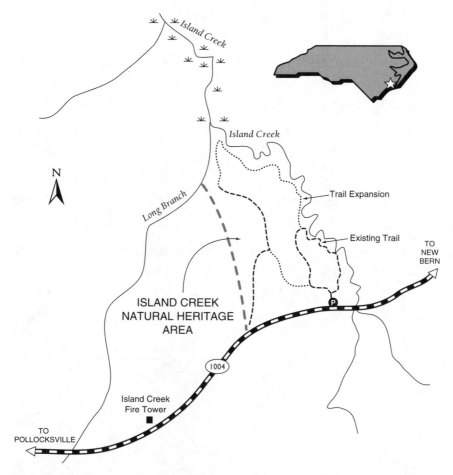

the beautiful marsh grasses that wave in the breezes and stir in the rising and falling of the tides. This rich estuary, on which the vast bulk of aquatic life depends, makes Cedar Point a wonderful trail for birders. The 1.5-mile, double loop trail has three elaborate blinds constructed to shield hikers from the sharp eyes of hawks, ospreys, and other local wildlife

The trail leaves the parking lot in two directions. The trail to the left leads to the small loop of the trail, where one blind is available. This walk takes less than 1 hour. The trail to the right starts the longer loop, with two blinds. It joins the small loop, too, and the total hike can take up to 2 hours, especially if you've remembered to take binoculars or chosen to picnic in a blind while you take in the view. The trail passes through pine and hardwood forests and crosses tidal marshlands on seven extensive cypress boardwalks and two bridges. Interpretive signs explain wetland ecology.

The **Island Creek Trail** is a 1-hour or less walk of about 1 mile through

Island Creek Trail, Croatan National Forest.

an unusual coastal virgin forest. Cypress trees were logged extensively in the Croatan and the coastal area, but this trail is the best place to see these impressive old trees with their knees protruding out of the water. The Island Creek forest is a rare ecosystem, and geologically unique. The 8 square miles of creek drainage are underlain with a marine limestone called the Castle Hayne Formation. The underlying alkaline rock neutralizes the normally acid soil and provides a base for the plant community. Twelve types of plant community have been identified here.

The path is contained in an isolated, triangular parcel of national forest land that borders Island Creek immediately before it empties into Muddy Cove and the Trent River. By late 1996, rangers say another mile or more of trail will be added, creating a double loop up to 2.5 miles in length extending farther along Island Creek. The map that accompanies this entry includes the best guess as to how this addition will look.

The Island Creek Trail was created in 1967 by a joint effort between the local Trent River Garden Club and Forest Service. The trail and the upcoming expansion lie within a 146-acre tract that is designated a North Carolina Natural Heritage Area.

51 NAGS HEAD WOODS NATURE CONSERVANCY TRAILS

Overview

The Nags Head Woods preserve is a triumph of preservation, the kind of undisturbed woodland that is the best anchor for North Carolina's migrating barrier islands. About 1,100 acres of Nags Head Woods have been owned or managed by The Nature Conservancy since 1978. In 1981 Congress named the forest a National Natural Landmark. The tract straddles the state border between the towns of Nags Head and Kill Devil Hills.

The town of Nags Head was initially the only entity willing to support the idea of a nature preserve in Nags Head Woods. The town's decision to lease the acreage to The Nature Conservancy was unprecedented, as was its assistance in the 1993 purchase of 400 additional acres and construction of the Sweetgum Swamp Trail.

Nags Head Woods is located where northern and more southern plant species mesh. Abrupt drops from high dunes to watery ponds and swamps further enhance the unique mix of habitats, and plant and animal combinations. Such ecological diversity and the size of this unmolested woodland make it one of the most significant stands of maritime forest on the North Carolina coast.

Research suggests that the forest had its beginning up to 1,000 years ago. With many trees 300 to 400 years old, and the oldest live oak in the

A massive live oak in the maritime forest at Nags Head Woods.

forest thought to be 500 years old, Nags Head Woods offers a pristine experience of a barrier island wilderness. Barrier islands are usually sandy, migrating ecosystems sparsely covered with plants. A coastal forest such as the one saved here requires a substantial fresh water table and a layer of topsoil, both found at Nags Head Woods. Large dunes parallel to the beach, some just under 100 feet high, have sheltered the site, keeping out the salty winds and spray that would have prohibited the birth of a forest, especially one where beeches, oaks, hickories, and maples grow. And under the forest is the largest of the Outer Banks' freshwater aquifers, a fact that accounts for the thirty-four ponds in the woods, many located along the trail network.

Visiting hours for the preserve vary by season, so call ahead. At the busiest times, the preserve limits trail use, due to staff constraints and overuse. A program of field trips is led by an environmental education specialist and an intern. A variety of other programs exist, including children's nature camps, teacher training workshops, internships, and classes for school groups. The preserve's 2,000-square-foot visitor center contains an exhibit room where interpretive and interactive displays are under development. A gift shop features field guides, T-shirts, and other items.

The fragility and sensitivity of the preserve dictates that hikers must stay on trails, and that no plants or animals be disturbed or collected without written permission from preserve managers. No fishing, firearms, smoking, mountain bikes or pets are permitted. Park only in designated areas. Use of the trails is free, but hikers must register and familiarize themselves with regulations before setting out. A hiking donation is appreciated. And larger but still modest contributions are encouraged by entitling the contributor, as a member, to receive the preserve newsletter, the state chapter newsletter, and The Nature Conservancy's news magazine.

The Nature Conservancy (TNC) is an international, private, nonprofit organization headquartered in Arlington, Virginia. The organization works with scientists to locate significant, threatened environments and coordinates funding to purchase those lands, as it has Nags Head Woods and Bluff Mountain, in northwestern North Carolina. The Conservancy's network of 1,500 preserves is the largest system of private nature preserves in the world.

Some TNC-purchased property is transferred to other agencies. It also accepts conservation easements that permit land to continue in private ownership and/or management, while the owners receive tax credits for their pledge of preservation in perpetuity. The North Carolina TNC group has protected more than 337,000 acres.

General description: Four trails explore The Nature Conservancy's pristine, 1,400-acre maritime forest preserve in the northern Outer Banks. A short nature trail flanks the visitor center, but a circuit of the Sweetgum Swamp Trail and the Blueberry Ridge Trail is the premier nature walk on North Carolina's barrier islands. There's also a 2.2-mile out-and-back hike to the edge of Albemarle Sound on the Town Trail.

Length: 0.3 mile for the Center Trail; 3.5 miles for the Sweetgum Swamp/Blueberry Ridge circuit; and 2.2 miles round-trip for the Town Trail.

Degree of difficulty: Easy to moderate.

Maps: USGS Roanoke Island and Manteo quads. The preserve sells nice brochures for the Center Trail and Sweetgum Swamp Trail and offers a rudimentary map of the entire system.

Elevation gain and loss: Numerous changes in elevation over dunes, up to 80 feet.

Trailhead elevation: Just above sea level.

Water availability: No drinking water on trails. The preserve's visitor center has water and restrooms. At the Nags Head Town Park trailhead for the preserve's newest trail, water and restrooms are available. Businesses that line U.S. Highway 158 in this popular beach vacation area may provide water.

For more information: Nags Head Woods Ecological Preserve, Kill Devil Hills. Also contact the Dare County Tourist Bureau. See Appendix C.

Finding the trailhead: The preserve is about 90 miles south of Norfolk, Virginia, and 225 miles east of Raleigh, North Carolina. Take U.S. Highway 64 from Raleigh, across the Croatan Sound to Roanoke Island, then over Roanoke Sound to Bodie Island. Go north on U.S. Highway 158 to milepost 9.5 and turn left onto West Ocean Acres Drive. Reach the preserve office in about 1 mile, on the left.

The preserve's Town Trail starts at Nags Head Town Park. Turn west on Barnes Road from US 158 at milepost 10.5. Go about 0.5 mile, almost to the end of the road, and pull into the parking lot on the left. The trail starts at a covered signboard on the right side of the parking lot.

The hikes: Three of four trails begin behind the preserve visitor center at the steps. The blue arrow-marked **Center Trail** is a 0.25-mile nature trail that ventures across a bridge from the visitor center and crosses two others as it makes a loop. The brief walk can take a half hour if you purchase the brochure at the visitor center and involve yourself in the fascinating details of how this microclimate works.

The **Sweetgum Swamp Trail** branches left about halfway through the Center Trail, at station 5, where a red trail marker points left. The 2-mile, red arrow-marked trail creates a more than 1-hour hike. The guidebook pictures many of the plants and animals. The trail reaches a power line and follows it for about 600 feet. It turns left back into the forest on a faint logging road, where pink lady's slipper orchids can be seen in the spring. Ferns are an obvious part of the woods ecosystem. Species include royal fern, cinnamon fern, Virginia chain fern, and, in the ponds, the tiny, aquatic mosquito fern, which floats. The woods are a meeting point for northern and southern species. Spanish moss and longleaf pine reach their northern limits here. So do the green orchid and the nonpoisonous yellow-lipped snake.

The trail continues over dunes and past seasonal ponds, and turns right off the old logging road (which continues straight ahead). The path has now

51 NAGS HEAD WOODS
NATURE CONSERVANCY TRAILS

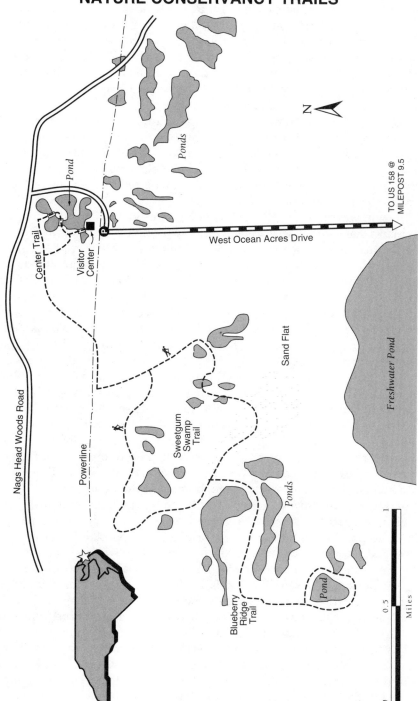

grown in to be an intimate trail. Go straight.

The depths of the freshwater ponds you encounter here fluctuate dramatically with the seasons. They fill to 3 feet deep in the winter and fall and can be nearly dry in lean years. Plant matter growing on the surface of the ponds attracts wood ducks. Other residents include otters. More usual types of birds, ospreys and gulls, wheel overhead, and the forest attracts red-shouldered hawks. The ponds also attract a variety of herons, and during spring and fall bird migrations, are an important stopping point in a landscape otherwise dominated by sand.

The Sweetgum Swamp Trail crosses a number of old dunes on steps, showcasing a typical forest ecosystem of loblolly pine, sweet pignut hickory, and southern red oak, depending on where you look. There's also sassafras, dogwood, American holly, and blueberry bushes. In the wet flats between the dunes sweet gum grows, along with red maple and black gum, both more often seen far from the coast.

As you walk the trail, the guidebook invites you to consider how various plants survive the occasional windblown coating of salt spray from the east. Notice any brown pine needles? This is salt burn, a phenomenon many people notice along snow-country highways where road salt has been thrown by snowplows onto nearby evergreens. This area of salt-resistant vegetation shelters the less-tolerant deciduous trees to the west.

The path crosses a bridge over a freshwater pond, wanders between two others, and skirts two more ponds. The largest of the woods' ponds continues to be used as a water source for nearby towns. The trail surmounts a dune and descends more stairs as it emerges from the woods onto an open sand flat. To avoid impacting pioneering plants, called sand binders, in this barren area, follow TNC's oak-leaf plaques across the sand past species such as woolly beach heather, here at its southern limit.

Back in the forest, the trail reaches the **Blueberry Ridge Trail**, which branches south at an orange arrow. The main path rises beyond that and follows a ridgecrest between two ponds. It then rejoins the old logging grade for a left turn back to the visitor center. The Blueberry Ridge Trail, a 1.5-mile, orange arrow-blazed loop, branches into a final loop that circles a pond. The trail stays largely on a ridge and provides some of the most scenic pond and forest views in the preserve. At one point, the path descends to pond level and crosses a bridge over a wetland. Retrace your steps, and return via the section of the Sweetgum Swamp Trail you have yet to hike and head back to the visitor center for a total hike of 3.5 miles.

The preserve's **Town Trail** adds an element of convenience for hikers: the preserve office doesn't need to be open for hikers to use the trail. The path begins at Nags Head Town Park with its playground, restrooms, water, picnic tables, and pavilion. The trail heads roughly southwest for 1.1 miles (2.2 miles round-trip) to Albemarle Sound. On the way, it traverses all of the woods' different habitats, including the power line and the woods road. It first crosses an area of dunes, then enters the forest before terminating beside a small strip of salt marsh on the sound.

APPENDIX A

APPALACHIAN TRAIL HIKES, MILEAGE LOG, AND EASTERN BOUNDARY – GREAT SMOKY MOUNTAINS NATIONAL PARK

The mileage log that follows is more than a list of landmarks on the Appalachian Trail (AT) in North Carolina. Scattered throughout the data you'll find detailed recommendations for day hikes and backpacking trips that are among the best in North Carolina and the East. And more than the AT is covered. The names of suggested trails, including one wheelchair-accessible hike, are highlighted, so even if you're not hiking from border to border on the AT, be sure to scan this appendix.

The hike descriptions imbedded in the chart below contain much the same information you find in entries throughout the rest of the book.

N to S	S to N	
0.0	313.7	Trailhead on US 19-E, between Roan Mountain, TN, and Elk Park, NC

Between Carvers Gap and Elk Park, the 13 miles of the AT are a classic hike and overnight trip. See Hike 1 in this book for an extensive description of the **Southern Balds** section of trail.

N to S	S to N	
0.5	313.2	Apple House Shelter
0.6	313.1	Spring
2.6	311.1	Doll Flats
5.0	308.7	Hump Mountain
5.9	307.8	Bradley Gap
6.5	307.2	Little Hump Mountain
8.3	305.4	Yellow Mountain Gap /Overmountain Shelter
10.0	303.7	Roan Highlands Shelter
11.4	302.3	Grassy Ridge
13.0	300.7	Carvers Gap, TN 143, NC 261

For more on the Appalachian Trail south from Carvers Gap over Roan Mountain, see Hike 7, the **Cloudland Trail**.

N to S	S to N	
14.3	299.4	Roan High Knob Shelter
14.9	298.8	Roan High Bluff
15.8	297.9	Ash Gap
17.6	296.1	Hughes Gap
18.9	294.8	Little Rock Knob
19.7	294.0	Clyde Smith Shelter

This shelter was named after the late AT trail volunteer Clyde Smith. See Hikes 7 and 12 for more about his life and work.

APPALACHIAN TRAIL, SOUTHERN BALDS

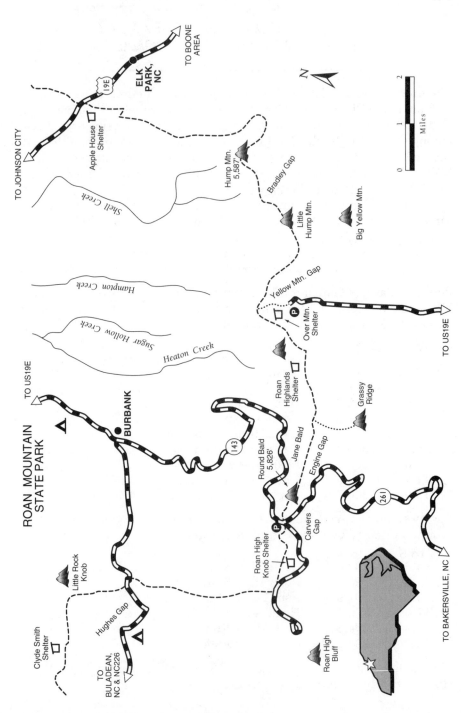

ROAN MOUNTAIN STATE PARK

TO JOHNSON CITY

TO BOONE AREA

ELK PARK, NC

19E

Apple House Shelter

Shell Creek

Hump Mtn. 5,587'

Bradley Gap

Little Hump Mtn.

Big Yellow Mtn.

Hampton Creek

Sugar Hollow Creek

Heaton Creek

Yellow Mtn. Gap

Over Mtn. Shelter

TO US19E

TO US19E

BURBANK

143

Roan Highlands Shelter

Grassy Ridge

Round Bald 5,826'

Jane Bald

Engine Gap

261

Carvers Gap

Roan High Knob Shelter

Little Rock Knob

Hughes Gap

Clyde Smith Shelter

TO BULADEAN, NC & NC226

Roan High Bluff

TO BAKERSVILLE, NC

N

Miles

0   1   2

APPALACHIAN TRAIL

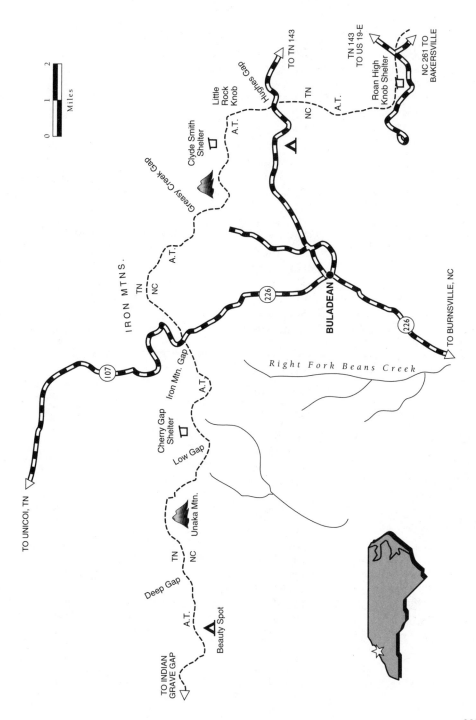

N to S	S to N	
20.8	292.9	Campsite
21.6	292.1	Greasy Creek Gap
24.2	289.5	Stream
25.7	288.0	Iron Mountain Gap, TN 107, NC 226
26.9	286.8	Little Bald Knob
28.4	285.3	Cherry Gap Shelter
29.4	284.3	Low Gap
31.1	282.6	Unaka Mountain
32.1	281.6	FR 230
32.7	281.0	Deep Gap
34.0	279.7	Beauty Spot Gap
34.2	279.5	Beauty Spot
35.4	278.3	FR 230
36.5	277.2	Indian Grave Gap
40.6	273.1	Curley Maple Gap Shelter
43.5	270.2	Nolichucky Expeditions
44.8	268.9	Nolichucky River; **Erwin, TN**
48.1	265.6	Temple Hill Gap
50.5	263.2	No Business Knob Shelter
50.7	263.0	Spring
54.4	259.3	Ogelsby Branch
55.0	258.7	Spivey Gap, US 19-W
55.5	258.2	Campsite
55.6	258.1	High Rocks
57.3	256.4	Whistling Gap
59.2	254.5	Little Bald
60.2	253.5	Campsite
60.6	253.1	Bald Mountain Shelter
61.5	252.2	Big Stamp
61.7	252.0	Big Bald
62.5	251.2	Spring
64.5	249.2	Low Gap
65.8	247.9	Street Gap
68.0	245.7	Sams Gap, US 23
69.7	244.0	High Rock
70.2	243.5	Hogback Ridge Shelter
71.3	242.4	Rice Gap
72.3	241.4	Big Flat
72.9	240.8	Frozen Knob
75.7	238.0	Boone Cove Road
76.2	237.5	Devil Fork Gap, NC 212
78.0	235.7	Campsite
78.9	234.8	Flint Mountain Shelter
81.6	232.1	Spring
82.9	230.8	Big Butt
84.8	228.9	Jerry Cabin Shelter

APPALACHIAN TRAIL

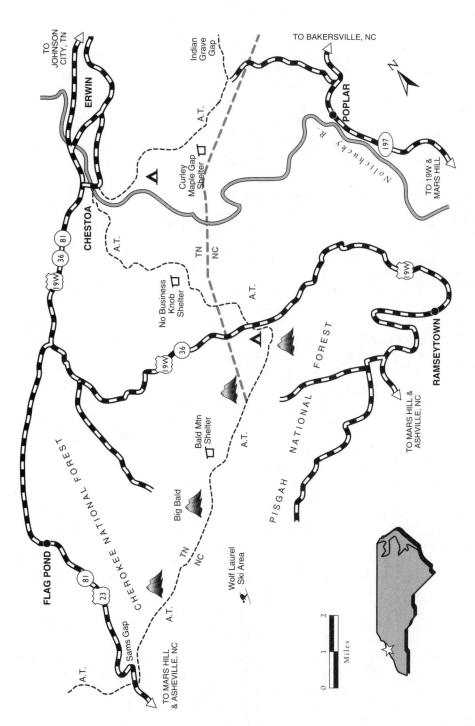

TO JOHNSON CITY, TN

ERWIN

TO BAKERSVILLE, NC

Indian Grave Gap

A.T.

Curley Maple Gap Shelter

POPLAR

197

Nolichucky R.

TO 19W & MARS HILL

N

CHESTOA

36 — 81

19W

A.T.

TN
NC

A.T.

No Business Knob Shelter

19W — 36

A.T.

Bald Mtn Shelter

Big Bald

PISGAH   NATIONAL   FOREST

19W

RAMSEYTOWN

TO MARS HILL & ASHVILLE, NC

Wolf Laurel Ski Area

CHEROKEE   NATIONAL   FOREST

FLAG POND

81

23

Sams Gap

TN
NC

A.T.

A.T.

TO MARS HILL & ASHEVILLE, NC

Miles

2

1

0

N to S	S to N	
87.3	226.4	Spring
88.2	225.5	Blackstack Cliffs
88.5	225.2	Spring
90.2	223.5	Camp Creek Bald, side trail to fire tower
91.5	222.2	Little Laurel Shelter
94.8	218.9	Old Hayesville Road
96.4	217.3	Allen Gap, NC 208, TN 70, water
98.6	215.1	Spring
100.1	213.6	Spring Mountain Shelter
101.8	211.9	Hurricane Gap
102.8	210.9	Rich Mountain Fire Tower Side Trail
105.2	208.5	Tanyard Gap, US 25/70
106.2	207.5	Campsite
107.8	205.9	Pump Gap
109.7	204.0	Lovers Leap Rock
111.1	202.6	US 25/70, NC 209; **Hot Springs, NC**

Hot Springs is an AT town with a choice day hike and overnight backpack trip on the trail. Like Damascus, Virginia, this is a tiny mountain burg where backpackers pick up supply packages at the local post office. Hot Springs is a nice place to visit for AT devotees, in part because the town has a rich history as a thermal spa. Hikers can take advantage of the popular "cure," a soak in 100-degree water, (704) 622-7676.

Jesuit priests run a hikers hostel on Serpentine Avenue, with bunks, kitchen, and showers. Hikers Hostel, P.O. Box 7, Hot Springs, NC 28743; (704) 622-7366.

The hiking possibilities just east of town are wonderful additions to the AT. To avoid the hike out of downtown, park at the Silvermine Trailhead. To reach it, go east from Hot Springs on US 25/70 across the French Broad River Bridge and immediately turn right onto SR 1304. Turn left at the first intersection and follow the signs to the trailhead, where several circuit hikes are possible. The short, steep hike to **Lovers Leap Rock** is a 1.2-mile loop with spectacular views down to the French Broad from a legendary rock ledge. Walk back down the access road leading that leads to the parking area to the Nantahala Outdoor Center. Take the bridge there across Silvermine Creek and follow the AT along the French Broad River. At about 0.5 mile, the AT climbs over steep switchbacks to the Lovers Leap viewpoint. Beyond the view, take the orange-blazed Lovers Leap Trail left and descend to your car.

To cut the crowds, lessen the grade, lengthen the walk, and possibly make an overnighter out of it, start at the Silvermine trailhead and hike up the orange-blazed Lovers Leap Trail. Go left on the yellow-blazed Pump Gap Trail at the first switchback above the parking lot. The **Pump Gap Trail** forks; both branches reach the AT. Take the right fork, the easiest climb to the AT, and take a left. Go left on the other branch of the Pump Gap Trail for a 3-mile hike. To approach Lovers Leap Rock from a less

APPALACHIAN TRAIL

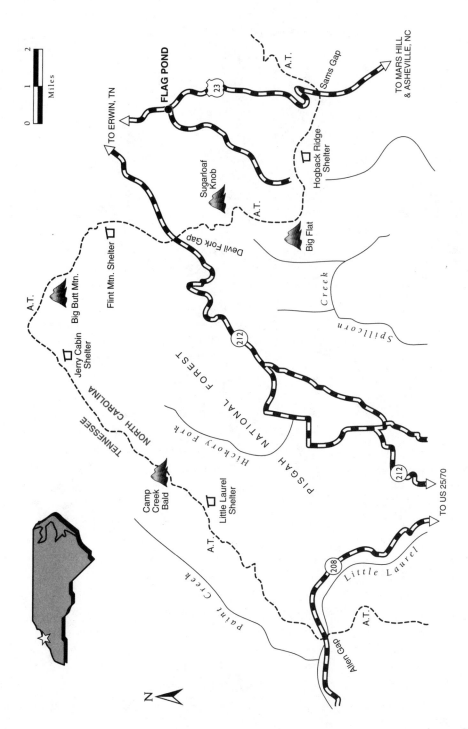

APPALACHIAN TRAIL

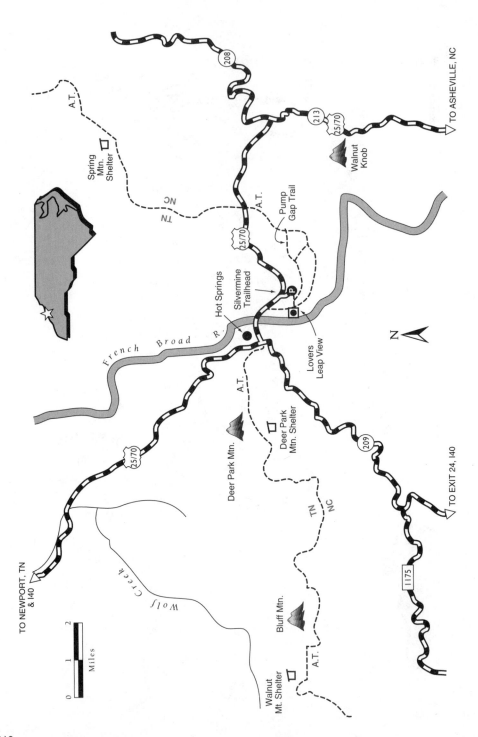

TO ASHEVILLE, NC

208

213

25/70

Walnut Knob

A.T.

Spring Mtn. Shelter

NC
TN

A.T.

Pump Gap Trail

25/70

Hot Springs

Silvermine Trailhead

P

Lovers Leap View

French Broad R.

N

A.T.

Deer Park Mtn.

Deer Park Mtn. Shelter

209

TO EXIT 24, I40

25/70

TN
NC

1175

TO NEWPORT, TN & I40

Wolf Creek

Bluff Mtn.

A.T.

Walnut Mt. Shelter

Miles
0   1   2

popular direction, go up the right branch of the Pump Gap Trail and go right on the AT to the view. Return to your car for a hike of about 4 miles.

N to S	S to N	
114.3	199.4	Deer Park Mountain Shelter
117.7	196.0	Garenflo Gap
120.0	193.7	Big Rock Spring
121.4	192.3	Bluff Mountain
123.8	189.9	Walnut Mountain Shelter
125.1	188.6	Lemon Gap, SR 1182, TN 107
125.6	188.1	Roaring Fork Shelter
130.5	183.2	Max Patch Summit
131.3	182.4	Max Patch Road, SR 1182

Max Patch is one of the state's outstanding balds and a perfect day hike. The view from the top, 4,629 feet, is noteworthy because Mount Mitchell and high peaks rise on one side, and the rippled Smokies bulk massively on the other.

The purchase of Max Patch by the Forest Service in September of 1982 eliminated a 3.8-mile section of trail that followed a dusty public road. A new, scenic portion of the AT was built over the peak in 1984. To create a circuit over the summit, the Forest Service opened new access trails to the AT in September 1995. The preferred map for this hike is the Forest Service Harmon Den Trail Map.

To reach the trailhead from the Hot Springs area go south from Hot Springs on NC 209 for about 7.5 miles to a right turn onto SR 1175. Go about 4 miles to a right turn onto SR 1181. Follow that to a T-junction with SR 1182 and go right. The parking area is about 3 miles on the right beyond where the AT crosses the road. To reach the trail from the south take Exit 24 on I-40 about 22 miles west of Asheville and go north on NC 209 to SR 1175.

Instead of hiking up and back on the AT, the new trails permit a circuit over the summit. The 1.3-mile, moderately strenuous hike is best tackled from the trail that rises to the left, an old road grade. The trail to the right, though more gradual, joins the AT below Troublesome Ridge, a steep pitch that climbs to the top over many wooden steps.

N to S	S to N	
134.0	179.7	Brown Gap
136.9	176.8	Deep Gap, Groundhog Creek Shelter

Between Brown Gap and Deep Gap, in the Harmon Den area, the **AT, Rube Rock,** and **Groundhog Creek trails** form a triangular circuit hike of 10.3 miles. This hike lies in the 1920s-logged Cold Springs Creek drainage, the tract to the west as you drive up Max Patch Road. A CCC camp was set up in the area and much of the current route of the AT between Max Patch and I-40 was built between 1936 and 1938.

APPALACHIAN TRAIL

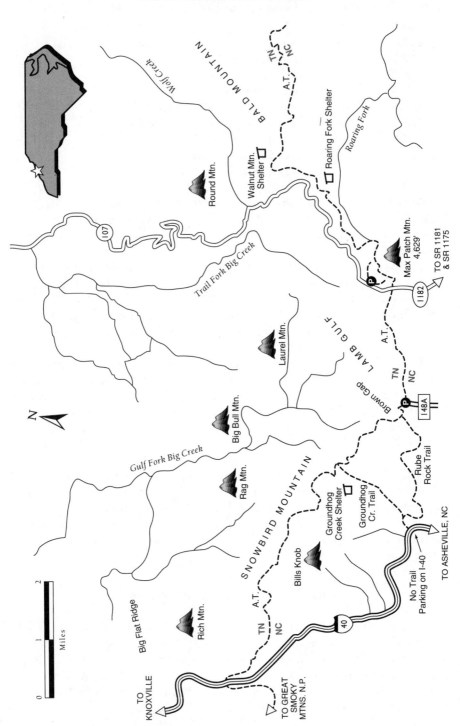

Wolf Creek

BALD MOUNTAIN

TN
NC
A.T.

Roaring Fork Shelter

Roaring Fork

Round Mtn.

Walnut Mtn.
Shelter

107

Trail Fork Big Creek

Max Patch Mtn.
4,629'

P

1182

TO SR 1181
& SR 1175

Laurel Mtn.

LAMB GULF

A.T.

Brown Gap

TN
NC

P

148A

Big Bull Mtn.

Rube
Rock Trail

Gulf Fork Big Creek

Rag Mtn.

SNOWBIRD MOUNTAIN

Groundhog
Creek Shelter

Groundhog
Cr. Trail

N

Bills Knob

No Trail
Parking on I-40

TO ASHEVILLE, NC

Big Flat Ridge

Rich Mtn.

A.T.

TN
NC

40

2

1

Miles

0

TO
KNOXVILLE

TO GREAT
SMOKY
MTNS. N.P.

Backpacker on the Appalachian Trail Balds— with less than ideal equipment.

To reach the start of this hike in Brown Gap leave I-40 about 39 miles west of Asheville at the Harmon Den exit (7). Turn right on FR 148, Cold Springs Road. In 3 miles make the first left on FR 148A at the Harmon Den parking area, and drive to the top of the ridge where the AT crosses the road, about 1.2 miles from the turn. Start the hike there. From Hot Springs go south on NC 207 for about 7.5 miles and turn right onto SR 1175. Go about 4 miles to a right turn onto SR 1181. Follow that to a T-junction with SR 1182 and go left. Take the next right, FR 148 (Cold Springs Road). Follow FR 148 to the next right onto FR 148A, and drive to the AT at the top of the ridge.

This is an unusual walk because the hike starts high (on the AT), descends to a low point, climbs back to a high point then descends to the trailhead. Follow the AT west out of Brown Gap and at 0.6 mile, go left on the Rube Rock Trail. The rugged, steep path descends to the junction with the Groundhog Creek Trail. On the way, the trail joins FR 358A. Turn right on the road (a left goes back to Brown Gap) and after 0.5 mile, go left on the woods path again. The trail follows Rube Rock Branch and then descends into Hall Branch. About 1,800 feet below the AT, the Rube Rock Trail turns onto an old railroad grade and parallels I-40 before reaching a T-junction with the Groundhog Creek Trail, 5.1 miles from the start of the hike.

To the left, the Groundhog Creek Trail leads to a unique trailhead: I-40 (where parking is illegal). Turn right and follow the logging grade uphill along Groundhog Creek to the AT, 2.3 miles and 1,000 feet above. The

Groundhog Creek Shelter is located at 7.2 miles. The AT is 0.2 mile farther, at 7.4 miles. Turn right on the AT. Brown Gap is 2.9 miles ahead, a round-trip of 10.3 miles.

N to S	S to N	
138.9	174.8	Campsite
139.4	174.3	Snowbird Mountain
140.9	172.8	Spanish Oak Gap
141.8	171.9	Painter Branch
144.1	169.6	Waterville School Road
144.7	169.0	I-40
144.9	168.8	Pigeon River
145.2	168.5	State Line Branch
146.5	167.2	Davenport Gap, NC 284, TN 32; **Eastern Boundary, Great Smoky NP**

GREAT SMOKY MOUNTAINS NATIONAL PARK

Hikers on this trail and elsewhere in **Great Smoky Mountains National Park** should realize that this is one of the nation's busiest parks. Any hike on the AT can be crowded if you go at the wrong time, so choose the time of year carefully. And remember that use of shelters and campsites can be problematical too.

Campers are required to have an overnight permit that stipulates where and when they'll be camping—in essence, a campsite reservation system. Permits can be obtained by self-registering at any ranger station. But some shelter and campsite spaces are rationed. If you intend to camp at one of those sites, you must phone in your registration to be sure there is space. Failure to do so is a ticketable offense. The best bet is to call the Backcountry Reservation Office (8 a.m.-6 p.m.; (615) 436-1231) a month in advance.

Backcountry camping regulations limit group size to 8 and allow only one consecutive night of camping at a shelter and 3 nights at a backcountry campsite. Every shelter has a small number of spaces reserved for through hikers, and short-distance backpackers get the rest. Campers must stay in designated sites and follow their itinerary. Do not reserve more space than needed and call to cancel if your plans change; failure to do so keeps other campers from using your space. Besides possessing your backcountry permit, you must camp and build fires only in designated sites. No tents are permitted at shelter sites (except by through hikers who have no choice; call to clarify this regulation). When not being carried or consumed, all food must be hung at least 10 feet off the ground to avoid tempting bears. All human feces must be buried at least 6 inches and all toilet use must take place at least 100 feet from campsites and water sources. Do not use soap to wash anything in a stream. Firearms and pets are prohibited.

From the area of Davenport Gap, on the northern side of the park, the AT provides a **hike to Mount Cammerer**, site of an old fire tower. The Yosemite-style tower, rare in the East, was built by the CCC in 1930s. Until recently, the tower was in jeopardy of being lost to time and weather on this 5,025-foot peak. Luckily, contributions provided funds and in summer 1995 the tower was repaired and rededicated. Today hikers can use its catwalk to enjoy a panoramic view.

The strenuous hike can start at the AT trailhead (5.8 miles one-way), but the National Park Service recommends starting at nearby Big Creek Ranger Station to avoid auto break-ins and vandalism. Take I-40 west from North Carolina into Tennessee and leave the interstate at Exit 451, Weaverville. Turn back under the interstate and cross the Pigeon River. Turn left along the river, pass the CP&L power plant, then Mountain Mama's Market (last supplies) and 100 yards later come to a crossroads. Davenport Gap is 1 mile or so to the right. Straight across the intersection, it's not far to Big Creek Ranger Station and the start of the Chestnut Branch Trail.

Leaving Big Creek on the Chestnut Branch Trail, you reach the AT in 2 miles (the Davenport Gap Shelter is 1 mile to the right). Going left, the Lower Mount Cammerer Trail intersects on the right at 2.9 miles. Just past the Lower Mount Cammerer Trail on the way up, a side trail branches left to a spring at 3.2 miles, and another is located on the right at 4.8 miles, just beyond an uphill site used by the CCC. At 5.3 miles, the Mount Cammerer Trail leads right 0.6 mile to the tower. For those who want to camp, the Davenport Gap Shelter is only 3 miles into the hike, and the Cosby Knob Shelter is 2.8 miles beyond the side trail to the Cammerer Tower, or 8.1 miles from the trailhead.

The 7.8-mile Lower Mount Cammerer Trail, which links the AT to Cosby Campground in Tennessee, is a wonderful return route for a 21.5-mile circuit backpack trip. To make this circuit, turn right on the Low Gap Trail at 7.4 miles just beyond Mount Cammerer and before Cosby Knob Shelter. The Low Gap Trail descends in 2.5 miles to the Lower Mount Cammerer Trail. Follow that back to a left on the AT, then go right on the Chestnut Branch Trail back to your car for a three-day backpack trip. If you make the above circuit hike, there is a designated backcountry campsite on the Lower Mount Cammerer Trail for the second night.

N to S	S to N	
147.4	166.3	Davenport Gap Shelter
149.6	164.1	Spring
151.2	162.5	Spring
151.7	162.0	Mount Cammerer Side Trail
154.5	159.2	Cosby Knob Shelter
155.0	158.7	Cosby Knob
158.4	155.3	Snake Den Ridge Trail
160.3	153.4	Mount Guyot Side Trail
160.4	153.3	Guyot Spring
162.2	151.5	Tri-Corner Knob Shelter

GREAT SMOKIES

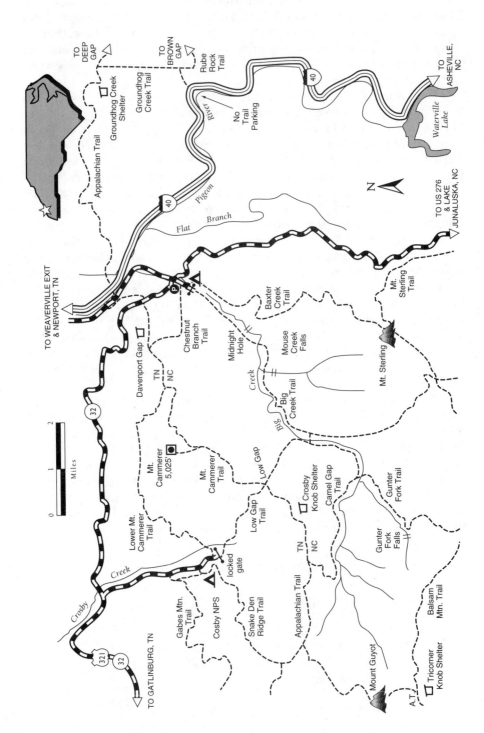

GREAT SMOKIES

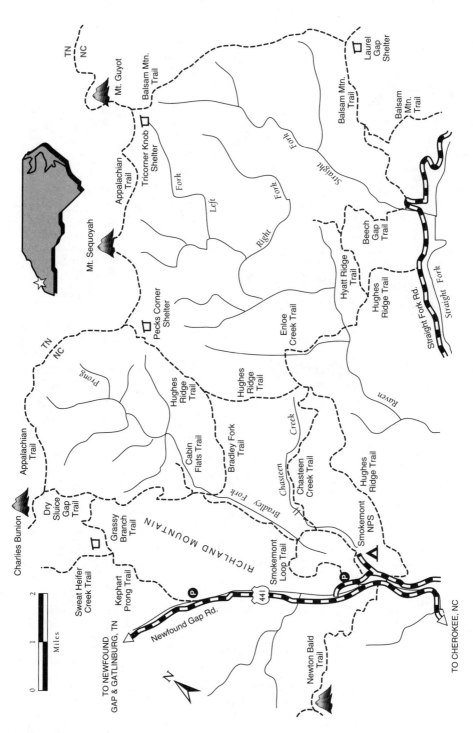

TN
NC

Mt. Guyot

Balsam Mtn. Trail

Laurel Gap Shelter

Balsam Mtn. Trail

Balsam Mtn. Trail

Appalachian Trail

Tricorner Knob Shelter

Mt. Sequoyah

Fork

Left Fork

Right Fork

Straight Fork

Beech Gap Trail

Straight Fork

Pecks Corner Shelter

Hyatt Ridge Trail

Hughes Ridge Trail

Straight Fork Rd.

TN
NC

Prong

Enloe Creek Trail

Appalachian Trail

Hughes Ridge Trail

Hughes Ridge Trail

Raven

Charlies Bunion

Dry Sluice Gap Trail

Grassy Branch Trail

Cabin Flats Trail

Bradley Fork Trail

Chasteen Creek

Chasteen Creek Trail

Hughes Ridge Trail

Sweat Heifer Creek Trail

Kephart Prong Trail

RICHLAND MOUNTAIN

Bradley Fork

Smokemont Loop Trail

Smokemont NPS

Newfound Gap Rd.

441

TO NEWFOUND GAP & GATLINBURG, TN

N

Newton Bald Trail

TO CHEROKEE, NC

2

1

Miles

0

317

GREAT SMOKIES

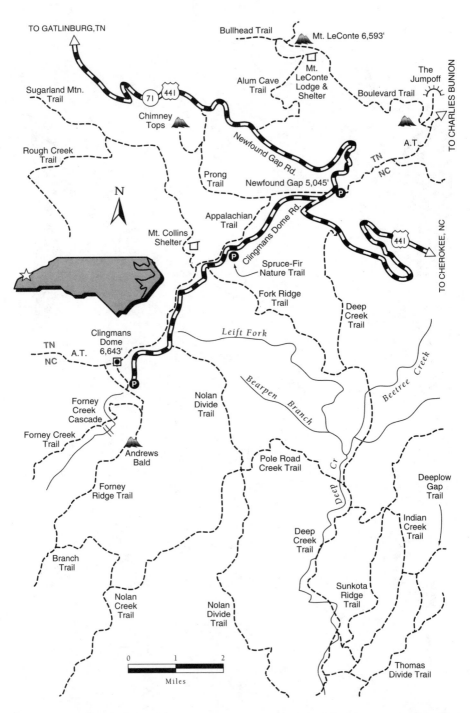

TO GATLINBURG,TN

Bullhead Trail

Mt. LeConte 6,593'

Sugarland Mtn. Trail

71 441

Alum Cave Trail

Mt. LeConte Lodge & Shelter

The Jumpoff

Boulevard Trail

TO CHARLIES BUNION

Chimney Tops

Rough Creek Trail

A.T.

Newfound Gap Rd.

Prong Trail

Newfound Gap 5,045'

TN
NC

N

Appalachian Trail

Clingmans Dome Rd.

P

441

TO CHEROKEE, NC

Mt. Collins Shelter

P

Spruce-Fir Nature Trail

Fork Ridge Trail

Deep Creek Trail

Leift Fork

Clingmans Dome 6,643'

TN
NC

A.T.

P

Nolan Divide Trail

Bearpen Branch

Beetree Creek

Forney Creek Cascade

Forney Creek Trail

Andrews Bald

Pole Road Creek Trail

Deep Cr

Deeplow Gap Trail

Forney Ridge Trail

Indian Creek Trail

Branch Trail

Deep Creek Trail

Nolan Creek Trail

Nolan Divide Trail

Sunkota Ridge Trail

Thomas Divide Trail

0   1   2
Miles

N to S	S to N	
163.2	150.5	Mount Chapman
164.7	149.0	Mount Sequoyah
167.4	146.3	Pecks Corner Shelter
168.7	145.0	Bradleys View
172.0	141.7	The Sawteeth
173.9	139.8	Charlies Bunion
174.8	138.9	Icewater Spring Shelter (through-hikers only)
175.1	138.6	Boulevard Trail
177.8	135.9	Newfound Gap, US 441

Newfound Gap, though a truly popular place to start a hike, is nevertheless the best way to reach a few of the Smokies' most spectacular viewpoints. Heading north, strenuous day hikes reach three awesome views: The **Jump-Off, Charlies Bunion,** and **The Sawteeth.** Newfound Gap is reached on US 441, 16 miles south of Gatlinburg, Tennessee, and 20 miles north of Cherokee, North Carolina. Leaving the Gap, the trail is impressively graded; it was one of the first built-from-scratch sections of the AT, artfully excavated by the CCC. The trail slides gradually from gap to gap and reaches the Boulevard Trail at 2.7 miles. This is an evergreen ridge that leads in 5.3 miles to the summit of Mount LeConte, 6,593 feet. The LeConte Lodge, open late March into November, is the closest thing in the South to the alpine huts of Europe (LeConte Lodge, P.O. Box 350, Gatlinburg, TN 37738; (615) 429-5704). There is also a shelter on the peak. The summit provides great views of the main ridge of the Smokies along the North Carolina border.

To reach The Jump-Off (6,100 feet), go left on the Boulevard and in 0.1 mile turn right. The trail crosses 6,150-foot Mount Kephart, and at 0.9 mile reaches a clifftop view looking down more than 1,000 feet. The round-trip hike is 5.4 miles.

Continuing north on the AT, the trail reaches the start of a fire denuded ridgecrest at 3.6 miles. At 3.8 miles in the heart of this area are the two peaks that make up Charlies Bunion, a great picnic spot for a 7.6-mile round-trip hike. Extending the hike another 1.2 miles one-way (for a 10-mile round-trip) permits a traverse of The Sawteeth, a serrated spine with an alpine feel.

N to S	S to N	
179.5	134.2	Indian Gap
182.3	131.4	Mount Collins Shelter
184.5	129.2	Mount Love
185.7	128.0	Clingmans Dome

The easiest hike from the **Clingmans Dome** parking area (7.6 miles west of Newfound Gap on the Clingmans Dome Road), is the 0.7-mile paved trail to the spiralling, grandiose view tower atop the peak, highest in Great Smoky Mountain National Park at 6,643 feet. The easiest longer hike is the popular trip to **Andrews Bald**. This bald, like others near Roan

GREAT SMOKIES

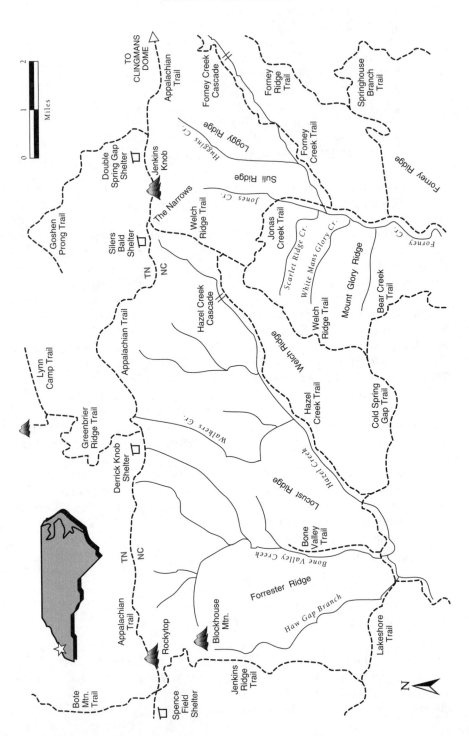

Miles
0 1 2

TO CLINGMANS DOME

Appalachian Trail

Forney Creek Cascade

Forney Ridge Trail

Springhouse Branch Trail

Loggy Ridge

Huggins Cr.

Double Spring Gap Shelter

Jenkins Knob

Forney Creek Trail

Forney Ridge

Sull Ridge

Jones Cr.

Goshen Prong Trail

The Narrows

Welch Ridge Trail

Silers Bald Shelter

Jonas Creek Trail

Scarlet Ridge Cr.

White Mans Glory Cr.

Mount Glory Ridge

Forney Cr.

TN NC

Hazel Creek Cascade

Welch Ridge Trail

Bear Creek Trail

Appalachian Trail

Welch Ridge

Lynn Camp Trail

Hazel Creek Trail

Cold Spring Gap Trail

Greenbrier Ridge Trail

Walkers Cr.

Derrick Knob Shelter

Locust Ridge

Hazel Creek

Bone Valley Trail

TN NC

Bone Valley Creek

Forrester Ridge

Appalachian Trail

Rockytop

Blockhouse Mtn.

Haw Gap Branch

Lakeshore Trail

Bote Mtn. Trail

Jenkins Ridge Trail

Spence Field Shelter

N

320

Mountain, is maintained to preserve its grassy ecosystem (see Hike 1). Like other balds, its pastures were likely preserved by cattle grazing.

The trail to Andrews Bald, called the Forney Ridge Trail, leads south from the parking area. Pass the junction on the right with the Clingmans Dome Bypass Trail at 0.1 mile (it reaches the AT in 1 mile). Continue left and take the Forney Creek Trail right at 0.9 mile. For the next 0.5 mile, the Forney Ridge Trail passes through lush Canadian-zone forest of ferns and moss. You'll emerge into Andrews Bald, with great views over the Nantahala National Forest to the south, at about 1.6 miles. A rudimentary spring is located on the southwest corner of the bald. To find it, hike about 0.2 mile across the bald, and near the lower end of the meadow, turn right along the edge.

Silers Bald is another good hike from the parking lot at Clingmans Dome. The hike is much more strenuous; on the way, hikers cross craggy ledges of the Narrows. Take the Clingmans Dome Bypass Trail from the parking and go left on the AT at about 1 mile. Pass the Double Spring Gap Shelter at 3.5 miles, and spectacular views of upcoming Silers Bald from Jenkins Knob at 4 miles (a nice turnaround point for an 8-mile round-trip). Immediately negotiate the alpine crags of the Narrows, and reach Silers Bald at 5 miles. Silers Bald Shelter is another 0.3 mile, just past a trail that leads right 100 yards to a spring.

N to S	S to N	
188.6	125.1	Double Spring Gap Shelter
190.1	123.6	Silers Bald
190.3	123.4	Silers Bald Shelter
193.0	120.7	Buckeye Gap
195.6	118.1	Sams Gap
195.8	117.9	Derrick Knob Shelter
196.9	116.8	Sugar Tree Gap
199.3	114.4	Mineral Gap
200.0	113.7	Beechnut Gap
200.3	113.4	Thunderhead (east peak)
200.9	112.8	Rocky Top
202.1	111.6	Eagle Creek Trail to Spence Field Shelter; Bote Mountain Trail
204.6	109.1	Russell Field Shelter
205.5	108.2	Little Abrahams Gap
206.9	106.8	Devils Tater Patch
207.2	106.5	Mollies Ridge Shelter
208.1	105.6	Ekaneetlee Gap
209.5	104.2	Doe Knob
211.8	101.9	Birch Spring Shelter
213.0	100.7	Shuckstack
217.0	96.7	Little Tennessee River, Fontana Dam; **Southern Boundary of Great Smoky Mountains National Park**
217.4	96.3	Fontana Dam Visitors Center

GREAT SMOKIES

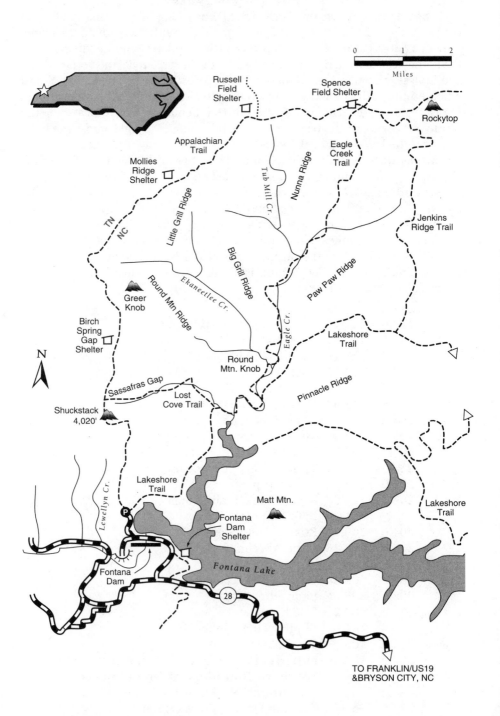

Miles
0   1   2

Russell Field Shelter

Spence Field Shelter

Rockytop

Appalachian Trail

Eagle Creek Trail

Nunna Ridge

Mollies Ridge Shelter

Tub Mill Cr.

Little Grill Ridge

Jenkins Ridge Trail

TN
NC

Ekaneetlee Cr.

Big Grill Ridge

Paw Paw Ridge

Round Mtn Ridge

Greer Knob

Eagle Cr.

Lakeshore Trail

N

Birch Spring Gap Shelter

Round Mtn. Knob

Sassafras Gap

Lost Cove Trail

Pinnacle Ridge

Shuckstack
4,020'

Lewellyn Cr.

Lakeshore Trail

Matt Mtn.

Lakeshore Trail

Fontana Dam Shelter

P

Fontana Dam

Fontana Lake

28

TO FRANKLIN/US19
&BRYSON CITY, NC

North from Fontana Dam (highest dam in the East), the AT offers a strenuous hike to the top of **Shuckstack,** climbing 3,500 feet in 4 miles, then making a circuit back to the parking area on the Lost Cove and Lakeshore Trails. To reach the trailhead take US 19 and NC 28 west of Bryson City for 39 miles. About 3 miles past Fontana Village, cross the dam and park at the AT parking area. If the road across the dam is not open, park in the visitor parking on the east side of the dam and walk across. (Just across the dam, a road goes left to a great view of the impoundment.)

The trail crosses Little Shuckstack to Shuckstack at 4 miles, then descends to Sassafras Gap at 4.3 miles. Go right on the Lost Cove Trail, pass a backcountry campsite, and reach Eagle Creek and the Lakeshore Trail at 7.8 miles. Another backcountry campsite is not far up the Eagle Creek Trail. Turn right and follow the Lakeshore Trail 5.5 miles back along Fontana Lake for an approximately 14-mile hike. Reversing the direction makes the hike easier.

N to S	S to N	
217.7	96.0	Fontana Dam Shelter
218.8	94.9	NC 28; **Fontana Dam**
221.5	92.2	Walker Gap
222.9	90.8	Black Gum Gap
224.3	89.4	Cable Gap Shelter
225.2	88.5	Yellow Creek Gap
		Yellow Creek Mountain Road
227.6	86.1	Cody Gap
228.4	85.3	Hogback Gap
230.2	83.5	Brown Fork Gap
230.4	83.3	Brown Fork Gap Shelter
231.8	81.9	Sweetwater Gap
232.8	80.9	Stecoah Gap,
		Sweetwater Creek Road, NC 143

From Stecoah Gap, the AT makes a nice day or overnight hike to **Cheoah Bald** and Sassafras Gap Shelter. The strenuous hike has awesome views atop the grassy, 5,062-foot summit, about 5.5 miles. To reach the trailhead, go northeast from Robbinsville about 8.6 miles on NC 143, or northwest of Franklin on NC 28. Just past Stecoah, turn left on NC 143 and reach the trailhead in about 3 miles.

Leaving the gap, the trail switchbacks and gains the ridgecrest in the first 0.5 mile. It passes through Simp Gap at 2.1 miles. At Locust Cove Gap, 3.1 miles, a spring is 500 feet to the right. The summit of the bald, and a view trail left, are about 5.5 miles from the start. Beyond the peak, the trail dips along a sharp ridge and leads to Sassafras Gap at 6.7 miles. A spring and a shelter are off to the right. The great view and shelter make this a worthwhile 13.4-mile overnighter.

APPALACHIAN TRAIL

TO SMOKIES

Eagle Creek

A.T.

FONTANA VILLAGE

Bee Cove Lead

Cable Gap Shelter

28

A.T.

Yellow Creek Gap

Tuskeegee Creek

Big Elk Knob

Sawyer Creek

Fontana Lake

Great Smoky Mountains

N

Stecoah Creek

Meetinghouse Mountain

Brown Fork Gap Shelter A.T.

28

STECOAH

143

Stecoah Gap

Shell Stand Creek

Rock Creek

Panther Creek

TO US 74 & FRANKLIN

A.T.

Franks Creek Lead

Franks Creek

Bert Creek Lead

Bert Creek

Cheoah Bald 5,062'

Sassafras Gap Shelter

A.T.

Rufus Morgan Shelter

TO BRYSON CITY

TO ROBBINSVILLE

Leadbetter Creek

Nantahala River

Silvermine Creek

Wesser Creek

NANTAHALA

BEECHERTOWN

Queens Creek

Wesser Bald Shelter

Wesser Bald 4,627'

TO ANDREWS

19 129 74

1310

BRIERTOWN

1365

Tellico Gap

Dicks Creek

Cold Spring Creek

A.T.

KYLE

1397

TO FRANKLIN

0   3   6
Miles

324

N to S	S to N	
234.9	78.8	Simp Gap
235.9	77.8	Locust Cove Gap
238.3	75.4	Cheoah Bald
239.5	74.2	Sassafras Gap Shelter
240.4	73.3	Swim Bald
243.3	70.4	Grassy Gap
244.8	68.9	Wright Gap
246.4	67.3	US 19, Nantahala River; **Wesser, NC**
247.2	66.5	A. Rufus Morgan Shelter
250.5	63.2	Jumpup Lookout
252.1	61.6	Wesser Creek Trail, Wesser Bald Shelter
252.2	61.5	Spring
252.9	60.8	Wesser Bald
254.3	59.4	Tellico Gap, SR 1365

The short, strenuous climb from Tellico Gap to a refurbished firetower on **Wesser Bald** is a memorable day hike that can also be an overnight trip. To reach the trailhead, go northeast from Andrews or southwest from Bryson City on US 19/129. Just south of the Nantahala Gorge and the town of Nantahala turn east along the Nantahala River on SR 1310. At 5 miles turn left onto SR 1365 and park in Tellico Gap at 4.1 miles. From Franklin go west on US 64 for 3 miles and turn right at a Wayah Bald sign. Take the first left onto Wayah Road (SR 1310). Pass Nantahala Lake and Kyle and turn right at a sign that reads "Tellico Gap."

The trail leaves the gap and rises beside a gated gravel road that also reaches the firetower. The trail attains a crag at the peak (4,627 feet) at 1.4 miles, and a side trail leads to an observation deck on a fire tower (a 2.8-mile round-trip). A campsite is located at 2 miles, and 0.1 mile beyond, a trail to leads to a spring. At 2.2 miles, a short trail leads left to the new Wesser Bald Shelter, built in 1994. The shelter, nearby campsites, and a fine spring make this a good overnight backpack trip, especially at off times of year. From the shelter, a nice view at Jumpup is another 1.6 miles.

N to S	S to N	
255.7	58.0	Campsite
256.0	57.7	Side trail to Rocky Bald Lookout
257.2	56.5	Copper Ridge Bald Lookout
257.9	55.8	Cold Spring Shelter
259.1	54.6	Burningtown Gap, SR 1397
261.4	52.3	Licklog Gap
263.2	50.5	Campsite
263.6	50.1	Wayah Bald

Incredible Wayah Bald (5,200 feet) is reached by road and is an easy barrier-free trail. The AT and Bartram Trail meet on its summit. A paved, 0.3-mile trail leads from the parking area to the top of the mountain. To reach the peak take US 64 west from Franklin. In 3 miles, turn right at the

Wayah Bald sign. Take the first left on Wayah Road (SR 1310). Go 9 miles to Wayah Gap and turn right on the gravel FR 69. The parking area near the Wayah Bald tower is 4.5 miles from there. The summit structure, a National Historic Landmark, is a CCC-built fire tower dedicated to John B. Byrne, a former Nantahala National Forest supervisor who suggested the 81-mile route for the AT through this part of the forest.

N to S	S to N	
265.5	48.2	Wine Spring
266.0	47.7	FR 69

The AT south from Wayah Gap to **Siler Bald** is a nice hike. The trail leaves the road just east of the gap and passes the Wayah Crest picnic area. At 1.7 miles, a blue-blazed side trail goes left, the first leg of a loop that passes Siler Bald Shelter (at 0.6 mile) and returns to the AT 0.5 mile farther south. The entire side trail is 1.1 miles. Where the first trail goes left to the shelter, a 0.2-mile spur leads right to expansive views on the summit of Siler Bald (5,216 feet). The entire day hike, including the bald and shelter loop, is 3.7 miles.

N to S	S to N	
267.8	45.9	Wayah Gap, SR 1310
270.0	43.7	Siler Bald Shelter
271.7	42.0	Panther Gap
272.8	40.9	Campsites
273.7	40.0	Winding Stair Gap, US 64; Franklin, NC
276.8	36.9	Wallace Gap, Old US 64
277.4	36.3	Rock Gap, Standing Indian Campground

Standing Indian Campground and the Wayah Ranger District's Backcountry Information Center is **one of the best hiking destinations in North Carolina's southwest mountains**. It is one of the few places where you can actually make a loop hike on the AT.

There are short day hikes in the area, including the **Big Laurel Falls Trail**. This family day hike leads 1 mile round-trip to a waterfall, beginning on FR 67, 5 miles past the Backcountry Information Center. The easy to moderate trail runs along an old railroad grade. At the split, the right fork leads to the waterfall.

The best of the more rugged day hikes is a 5-mile out-and-back from Deep Gap to spectacular views at Standing Indian. There are also circuit hikes, including a 25-mile circle from the Backcountry Information Center. This is one of the best places on the AT to get a multi-day feel for the trail and be able to park your car in a safe spot.

Fantastic scenery ups the appeal of this area. This section is among the most scenic on the entire 2,000-mile route. Many of the hikes lie in the **Southern Nantahala Wilderness**, a 24,000-acre tract in North Carolina and northern Georgia. The preferred map for hikes in this area is the Southern Nantahala Wilderness/Standing Indian Basin trail map.

The shortest day hike leaves Deep Gap, not the information center. To find the trailhead turn from US 64 onto FR 71 about 12 miles south of Franklin (less than 0.5 mile south of the Macon and Clay County line). FR 71 reaches Deep Gap, 4,341 feet, in 6 miles. This hike is strenuous but part of it follows an old logging grade. The AT passes Standing Indian Shelter at 0.8 mile. At 2.4 miles, a side trail reaches a spring on the left. In another 300 feet, the **Lower Ridge Trail** crosses, dropping left to Standing Indian Campground in 4.2 miles and leading right in 600 feet to the vista from the 5,499-foot summit of **Standing Indian**. The round-trip is 5 miles.

All of the hikes below start at the Backcountry Information Center beside Standing Indian Campground. To reach it, drive 10 miles west of Franklin on US 64 and turn left onto the Wallace Gap Road (Old Highway 64). In 2 miles turn right onto FR 67 toward Standing Indian Campground to reach the Backcountry Information Center in another 2 miles. A perfect overnight backpacking trip climbs from the **Kimsey Creek Trail**, traverses a portion of the AT over Standing Indian and returns on the Lower Ridge Trail for a 10.8-mile hike. Leave the information center on the blue-blazed Park Creek Trail and cross the bridge into Standing Indian Campground. Go right on the Park Creek Trail and take the first blue-blazed trail leading left.

This hike is moderately strenuous, climbing gradually along a trout stream. At 4.2 miles, it turns along the AT, and at Standing Indian (about 6.7 miles) goes left down the switchbacking Lower Ridge Trail to the information center. This circuit has an elevation gain and loss of just over 4,000 feet.

Another circuit just north of the Kimsey Creek/Lower Ridge hike climbs the **Park Creek Trail** to Park Gap and descends back to the information center on the **Park Ridge Trail** for a 10-mile hike. To make this circuit follow the blue-blazed trail away from the information center and go right on the Park Creek Trail after crossing the Nantahala River. The trail follows the river, passing left turns to Kimsey Creek and Park Ridge trails. Portions of the trail lie on an old railroad grade used during extensive logging in the 1900s. The trail passes a log dam at about 1 mile and turns left from the river and ascends Park Creek at about 1.5 miles. On the way up the mossy stream, a connector trail goes left to the Park Ridge Trail. A left here shortens the circuit to 5.4 miles. At Park Gap, about 6 miles, go left onto the Park Ridge Trail and descend past the connector and back to the parking area at 10 miles. The elevation gain and loss on the hike, which tops out at 4,200 feet, is about 1,700 feet.

The lengthiest hike in the area, and the finest AT experience, starts at the information center and goes east or west. East it climbs the 2-mile **Long Branch Trail**, traverses the AT between Glassmine Gap and Standing Indian, and descends on either the Long Branch or Kimsey Creek Trails. The hike is about 24.2 miles. Using Lower Ridge Trail, the hike is about 21.5 miles. There are many campsites on the way (Beech Gap, Betty Creek Gap, and Mooney Gap), and 3 shelters (Standing Indian, Carter Gap, and Bigspring Gap). One of the best views on the entire hike is at Albert Mountain (5,250 feet). An interpretive sign describes the Coweeta Experimental Forest visible below.

APPALACHIAN TRAIL

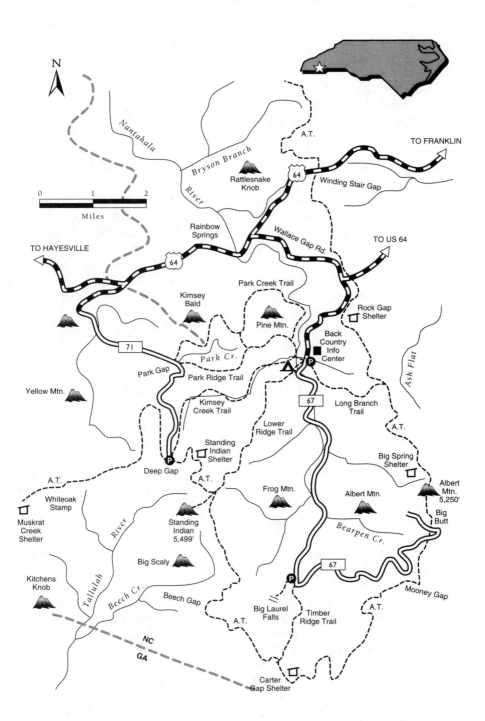

N

TO FRANKLIN

TO HAYESVILLE

TO US 64

Nantahala River

Bryson Branch

Rattlesnake Knob

A.T.

64

Winding Stair Gap

Rainbow Springs

Wallace Gap Rd.

64

0   1   2
Miles

Park Creek Trail

Kimsey Bald

Pine Mtn.

Rock Gap Shelter

Back Country Info Center

Ash Flat

71

Park Cr.

Park Gap

Park Ridge Trail

67

Long Branch Trail

Yellow Mtn.

Kimsey Creek Trail

Lower Ridge Trail

A.T.

Big Spring Shelter

A.T.

Standing Indian Shelter

P

Deep Gap

A.T.

Frog Mtn.

Albert Mtn.

Albert Mtn. 5,250'

Whiteoak Stamp

Muskrat Creek Shelter

River

Standing Indian 5,499'

Bearpen Cr.

Big Butt

Big Scaly

67

Kitchens Knob

Tallulah

Beech Cr.

Beech Gap

P

Big Laurel Falls

Timber Ridge Trail

A.T.

Mooney Gap

NC
GA

A.T.

Carter Gap Shelter

World Traveller Books & Maps

400 S. Elliott Road, Chapel Hill, NC 27514
Telephone 919.933.5111   Fax 919.933.532
Internet http://www.travelbookshop.com

Fall Travel Talk Schedule

Taos & Santa Fé	Waltraud Bastia	9/17/96
Tour of Spain	Alvin Tonkonagy	9/24/96
Temples & Gardens of Japan	Norris Johnson	10/1/96
Voyage to Hong Kong	Bill Brooks	10/8/96
Small Coffee Co-ops in Costa Rica	Deborah Hilgenberg	10/15/96
Tour of Turkey and Greece	Marilyn Vine	10/22/96
Portland and Central Oregon	Ross Pipes	10/29/96
Christmas Shopping: Chicago & New York	Ross Pipes	11/5/96
Alaska: A Different Approach	Dr. Harrie Chamberlin	11/12/96
Cuzco & Machu Picchu	Hélène Montgomery	11/19/96

All talks begin at 7 p.m. Admission is free and the talks are held in the bookshop. Speakers are customers who enjoy sharing their pictures and travel experiences with other customers. Call for more information.

World Traveller Books & Maps

400 S. Elliott Rd.
Chapel Hill, NC 27514

Fall Travel Talk Schedule

N to S	S to N	
277.5	36.2	Rock Gap Shelter
280.0	33.7	Glassmine Gap
282.8	30.9	Big Spring Shelter
283.4	30.3	Albert Mountain
283.7	30.0	Bear Pen Trail, FR 67
284.8	28.9	Spring
285.0	28.7	Mooney Gap, FR 83
285.9	27.8	Betty Creek Gap
289.6	24.1	Carter Gap Shelter
290.0	23.7	Timber Ridge Trail
292.8	20.9	Beech Gap
295.7	18.0	Lower Ridge Trail, Standing Indian Mountain
297.3	16.4	Standing Indian Shelter
298.1	15.6	Deep Gap, FR 71
300.2	13.5	Wateroak Gap
301.1	12.6	Chunky Gal Trail

The **Chunky Gal Trail** offers a nice AT-related day hike. The trail leaves the AT heading west, crosses Chunky Gal Mountain, and ends at Tusquitee Bald on the Rim Trail in 22 miles. The best way to hike part of the trail is to start on US 64 (about 17 miles west of Franklin) and hike the 5.5 miles from there to the A.T. over Chunky Gal Mountain (with nice views at 4.8 miles). The 11-mile hike is strenuous, with plentiful ups and downs between Glade Gap and the AT.

For a nice overnight backpacking trip from here, hike south on the AT another mile and spend the night at Muskrat Creek Shelter. The round-trip backpack trip is 13 miles. Chunky Gal Mountain got its name from an Indian legend: A chubby girl fell in love with a boy from a different tribe. When he was banished by her parents, she followed the boy into the wilds.

N to S	S to N	
301.4	12.3	Whiteoak Stamp
302.1	11.6	Muskrat Creek Shelter
303.0	10.7	Sassafras Gap
304.9	8.8	Bly Gap
305.1	8.6	**North Carolina-Georgia Line**
306.9	6.8	Rich Cove Gap
307.1	6.6	Campsite
308.1	5.6	Blue Ridge Gap
308.7	5.0	As Knob
309.4	4.3	Plumorchard Gap Shelter
310.5	3.2	Bull Gap
311.9	1.8	Cowart Gap
312.1	1.6	Stream
312.6	1.1	Campsite
313.7	0.0	Dicks Creek Gap, US 76

APPALACHIAN TRAIL

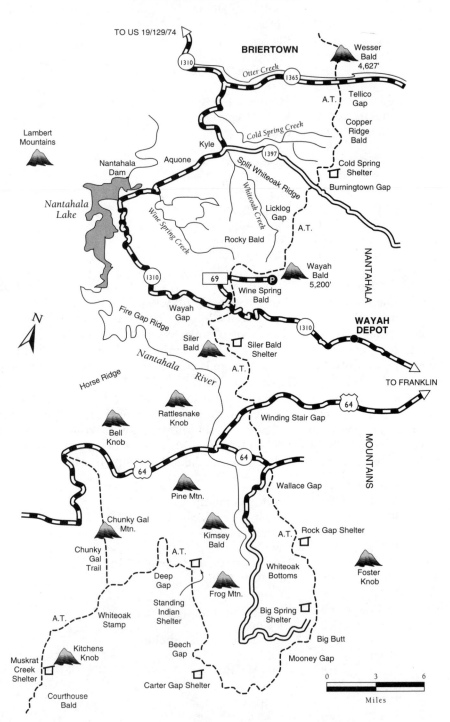

TO US 19/129/74

BRIERTOWN

1310

Otter Creek

1365

Wesser Bald 4,627'

A.T.

Tellico Gap

Cold Spring Creek

Copper Ridge Bald

Lambert Mountains

Kyle

Nantahala Dam

Aquone

1397

Split Whiteoak Ridge

Cold Spring Shelter

Burningtown Gap

Nantahala Lake

Whiteoak Creek

Licklog Gap

Wine Spring Creek

Rocky Bald

A.T.

1310

69 P

Wayah Bald 5,200'

Wine Spring Bald

NANTAHALA

Fire Gap Ridge

Wayah Gap

Siler Bald

Siler Bald Shelter

1310

WAYAH DEPOT

Horse Ridge

Nantahala River

A.T.

TO FRANKLIN

Rattlesnake Knob

Bell Knob

Winding Stair Gap

64

64

64

Wallace Gap

MOUNTAINS

Pine Mtn.

Chunky Gal Mtn.

Kimsey Bald

A.T.

Rock Gap Shelter

Chunky Gal Trail

A.T.

Deep Gap

Whiteoak Bottoms

Foster Knob

A.T.

Whiteoak Stamp

Standing Indian Shelter

Frog Mtn.

Big Spring Shelter

Muskrat Creek Shelter

Kitchens Knob

Beech Gap

Big Butt

Mooney Gap

Courthouse Bald

Carter Gap Shelter

0   3   6

Miles

N

APPENDIX B *THE HIKER'S CHECKLIST*

Hikers realize the importance of a good checklist once they are on a wilderness trail about 15 miles from the trailhead and discover they have forgotten an important item. What you forget may be only an inconvenience—or a serious need. A good checklist will help you remember the essentials.

   The list below is only a suggested list. Use it to create your own, based on the nature of the hike and your personal needs. Items will vary depending on whether you are camping near your vehicle or backpacking to remote places, and how long you plan to stay. If you are carrying supplies on your back, select items judiciously. Weight is an important factor.

Clothing
- ☐ dependable rain parka
- ☐ windbreaker
- ☐ thermal underwear
- ☐ shorts
- ☐ long pants
- ☐ cap or hat
- ☐ wool shirt or sweater
- ☐ warm jacket
- ☐ extra socks
- ☐ underwear
- ☐ lightweight shirts
- ☐ T-shirts
- ☐ gloves
- ☐ belt

Footwear
- ☐ comfortable hiking boots
- ☐ lightweight camp shoes
- ☐ aqua shoes or sandals

Bedding
- ☐ sleeping bag
- ☐ foam pad or air mattress
- ☐ pillow (deflating)
- ☐ ground cloth (plastic or nylon)
- ☐ dependable tent

Cooking
- ☐ 1-quart plastic water container
- ☐ 1-gallon collapsible water container for camp use
- ☐ backpack stove with extra fuel
- ☐ funnel
- ☐ aluminum foil
- ☐ cooking pot
- ☐ bowl or plate
- ☐ spoon, fork, knife, spatula
- ☐ matches in waterproof container

Food and Drink

- ☐ cereal
- ☐ bread and/or crackers
- ☐ trail mix
- ☐ margarine
- ☐ powdered soups
- ☐ salt, pepper, spices
- ☐ main course meals
- ☐ snacks
- ☐ coffee, tea, hot chocolate
- ☐ powdered milk
- ☐ drink mixes

Photography

- ☐ camera
- ☐ film
- ☐ accessories
- ☐ large plastic zipper bag

Miscellaneous

- ☐ maps, compasses
- ☐ toilet paper
- ☐ toothbrush
- ☐ water filter or purifier
- ☐ first-aid kit
- ☐ survival kit
- ☐ pocket knife
- ☐ insect repellent
- ☐ flashlight, with spare batteries and bulb
- ☐ candles
- ☐ small trowel or shovel
- ☐ extra plastic bags to pack out trash
- ☐ biodegradable soap
- ☐ towel/washcloth
- ☐ waterproof covering for pack
- ☐ binoculars
- ☐ watch
- ☐ sewing kit
- ☐ fishing gear and license

APPENDIX C *RESOURCES FOR MORE INFORMATION*

The trail entries in this book contain various addresses for information, but not every state or national park or ranger district in North Carolina is covered there. Below is a directory to most trail-related agencies in the state.

National Parks

The Blue Ridge Parkway
400 BB&T Building
Asheville, NC 28801
(704) 271-4779
(704) 298-0398 (recorded information and mailing requests)

Asheville Ranger District
51 Ranger Drive
Asheville, NC 28805
(704) 298-0262

Bluffs District
Route 1, Box 263
Laurel Springs, NC 28644
(910) 372-8568

Gillespie Gap Ranger District
Route 1, Box 798
Spruce Pine, NC 28777
(704) 765-6082

Great Smoky Mountains National Park
107 Park Headquarters Road
Gatlinburg, TN 37738
(615) 436-1200 (recorded information)
(615) 436-1231 (backcountry reservations)

Guilford Courthouse National Military Park
2332 New Garden Road
Greensboro, NC 27410
(910) 288-1776

National Forests

Supervisor's Office
National Forests in North Carolina
P.O. Box 2750
Asheville, NC 28802
(704) 257-4200

Croatan National Forest

District Ranger
USDA Forest Service
141 East Fisher Avenue
New Bern, NC 28560
(919) 638-5628

Nantahala National Forest

Cheoah Ranger District
USDA Forest Service
Route 1, Box 16-A (on US 129 north of Robbinsville)
Robbinsville, NC 28771
(704) 479-6431

Highlands Ranger District
USDA Forest Service
2010 Flat Mountain Road
Highlands, NC 28741
(704) 526-3765
Visitor Information Center
(704) 526-3462

Tusquitee Ranger District
USDA Forest Service
201 Woodland Drive (on US 19 south of Murphy)
Murphy, NC 28906
(704) 837-5152

Wayah Ranger District
USDA Forest Service
90 Sloan Road (on US 64 west of Franklin)
Franklin, NC 28734
(704) 524-6441

Pisgah National Forest

French Broad Ranger District
USDA Forest Service
P.O. Box 128
Hot Springs, NC 28743
(704) 622-3202

Grandfather Ranger District
USDA Forest Service
Rt. 1, Box 110A
Nebo, NC 28761-9707
(704) 652-2144

Pisgah Ranger District
USDA Forest Service
1001 Pisgah Highway
(2 miles north of Brevard on US 276)
Pisgah Forest, NC 28768
(704) 877-3265

Toecane Ranger District
USDA Forest Service
P.O. Box 128 (on 19-E Bypass)
Burnsville, NC 28714
(704) 682-6146

Uwharrie National Forest

District Ranger
USDA Forest Service
Route 3, Box 470 (2 miles east of Troy on NC 27)
Troy, NC 27371
(910) 576-6391

National Seashores

Cape Hatteras National Seashore
Route 1, Box 675
Manteo, NC 27954
(919) 473-2111

Cape Hatteras Visitor Center
(919) 995-4474

Cape Lookout National Seashore
131 Charles Street
Harkers Island, NC 28531
(919) 728-2250

Wildlife Refuge

Pea Island National Wildlife Refuge
Refuge Manager
Alligator River National Wildlife Refuge
P.O. Box 1969
Manteo, NC
(919) 473-1131

State Parks

North Carolina Department of Environment, Health, and Natural
Resources
Division of Parks and Recreation
P.O. Box 27687
Raleigh, NC 27611-7687
(919) 733-7275 [733-PARK]

Crowders Mountain State Park
522 Park Office Lane
Kings Mountain, NC 28086
(704) 853-5375

Eno River State Park
6101 Cole Mill Road
Durham, NC 27705-9275
(919) 383-1686

Hanging Rock State Park
P.O. Box 278
Danbury, NC 27016
(910) 593-8480

Morrow Mountain State Park
49104 Morrow Mountain Road
Albemarle, NC 28001
(704) 982-4402

Mount Jefferson State Park
P.O. Box 48
Jefferson, NC 28640
(910) 246-9653

Mount Mitchell State Park
Route 5, Box 700
Burnsville, NC 28714
(704) 675-4611

Pilot Mountain State Park
Route 3, Box 21
Pinnacle, NC 27043
(910) 325-2355

State Parks

Roan Mountain State Park
Route 1, Box 236
Roan Mountain, TN 37687
(423) 772-3303 / (800) 250-8620

Stone Mountain State Park
Route 1, Box 17
Roaring Gap, NC 28668
(910) 957-8185

Taunenbaum Park
(910) 545-5315

William B. Umstead State Park
Route 8, Box 130
Raleigh, NC 27612
(919) 787-3033

Other Sources and Trail Organizations

Appalachian Trail Conference
P.O. Box 807
Harpers Ferry, WV 25425
(304) 535-6331

Bald Head Island Conservancy
(910) 457-0089

Bald Head Island Ferry
Reservations
(910) 457-5003

Bald Head Island
5079 Southport Supply HWY
Southport, NC 28461
(800) 234-1666

Blowing Rock Chamber of Commerce
Box 406
Blowing Rock, NC 28605
(704) 295-7951

Boone Area Chamber of Commerce
208 Howard Street
Boone, NC 28607
(704) 264-2225

Bur-Mil Park
(910) 545-5300

Other Sources and Trail Organizations

Chimney Rock Park
P.O. Box 39
Chimney Rock, NC 28720
(704) 625-9611

Dare County Tourist Bureau
(800) 446-6262

Office of the Duke Forest/Duke University School of the Environment
Box 90332
Durham, NC 27708-0332
(919) 613-8013

Grandfather Mountain
P.O. Box 129
Linville, NC 28646
(704) 733-2013
(800) 4MT-PEAK

Greensboro Parks and Recreation Department
211 North Greene St.
Greensboro, NC 27401
(910) 373-2574
(mailing address will change in fall 1996, phone will stay the same)

Greensboro Natural Science Center
(910) 288-3769

High Point Parks and Recreation Department
221 Nathan Hunt Drive
High Point, NC 27260
(910) 883-3469

Horne Creek Farm Visitor Center
(910) 325-2298

Lake Brandt Marina Office
(910) 545-5333

McApline Greenway Park Office
(704) 568-4041

Mecklenberg County Park and Recreation Department
5841 Brookshire Blvd.
Charlotte, NC 28216-2403
(704) 336-3854

Other Sources and Trail Organizations

Nags Head Woods Ecological Preserve
The Nature Conservancy
701 West Ocean Acres Drive
Kill Devil Hills, NC 27948
(919) 441-2525

North Carolina Bartram Trail Society
Route 3, Box 406
Sylva, NC 28779

Piedmont Environmental Center
1220 Penny Road
High Point, NC 27265
(910) 883-8531

Raleigh Parks and Recreation Department
P.O. Box 590
Raleigh, NC 27602
(919) 890-3285

Winston-Salem Parks and Recreation Department
836 Oak St., Suite 200
Winston-Salem, NC 27101
(910) 727-2063

APPENDIX D: *TRAIL RELATED INTERNET ADDRESSES*

As more and more organizations go on-line, the existing wealth of World Wide Web sites of interest to hikers is sure to explode. Besides the homepages below, be sure to search Internet indexes such as NetScape, Lycos, and Yahoo using trail-related keywords.

Appalachian Mountain Club homepage - New England-based, oldest trail organization in US, with great links to other resources - http://www.lehigh.edu/~ludas/amc.html

Appalachian Trail homepage - all kinds of features - http://www.fred.net/kathy/at.html

AT page from the National Park Service - http://www.nps.gov:80/parklists

AT articles from summer 1995 in the Raleigh News & Observer - see the newspaper's listing below.

Backcountry homepage - all kinds of topics of interest to hikers - http://10.datasys.swri.edu/Overview.html

Backpacker Magazine, current issue and archived articles, is available online through America Online. E-mail is: BPeditor@aol.com

Blue Ridge Parkway - http://www.nps.gov.80/parklists/index/blri.html

Bur-Mil Park in Greensboro - http://www.greensboro.nc.us/frontier/gol/greensboro/parks/burmilpark.html

Cape Hatteras National Seashore - http://www.nps.gov.80/parklists/index/caha.html

Cape Lookout National Seashore - http://www.nps.gov.80/parklists/index/calo.html

Cary Greenways - http://www.geo,duke.edu/cary.htm

Chapel Hill Parks & Recreation - http://ils.unc.edu/TOCH/prkrec/title.html

Charlotte and Community Parks and Recreation - http://www.coe.uncc.edu/~dak/Charlotte_Park_Rec.html

Clingman's Dome homepage - great links to other resources - http://www.inch.com/~dipper/tn.html

Crowder's Mountain State Park - http://ils.unc.edu/parkproject/crmo.html

Duke Forest - address later

Eno River State Park - http://ils.unc.edu/parkproject/enri.html
Hiking trails in Eno River S.P. - the park's maps and brief descriptions, directions - http://www.geo.duke.edu/hiking.htm
Another Eno homepage - http://www.geo.duke.edu/enowelco.htm

GORP: Great Outdoor Recreation Homepages - information on all kinds of outdoor topics - http://www.gorp.com/default.htm

GORP's North Carolina homepage - http://www.gorp.com/gorp/location/nc/nc.htm

Grandfather Mountain - http://www.grandfather.com - planned for 1996 or after

Great Smokies -

National Park homepage - http://www.nps.gov.80/parklists/index/grsm.html

GORP's Great Smokies homepage - http://www.gorp.com/gorp/resource/us_national_park/tn_great.htm

The Raleigh News & Observer's Smokies homepage - http://www.nando.net/smokies/smokies.html

Guilford Courthouse National Military Park - http://www.nps.gov.80/parklists/index/guco.html

Hanging Rock State Park - http://ils.unc.edu/parkproject/haro.html

Lycos - http://lycos.cs.cmu.edu/ - a Web index to search for hiking-related keywords.

Medoc Mountain State Park - http://ils.unc.edu/parkproject/memo.html

Morrow Mountain State Park - http://ils.unc.edu/parkproject/momo.html

Mount Jefferson State Park - http://ils.unc.edu/parkproject/moje.html

Mount Mitchell State Park - http://ils.unc.edu/parkproject/momi.html
Mount Mitchell homepage - http://www.inch.com/~dipper/nc.html

National Park Service homepage - http://www.nps.gov

National Park Service homepage for North Carolina national parks, with links to individual park pages, is - http://www.nps.gov:80/parklists/nc.html

National Weather Service - with links to NWS forecast and recording offices - http://www.nws.noaa.gov

NetScape - a Web index to search for hiking-related keywords - address later

North Carolina Encyclopedia - This on-line resource to the state is maintained by the Government and Business Services Branch of the State Library of NC and contains a wide array of information including overviews of geography and weather, profiles of state and county governments, communities, educational institutions and more. http://hal.dcr.state.nc.us/nc/cover.htm -

North Carolina National Forests on GORP - see U.S. Forest Service

North Carolina State Parks - with links to information-packed pages for all the parks and Natural Heritage Program, plus e-mail adresses - http://ils.unc.edu/parkproject/ncparks.html

North Carolina State University Recreation Resources Service - lists of park and recreation agencies and all types of published outdoor recreation research and features - http://www2.ncsu.edu/ncsu/forest_resources.rrs.html

North Carolina Department of Commerce - Travel & Tourism information and press releases, many about the outdoors, are available if you click "search WW pages" and type in "travel and tourism." http://www.commerce.state.nc.us

Pilot Mountain State Park - http://ils.unc.edu/parkproject/pimo.html

Piedmont Appalachian Trail Hikers - Appalachian Trail Conference member club - http://www.ansouth.net/~dchildre/path.htm

Potomac Appalachian Trail Club - a wonderful, link-filled Website - http://io.datasys.swri.edu/PATC/patc.htm

Raleigh Greenways homepage - http://www.geo.duke.edu/raleigh.htm

Raleigh Greenway's guidebook pages - maps, trail desriptions, etc.- http://www.geo.duke.edu/ratrails.htm

Raleigh News & Observer - the state's most extensively online newspaper - has a variety of sites and services for those with outdoor interests. A summer 1995 series on hiking the Appalachian Trail is available at - http://www.nando.net/AT/ATmain.html

Raven Rock State Park - http://ils.unc.edu/parkproject/raro.html

South Mountains State Park - http://ils.unc.edu/parkproject/somo.html

Stone Mountain State Park - http://ils.unc.edu/parkproject/stmo.html

Tannenbaum Park in Greensboro - mentioned in entry for Guilford Courthouse National Military Park - http://www.greensboro.nc.us/frontier/gol/greensboro/parks/tprk.html

Triangle Greenways Council - a citizens group promoting and informing the public about Triangle greenways - http://www.geo.duke.edu/tgc.htm

The Weather Channel - the quintessential stop for weather fans - has a weather forum on Compuserve and an ever-expanding homepage at - http://www.weather.com

U.S. Forest Service - http://www.fs.fd.us/homepage.html
National Forests on GORP - http://www.gorp.com/gorp/resource/us_national_forest/main.htm
North Carolina National Forests on GORP - http://www.gorp.com/gorp/resource/us_national_forest/nc.htm

Weathernet - a wonderful clearinghouse for links to all kinds of weather information - http://cirrus.sprl.umich.edu:80/wxnet

Yahoo - http://www.yahoo.com/ - a Web index to search for hiking-related keywords.

ABOUT THE AUTHOR

Randy Johnson divides his time between Greensboro, where he is senior editor of United Airlines inflight magazine *Hemispheres,* and his home in the mountains near Banner Elk. Having conducted backcountry research for the Forest Service and the Appalachian Mountain Club, in 1978 he established the backcountry management program at Grandfather Mountain, including a much-praised hiking permit system. He oversaw the reconstruction of Hi-Balsam Shelter and new trails, especially the Cragway and the Profile trails during his tenure at Grandfather, and acted as design consultant for the Blue Ridge Parkway's Tanawha Trail.

Johnson has written and spoken widely on trail management and user fees, with a recent article in A 1996 *International Journal of Wilderness.* His articles and photos on travel, skiing, and environmental topics have appeared in national publications, including *The Atlanta Journal-Constitution, The Boston Globe, The Charlotte Observer, The Raleigh News & Observer, Ski, Skiing, Snow Country, Diversion, Backpacker,* and many others. He's the author of another FalconGuide, *Hiking Virginia,* and *Southern Snow: The Winter Guide To Dixie.*

Johnson is a member of the Society of American Travel Writers and the North American Ski Journalists Association, and the winner of North Carolina Press Association Awards during his long association with *The Mountain Times.*